Biblical Interpretation

Principles and Practice

Studies in Honor of Jack Pearl Lewis

F. Furman Kearley,
Edward P. Myers,
and
Timothy D. Hadley,
Editors

Biblical Interpretation

Jack Pearl Lewis
B.A., M.A., S.T.B., Ph.D., Ph.D.

Biblical Interpretation
Principles and Practices

Studies in honor of
Jack Pearl Lewis
Professor of Bible
Harding Graduate School of Religion

F. Furman Kearley,
Edward P. Myers,
and Timothy D. Hadley, Editors

BAKER BOOK HOUSE
Grand Rapids, Michigan 49506

Copyright 1986 by
Baker Book House Company

ISBN: 0-8010-5472-9

Third printing, March 1987
(with updated bibliography)

Library of Congress
Catalog Card Number: 85-073721

Scripture references marked KJV are from the King James Version. Those identified as RSV are from the Revised Standard Version, copyright 1946, 1952, 1971 by Division of Christian Education of the National Council of the Churches of Christ in the United States of America; those identified as NAS are from New American Standard Bible, copyright 1960, 1962, 1963, 1968, 1971, 1972, 1973, 1975, 1977 by The Lockman Foundation. Those quotations not otherwise identified are the author(s') own translation.

Printed in the United States of America

Contents

Preface

In November 1980 a proposal was made to interested individuals about the possibility of producing a festschrift to honor our teacher, friend, and colleague—Dr. Jack P. Lewis. We believed there was ample time to produce the volume before Dr. Lewis's sixty-fifth birthday on March 13, 1984. Although various delays have kept us from making that deadline, this has not swayed us from our original intent.

We express sincere appreciation to several people for their help at various stages. Delno Roberts proofread almost all the chapters and assisted in making many valuable suggestions. Ken Berry and Joel Elliott proofread and checked references for accuracy. Amy Burks not only proofread the text but retyped some portions to make them more readable for the typesetter. Jim Howard, minister for the White Station Church of Christ in Memphis, Tennessee, assisted in putting final touches on the entire project and served as a messenger when necessary to Jack Lewis's wife, Annie May. We also thank Annie May Lewis for the bibliography of her husband's writings. The editors would also like to express appreciation to our wives—Helen Kearley, Janice Myers, and Nan Hadley—for being patient and supportive in a project that has taken so much time.

Finally we give special thanks to those who contributed so generously of their time, talent, and energy to produce the articles that fill this volume. May their work be an appropriate tribute to honor Jack P. Lewis.

F. Furman Kearley
Edward P. Myers
Timothy D. Hadley

The Life and Work of Jack P. Lewis

James E. Howard

Jack Pearl Lewis was born March 13, 1919, in Midlothian, Texas, a town thirty miles southwest of Dallas. He was one of four sons and one daughter born to Pearl Gaunce and Anna Elizabeth Holland Lewis. With the scarcity of money and the demands of the farming life, it was not easy in those days to get a formal education. It is significant, therefore, that Jack's grandfather, William Donald Lewis, and his grandmother, Amanda Jane Hackworth both attended college and sent six sons and a daughter to universities. Jack's mother was privileged to attend Gunter Bible College for two years and Denton Normal for one year. Jack's father found it difficult to leave the rigors of farming for a formal education himself, but he believed in education and made the sacrifices necessary to see that his children had educational opportunities.

Influences which were to shape Jack's life were early at work. Lewis was a serious student—in school, at home, and at church. His father was an elder in the Midlothian Church of Christ until his death in 1952. There in 1929 Jack was baptized into Christ by G. A. Dunn, Sr. In home and in church Jack acquired an insatiable thirst for knowledge of the Word of God which would characterize him throughout his life. This quest for learning was not Jack's alone but belonged also to other members of the family, especially to his older brother, LeMoine.

After graduation from Midlothian High School in 1936 at the age of seventeen, Jack entered Abilene Christian University. He majored in Bible and Greek and achieved an exemplary record which would later open the door to Harvard University and his continuing quest for learning. Because these were depression years, financing a private-college education

11

was not an easy task. Beginning in the summer before his junior year, Jack sold books and Bibles for the Southwestern Company to put himself through school—a practice that continued through four subsequent summers. Although many young men thus financed their educations, book selling was one of the most physically-demanding and emotionally-draining summer vocations. The experience taught Jack to be self-reliant and independent. He learned to deal with all sorts of people and all kinds of situations. He sold books in places as geographically diverse as Port Arthur, Texas; Portsmouth, Ohio; Evansville, Indiana; and Harrisburg, Pennsylvania. He encountered roaches on the Gulf Coast and bed bugs in Ohio. The discipline and rigors of Jack's book selling were symbolized by his practice of sending in to the company on Saturday all moneys collected the preceding week so he would be forced to sell on Monday morning or go hungry. Although many of the people whom he met were poor, he found them to be hospitable. Those hard summers brought many opportunities to work and worship with small struggling churches as well as to develop friendships that would last many years.

After graduating from Abilene Christian with a B.A. degree in 1941, Jack preached for the Church of Christ in Throckmorton, Texas, during 1941 and 1942. Then he moved to Huntsville, Texas, to serve as minister of the Church of Christ until 1944 and meanwhile pursued the M.A. degree in English at Sam Houston Teachers' College. His thesis dealt with the use of poetry in sermons comparing John Wesley, Alexander Campbell, and N. B. Hardeman. On August 3, 1943, he married Lynell Carpenter who passed away in 1975. To that union were born two sons, John Robert and Jerry Wayne. On November 23, 1978, Jack married Annie May Alston, a long-time friend and librarian at the Harding Graduate School of Religion.

In September of 1944 Jack entered the Harvard Divinity School. He had been preceded there three years earlier by his brother LeMoine. It proved to be a long way from Midlothian, Texas, to Boston, Massachusetts. While the adjustment was not an easy one, the discipline acquired by years of serious study and demanding work stood Jack in good stead. What more promising educational setting could be found for one whose hunger and thirst for knowledge were great? At Harvard he was privileged to sit at the feet of world-renowned scholars in biblical studies and related areas. Included in this list of his mentors were Robert Pfeiffer (Old Testament), Edwin Broome (Hebrew), Arthur Darby Nock (History of Religion), Dean Willard Sperry (Preaching and Ministry), Henry Cadbury (New Testament), Harry Wolfson (Judaism), and George LaPiana and George H. Williams (Church History). The Bachelor of Sacred Theology degree was received in 1947 and the Doctor of Philosophy in New Testament degree was awarded in 1953. Dr. Lewis achieved an enviable academic record during the years at Harvard. He came away from the Harvard years with a broad and thorough academic education and also a personal faith which stood strong against the buffeting of the radical historical criticism applied to the Scriptures. Dr. Lewis describes the Harvard of that era as a free atmosphere in which men of widely divergent views could study. One was not required to subscribe to any particular belief. His education was not limited to the formal classroom setting but included many hours of informal give-and-take discussion with professors and fellow-students of religious persuasions broad enough to run the whole spectrum.

If the intellectual demands of obtaining a Ph.D. from Harvard were trying, the physical logistics for Jack Lewis were no easier. During his first year he and his wife rented a room with kitchen privileges in Cambridge relatively close to the university. But subsequent years were a different story. Lewis committed himself to work with the struggling Church of Christ in Providence, Rhode Island, some forty miles from Harvard. After the first year, the Lewises moved to Providence to more effectively serve the church. To attend classes at Harvard three days a week it was necessary to make the twenty-minute trip to the Providence train station, an hour's train ride to the South Station in Boston, then a ten-minute subway ride, and finally a fifteen-minute walk to Andover Hall. One would really have to desire an education to survive that routine. But to make matters worse critically-important classes were offered the other two days of the week.

In 1944 the church in Providence was small and struggling. The congregation consisted of fifteen to twenty-five people who gathered Sunday afternoon for worship in Parlor A of the Biltmore Hotel. Only one or two were native New Englanders. The others had migrated from all over the country. Many members were in military service during those war years. Lewis not only preached and taught but also made a special effort to visit in the homes of members and visitors. He took seriously the classroom advice of Dean Willard Sperry that the preacher should be in the home of every family at least twice a year so that in time of crisis he could go to them as a friend and not as a stranger. In the summer, vacation Bible schools were held in area congregations preceded by door-to-door invitations. These Bible schools were combined with gospel meetings in the evenings. The work was slow and difficult. Many evangelistic methods were tried including telephone directory and newspaper advertising, correspondence courses, gospel meetings, teaching husbands and wives of members, and opening one's home to all.

A major problem faced by the church in Providence was the lack of a church building. After years of meeting weekly in the Biltmore, the church was given the opportunity to bid on the building of a defunct

Swedish Lutheran church. Under Lewis's leadership the church had been accumulating a building fund. The church was fortunate to purchase the property for a high bid of $4,004. The building was in need of extensive repairs and renovation and the small group of committed disciples worked diligently with their own hands to make it useable. During one of his summers Jack traveled hundreds of miles throughout the South seeking the funds necessary to refurbish the building. He discovered how disillusioning it is both to have one's plea refused and to have positive responses only to wait in vain for the committed funds to arrive. There were, however, caring congregations and individuals that did give to this important ministry. The building opened important doors for the church to reach into the community. Again friendships developed that would stay with Jack throughout his life.

In the fall of 1950 the Lewises moved to Cincinnati where Jack pursued a Ph.D. in Old Testament at Hebrew Union College. From there he returned to Cambridge in 1952 to defend his doctoral dissertation in New Testament at Harvard. With the conferring of the degree the following year he became the first individual of the churches of Christ in his generation to complete a Ph.D. from Harvard in the History and Philosophy of Religion. The work at Hebrew Union was quite different from that at Harvard. Lewis received a $2,400 per year interfaith fellowship to make his studies possible. His work involved intensive study of Hebrew and he sat under such outstanding scholars as Sheldon Blank, Elias Epstein, and Samuel Sandmel. Cordial relations were enjoyed not only with the faculty but also the rabbinic students. During the Hebrew Union stay Lewis preached for the Garrard Street Church of Christ in Covington, Kentucky.

After three years of residence in Cincinnati, Dr. Lewis and his family in 1954 moved to Searcy, Arkansas, where he accepted a teaching position with Harding University. That relationship has continued unbroken for more than thirty years. After teaching Bible in Searcy for four years, Lewis moved to Memphis where he was a charter faculty member of the Harding Graduate School of Religion. In 1962 he completed his Old Testament dissertation and received the Ph.D. from Hebrew Union College. During his tenure with Harding he has received numerous honors and published the major works listed in the accompanying bibliography. In 1967–68 he received a coveted fellowship grant from the American Schools of Oriental Research to study in Jerusalem. In 1968 he received the Twentieth Century Christian Education award in recognition of his "scholarly research, profound writing, and inspirational teaching." He served on the translation committee for the New International Version of the Bible. In 1983 he was chosen Senior Fellow at the W. F. Albright Institute for Archaeological Research in Jerusalem. He serves on the editorial boards of *Restoration Quarterly* and *Journal of Hebraic Studies* and is

14

a member of the Board of Directors of University Christian Student Center, Oxford, Mississippi. He served as president of the Southern section of the Evangelical Theological Society 1969–70. During his years in Memphis he has filled many pulpits and appeared on numerous college and university lecture programs. He is uniquely qualified in the area of biblical studies, having taught more than thirty courses in this field. Special areas of expertise include biblical archeology, versions of the Bible, and church organization, spheres in which he has lectured and written extensively and practically. He has been designated to occupy the first endowed chair of Biblical Studies at Harding University, a position generously made possible by R. Walton Lipsey in memory of his beloved wife Margaret. He has led tour groups around the world, having made twenty-five trips to the Holy Land in addition to trips made to Scandinavia, Spain, the British Isles, Eastern Europe, and Alaska. He serves as an elder and member of the missions committee of the Church of Christ at White Station, a church of which he has been a part since moving to Memphis in 1958. His loyal and dedicated wife, Annie May, sharing his quest for knowledge, excellence in teaching, and zeal for Christian service, always stands by his side.

It is true, though, that a man's life is never adequately chronicled by the enumeration of the external events, the facts of public record, of his life. Such is surely the case with Jack Lewis. Those of us who have been privileged to sit at his feet or to have been influenced by his life in some other way have come to know a man whose life is characterized by seriousness of purpose and humility of spirit. We have come to know Dr. Lewis as an extremely well-organized, proficient lecturer gifted with the ability to pass on to his students a wealth of valuable knowledge thus opening their eyes to exciting new vistas of God's Word. We have come to know him as a generous-hearted man as evidenced by his creation some years ago of the P. G. and Anna Lewis Library Endowment Fund for the Library of the Harding Graduate School of Religion, a fund which will insure adequate resources for learning for young men and women long after he is gone. We have come to know him as a Christian gentleman unentangled with the passing fads of this present world and urgently pursuing and excitedly anticipating the eternal fellowship with the Father in the life to come. The right values of his life are well summed up in the brief essay which he penned some years ago titled "My Day in the Park:"

In Joshua Loth Liebman's widely read book, *Peace of Mind*, he compares life to a day spent in the park. Some have a whole day for the joys and pleasures there to be found; others can go only for a few hours. But whether it be for only an hour or for a whole day, the journey to the park is a glorious experience which one cannot spurn because his time is shorter than others.

Though it passed so swiftly that I wonder where it went, my day in the park has been a long one—now extended beyond three-score years. It is a day filled with memories of those of much briefer days: those of the infant brother who had only a few hours; those of the young girl who in grade school took lockjaw from a compound fracture of an arm; those of the college mate who suffered hydrophobia from a dog bite; those of the many friends who marched away to war never to return; and those of scores who have been cut off in automobile accidents.

In my youth children were not shielded from the facts of birth and death. The two events were often not separated for mother and child. Children were born in the bedroom at home, and brothers and sisters saw the new arrival quite shortly afterward. Winter brought pneumonia; summer had its cases of scarlet and typhoid fever, and its cases of other cripplers and killers. Funerals were community occasions and the whole family attended whether the passing one was another family member or a fellow community member. The age of the baby sitter had not arrived. Who was taken from us and who stayed lay in the hands of a Providence no more then to be explained than now. Who knows what benefit to society those who had only a few hours in the park could have been?

The park has for me been a very large one. The horizons of the slightly rolling lands of Ellis County, Texas, with their rows of cotton have proved not to be the limits of the park. An uncurbed restlessness has carried me around the world, and to most of the continents of the earth. Even yet the mention of a new place touches off a curiosity to see what is over there. Were there no other reason for the journey to heaven, I have to see what is there. I find within myself the call, "Your day here is nearly over. It soon will be time to go to a larger park!" With the Grace of God, I have to see that park!

This is the Jack Lewis who has touched our lives, whom we know and love, and to whom the articles of this volume are gratefully dedicated.

A Dean's Tribute to Jack P. Lewis

Harold Hazelip

I first met Jack P. Lewis in 1967, when I came to Harding Graduate School to be interviewed for a teaching position. The occasion was an autograph party marking the publication of his *The Minor Prophets* by Baker Book House. I recall that Jack was quiet—almost shy—and unassuming. His conversation was terse but genial.

Jack Lewis as a Student

Jack's doctorates from Harvard and Hebrew Union indicate his quest as a student. He wanted to study under the opinion-shapers, the writing scholars, rather than learn their views secondhand.

Jack has an inquiring mind, a natural curiosity about everything. He is interested in education at every level. His shirt pocket is always stuffed with three-by-five cards to facilitate jotting down notes while listening to a speech or recording an observation during a conversation.

He is in his study from 8 A.M. until 6 P.M., with precisely one hour for lunch, five days each week. Every book in his carefully chosen library has become his personal companion. Jack is too frugal to buy and shelve books that he does not read. Each evening after dinner is a time to study and write, unless there is a social occasion. His life is routinized, and the center of the routine is study.

Jack Lewis as a Teacher

Jack is a demanding teacher and expects the enrollee to be a student.

Some pupils comment that if they drop their pencils, they miss a half-page of notes from his rapid delivery. When alumni return for visits, they applaud him for having taught them serious study habits.

A genuine pioneer in graduate education within the churches of Christ, Jack began work with Harding University in 1953 and was on the original faculty of Harding Graduate School in Memphis. He has taught thirty-five different graduate-level courses, although his top priority is the Minor Prophets. He teaches and writes in other areas principally to respond to needs as they arise.

Jack is not primarily a preacher but rather a teaching and writing scholar. I have never heard him deliver a speech that was not from a full manuscript—even in chapel.

No task is too hard for Jack if it needs to be done. He will ardently chase a footnote until it is verified. He always attends the national meetings of the learned society closest to his profession and is a frequent contributor to the scholarly community from his own research.

Whatever the Bible says is final to Jack Lewis. His basic commitments are never shaded. He is the same everywhere—whether surrounded by critical scholars or unlettered beginners.

Jack Lewis as a Person

Jack is a person of complete integrity. He loves his family and his values are simple and straightforward.

He had a very frugal boyhood, and his father required hard work of his sons. Yet Jack has not hoarded what he has earned. Each year he gives, from his modest salary and his income as a tour-host, five to ten thousand dollars to an endowment fund at Harding Graduate School library, in memory of his parents. The interest from this fund now provides about eight thousand dollars for book purchases annually. These gifts are in addition to Jack's contributions to his home church, where he serves as an elder.

Jack has owned only two cars in the eighteen years I have known him. The first was replaced because it literally died. Both were stripped-down models. He has no interest in radios, automatic transmissions, and the like: cars are for transportation. Weather permitting, he walks the two-mile round trip to work each day and does it twice, since he goes home for lunch.

Jack has not always been appreciated at a distance, perhaps because he has no knack as a politician. But people who know him appreciate his singleness of aim: to love God with all his mind (especially his mind), his heart, and his soul—and to love every neighbor as himself.

Tributes from Former Students

Bill Flatt, Compiler

I am glad to pay tribute to Dr. Jack P. Lewis, an outstanding Christian man, a sacrificial and dedicated Christian worker, a Christian scholar, and a master teacher. I have known him for some twenty-five years, and my admiration and respect for him continue to grow. If there has been one teacher who merely by his presence has added prestige, scholarship, and respect to the Harding Graduate School of Religion, that teacher would be Jack Lewis. His dedication and scholarship give everyone a goal toward which to strive.

During the last few months, I have contacted several former students of Dr. Lewis and asked them for comments about him. What do they say?

In short, they appreciate him very much. Dr. Furman Kearley, director of Graduate Bible Studies at Abilene Christian University, writes, "I highly regard Dr. Jack Lewis as a teacher, a Christian scholar, and a prolific writer of very beneficial materials. In my estimation, the church and higher Christian education are extremely fortunate that brother Lewis chose to teach and write." Dr. Allan Isom, assistant chairman of the Bible Department of Harding University, says that he appreciates Dr. Lewis's ongoing concern for developing scholarship in his students—his going beyond the call of duty to help students obtain information and develop the skills needed to translate the Bible and write papers worthy of retaining in one's files. Leon Crouch, Bible professor at Lubbock Christian College, comments that although Jack Lewis has always been more interested in helping students learn than in being popular, he is still one of the favorites of students. Becky Amole, campus ministry worker, mentions Dr. Lewis's dedication to scholarly study, his interest in students, and his

19

work with campus ministries. Dr. Neale Pryor, vice-president for academic affairs at Harding University, rates him as one of the most influential teachers in his graduate work. Dr. Paul Pollard, professor of New Testament at Harding University, writes that he especially appreciates Dr. Lewis as "a very down-to-earth, warm, likeable person." James A. Jones, a professional counselor in Atlanta, Georgia, says that Dr. Lewis is one of the most objective persons he knows. Several of these same attributes were mentioned by many alumni.

Others expressed such ideas as the following:

He never let you forget that the love of God is a triad of heart, soul, and mind.

Always extremely well prepared for class lectures, he did a good job relating what he had prepared in the classroom.

He does not want to compromise the truth simply to maintain the traditions or the status quo.

He stayed with the job in times of discouragement.

He believed that no truth should be feared.

He pulled from me an ability to meet the challenges of scholarly work that before I had thought impossible for me.

He has devoted himself to the ministry of study. His students and his writings will make a lasting impact for years to come.

He taught us how to be true disciples by his own submission to the Master Teacher.

He is a combination of firm commitment to the Bible as God's inerrant Word and a commitment to restoring the goal or object to which it points.

He is always the same, always helpful, always encouraging, always humble.

He is able to state things concisely. He is always honest with the Scriptures.

Dr. Terry Bell, minister of the Hillcrest Church in Abilene, Texas, writes, "I was able to watch his faith in action at the White Station Church. It was a great example to me to see such an established scholar so involved with evangelism in the local church." Jim Howard, minister of the White Station Church, says, "Dr. Lewis has been a faithful member of the church of Christ at White Station in Memphis since 1958. In January 1984 he was selected to serve as an elder of this congregation. Through the years he has served the church in a number of significant areas, particularly as a member of the missions committee and as a teacher in the adult Bible School program." No wonder so many people appreciate Dr. Lewis!

Former students of Dr. Lewis not only appreciate his personal qualities; they also learned a great deal from him. Dr. Dowell Flatt, chairman of the Bible Department at Freed-Hardeman College, writes that he learned from Dr. Lewis to examine each item on the basis of the evidence. Mike Cope, minister of the College Church in Searcy, Arkansas, learned of the responsibility he had to dig in and study to make sure that his message was indeed the message of God. He kept emphasizing that we learn in order to be more responsible with the text. Cecil May, Jr., president of Magnolia Bible College, mentions that Dr. Lewis taught him to use historical background, language study, and context to understand the Scripture. Ed Short, missionary to Taiwan, writes that Dr. Lewis thinks the ministry of study is intended to edify God's people and that if one does not find an answer to a question about a biblical topic, he should be patient and continue to study. Allen Black, professor of New Testament at the Harding Graduate School of Religion, mentions Dr. Lewis's emphasis on using the very best tools and methods in biblical study. Harold Shank, a minister in Milwaukee, Wisconsin, mentions Dr. Lewis's appreciation for archeology. Evangelist Jerry Jones learned the significance of research from Dr. Lewis. James Hinkle, Bible professor at York College, learned never to be pretentious. Arlin Hendrix, a missionary to France, learned to stick to the subject at hand and state his thoughts concisely and honestly. Vernon Boyd, a minister in Southfield, Michigan, remembers Dr. Lewis's emphasis on giving one's best to the Lord. Dwight Albright, a missionary to Japan, says that he learned from Dr. Lewis the lesson of accepting the circumstances of life and working with them for the Lord. Others mentioned all these lessons as well as additional points such as the following: to plunge oneself straight to the heart of the primary sources; to emphasize the essential in teaching and preaching; to discipline oneself and demand excellence; to look at all sides of an issue; to realize that no person has an absolute knowledge of absolute truth; to learn to explain truth to the trained and untrained mind; to persevere in study; to expect much from students; to work and study hard; to be honest; and to think for oneself. Jimmy Moffett, long-time minister of the Raleigh Church of Christ in Memphis, sums it up well by saying that he learned from Dr. Lewis to "put up or shut up!"

Alumni also remember several humorous incidents connected with Jack Lewis:

> One wrote about Dr. Lewis's collection of "garish coats and ties. It did not seem to bother him if the tie did not match the coat."
> Dr. Allan Isom recalled a day when Dr. Lewis came to class and began lecturing on Isaiah, only to find out from the students that the class was on eschatology. He immediately went to his office downstairs, retrieved his class notes on eschatology, and began lecturing as he came up the stairs, down the hallway, and into the classroom, never missing a beat.
> Becky Amole recalls how delighted she once was to catch Dr. Lewis at home in overalls, sanding a piece of furniture out in the carport.

Dr. Paul Pollard writes of a Christmas party where students had a chance to mock the teachers, who then had their turn to reply. Dr. Lewis advised one student that he needed a little less chuckle and a lot more buckle.

Dr. Dowell Flatt mentions singing Hebrew songs with Dr. Lewis and goodheartedly adds that he has heard many who "sing by ear through the nose," but that Dr. Lewis received the blue ribbon on that.

Cecil May once asked Dr. Lewis how many students were enrolled in the Harding Graduate School of Religion. Lewis's reply was, "Oh, about two percent of the enrollment," and then added that the figure might be "a little high."

Ed Short says that once after Dr. Lewis had preached a sermon on the Greek word *teleios* (perfect), one of the brethren turned to him and said, "That was an interesting sermon, but I sure wish you would *teleios* [tel-li-us] what you are talking about!"

Vernon Boyd said that it is humorous for him to remember how he had the constant feeling in Jack Lewis's classes that if he dropped his pencil in class while taking notes, he would fail the course.

Jimmy Moffett remembers that one day in chapel a preacher was introducing one of the foremost "promoters" among them. He got carried away and said that if you took this man up in an airplane and kicked him out over a city that had no church, in six weeks he would have three thousand in Sunday school. Sitting next to Jimmy, Dr. Lewis said under his breath, "I hope he doesn't land on Mars Hill." All of these former students relate these humorous incidents out of a deep respect for the man and his work.

There is no doubt that Dr. Jack Lewis has left his mark on hundreds of preachers and teachers of the gospel of Christ—and indeed upon the entire Restoration Movement. His Christian character, tireless efforts, emphasis on honesty and integrity, and steadfast devotion to Christ have not only meant so much in the past but will continue to contribute toward the work of the Lord. Jack P. Lewis, we salute you. We appreciate you and hope you have many more enjoyable and productive years in the service of the Lord.

List of Contributors

Ted Carruth (Ph.D., Baylor University), Professor of Bible, David Lipscomb College, Nashville, Tennessee.

Larry Chouinard (Ph.D. candidate, Fuller Theological Seminary), Minister of the Woodland Hills Church of Christ, Woodland Hills, California.

Leon Crouch (Th.D., Toledo Seminary; D.Min., Luther Rice Seminary), Professor of Bible, Lubbock Christian College, Lubbock, Texas.

Joel Elliott, Ph.D. candidate, Baylor University, Waco, Texas.

Ian A. Fair (Ph.D., University of Natal, South Africa), Dean, College of Biblical Studies, Abilene Christian University, Abilene, Texas.

Everett Ferguson (Ph.D., Harvard University), Professor of Bible and Church History, College of Biblical Studies, Abilene Christian University, Abilene, Texas.

Bill Flatt (Ed.D., Memphis State University), Registrar and Professor of Counseling, Harding Graduate School of Religion, Memphis, Tennessee.

Timothy D. Hadley (Ph.D. candidate, Hebrew Union College–Jewish Institute of Religion), Associate Professor of Bible and Biblical Languages, Lubbock Christian College, Lubbock, Texas.

Harold Hazelip (Ph.D., University of Iowa), Dean and Professor of Christian Doctrine, Harding Graduate School of Religion, Memphis, Tennessee.

James E. Howard (Ph.D., Baylor University), Pulpit Minister, White Station Church of Christ, Memphis, Tennessee.

F. Furman Kearley (Ph.D., Hebrew Union College–Jewish Institute of

Religion), Editor, *Gospel Advocate;* Minister, Church of Christ, Monahans, Texas. Formerly, Director of Graduate Studies, College of Biblical Studies, Abilene Christian University, Abilene, Texas.

Raymond C. Kelcy (Th.D., Southwestern Baptist Theological Seminary), Chairman, Bible Department, Oklahoma Christian College, Oklahoma City, Oklahoma.

Annie May Lewis, (A.M., University of Chicago), Librarian Emeritus, Harding Graduate School of Religion; wife of Jack P. Lewis, Memphis, Tennessee.

LeMoine Lewis (Ph.D., Harvard University), Professor of Bible, College of Biblical Studies, Abilene Christian University, Abilene, Texas; brother of Jack P. Lewis.

Hugo McCord (Th.D., New Orleans Baptist Theological Seminary), Professor of Bible (retired), Oklahoma Christian College, Oklahoma City, Oklahoma.

John McRay (Ph.D., University of Chicago), Director of Graduate Studies and Professor of New Testament, Wheaton Graduate School, Wheaton, Illinois.

Clyde M. Miller (M.Th., Harding Graduate School of Religion), Professor of Bible, David Lipscomb College, Nashville, Tennessee.

Charles F. Myer, Jr. (Ph.D., University of Pennsylvania), Dean and Professor of Bible and Biblical Languages, Northeastern Christian College, Villanova, Pennsylvania.

Edward P. Myers, (M. Phil., Ph.D., Drew University), Academic Dean, Alabama Christian School of Religion, Montgomery, Alabama.

Carroll D. Osburn (Ph.D., University of St. Andrews), Chairman, Department of Religion, Pepperdine University, Malibu, California.

Frank Pack (Ph.D., University of Southern California), Professor of Bible, Pepperdine University, Malibu, California.

Neale Pryor (Th.D., New Orleans Baptist Theological Seminary), Vice-President, Harding University, Searcy, Arkansas.

Don Shackelford, (Th.D., New Orleans Baptist Theological Seminary), Professor of Bible, Harding University, Searcy, Arkansas.

J. D. Thomas (Ph.D., University of Chicago), Professor of Bible (retired), Abilene Christian University, Abilene, Texas.

Jack W. Vancil (Ph.D., Dropsie College for Hebrew and Cognate Learning), Professor of Old Testament, Harding Graduate School of Religion, Memphis, Tennessee.

Duane Warden (Ph.D. candidate, Duke University), Associate Professor of Bible and Biblical Languages, Ohio Valley College, Parkersburg, West Virginia.

John T. Willis (Ph.D., Vanderbilt University), Professor of Old Testament, College of Biblical Studies, Abilene Christian University, Abilene, Texas.

John F. Wilson (Ph.D., University of Iowa), Dean, Seaver College; Professor of Religion, Pepperdine University, Malibu, California.

List of Abbreviations

In general, abbreviations follow styling outlined in *Journal of Biblical Literature* 95 (1976): 331–346.
Abbreviations used in bibliographic sections are as follows:

AASOR   *Annual of the American Schools of Oriental Research*
AB   *Anchor Bible*
AnBib   *Analecta Biblica*
AOAT   *Altorientalische Texte zum Alten Testament*
AOS   *American Oriental Series*
ASOR   *American Schools of Oriental Research*
ATR   *Anglican Theological Review*
BA   *Biblical Archaeologist*
BArRev   *Biblical Archaeology Review*
BASOR   *Bulletin of the American Schools of Oriental Research*
BETS   *Bulletin of the Evangelical Theological Society*
BibSac   *Bibliotheca Sacra*
BT   *The Bible Translator*
CBQ   *Catholic Biblical Quarterly*
CHB   *Catholic Historical Bulletin*
CT   *Christianity Today*
EvQ   *Evangelical Quarterly*

ExpTim	*Expository Times*
GTJ	*Grace Theological Journal*
HUCA	*Hebrew Union College Annual*
IB	*Interpreter's Bible*
IDB	*The Interpreter's Dictionary of the Bible*
IEJ	*Israel Exploration Journal*
Int	*Interpretation*
ISBE	*International Standard Bible Encyclopaedia*
JAOS	*Journal of the American Oriental Society*
JBL	*Journal of Biblical Literature*
JETS	*Journal of the Evangelical Theological Society*
JNES	*Journal of Near Eastern Studies*
JSOT	*Journal for the Study of the Old Testament*
JTS	*Journal of Theological Studies*
NICOT	*New International Commentary on the Old Testament*
NovT	*Novum Testamentum*
NTS	*New Testament Studies*
OR	*Orientalia*
PEQ	*Palestine Exploration Quarterly*
RQ	*Restoration Quarterly*
TToday	*Theology Today*
VT	*Vetus Testamentum*
WTJ	*Westminster Theological Journal*
ZAW	*Zeitschrift für die Alttestamentliche Wissenschaft*
ZNW	*Zeitschrift für die Neutestamentliche Wissenschaft*

Part One

Introduction to Biblical Interpretation

1

Disciplines Related to Biblical Interpretation

Ian A. Fair

The Nature and History of Biblical Interpretation

Perhaps the term most widely used to describe the science of biblical interpretation is *hermeneutics*. This term is derived from the Greek *hermēneuo* meaning "to translate, interpret, or explain." Although most agree with this general definition of the term, some confusion enters the discussion since there are numerous opinions concerning the dynamic of hermeneutics. In view of the fact that there is no universal agreement concerning either this dynamic or the precise use of the word, in this study the term *biblical interpretation* will be used for the broader principles of interpretation, reserving the term *hermeneutics* for the principles involved in the final process of interpretation to be discussed in the last section of this study.[1]

As a discipline, biblical interpretation has had a long and interesting history, always subject in its methodology to the vicissitudes of philosophy and theology.[2] From the early church fathers through the Middle

1. This narrower understanding of the term *hermeneutics* is suggested by A. Malherbe, "An Introduction: The Task and Method of Exegesis," RQ 5 (1961), 166–178; D. H. McGaughey, "The Problem of Biblical Hermeneutics," ibid., 251–256; and J. Muilenberg, J. C. Rylaarsdam, and K. Stendahl, "Problems in Biblical Hermeneutics," JBL 77 (1958): 18–38. E. F. Harrison, "Exegesis," *Baker's Dictionary of Theology* (Grand Rapids: Baker, 1960), p. 204; and W. C. Kaiser, Jr., *Toward an Exegetical Theology* (Grand Rapids: Baker, 1981), p. 47, use the term *hermeneutics* in the broader sense of the "ruling principles of biblical interpretation."

2. Excellent reading on this subject can be found in R. N. Soulen, *Handbook of Biblical Criticism*, 2nd ed. (Atlanta: John Knox, 1981); W. G. Kümmel, *The New*

Ages, four types of interpretation of the biblical text prevailed: literal, allegorical, anagogic (ultimate spiritual meaning), and tropological (moral meaning). During the Protestant Reformation, however, there was a movement away from the early allegorical interpretation and later medieval priority of tradition to a position where the literal sense of Scripture became central to biblical interpretation.

The Enlightenment mood, however, introduced a new perspective into biblical interpretation that saw two conflicting developments emerge. On the one hand, an extreme position developed where Scripture was conceived of as nothing more than ordinary literature. It was interpreted on the same level as profane literature through the canons of reason. On the other hand, Scripture was regarded as totally different from profane literature and, as sacred literature, was held aloof from the normal channels of investigation. This unfortunate bifurcation of Scripture into either sacred or profane has plagued theology ever since the eighteenth century and has ultimately led to methodological confusion.

With each philosophical or theological direction in biblical interpretation, there has been a key principle determining the direction and methodology adopted. For Luther, the key was the doctrine of justification by grace through faith alone. Everything had to be interpreted through this screen. For ultraconservative or fundamentalist interpretation, the key has most often been an extreme view of verbal-dictation inspiration. Accordingly, an excessively literal interpretation of the text has predominated with little appreciation being given to figurative, poetic, or apocalyptic expression. In more recent times, H. G. Gadamer argued that the key to interpretation is the understanding of the interpreter. Gadamer rejected the view that a text has any autonomous meaning apart from the cognitive understanding of the interpreter. M. Heidegger and R. Bultmann had already developed this emphasis to the point that the existential being of the interpreter was paramount to interpretation. The key principle of interpretation for Bultmann became demythologization, whereby the horizons of a text are reduced to the horizons of the interpreter.

A more recent development has been the advent of the New Hermeneutic in the hands of E. Fuchs and G. Ebeling, who have drawn the formulations of Heidegger, Bultmann, and Gadamer into a new phenomenology of understanding. The New Hermeneutic grew out of the neo-orthodox view that conceived of Scripture as containing the Word of

---

Testament: The History of the Investigation of its Problems (Nashville: Abingdon, 1972); P. J. Achtemeier, *An Introduction to the New Hermeneutic* (Philadelphia: Westminster, 1959); and I. H. Marshall, "Introduction," *New Testament Interpretation* (Grand Rapids: Eerdmans, 1977). This last work is an exceptionally fine introduction to the nature and task of biblical interpretation.

God made present to the world through the word of proclamation. The New Hermeneutic agrees with Gadamer that there is no objective meaning in a text beyond the meaning of the language of the text to the interpreter. What is known as the "hermeneutic circle" is introduced at this point, whereby, it is claimed, the subjective presuppositions of the interpreter play a significant role in interpretation and influence the meaning of the text as much as the interpreter is influenced by the text.[3] Much is made of the "language-event," emphasizing the relationship between language and meaning. The key to the New Hermeneutic is that the language of Scripture ceases to be mere language with its own fixed cognitive meaning and becomes instead a dynamic language-event that creates faith and its own new meaning in the hearer-interpreter. The controlling principle in the New Hermeneutic is an outgrowth of the Lutheran doctrine of justification by faith alone. Faith is the subjective creation of the language-event and not the product of rational analysis and an objective word meaning.

The traditional problem confronted by biblical interpretation has lain in the tension that exists between the objective historical nature of the text and the subjective contemporaneousness of the interpreter. In some extreme interpretations, the former pole—the historical dimension of the text—has been denied or negated. On the other hand, an ultraconservative interpretation can overlook the contemporary dimension of meaning and the symbolism of language in favor of a literal interpretation.

A balanced approach to interpretation will seek to preserve both poles. It will approach the text with a high regard for the inspiration of God's Word. As G. B. Caird has expressed it, the interpreter will approach the text with the view that lives "must be lived under the authority of the word of God, and that this word is spoken in Scripture."[4] Caird also emphasizes that there is "no access to the word of God in the Bible except through the words of those who claim to speak in his name."[5] Contrary to Gadamer, Caird maintains there can be no meaning for a text other than the meaning intended by the writer.[6] At the same time, a balanced interpretation will also seek, through the symbolism of language, to find meaning in the text for the contemporary situation of the interpreter, so that the interpreter will himself be challenged in his subjective existence by the historical meaning of the text.

3. For discussion on the subjective aspect of the hermeneutic circle see below under the section entitled "The Task of Hermeneutics." Cf. also Kaiser (note 1), pp. 31, 34ff, 46ff.

4. G. B. Caird, *The Language and Imagery of the Bible* (Philadelphia: Westminster, 1980), p. 1.

5. Ibid., p. 61.

6. Ibid.

The New Hermeneutic is correct in drawing attention to the fact that true interpretation cannot be permitted to degenerate into a discipline whereby the interpreter simply masters or objectifies the text and studies it purely in its historical setting. But neither should interpretation slide to the point that the interpreter masters the text with only his own subjective meaning. True interpretation, therefore, can only arise from that situation where the interpreter and his being are challenged by both the historical text and its contemporary significance. However, the overriding principle will always be that it is the text in its historical context that provides the parameters or horizons of meaning. No meaning may be imported into the text that is extraneous to the text. The interpreter may not, in the words of Caird, "penetrate to a meaning more ultimate than the one the writers intended."[7] The dynamic relationship between text and contemporary application, wherein the objectivity of the text and the subjectivity of the interpreter are both preserved, can be maintained only when the direction of interpretation is *from* the historical interpretation of the text *toward* the subjective context of the interpreter. In other words, "meaning" is that understanding found in a text in its historical context through a grammatical-historical investigation of the text. The "significance" (or application) of that text to the interpreter's contemporaneous interest is that which grows out of the dynamic arising when the historical meaning of the text meets the new person, time, situation, or idea.[8]

Having drawn the distinction between the terms *meaning* and *significance* in biblical interpretation, some of the ruling principles of interpretation can now be introduced. The first principle is the presupposition regarding the nature and authority of Scripture as the Word of God. While this presupposition should not permit the interpreter to introduce his subjective interests into the meaning intended by the original author, it does reflect on how the interpreter ultimately finds significance in the historical meaning of the text and thus does involve one in some form of "hermeneutic circle." The impact of this presupposition will be developed under the section titled "The Task of Hermeneutics."

It is the task of yet another ruling principle of biblical interpretation to control subjective interests as the interpreter is confronted by a text. This principle is known as "biblical exegesis." Exegesis is the discipline whereby the interpreter searches for the historical meaning of the text.

Having established the historical meaning through exegesis, the interpreter then seeks to explain the significance or application of the historical meaning to his own contemporary context. This final discipline or principle of interpretation is called hermeneutics. In this manner it can

---

7. Ibid.
8. For discussion on the distinction between "meaning" and "significance" cf. E. D. Hirsch, Jr., *Validity in Interpretation* (New Haven: Yale University, 1967), pp. 8ff.

be said that exegesis must always precede hermeneutics, and that exegesis is the basic discipline of theology.[9] Exegesis must always govern theology. In the same manner, it should also be understood that exegesis must always precede and govern homiletics or proclamation.

The Task of Biblical Exegesis

Exegesis is fundamentally a critical examination of a text, whereby the researcher, using a variety of tools or critical disciplines, seeks to penetrate behind a text to the original meaning of the original author as he addressed his original constituency.[10] R. P. Martin observes:

> To practice exegesis in regard to the New Testament literature is to enquire what was the meaning intended by the original authors. The process is one of uncovering that meaning, and the technique is known as heuristics, i.e. the study which explains how to discover the sense of a passage of Scripture. This is to be the interpreter's primary aim, requiring that his approach to Scripture be one of honest enquiry and a determined effort to find out the intended meaning of the author for his day.[11]

This task is never a simple one, as the exegete seeks to bridge the centuries between the text and his own historical context. The difficulty of the task, however, is neither new nor unique, nor one that should cause the exegete to retreat in dismay. It is simply the task faced by every careful historian. In fact, Malherbe correctly observes that "the task of the exegete is, first and foremost, an historical one."[12] Citing J. J. Mays, *Exegesis as a Theological Discipline*, he observes that the use of historical and philological tools defines the exegete clearly as a historian rather than a theologian.[13] The task of exegesis, therefore, begins with a careful, critical examination of the text in its historical context, paying attention to the political, cultural, religious, and philosophical milieu.

Since language is an integral part of the historical milieu of a text, another dimension of this historical investigation must always include an analysis of the text's language. Grammatical, syntactical, and lexical considerations should figure significantly in exegesis. Therefore, the task of exegesis can be defined as a careful, critical, historical investigation of a text, whereby the text is examined historically, contextually, gram-

9. Malherbe (note 1), pp. 169–178.
10. Cf. R. P. Martin, "Approaches to New Testament Exegesis," *New Testament Interpretation*, I. H. Marshall, ed., pp. 220–251.
11. Ibid., p. 220.
12. Malherbe, p. 169.
13. Ibid.

matically, syntactically, lexically, and biblically. The descriptive term given to this approach is the grammatico-historical method of exegesis.[14]

The Components of Biblical Exegesis

The grammatico-historical method is one that seeks to take seriously the twofold nature of Scripture, admitting to both its human (profane) and divine (sacred) dimensions. Conservative theology today views Scripture as the divinely inspired Word of God that contains God's message, or revelation, in human form of expression. This view suggests that one hold a high view of Scripture that admits to God's inspiration or superintendence, but also recognizes that this message has been transmitted in human language, idiom, and literary form.[15]

Prior to the Enlightenment of the seventeenth and eighteenth centuries, the human dimension of Scripture, although acknowledged, did not play a significant role in biblical interpretation, and the Scriptures by and large were accepted uncritically. The partial reason for this lay in the fact that scholars prior to the Enlightenment did not have adequate tools available for critical research. The Renaissance, however, introduced a desire to press back into the literature of antiquity, and this, together with the Enlightenment mood, awakened the desire of scholars to look upon the Scriptures not only as the sacred literature of the church but also as the literature of antiquity. In fact, the Enlightenment introduced a significant change in regard to concepts concerning the nature of Scripture. This attitude, although healthy in some ways, became destructive in the hands of radical scholars. Rationalism had led many to dispense with the need for acknowledging any supernatural intervention in human affairs. Consequently, through a radical application of the canons of reason, the Scriptures were stripped of their supernatural or divine dimension and

14. It is not the purpose of this chapter to discuss the history of biblical interpretation, nor to discuss the relative merits of a variety of different methods of biblical interpretation. Space does not permit this luxury. For such discussion see Martin, "Approaches . . ." in *New Testament Studies*, pp. 220ff.; F. F. Bruce, "The History of New Testament Study," *Ibid.*, pp. 21ff.; and Soulen, "Biblical Criticism," *Handbook*, p. 27.

15. In recent years much discussion has been conducted in both evangelical and ecumenical circles as to the true nature of Scripture. The student is referred to the following works for detailed discussion on this matter: F. F. Bruce, *The New Testament Documents, Are They Reliable?* (Grand Rapids: Eerdmans, 1960); J. M. Boice, ed., *The Foundation of Biblical Authority* (Grand Rapids: Zondervan, 1978); R. Pache, *The Inspiration and Authority of Scripture* (Chicago: Moody, 1969); C. H. Pinnock, *A Defense of Biblical Infallibility* (Philadelphia: Presbyterian and Reformed, 1969); P. J. Achtemeier, *The Inspiration of Scripture* (Philadelphia: Westminster, 1980); H. Lindsell, *The Battle for The Bible* (Grand Rapids: Zondervan, 1976); and S. T. Davis, *The Debate About The Bible* (Philadelphia: Westminster, 1977).

became simply a human product, operating solely on the level of the horizontal plane of reason.

Although post-Enlightenment biblical research, by adopting these rationalistic or humanistic presuppositions, led ultimately to an anthropocentric view of Scripture, it also brought with it a new awareness of the real dual nature of Scripture and ultimately a healthy, critical approach to Scripture.[16] Soulen observes that with the awakening of a critical attitude toward literature in general and the concurrent rise of critical-historical consciousness, there "came a flood of philological, historical, and literary questions regarding the text: date, place, authorship, sources, intention. . . ."[17] It is this critical attitude toward the text, with its resultant critical questions, that has been healthy for biblical research. (It should be emphasized here that a critical attitude toward the text does not mean that the scholar has to surrender a high view of Scripture and adopt an anthropocentric view of its text.) When, as a result of this critical approach, it was realized that the Scriptures were presenting God's Word through the medium of common literary expression, full of the richness and idiom of the language of the period of the text, many doors were opened to a deeper and more meaningful understanding of the text.

This method of critical research stemming from the Enlightenment is known today as Biblical (or Historical) Criticism. As has already been indicated, when conducted along the lines of anthropocentric presuppositions, Biblical Criticism can produce a negative result and attitude toward the Scriptures. However, this negative approach is not necessarily axiomatic, for the questions raised by Biblical Criticism—questions concerning date, place, authorship, sources, genre, and intention—are valid concerns that in careful hands can yield meaningful answers for biblical research. The critical point hinges on the presupposition that one brings to the research. When the researcher approaches the text with a presupposition that permits God's actions in history to be viewed as part of history and that permits men to record God's Word under the inspiring

---

16. This is not the place to debate the problems of an anthropocentric view of history, nor the historical dimension of Scripture. Suffice it to draw attention to the work of W. Pannenberg who, together with others, has emphasized in contemporary theology that God has revealed himself in history and that history is a reliable avenue of revelation and faith. See W. Pannenberg, ed., *Revelation as History* (New York: Macmillan, 1968). Pannenberg has also drawn attention to the faulty historical methodology of the Enlightenment mood, and has observed that it is not the task of the historian to determine what could, or could not, take place in history, but to report and discuss the evidence of what has taken place. See W. Pannenberg, *Jesus—God and Man* (London: SCM, 1968), pp. 97f., 109. Cf. also the discussion on history in C. Brown, ed., *History, Criticism and Faith* (Leicester, England: Inter-Varsity, 1977), and C. E. Braaten, *New Directions in Theology Today, History and Hermeneutics* (London: Lutterworth, 1968).

17. Soulen (note 2), p. 27.

guidance of the Holy Spirit, the results of Biblical-Historical Criticism can be positive and rewarding.

Traditionally, this approach has been divided into two categories: Lower Criticism and Higher Criticism. The term *lower* is somewhat unfortunate in that it implies some inferiority, which is misleading. It refers to what is now more appropriately called *Textual Criticism*, that discipline that seeks to establish, or reconstruct, the original wording of a text.[18] By careful and disciplined research, the textual critic compares and evaluates the multitude of manuscripts, translations, and fragments available to him, in an attempt to approach as accurately as possible the wording of the original text. Great strides in this area of critical study have been made over the last few centuries, so that today the scholar has access to accurate and carefully produced texts with critical footnotes known as "critical apparatuses." These devices and other research tools make it possible for biblical researchers to approach a text with a high degree of confidence that they are working with the precise words (or sufficiently close to the words) originally penned by the author. No serious biblical interpretation should be conducted in a text without first having critically established that the text is the best one available. Textual Criticism also helps the researcher to trace the history of the transmission of the text through the centuries and thus to identify theological presuppositions that may have altered or affected the wording.

The second category of critical biblical research—Higher Criticism— refers to the remainder of the disciplines directed toward the inherent qualities of the text. They are commonly identified as Historical Criticism, Literary Criticism, Source Criticism, Form Criticism, Redaction Criticism, and Tradition Criticism.

Historical Criticism or, more appropriately, the historical-critical method of research, has often been used erroneously as a synonym for the whole field of Biblical Criticism.[19] Furthermore, it has also unfortunately most often been identified with a narrow form of biblical research that moves out of an anthropocentric presupposition.

> Strictly speaking, the term HCM [historical-critical method] refers to that underlying principle of historical reasoning which came to full flower in the 19th cent., viz., that reality is uniform and universal, that it is accessible to human reason and investigation, that all events historical and natural occurring within it are in principle comparable by analogy, and that man's contemporary experience of reality can provide the objective criteria by which what could or could not have happened in the past is to be

18. Ibid., pp. 161ff. For a recent discussion of the various disciplines within Biblical Criticism and their application in Biblical exegesis cf. J. H. Hayes and C. R. Holladay, *Biblical Exegesis* (Atlanta: John Knox, 1982).

19. Soulen, p. 78.

determined. . . . If HCM by definition rules out the Divine as a causative factor in history, of what help can it be to the Church in understanding the Bible which views God and history precisely in that way?[20]

In an exceptionally fine study, G. Maier has shown that an extremely narrow and radical approach to Historical Criticism has in fact "plunged theology into an endless chain of perplexities and inner contradictions."[21] The supposedly "scientific" approach has been more critical than historical and has removed from the text the very thing it had sought to find, namely, the Word of God. Maier argues that the historical-critical method, when pursued in this manner, has come to a dead end. Maier does not rule out an historical approach but suggests a more balanced procedure, which he describes as the "Historical-Biblical method." Such an approach to the Bible, he maintains, takes history seriously while permitting a supernatural intervention into human affairs.[22]

Historical Criticism can, however, also have reference to the field of biblical research that seeks to investigate the historical context of the text, establish its date, and determine the circumstances surrounding the writing of the text.[23] This kind of research is absolutely essential to a correct interpretation of the text. It is only through understanding its historical background that the religious, political, and cultural milieu of a text can be appreciated and that the problems or themes being developed in the text can be understood. For example, without seeking to understand the historical, political, cultural, and religious contexts of Revelation, a researcher is not in a position to appreciate the problems being addressed by the author, John. Failure to grasp these matters will lead to fanciful speculation without the necessary objective checks and balances provided by the historical context of Revelation. Missing these checks and balances causes one, in Caird's words, to "penetrate to a meaning more ultimate than the one the writers intended."[24]

Literary Criticism is closely associated with Historical Criticism. As the term is defined by some scholars, this type of research is a broad concept that covers several disciplines involved in the critical analysis of the text as a literary product.[25] In this broad sense Literary Criticism seeks to

20. Ibid.
21. G. Maier, *The End of the Historical-Critical Method* (St. Louis: Concordia, 1977), p. 11.
22. Ibid., pp. 50ff. Along similar lines to Maier, Pannenberg has argued against Barth and Neo-Orthodoxy that the problem for theology is not history, but the faulty positivistic anthropocentric historical method theology inherited from the Enlightenment mood. Pannenberg, *Jesus—God and Man*, passim, *Revelation as History*, passim, *Basic Questions in Theology*, Vol. 1 (Philadelphia: Fortress, 1970), passim.
23. Soulen, p. 78.
24. Caird, p. 61.
25. Soulen, pp. 113ff.

investigate all the literary features of a text, such as sentence structure, the internal arrangement of the text, its sources and redactional concerns, in addition to the literary genre of the text. W. Beardslee observes that

> . . . any kind of literary criticism of the New Testament means setting the New Testament in the context of other literature and perceiving it as literature. It means trying to understand the Biblical books by methods of approach and standards which can be useful in the study of other writings as well.[26]

Literary Criticism, however, as discussed here, is understood in the narrower sense of literary form, where the researcher studies such matters as genre and the form of the text.[27] The "literary critic," as we are defining the term, asks questions that seek to understand the overall character of the text. What kind of literature is this—historical narrative, poetry, parable, allegory, apocalyptic, epistle, religious treatise, or what? What function does this literary form serve? How does this literary form intend itself to be understood? It is only when such questions concerning literary form have been asked that the researcher is in a position to know how to evaluate or understand the text. Failure to ask them leads, for instance, to an overliteral interpretation of figurative language. This is especially true in the case of Revelation, where language that is so obviously apocalyptic and figurative has been alternately understood as either historical narrative or literal language, resulting in farfetched and speculative eschatological views of the end of the world.

Besides form, there are yet other literary questions that can be asked of a text. These concern the sources from which the author drew his ideas, how he has used or combined these sources to achieve his purpose, and/or how the component parts of a verse or text are structured and relate to one another. Although indeed matters of literary concern, they will be considered under the remaining categories of Biblical Criticism:

Source Criticism is a particular focus of Literary Criticism that seeks to identify and delineate the separate sources within a text or pericope. Originating in a particular critical approach to studies of the Pentateuch

26. W. A. Beardslee, *Literary Criticism of the New Testament* (Philadelphia: Fortress, 1970), p. 3. Cf. also N. Habel, *Literary Criticism of the Old Testament* (Philadelphia: Fortress, 1971).

27. Ibid., p. 3. Beardslee approaches Literary Criticism more from the narrower sense described above, whereas Habel discusses it in regard to the OT more from the broader sense. Both approaches are a valid method of considering the literary nature of the text, the difference between the two being more a matter of focus. There appears to be little unanimity as to the exact definition and practice of Literary Criticism. Most scholars, however, agree that it is in some form the analysis of a text along literary lines.

known as the Documentary Hypothesis, Source Criticism has spread to a study of all of the books of the Bible, and in the New Testament to the synoptic Gospels in particular. Soulen observes that "sometimes it [source criticism] was carried to absurd extremes, with multiple sources purportedly lying behind a single verse."[28] But such extremes are not always characteristic of this type of study. Careful analysis of the sources and components of a text has made significant contributions to exegetical research. Our appreciation of the interrelationship of the Synoptics, especially in their unity and diversity, has been deepened by the application of Source Criticism. The identification of apocalyptic sources within a text, especially within such texts as Matthew 24:29–31, has opened the way to a better understanding of the passage.

Form Criticism is related to source criticism, but it presses beyond the text itself to the situations or conditions in the life of the church that gave rise to the written text. This delving to the oral stratum that formed the basis of the written text, unlike Literary Criticism, is more concerned with the oral history of the text than its literary characteristics.[29] In recent years there has been a growing appreciation for that period of oral tradition that lay behind the literary appearance of the written text. The "form critic" seeks to identify those sociological or religious conditions that gave rise to the use and memory of certain religious concepts. This careful study of the *Sitz im Leben* (life situation) of the text helps the biblical student appreciate how the concept conveyed in the text related to the life situation of the church. It also clarifies the dynamic process responsible for the remembering and recording of the text, thus leading to a deeper understanding about the significance of the thought conveyed in the text to the total life situation of the early community.

Redaction Criticism recognizes the one obvious weakness in Form Criticism, which is by its very nature fragmentary, working predominantly with isolated sources.[30] Form Criticism thus tends to lose sight of the overall nature and purpose of a written work. It is for this reason that biblical scholars began to pay attention to the overall theological interest or *tendenz* of a text. This method of study

> . . . seeks to lay bare the theological perspectives of a Biblical writer by analyzing the editorial (redactional) and compositional techniques and

28. Soulen, p. 114.
29. Cf. Soulen, pp. 71ff; E. V. McKnight, *What Is Form Criticism?* (Philadelphia: Fortress, 1969); and G. M. Tucker, *Form Criticism of the Old Testament* (Philadelphia: Fortress, 1971).
30. For discussion of the limitations of Form Criticism see S. H. Travis, "Form Criticism," *New Testament Interpretation*, I. Howard Marshall, ed., pp. 151ff.; and D. Guthrie, *New Testament Introduction, The Gospels and Acts* (Chicago: InterVarsity, 1966), pp. 189ff.

interpretations employed by him in shaping and framing the written and/
or oral traditions at hand.[31]

Form-critical studies often left one with the opinion that the writer of a
text was more of an editor who collected a variety of sources and put them
together in some scissors-and-paste manner. "Redaction critics" recognize that the author had a more active role and more intense interest, not
only in collecting but also in shaping the sources as he worked with them
to produce his theological theme or purpose. Redaction Criticism, therefore, seeks to identify the writer's theological purpose and then explain
how the writer has used his sources to produce that theological emphasis.

Each of the disciplines thus far discussed develops a particular focus
on the text within the general methodology of Biblical Criticism. Textual
Criticism focuses on the textual validity of the text, Literary Criticism on
its literary characteristics. Source Criticism tackles the sources identifiable within the text, and Redaction Criticism searches for the theological
purpose developed by the author as he used the material and resources
available to him.

Tradition Criticism, or the traditio-historical method of study, is yet one
other discipline that needs attention. Here the focus is "the study of the
history of oral traditions during the period of their transmission."[32]
Whereas Form Criticism focused on the community's *Sitz im Leben* that
was responsible for the production or remembrance of a religious concept, the traditio-historical method investigates the history of the tradition's transmission up to the point of its written form. In the area of New
Testament studies, the focus has been mainly the ongoing history of liturgical formulas, hymnic fragments, baptismal formulas, and so on, which
ultimately became part of the written text. In regard to the Old Testament, the direction of study has been the formation and transmission of
the traditions that eventually solidified into the Credo of Israel. In both
New and Old Testament emphases, the traditio-historical researcher
seeks to trace and understand the development and transformation of
traditions as they were used and reused, until ultimately worked into the
text under the hand of a redactor. Tradition Criticism thus stands between
Form Criticism (the study of the *Sitz im Leben* of a source or tradition) and
Redaction Criticism (the ultimate working of the source or tradition into
the theological purpose of the redactor).

In concluding this section on Biblical Criticism as a major component
of scriptural interpretation, it is necessary to reemphasize certain points.

---

31. Soulen, pp. 165., and N. Perrin, *What Is Redaction Criticism?* (Philadelphia:
Fortress, 1969).

32. Soulen, pp. 200f., and W. E. Rast, *Tradition History and the Old Testament*
(Philadelphia: Fortress, 1972).

First, Biblical Criticism, when carried out via anthropocentric and philosophic presuppositions, can have a negative effect upon Scripture. In fact, it can destroy that which it seeks to find and understand, namely, the Word of God. But this need not be the case. When conducted with sound respect for the inspiration of God's Word, Biblical Criticism can provide much valuable information and insight into a text. Its application supplies valuable questions that can assist the scholar to lead out of a text the meaning built into it by its original writer.

Second, although the different forms of Biblical Criticism are separate disciplines, they are all interrelated in their concerns for the text as a literary product. Each merely focuses on a different aspect of the text and, through specialized questions, techniques, and methods of analysis, is interested in uncovering the whole meaning of the text as a literary unit.

The Method of Biblical Exegesis

Having considered the components of exegesis in some detail, it now remains to coordinate the steps involved in the historical analysis, or exegesis, of a text. In this process the researcher applies all of the techniques and questions discussed above.[33]

Delineating and Verifying the Text

The first step involves a consideration of the text itself. Every effort must be made through the discipline of Textual Criticism to establish and delineate the text under consideration. Through the study of reliable Greek or Hebrew texts and their critical apparatuses, the researcher seeks to establish that the text he is using comes closest to the original words penned by the author. Delineating the text has reference to making sure that the pericope being studied includes all of the words or phrases necessary to a complete understanding of the text and that a unity of thought, or the totality of one thought, is included in this pericope. The researcher has several techniques available to him for this purpose. He can consult the paragraphing of a reliable translation that sets the text out in paragraphs (the Revised Standard Version is a good example of such a text). He can consult the Greek and Hebrew text in this regard. Good critical commentaries and introductory studies will also be of help. The researcher capable of using the original language can also diagram the pericope and the surrounding verses in an effort to delineate accurately the opening and closing statements of the pericope.[34]

33. The student is encouraged to read the article by Malherbe referenced in note above, and to refer to the article by Muilenberg under the same note 1.

34. Cf. the chapter in this volume by F. Kearley for the information on diagraming, and J. D. Grassmick, *Principles and Practice of Greek Exegesis* (Dallas: Dallas Theological Seminary, 1974).

Defining the Contexts

Following the steps necessary in delineating and verifying the text, the researcher seeks to define the larger and immediate contexts of the pericope being researched. Here Redaction Criticism supplies some valuable questions: What is the theological purpose or interest of this work? What is the writer attempting to say through this work to his readers? What major themes are developed in this work? Historical Criticism also asks valuable questions: What are the historical, sociological, political, and religious contexts of this work? Having established the larger context of the pericope being studied, the researcher seeks to establish the immediate context of the pericope: How does this pericope relate to the thoughts immediately surrounding it? What major thought is it developing? How do these thoughts relate to the overall or larger context? The answers to these questions supply some of the fundamental checks and balances to subjective interpretations and consequent abuse of the text. A further helpful contextual investigation is an examination of contexts parallel to the one being studied. The researcher first considers parallel contexts in other writings of the same author. He then researches similar writings within the biblical canon. Finally he researches extra-biblical parallel contexts. Comprehensive concordances for the Bible and related literature are available for this purpose.

Identifying Background and Foreground

Closely related to establishing the context is the consideration of the background and foreground of the pericope. Background questions ask: From where did the writer draw his illustrations? What kind of influences did past writings or religio-philosophical ideas have upon the writer? These are questions of vital interest to the researcher. Answers from Historical-, Source-, Form-, and Tradition-Criticism open possibilities to background information. In literature incorporating apocalyptic sources, such as Revelation, background research is invaluable to a proper understanding of the text.

How the text was used by later Jewish or Christian writers supplies foreground context. This research explains how those closer in time to the text understood and used it. This historical perspective, when considered through a critical understanding of the theological problems of later writers, aids the researcher in understanding how the significance of the text has been perceived through history.

Establishing the Writer's Intention

It is imperative that the researcher establish how a writer intended his literature to be understood. Literary Criticism and its questions of form or genre are indispensable in this regard. It is only after the researcher has established what kind of literature he is studying that he can fathom its meaning. Figurative literature, or symbolic-mythological material, must be studied differently from literal or historical-narrative writing.

Studying the Language

After having made every effort to understand the contexts of a pericope and the form of literature used by the writer, the researcher is now in a position to consider the language of the text. Through careful philological and grammatical analysis, the researcher makes a translation of the text. Every significant word and syntactical construction is researched through lexicons, word studies, and other grammatical and philological tools. The researcher's translation and syntactical study should be checked against other major translations and critical studies of the grammar and syntax.

Comparative Research

Only after the researcher has made every effort to understand the text through the above avenues of study should consideration be given to other modern detailed exegetical treatments of the text. Research into comparative exegetical studies can reveal problems connected with the text that the researcher might not have identified and shows how these problems have been addressed from a variety of theological perspectives. This sharpens the researcher's appreciation of the text and its problems and indicates further avenues of consideration and research. Such detailed exegetical studies can be found in scholarly journals, critical commentaries, and other scholarly works.

When all of the above research possibilities have been carefully considered, the researcher makes a synthesis and paraphrase of his results. Malherbe remarks regarding this synthesis that ". . . this discipline will unite disparate elements, and will show a new dimension in the text itself. Here the task of exegesis ends, and that of hermeneutics takes over to place the text and its message in the total context of theology and its relevance to present-day man."[35]

The Task of Hermeneutics

At the outset of this study, the term *hermeneutics* was reserved for the final stage of biblical interpretation, wherein the interpreter relates the historical meaning of the text to his own contemporary context. Any discussion of hermeneutics in the contemporary theological climate thrusts one immediately into dialogue with the New Hermeneutic. Taking up the directions indicated by Heidegger, Bultmann, and Gadamer— that it is impossible to engage in hermeneutics without some "pre-under-

---

35. Malherbe, p. 178.

standing" of the text[36]—the New Hermeneutic makes much of the dynamic of the subjective role of the interpreter in the process of interpretation. Brief comments have already been made on one matter of concern in this process, namely, a "hermeneutic circle," in which it is argued that the interpreter begins with a pre-understanding of the text that ultimately shapes his final interpretation. That some form of hermeneutic circle exists should not be denied, but neither should the subjective element of the hermeneutic circle unduly unsettle the interpreter since we have already observed that it is the role of exegesis to establish checks and balances against excessive subjectivism. Nevertheless, some further comment on the matter of presupposition and a hermeneutic circle is incumbent at this point.

Malherbe has correctly observed, concerning the problem of presuppositions, that one should not resist the concept of presuppositions in biblical interpretation. It is not the existence of the presupposition that is the real issue, but the validity of the presupposition.[37] McGaughey admits to the existence of some form of presupposition when he notes that the primary principle or presupposition that one confronts in hermeneutics is one's attitude toward the role of Scripture as revelation or authority.[38] He observes concerning the "conservative"[39] view of Scripture that it accepts the Bible as authoritative revelation.[40] Naturally this presupposition has considerable impact on conservative hermeneutics. McGaughey maintains that "one's hermeneutic principles are always determined by one's concept of the Biblical records and their relation to the problem of revelation."[41]

It is not the task of this study to analyze the validity of the various presuppositions regarding the role or authority of Scripture. The point at issue here is that one's hermeneutic is significantly influenced by one's presupposition concerning the role of Scripture. For example, classical Historical Criticism could not see beyond a presupposition that limited the role of the text to that of merely an historical document. Hence it could not proceed beyond a purely historical analysis. Bultmann cor-

---

36. R. Bultmann, *Essays* (New York: Macmillan, 1955), p. 239. Bultmann argues that "A comprehension—an interpretation—is, it follows, *constantly oriented to a particular formulation of a question, a particular 'objective'*. But included in this is the fact . . . that it is *governed always by a prior understanding of the subject*, in accordance with which it investigates the text."

37. Malherbe, p. 170.

38. McGaughey, pp. 251ff.

39. The term "conservative" is an unfortunate one that is at best ambiguous. However, when considered in the context of such terms as "liberal," "neo-orthodox," or "existential," it is expressive of a general view of Scripture that seeks to emphasize some form of divine initiative or super-intendence in the production of Scripture.

40. McGaughey (note 1), pp. 255f.

41. Ibid., p. 256.

rectly observed that liberal theology consequently failed in that it did not ask what its research said "for me."[42] As opposed to this liberal view, which considered the Scriptures merely as historical text, a more balanced view of Scripture understands the text as a record of God's revelation of his nature and his word for man. This revelation, it is held, has been made in the context of history, but not simply an ordinary kind of history. God's revelation is in a history broken open and given meaning and direction by the person and significance of Jesus. It is through Jesus and the circumstances surrounding Jesus that God has finally revealed his will to man. The Bible is the record of this revelation in history. Malherbe observes that "in Christ a new meaning of history is revealed—revealed in the first century, but with validity for all time. This presupposition was also that of the writers of the NT."[43]

This understanding of the nature of Scripture as the record of God's revelation in history is the fundamental presupposition of the method of biblical interpretation set forth in this study. It is the responsibility of biblical interpretation, therefore, to approach the Scriptures as the source of such revelation in history. Through the practice of biblical exegesis, the attempt is made to understand the meaning of this revelation in its original context.[44] When this historical meaning has been established, the task of exegesis is completed, but that of biblical interpretation is only begun. The consequent task of reflecting on the contemporary significance of the historical meaning moves one from the discipline of exegesis to that of hermeneutics. Malherbe and Stendahl concur that it is at this point that the task of the exegete ends and the task of the systematic theologian begins.[45]

Hermeneutics—as the term is here being used to refer to the final stage of biblical interpretation—is therefore not the task of the historical exegete, but that of the preacher or systematic theologian. In this regard Stendahl observes, "It is here the student of biblical material leaves off and the theologian has to take over if we want to answer the question what all this 'means' to the Church."[46] He further observes that "such contemporary relevance is quite different from the 'meaning'" of the original text.[47] The tasks of the preacher and the theologian concerning the text are similar, although the theologian focuses on a general or broad audience, while the preacher focuses on a specific and narrower audience.

42. R. Bultmann, "Die Bedeutung des Alten Testaments für den christlichen Glauben," *Glauben und Verstehen*, Vol. I (Tübingen: Verlag J. C. B. Mohr, 1958), p. 317.
43. Malherbe, p. 171.
44. Muilenberg, (note 1), p. 19.
45. Malherbe, p. 178, and Stendahl, pp. 37f.
46. Stendahl, p. 37.
47. Ibid., p. 38.

Both in their own discipline seek to move their audience from the historical text to contemporary involvement with the text.

As the systematic theologian directs his attention to translating the meaning of a text to his audience and so begins the process of hermeneutics, further ruling principles of interpretation must be developed "whereby the relevant and authoritative aspects of Scripture can be separated from the incidental and non-authoritative."[48] Through a careful analysis of the exegetical findings, the theologian suggests a hypothesis concerning the text as to its normative or incidental nature. This hypothesis is then evaluated against the "analogy of Scripture."[49] By this term is meant the overall theological context of Scripture as previously determined through careful exegetical study and synthesis. Although not using the same terminology, B. Childs speaks of hermeneutics within the context of the Christian canon. He observes:

> The challenge of the Christian interpreter in our day is to hear the full range of notes within all of Scripture, to wrestle with the theological implication of this biblical witness, and above all, to come to grips with the agony of our age before a loving God who still speaks through the Prophets and Apostles.[50]

In other words, the exegetical hypothesis is carefully analyzed and evaluated in the context of other scriptural hypotheses. L. Goppelt makes the following succinct observation regarding this relationship between exegesis and theology:

> New Testament theology not only gathers the theological conclusions of exegesis, but develops an overview, or better a view of the whole, that stimulates exegesis, and indeed, makes it possible at all. The study of the New Testament proceeds theologically and historically in a continual dialogue moving from matters of particular concern to the whole and back again from the whole to the particular.[51]

The end result of this careful process of analysis and evaluation through the analogy of Scripture is a statement concerning either the normative

48. McGaughey, p. 255. McGaughey discusses the ruling principles in hermeneutics adopted by various schools of biblical studies. In particular he focuses on the liberal, neo-orthodox, existential, and the conservative approach to hermeneutics.

49. W. Kaiser (note 1) develops this point extremely well in his chapter entitled "Theological Analysis." He discusses problems involved in using the "analogy of faith" (analogia fidei) or "Scripture by Scripture" principle (Scriptura Scripturam interpretatur), and suggests in their place the "analogy of (antecedent) Scripture" whereby a text is compared diachronically. Kaiser, pp. 131–140.

50. B. S. Childs, "Psalm 8 in the Context of the Christian Canon," Interpretation 23 (Jan. 1969): 20–31, and Biblical Theology in Crisis (Philadelphia: Westminster, 1970).

51. L. Goppelt, Theology of the New Testament, Vol. 1 (Grand Rapids: Eerdmans, 1981), p. xxv.

authority of the text or its existence as a circumstantial or incidental matter of biblical record. The task of the theologian is never closed, for this process of analysis and evaluation by the analogy of Scripture is always open to future exegesis and analysis.

The final stage of hermeneutics to be considered addresses the contemporary implications of the biblical text. This stage is also a matter of analogy. Here the theologian (most likely the preacher) seeks to determine what conditions or considerations within his own contemporary context might be analogous to the biblical context and message. In this manner the meaning and significance of the historical message of the original text is brought forward to "challenge" the contemporary analogous context of the interpreter. Thus the revelation of God and his will in the Bible, understood as a revelation in history broken open by the significant event of Jesus, is understood through exegesis and brought forward through hermeneutics to challenge contemporary man. The hermeneutic circle, which began with a presupposition concerning the authoritative role of Scripture, is completed as the interpreter is himself addressed by the text.

2

The Implication of Proper Principles of Biblical Interpretation for Christian Unity

Ted Carruth

Shortly before his death, Jesus prayed four times that his disciples be one.[1] The unity of believers that Jesus desired is analogous to the unity of the Father and the Son. At least three factors may be mentioned:

1. It is a unity that already exists. Jesus did not pray that they may "become" one, but that they may "continually be" one. The Father and the Son are one as a result of their nature. Believers are one because of a faith relationship that gives them a new nature.

2. It is a unity that does not completely identify the one as the other. In other words, the Father and the Son are one and yet remain different. There is diversity in their unity. The same is true of believers. It is not a unity by means of "cloning." However, in spite of not being completely reciprocal, each can be said to be "in" the other. The Father abiding in the Son does his works. The Son exists in the Father's being.

3. Further, it is a unity of resolve, goals, and affections. While organizational and doctrinal equanimity are admirable goals and can be impressive witnesses to the unity of the spirit, they are nonetheless merely outward forms. To have these does not insure the unity for which Jesus prayed. Stated differently, a group may be a team without being unified. Jesus had in mind something far more difficult. He desired a oneness of emotion, aim, and will.

---

1. John 17:11, 21, 23, 24 with neuter *hen.*

Not only did Jesus pray that all be one, he also took steps that would lead to the fulfillment of his prayer. First, his death destroyed the barriers that divided men from God, themselves, and others (Col. 1:19–22). Second, he gave a means, another comforter, the Spirit, by which the believer would be assisted to live within the unity that his death and resurrection had effected (John 16:12–15; 20:22–23). Third, Christ, through the Spirit, gave various gifts to men (Eph. 4:7) to equip "the saints . . . for building up the body of Christ, until we all attain to the unity of the faith and of the knowledge of the Son of God, to mature manhood, to the measure of the stature of the fulness of Christ" (Eph. 4:12–13, RSV). Through the exercise of these gifts, the statement of, the witnesses for, and the explanation of Christ's work was divinely directed to be written down, preserved, and transmitted to men so that the aim of Jesus would be fulfilled.

It is not within the purview of this essay to discuss the complex process of the inscripturation of the divine message. However, one does need to recognize that Scripture has come to man not because man is finite, but because man is a sinner. The Bible is a coherent redemptive message and must therefore be interpreted as a written statement of God's revelation regarding his redemption of his creatures.

Since the Bible is not just another religious book, but a document regarding God's act for man, which is the most profound thought and action in all of man's experience, every effort should be devoted to understanding and applying its message. If this is neglected, the aim of Jesus is thwarted.

To properly interpret the mind of the Spirit as conveyed in the thought of the writer, one must allow oneself to be conformed to the principles utilized by the Spirit. Inasmuch as one cooperates with the Spirit's principles and his guidance in those principles, progress is made toward the goal. Inasmuch as the Spirit's principles are distorted and abused, the process is hindered. Therefore, applying proper principles of interpretation means utilizing those means by which one can prepare for the Spirit's guidance. One does not obtain the Spirit by the use of these principles. One is merely able to open avenues by which the Spirit may instruct. Only by this means may one be able to apply the message and progress toward the attainment of Christ's aim. Although the unity of the Spirit was effected on the eternal plane by Christ, "unity of the faith" has not yet been attained on the earthly sphere. Since the task is unfinished, the body is still growing to fit the head.

Interpretive Tools and Attitudes

Cooperating with the Spirit's principles and guidance includes at least the following factors.

1. One needs to begin with the proper document, that is, what is commonly referred to as the canon. Those familiar with early church history cannot help but appreciate the labor expended to bring into existence the canon of sixty-six books. Men did not simply "decide" which books would be included, but they did follow the Spirit's guidance and recognized and accepted those books as God's revelation in Christ.

2. One also profits by being familiar with the Spirit's medium of communication—language. This necessitates learning the correct grammar, vocabulary, and usage of the vocabulary in order to understand the author's meaning so that it may be applied to oneself. For most people, since the Bible was written in a language different from their own, this requires additional language preparation, either by learning the original languages or by being cognizant of the factors involved when the message of one language is translated into another.[2] This is not to imply that God's message may not change the lives of those who are poorly equipped in semantics. However, faith does come "by hearing and hearing by the word of God." Therefore, when one is dependent upon the understanding of others for his own understanding of the Word, he needs to be cautious lest he confuse the message itself with another person's understanding of the message.

3. The best results for a clear understanding come from the use of the most accurate text. Since no autographed originals are available, one is dependent on what the Spirit has seen fit to preserve: copies, translations, quotations, and so on. The amount of material is indeed massive and therefore serves as a check and countercheck against faulty readings.

4. An awareness of the historical and cultural factors that served as both a backdrop and a stimulus for the author's work is also helpful. The authors did not write out of a vacuum. Questions involving introductory materials would be included here.

5. Since the Spirit utilized the way God has made men think and reason, it is to one's advantage to be aware of how the mind functions. These processes include what logicians term "fundamental laws," such as: (a) the law of identity or affirmation; (b) the law of contradiction or negation; (c) the law of the excluded middle; and (d) the law of continuous thought. From these laws, two conclusions are usually mentioned. First, truth regarding reality can be ascertained and can be agreed upon when men's minds act in accordance with the laws of thought; and, second, that which is implicitly contained in thought may be conveyed explicitly in language.[3]

2. Useful in this endeavor is J. Beekman and J. Callow, *Translating the Word of God* (Grand Rapids: Zondervan, 1974).

3. Among the resource materials are W. Hamilton, *Lectures on Metaphysics and Logic* (Boston: Gould and Lincoln, 1873); R. Whately, *Elements of Logic* (New York:

6. One benefits from the realization that everyone approaches the study of the Scriptures with his own set of complex circumstances and understandings. On one side are the personal factors or prejudices that affect the judgment of the interpreter. On the other side are the philosophical and theological assumptions or presuppositions that the interpreter shares with some others. Both play significant roles in the result of one's study. While some have attempted to approach the Scriptures strictly from a neutral stance, without presuppositions, the results have been disappointing. Instead of attempting to discard all influencing factors, one may take appropriate cautionary steps, as listed by Stanton[4]: (a) the awareness of the danger of prejudices and presuppositions; (b) the use of the historical-critical method[5]; and (c) allowing one's own presuppositions to be modified or even remolded by the text itself. One will not interpret the text as much as the text will interpret him.

7. An awareness of the hermeneutical principles that have been employed throughout the centuries is also desirable. Such a knowledge gives both positive and negative models. Of particular importance is distinguishing between the methods utilized by (a) Jesus and his immediate disciples; (b) his other interpreters in the New Testament; and (c) subsequent interpreters of the New Testament.[6]

Unifying Hermeneutical Principles

The New Testament writers treated the text of the Old Testament with a degree of freedom, selecting from the various textual traditions the one that best set forth the proper concept. For example, in a number of instances the wording of statements attributed to Jesus is drawn from the LXX as against the MT or known Targums. Subsequent interpreters do not have that prerogative. The New Testament authors also employed a number of diverse methods of interpretation current at the time. Among these are literalistic exegesis (historical-grammatical), *pesher* ("this" is "that") interpretation, *midrash* exegesis (some of Hillel's rules), and to some extent allegorical treatment. They shift from one to the other and do not sense any opposition of one method to another.

Harper and Brothers, n.d.); R. Smart, *An Introductory Logic* (New York: Macmillan, 1898); H. S. Leonard, *Principles of Reasoning* (New York: Dover, 1967); P. T. Geach, *Logic Matters* (Berkeley: Univ. of California, 1972).

4. G. N. Stanton, "Presuppositions in New Testament Criticism," in *New Testament Interpretation: Essays on Principles and Methods*, ed. by I. H. Marshall (Grand Rapids: Eerdmans, 1977), pp. 68–69.

5. An analysis of this approach and its principles is found in B. Ramm, *Protestant Biblical Interpretation* (Boston: W. A. Wilde, 1950).

6. Useful in this endeavor is R. N. Longenecker, *Biblical Exegesis in the Apostolic Period* (Grand Rapids: Eerdmans, 1975).

It is notable, however, that Jesus and the apostles utilized some principles not utilized by other New Testament writers and speakers. Because of their historic relationship, Jesus gave a unique place to the apostles in the explanation of the redemptive process. One example is the apparent absence of the *pesher* ("this," is "that" fulfillment motif or "mystery revealed" principle) type of exegesis in writers other than Jesus, the Twelve, and the apostle untimely born, Paul.[7] Being eyewitnesses of the life, death, and resurrection, the apostles could understand the Old Testament Christologically in a unique way. They thus used Jesus' own approach as a paradigm for their continued interpretative efforts of showing that "this" which was manifest in the person and work of Jesus, is "that," which was recorded in some event in the nation's history or prophetic message.

The uniqueness of Jesus as the true interpreter of the Old Testament and the distinctive place he gave the apostles in the explication of the Christ event are sufficient reasons to caution us against using their methods as a hard-and-fast set of hermeneutical rules. The authors of the New Testament were proclaiming a message. They were not giving a textbook on the science of hermeneutics. The acceptance of the Christological interpretation of the Old Testament and its fulfillment in Jesus produced the oneness that is described at certain points in the life of the church in the early chapters of Acts. It was the nonacceptance of this proclamation that resulted in the persecution, division, and heretical concepts that troubled the Christian movement of the first century.

The task of subsequent interpreters is unchanged, namely, to understand and apply the message of Christ's redemptive work in their own lives. The same Spirit is available for guidance. However, there is one restriction. An interpreter is solely dependent upon the text before him and does not possess the special eyewitness insights of the apostles. Therefore, it is all the more important to discern and conform to the principles utilized by the Spirit.

Almost twenty centuries have been devoted to that effort. It is customary to group this struggle into seven major schools or periods: Rabbinic; Alexandrian or allegorical; Antioch or literal; Scholastic; Reformation; Post-Reformation; and Modern.[8] The last of these may be divided into

7. Jude's use of 1 Enoch 1:9 may preclude this exception. However, Jude may have regarded the statement as true from a proverbial point of view. It is true whether or not it is derived from canonical scripture. See Longenecker, p. 204.

8. A history of interpretation before the twentieth century may be found in F. Farrar, *History of Interpretation* (London: Macmillan, 1886); G. H. Gilbert, *Interpretation of the Bible: A Short History* (New York: Macmillan, 1908); R. M. Grant, *A Short History of the Interpretation of the Bible* (New York: Macmillan, 1963). For the twentieth century consult H. Hahn, *The Old Testament in Modern Research* (Philadelphia: Fortress, 1966); S. Neill, *The Interpretation of the New Testament 1861–1961* (London: Oxford University, 1964); I. H. Marshall, ed., *New Testament Interpretation: Essays in Principles and Methods* (Grand Rapids, Eerdmans, 1977); J. Rogers and D. Mckim, *The Authority and Interpretation of the Bible: An Historical Approach* (New York: Harper and Row, 1979).

"old hermeneutics," which gives varying degrees of credibility to historic accounts, and "new hermeneutics," which largely concludes that the actual events are unrecoverable and/or unnecessary. Each of these approaches may be further subdivided, with additional or refined principles such as structuralism and the meaning of language, being currently evaluated.[9] The continuing search indicates that man needs to be extremely cautious in claiming that all the principles have been discerned.

Two trends emerge from the attempts made throughout Christian history to interpret the text. The first is negative, namely, division. The course of biblical studies is marked by clash and tragedies resulting from distortions and abuse. Incalculable damage has been done to Christ, his work, and those who both honor and dishonor him because of misinterpretation of the Bible. Superstition, antinomian license, hatred, fanaticism, and unyielding sectarianism are but a few of the results of misapplication. The Crusades, the witch hunts, the Spanish Inquisition, the persecution of Huguenots, the oppression by kings who regarded their position as a divine right, all illustrate the twisting of God's Word to fit Satan's designs. When an interpreter sets forth the wrong sense of God's Word, he hides the divine message so that it becomes Satan's word. The result: Scripture is used to destroy, not to save.

The second trend is positive. The bright spot in the disastrous drama is that in spite of all the aberrations that have developed through the centuries, none has been able to obscure God's message completely. The truths sufficient for man's response to God's grace have reached the fertile soil. Regardless of the failures of a particular period or school of interpretation, each has made contributions to the study of Scripture. In one way or another, each age or system serves as a corrective to the excesses of another period or school and continually adds to the wealth of insight into Scripture. Each age instructs, warns, and paves the way for perceiving the message in another light.

For example, the Rabbis invested their time on minute and insignificant details and thereby smothered the message. However, they rendered the invaluable service of preserving the text. The Fathers of the church were plagued by allegorical abuses that distorted the meaning. Yet today all are indebted to the insights of Irenaeus, Jerome, and Augustine, who plowed previously untouched soil and cut paths that would lead to clearer understanding. The Scholastics dealt with unnecessary speculation and overly systematized the material. Yet their contribution does not go unnoticed, since they, too, paved a way for greater things. While the

9. Consult for relevant bibliography A. C. Thiselton, "Semantics and New Testament Interpretation" in Marshall, *Essays*, pp. 75–104. For additional sources consult A. M. Johnson, Jr., *A Bibliography of Semiological and Structural Studies of Religion* (Pittsburgh: Clifford E. Barbour Library, 1979).

Reformation served to recall scholars to the text rather than to man's reason and tradition, it was hampered by its own pride. Hermeneutics of the Post-Reformation era was a new form of scholastic subtlety and systematization, yet it prompted renewed interest and research. The Modernists exhibit the concern of calling into question certain time-honored assumptions. Although such interests are regarded as the attack of an enemy, study has been stimulated to reconfirm what the Bible self-attests: it is the Word of God.

Thus, from the varied approaches and the varied attacks, the Scriptures themselves have nothing to fear. God's Word stands. Also, the continued results of changed lives and devotion to Christ also indicate that in spite of incomplete understanding or application, the power of the Word to effect conversion is not diminished. Although the Scriptures are violated and Christ and his work are dishonored when hermeneutics are incorrect, man's misdeeds cannot overcome God's designs. One need not think that unity will be achieved only if the proper principles have been intellectually perceived and expertly applied. God's ways outstrip all of man's machinations.

This is not to say that man should not continue his quest to discern and apply principles by which Christ will be set forth. This is the very point Paul makes in Ephesians 4:1–3. We are to be "eager to maintain the unity of the Spirit in the bond of peace" (RSV). All our interpretative efforts will not establish this unity, since it has already been effected by God in Christ. However, we are to expose and reject principles, attitudes, and methodologies that impair that unity.

Achieving the Bond of Peace

The above-mentioned trends are a result of two opposing factors. First, the cause for division always has been in man. The paradox of biblical interpretation is that even those who affirm the desire to use the principles that God has ordained for life under his dominion also desire self-autonomy. They wish to determine by man-made categories who or what the ultimate authority will be.[10] They establish "the system" to which all are to adhere, and in the end they stymie the acceptance of the power of the Word. When man begins the process of interpretation with his own reasoning abilities at the center, division will always result. This comment is not to be viewed as a rejection of reason and its use. It is only to say that the process of interpretation too often begins at the wrong place. Nor

10. C. Van Til, *A Christian Theory of Knowledge* (Nutley, N.J.: Presbyterian and Reformed, 1977) examines the factors involved. An evaluation and response to Van Til's views is found in *Jerusalem and Athens*, ed. by E. R. Geehan (Grand Rapids: Baker, 1971).

is it to be construed as supporting a mystical or subjective apprehension of truth. The power of the Word comes through the proclamation of the message in propositional statements about which man may study, ponder, and reason. However, the authority of these reasonable statements is not established by reason. If we begin with man and his categories, we cannot end with God. We end only with man's rational apprehension of God.

Instead, one must begin with God, who is all-sufficient and thus speaks with absolute authority. Although this is usually affirmed, not all interpreters mean the same things by the affirmation. The statement "God speaks with absolute authority" means that his Word has authority in and of itself. God does not need tradition or human reason to justify or establish what he says as true. His Word comes to man, who is not all-sufficient, with absolute authority. Furthermore, the all-sufficient God, when speaking to man with absolute authority, does not reveal everything about himself or even use infinite categories to explain this limited revelation. God reveals only what man needs to know and is capable of knowing. "For my thoughts are not your thoughts, neither are your ways my ways, says the LORD. For as the heavens are higher than the earth, so are my ways higher than your ways and my thoughts than your thoughts" (Isa. 55:8–9, RSV). God speaks to man in human terms and is understood by human rational powers, but his concepts are not established by human reason.

For example, before the fall, God communicated to man how to enjoy the divinely ordained system. Man did not "reason" that what God said was true, since there were no prior categories for determining whether or not one would die if the forbidden fruit was eaten. Man either accepted God's revelation (communication) or he rejected it. When tempted to become self-autonomous and under his own authority, man rejected the communication of God. The fall resulted. Though he still "knew" God in the sense that he was God's creature, he did not "know" God ethically. Man was a sinner.[11]

After the fall, God addressed man differently. In addressing man as sinner, God communicated two major points. First, he explained what man is—a sinner, one who is opposed to identifiable authority over himself. Man desires self-autonomy and therefore attempts to interpret facts apart from the revelation or communication of God. Second, God also indicated how man, being what he is, may understand and enjoy God's system. As God began to unfold his love to man the sinner, the process of inscripturation or explanation of that love began. The Bible alone explains God's redemption through Christ and how one may enjoy what God has done for man.

---

11. Ibid., p. 52.

The Fallacies of Self-Autonomous Man

The Bible was not written for man because man was finite, but because man was a sinner. Here centers the problem. Man's sense of self-autonomy, a principle that was first demonstrated by Adam and Eve in the Garden of Eden, causes one of two things:

1. Man will deny that he is a sinner. He may acknowledge that he is imperfect or even very wicked, but he will not admit that he really wants to be the ultimate authority. He will attempt to arrange the facts around him (that which God has established) according to his own thinking. However, this arrangement will always be biased to fit his desire for self-adequacy. He rejects the guidance (Scripture) that would enable him to place himself under God's authority. Instead, he substitutes his own system. The polytheistic accounts of Israel's neighbors regarding the beginning of the world, man, and the flood are cases in point. Likewise, some contemporary sociological and psychological explanations of why man does not sense that he has reached his highest potential also illustrate this attempt for self-autonomy. On the other hand, although man may accept the Scriptures as God's message of redemption, he may abuse it with his desire for ultimacy. He may delude himself by saying he is doing God's will, when in fact he is doing his own will in God's name. He will erect a system to explain or interpret the Word of God to others. In the end the system clouds the message and often becomes the substitute for the message.

For example, Jesus explicitly affirmed that he was self-attesting. Light bears witness to itself. True, the Baptist bore witness to Christ, but his witness did not establish him to be the Christ. It was what Jesus said and did that established him as the Christ. Again, reflection upon what he said and did is reasonable and rational, but such a systematization does not establish Jesus as the Christ. When men sought to use reason to demonstrate whether or not Jesus was the Christ, they invariably divided (John 6:41–43; 7:27–31; 9:24–34). When man does not submit to God as the rightful self-attesting authority and instead, desiring to be ultimate, attempts by his own abilities to establish authority, he destroys himself and others. Unity can never result.

The same thing occurs in the area of interpretation. One may devise a rational system to be used to understand Scripture. However, the principles involved are often confused with Scripture itself. Rabbinic exegesis is a case in point. Hillel devised seven rules of interpretation in order to bring cohesion to rabbinic efforts. Some of the rules were used by Jesus and the writers of the New Testament. However, the well-intentioned principles were used by some to bring about some very distorted conclusions.[12] Division results whenever man reasons and establishes in his own mind what God intended and then applies that system to all others.

---

12. Farrar, *Interpretation*, (note 8), pp. 19–20 cites examples.

2. Man will reject the idea that the solution for the destructive results of self-autonomy is submission to God as exemplified in Samuel's request, "Speak Lord, thy servant heareth." God enables the individual to perceive and utilize principles that lead to the enlightening of the soul. On the surface this may appear to rely upon pietism or a mystical encounter, and it would seem that there would be a multitude of voices. As Ramm[13] rightly observes, one of the most acute problems is how two Spirit-led men arrive at divergent interpretations. The answer is the realization that the Holy Spirit has spoken through the inscripturated Word, giving there the proper interpretation of the Christ event. He does not now give a refresher or special interpretation. There is no substitute for study, knowledge, and perseverance. Deep reverence for God involves a passion to know God's Word so that the truest interpretation comes forth. Since the truest interpretation is the one with the best justification, this necessitates equipping oneself in languages, history, culture, geography, psychology, and many other disciplines. By being submissive to God, one will eliminate many of the false principles that history has revealed. Above all, submission to God enables the message to come to the interpreter without the dominating force of man's self-autonomy, the most debilitating of all hindrances. This was the tragedy of Jesus' studious opponents: "[Ye] Search the scriptures; for in them [not in God] ye think you have eternal life . . ." (John 5:39, KJV). Study, methods, and principles without submission bring failure. Submission without investigation is vanity.

The process described in Ephesians 4:1–3 is not easy. The maintenance of "unity of the Spirit in the bond of peace" involves an arduous, continuous endeavor. God's people have been summoned to lead a worthy life through the hearing of the Word. That life is to be held in a spirit of lowliness and meekness, underscored with patience and forbearance toward one another in love. The call for an eagerness to maintain that unity stresses the fact that the task is ongoing and incomplete "until we attain to the unity of the faith . . ." (Eph. 4:13, RSV). The common denominator for establishing the oneness of Matthew the Publican and Simon the Zealot is Christ. As Christians submit to Christ, they learn; as they learn, they are humbled; as they are humbled, they become one.

13. Ramm (note 5), p. 61.

3

The Function of
Presuppositions and Attitudes
in Biblical Interpretation

Bill Flatt

Presuppositions and attitudes are involved in every aspect of biblical exegesis.[1] The interpreter must be able to distinguish between what a text means and what it means specifically to him.[2] Accurate exegesis is impossible without accurate presuppositions and attitudes.

Attitudes

Any interpreter's work is influenced by his own attitudes, prejudices, and personality. G. Stanton states, for example, that an optimist and a pessimist will interpret a literary or historical document differently.[3] A historian's political stance will alter his record of history. A young scholar in his efforts to be published may ignore contrary evidence or choose an irrelevant topic.[4] A favorite part of the Bible may be arbitrarily chosen as a yardstick for all other sections. Gadamer says that a complete detachment or unbiased stance is impossible: "Even a master of historical

1. F. F. Bruce, "The History of New Testament Study," *New Testament Interpretation* (Grand Rapids: Eerdmans, 1977), pp. 21–59.
2. E. D. Hirsch, Jr., *Validation and Interpretation* (New Haven: Yale University, 1967), p. 39.
3. G. M. Stanton, "Presuppositions in New Testament Criticism," *New Testament Interpretation* (Grand Rapids: Eerdmans, 1977), p. 61.
4. Ibid.

method is not able to remain completely free from the prejudices of his time, his social environment, his national position. . . ."[5]

Attitudes, conditioning, and prejudice are deeply seated, but they are not so great that they must inevitably determine the interpretation of a biblical text before it is read. One's mind does not have to be set in concrete. Although each person brings certain pre-understandings or hypotheses to the text, these may be altered by a critical encounter with the text. New hypotheses can and do appear.[6]

The interpreter may be tempted to read his own prejudgments into the text. Instead, he should use sound, consistent, sober, and honest principles and processes. His attitude should not prompt him to make exegetical conclusions with more certitude than are supported by his knowledge.[7] Avoiding unwarranted conclusions can be as difficult in scholarship as it is in everyday life. A husband, for example, may have a dominant attitude toward people in general. By nature, he either leads, dominates, or is inflexible. He may then come to a biblical text on family leadership, read it through his domineering glasses, and conclude that he has a biblical mandate to boss, to push, to coerce his wife, even to the point of "commanding" her love.

Correct biblical exegesis presupposes a sound attitude of objectivity, which in part is a measure of good mental health. A person without such healthy balance will read himself into the text and may not even be aware of what he is doing. Accurate exegesis cannot come from such an approach.

Presuppositions

Presuppositions have had a profound influence on biblical interpretation throughout history. An interpreter with doctrinal presuppositions looks for prooftexts to support his already-established doctrinal positions. Traditions also become part of one's explanation of a text. The parables, for example, are rich ground for such individual interpretations. Or a history of Jesus may be written in conjunction with the author's presuppositions about his life and works.

While one may disagree with R. Bultmann on many points, he seems correct when he says: "Every exegesis that is guided by dogmatic prejudices does not hear what the text says, but only lets the latter say what

5. J. M. Robinson, "Hermeneutic Since Barth," in *The New Hermeneutic*, ed. J. M. Robinson and J. B. Cobb (New York, 1974) pp. 1–77.

6. Hirsch, p. 261.

7. M. S. Terry, *Biblical Hermeneutics* (Grand Rapids: Baker, 1968), p. 151.

it[sic] wants to hear."[8] Even the textual critic may be influenced by his presuppositions when the text is ambiguous.

While all efforts should be made to avoid the influence of incorrect presuppositions, it is difficult for anyone to come to the text without certain preunderstandings. K. Barth emphasized that one such preunderstanding is to determine the meaning of the text for the original readers.[9] Some adaptation of the historical-critical method should be the starting point in exegesis.[10] A basic assumption of the historians is that evidence can be recovered and verified by reexamination of the data. It is also a well-accepted principle that when historical evidence is vague, one must not read into it his own views. It is easy for the historian to interpret the past in terms of his presuppositions and attitudes. A biblical scholar may choose by assumption, for example, not to see all of the evidence for causation. Thus, God may be excluded as a factor and all miracles denied as a possibility.[11] When one denies by assumption the possibility of God, however, he destroys the neutrality that is required of the scholar.[12]

It is also clear, as stated by E. Fuchs, that "in the interaction with the text with daily life we experience the truth of the New Testament."[13] However, the interpreter is in danger of becoming the measure of his own knowledge. Unless he is aware of his attitudes, he can merely be under a psychological illusion.[14] An interpreter may decide by his own will what he will get out of the text—the author's intended message or some other message. If one merely extracts his own meaning, he does not learn anything from the author. He does not feel what the author felt or know what he knew. Education has been torpedoed when the interpreter encounters not the author, but himself, his own preconceptions and prejudices.[15]

Formally Stated Presuppositions

Probably the best starting place for examining presuppositions is with those made by modern science, because biblical interpreters have to deal with these same presuppositions. G. Collins lists five assumptions of mod-

8. R. Bultmann, "Is Exegesis Without Presuppositions Possible? in *Existence in Faith*, ed. and trans. J. Smogden (London: Hodder and Stoughton, 1961, 1964), p. 343.

9. K. Barth, *The Epistle to the Romans* (New York: Oxford University, 1933, 1957), pp. 1–3.

10. E. Krentz, *The Historical-Critical Method* (Philadelphia: Fortress, 1975).

11. S. E. Morrison, "Faith of an Historian," *American Historical Review* 56 (1951): 290.

12. R. Grant, *A Historical Introduction to the New Testament* (London: Carl Lentz, 1963), p. 78.

13. E. Fuchs, "The Hermeneutical Problem," in *The Future of Our Religious Past*, ed. J. M. Robinson (London: SCM, 1971), p. 142.

14. J. C. Webber, "Language-Event and Christian Faith," *TToday* 21 (1965): 455.

15. Hirsch, p. 26.

ern science: empiricism, determinism, relativism, reductionism, and naturalism.[16]

1. *Empiricism* is said to be the objective examination of observable facts. The empiricist assumes that the only truth that can be accepted is available in observations that can be viewed through one's senses.[17]

2. *Determinism* is another basic assumption of modern science. Determinism is the belief that behavior is determined by some prior cause or causes. Thus, if the causes of behavior can be fully discovered, they can be predicted and controlled. To extreme determinists, individual freedom is an illusion.[18] Other determinists believe that humans have a little freedom, but that most behavior is molded by their environment. Extreme metaphysical determinists eliminate personal freedom to respond to divine guidance.

3. *Relativism* is a third assumption of modern science. This widespread view holds that there are no absolute truths, no constant values.[19] Such a view negates inspiration of the Bible and undermines its authority.

Philosophically, it is inconsistent to state that there are no absolute values, for in stating this, one *is* stating an absolute truth and is thus contradicting himself. Perhaps what the relativist wishes to say is that there are no absolute truths except the truth that there are no absolute truths.

4. *Reductionism* is the view that all human behavior can be reduced to small units that are easier to investigate than the whole.[20] Human actions may thus be reduced to conditioned responses, synapses, hormone actions, id impulses, or other basic units. It is thought that eventually all of these small bits and pieces will add up to a firm, well-established body of truth.

The temptation of reductionism is to resort to "nothing-butism." Human behavior studied in bit parts is thus nothing but animal behavior. Memory is nothing but a reaction in the brain. Belief in God is nothing but superstition. Conversion is nothing but a reaction to manipulative techniques of a preacher. A human is nothing but a machine which receives input from the environment, stores it in a memory system, and gives output in the form of responses. Another person becomes an "it" to be analyzed and used rather than a "thou" to be respected and understood.[21]

16. G. Collins, *The Rebuilding of Psychology* (Wheaton, IL: Tyndale House, 1980), pp. 75–77.

17. J. Shotter and A. Gauld, "The Defense of Empirical Psychology," *American Psychologist* 26 (1971): 460–66.

18. B. F. Skinner, *Beyond Freedom and Dignity* (New York: Alfred A. Knopf, 1971).

19. J. Kagan, "On the Need for Relativism," *American Psychologist* 22 (1967): 131–42.

20. Collins, p. 85.

21. M. Buber, *I and Thou* (New York: Rinehart, 1947).

While acknowledging that there is some value in reductionism as a method of science, it is inadequate as a complete explanation of reality. One cannot explain love, faith, hope, expectation, anger, beauty, or sin by finding the psychological or physiological foundation underlying such behavior.[22]

5. *Naturalism* is the view that man is alone in the universe, that there is no God.[23] All human behavior thereby results from natural forces. Expressing this view, Eric Fromm says that there is no meaning in life except the meaning that man gives it. The universe is indifferent to man's fate. There is no power that transcends him.[24] Transcendence has thus been set aside by the *a priori* assumption of naturalism, and humans work within a framework that limits its outlook strictly to that view.[25] The naturalist explains away all historical evidence that does not fit his assumptions, such as the evidence for the divinity of Jesus. The supernaturalist accepts such evidence.[26] "But surely this method," says G. H. Clark, "is not only the reverse of the Christian method, it is clearly the reverse of rational procedure as well."[27]

Collins is correct: the assumptions of modern science do influence us. For example, empiricism eliminates biblical revelation; determinism leaves little room for freedom of choice; relativism discards absolute truth; reductionism ignores the complexity and completeness of human beings; and naturalism renounces supernaturalism. Indeed, if these presuppositions of modern science are rigidly accepted, biblical Christianity is destroyed.

Yet this is not to say that the interpreter comes to the text as a blank slate, with no beliefs at all. B. Ramm states: "The scholar does not exist completely free from presuppositions, and completely delivered from any emotionally or culturally rooted disposition that would materially influence his interpretation."[28]

All presuppositions influence exegesis.[29]

An Expanded View

While Collins stated well the main presuppositions of modern science, they may be somewhat difficult for the minister to apply since he does not

22. D. M. McKay, *The Clockwork Image* (Downers Grove, IL: InterVarsity, 1974), p. 43.

23. Collins, p. 88.

24. E. Fromm, *Man For Himself* (New York: Rinehart, 1947), p. 445.

25. P. Tournier, *The Person Reborn* (New York: Harper & Row, 1966), pp. 24–25.

26. M. A. Jeeves, *The Scientific Enterprise and Christian Faith* (Downers Grove, IL: InterVarsity, 1969), p. 33.

27. G. H. Clark, "Miracles: History and Natural Law," *The Evangelical Quarterly* 12 (1940): 34.

28. B. L. Ramm, *Biblical Interpretation in Hermeneutics* by B. Ramm and others (Grand Rapids: Baker, 1967), p. 21.

29. Ibid., pp. 19–30.

often deal with such terms. There are other attitudes, beliefs, and/or assumptions that are also important for the person who is already a believer in God. An expanded list and discussion of these follows:

1. The interpreter must have a healthy and balanced attitude and mental condition. This is so vital that its absence can negate every other point that is discussed. If a person is mentally unbalanced or has an attitude that is significantly tilted in certain directions, this can distort his exegesis. Personality can likewise twist biblical interpretations. An example of this is the dominating person who looks for Scripture to justify his authoritarianism.

2. One should use adequate tools for exegesis. While everyone would agree that a knowledge of reading is essential for exegesis, it has also been traditionally recognized that a knowledge of the liberal arts and of Hebrew and Greek, as well as a theological education, are helpful. Barows says: ". . . there should always be in the church a body of men able to go behind the current versions of the scripture to the original tongues from which these versions were executed."[30] A knowledge of other languages is of great value to biblical scholars.

It is important that an exegete have a certain level of intellectual ability, a knowledge of certain necessary tools, and a willingness to use them. These tools start with the text of Scripture. Resources include works that deal with textual and historical matters, as well as standard grammars, lexicons, concordances, commentaries, Bible dictionaries, Bible encyclopedias, Bible atlases, and other specialized books and journals. The fact that such helps have sometimes been abused is no reason to forsake them.

In examining the text and related resources, one makes certain important presuppositions:

The true canon of Scripture has been established. Ramm states that theological considerations and Historical Criticism unite to settle the problem of canon.[31] The boundary of Scripture must be determined before one interprets it. This involves the question of what books belong in the Bible. If one does not have the correct canon, then exegesis is either inaccurate or incomplete.

The text we have is reliable. There are many manuscripts and numerous differences among them. The work of a textual critic is to determine the correct text: to determine what was the original wording of the Word of God. Ramm says that the number of "really important textual variations of the New Testament that cannot be settled with our present information is very small, and the manuscripts available from the

30. Ibid., p. 16.
31. B. Ramm, *Protestant Biblical Interpretation* (Grand Rapids: Baker, 1970), p. 7.

various caves around the Dead Sea show the remarkable purity of our present Old Testament text."[32]

The text of the Bible can be adequately translated and understood. If Scripture cannot be adequately translated, most people cannot read what God is saying. If it cannot be understood, none can grasp what God is trying to say.

Jack Lewis has made a tremendous contribution to the understanding of translations in his recent book on *The English Bible*.[33] In a recent article, Lewis stated that the idea of restoring New Testament Christianity involves making several assumptions, including the assumption that the text can be rendered into various vernaculars so that the common man can read about and know what his duties to God and humanity are. He further states that apart from the validity of this assumption—that there was a valid revelation of God's will and that the valid text for that revelation can be established—a Restoration Movement makes no sense. In general, Lewis continues, "the man who has become persuaded that there is not unity, authenticity, infallibility, and authority in Scripture has in time sought fellowship elsewhere,"[34]— not with the churches of Christ.

Historical (or Higher) Criticism deals with the character of the books of the Bible: authorship, date of composition, historical circumstances, authenticity of contents, and literary unity. Such studies may undergird faith. Proper exegesis also presupposes Textual and Literary Criticism of the document. It is at this point that exegesis begins. A canon has been determined, a text has been established, the framework of the books has been demonstrated, and rules of interpretation of the books have been selected. Exegesis, then, is the application of these rules to the books, and biblical theology is the result.

A sinner can understand the Word of God. This, too, is an important presupposition. Ramm presents a double-bind incongruity when he says that the first spiritual qualification of the interpreter is that he be born again.[35] Admittedly, one must desire to know God's message and must have a deep reverence for God, but it is not necessary that he be born again in order to understand. If such were a requirement, the Word of God could not lead a sinner to a new birth and to the kingdom of God. In such a case, a sinner could never read himself out of the world of darkness.

---

32. Ibid., pp. 8–9.
33. J. P. Lewis, *The English Bible: From KJV to NIV* (Grand Rapids: Baker, 1981).
34. J. P. Lewis, "What the Restoration Movement Has Accomplished." *Firm Foundation* 99 (March 2, 1982): 7.
35. Ramm, *Protestant*, p. 13.

3. Appropriate methods must be used in exegesis. All of the Bible must be considered; every verse must be understood in its context. Every text must be read according to an appropriate method.

Some of the assumptions of what is known as Historical Criticism cannot be accepted, but some sort of modified approach to this method can and should be accepted. This does not imply a lack of faith but actually demonstrates faith.[36] Historical Criticism, by closing the gap between the centuries when the Bible was written and the present time, allows the intended ideas to enlighten present reality. Historical Criticism is appropriate in that the Bible gives a witness to an historical event and raises a claim to historical truth.[37] Funk correctly states that historical study prevents too-rapid modernizing.[38]

There is a movement from the text to the interpreter and then back to the text. The text speaks to him, and he speaks to the text. Krentz concludes that:

> . . . in the community of scholarship that lives in the fellowship of the people of God, the errors that arise from human frailty can be corrected and the sin forgiven by God's grace. Then, biblical criticism will grow with faith into the full measure of the stature of Christ, his Gospel, his Word, and his Holy Scripture.[39]

G. E. Ladd argues that Historical Criticism should be used by biblical conservatives; they should purify it of its rationalist suppositions with the conviction that the Bible is the Word of God in the words of men.[40] The alternative to accepting some form of Historical Criticism is to accept tradition uncritically. This alternative is unthinkable for those who are committed to the Restoration Principle. It is difficult to accept the idea that what is historically false is theologically significant. Historical Criticism, however, must be sufficiently broad in methodology to allow the scholar full access to reality in history. If he excludes the possibility of God's acting in history, he is limiting his view and his evidence, and his conclusions will be inadequate and false.

Answering the Rigid Assumptions of Modern Science

A believer in God may accept all of the above premises and yet have his faith undercut by such false and limiting philosophical presuppositions

36. C. H. Schelkle, "Sacred Scripture in the Word of God," *Dogmatic Versus Biblical Theology* (Baltimore: Helicon, 1968), p. 17.

37. A. A. T. Ehrhardt, "The Theology of New Testament Criticism," *The Framework of the New Testament Story* (Cambridge: Harvard University, 1964), p. 3.

38. R. Funk, "The Hermeneutical Problem and Historical Criticism," *The New Hermeneutic* (New York: Harper & Row, 1964), pp. 183–84.

39. Krentz, p. 72.

40. G. E. Ladd, *The New Testament and Criticism* (Grand Rapids: Eerdmans, 1967).

as those listed by Collins as the assumptions of modern science. To adequately deal with these, the following presuppositions and/or beliefs are suggested:

Truth may reach beyond empirical observation. Objective and measurable data are useful but limited in scope. Truth exists that humans have never seen. It should not be assumed that truth cannot exist unless it can be empirically observed by the senses. There may be more in the universe than can be perceived through scientific methods, and one's observations of truth may be defective and/or incomplete.

Truth can be known. In his excellent article "Back to the Bible," C. Osburn assumes, among other things, that truth can be known. Other assumptions are that religion is historical rather than existential; that faith is involvement rather than rationalism (skepticism); that God is ultimate; that God has revealed himself and that his revelation is recorded in the Bible; that all of the Bible must be considered; that every verse must be understood in its context; that text must be read according to appropriate method; and that there is no privileged sanctuary for any fact or idea. He concludes: "Only when one understands what a text meant in the First Century will he be able to understand with clarity what are its implications for the present."[41]

Humans have some degree of free will. Though all people are conditioned and influenced by their past and present situations, each can make choices within certain limitations and boundaries.

There are absolute standards of right and wrong. Though one's understanding of truth is incomplete, absolute truth is not relative. Mankind's understanding of truth changes, but truth remains the same. The possibility of absolutes must not be ruled out by assumption. In God, there is absolute truth, love, goodness, perfection, sovereignty, and wisdom. The problem is in grasping these absolutes. Humans search the Bible for truth, for general principles that can guide their lives. All things are not equally probable.

There is more to a whole person and the unity of Scripture than can be perceived by studying individual parts of either. A person is more than the sum of hormone actions, conditioned responses, synapses, self-concept, id impulses, and other basic units that can be individually analyzed. Reductionism—analysis of parts—may not lead to total understanding of the whole. Accordingly, there is more to the message of the Bible than can be seen by focusing on its individual parts.

Truth may be expressed in various ways. Mathematical paradigms and stories are examples. Empirically oriented laboratory instruments may not be able to demonstrate God, but this does not disprove his existence.

41. C. D. Osburn, "Back to the Bible," *Alternative* (Spring 1979): 15–20.

Revelation can light man's path and should not be rejected by assumption.

A human is a physical, social, emotional, and spiritual being. Man is not just a computerized machine, although he has some machinelike characteristics. He is not just so many chemicals, although he is composed of various chemical substances. He is more than a member of the animal world, although he has certain characteristics in common with other animals. He is unique among them: a human being can think, feel, and act in ways no animal can.

God exists. On the basis of evidence in nature, one must at least assume the possibility of the supernatural—of God—before approaching Scripture. Man is not alone in the universe. There is a power that transcends him and helps him with his problems. An appropriate study of the Bible will lead one to faith, but not unless the student allows for the possibility of God's existence. If God is ruled out by assumption, and the Bible is fitted into this view, faith is ruled out by assumption.

God has revealed himself in history. The Bible is not primarily a handbook of doctrinal presuppositions; it is related to a particular people in a particular culture. Neither does Scripture necessarily use identical words with identical meanings from Old Testament to New Testament and from author to author. The Bible utilizes mystical or spiritual meanings. These are not arrived at apart from cultural and historical contexts but rather grow out of them. The Bible employs typology (Isa. 53; Exod. 14:21–31; Gal. 4; Heb. 6), but typology must not become the usual method of exegesis. The basis of typological exegesis lies in a belief in the unity of the Bible. But unless such exegesis grows out of a scholarly historical effort, its outcome may be limited only by the "resources and fertility of invention of the expositor."[42] Whatever further may be made of typology, it cannot be implored as a foundation for sound biblical exegesis.[43] Scripture is to be read as a man would read a letter from a friend. He tries to comprehend what the friend is saying, not what he wishes to read into the words. Before such understanding can come, it is necessary to apply to the documents of Scripture the tools of literary analysis one would use on any document.

The Bible is inspired by God and contains his revelation. Ramm states that divine inspiration is not an assumption but the demonstration of the theologian and the apologist.[44] If the Bible is not inspired by God, exegesis is rather meaningless.

---

42. J. T. Wilkinson, *Principles of Biblical Interpretation* (London: Epworth, 1960), p. 33.

43. A. Peake, *The Nature of Scripture* in Wilkinson, *Principles of Interpretation*, p. 50.

44. Ramm, *Protestant*, p. 7.

There is no privileged sanctuary for any fact or idea. Osburn notes that this is a presupposition with many implications. For example, when science, another person, or theology is considered a privileged sanctuary for facts or ideas, the theology, the other person's ideas, or science becomes the screen through which one reads the Bible. If the Bible does not fit the predetermined ideas, it is altered. An illustration of the limiting effects of such assumptions in this century is Bultmann's dedication to science. Since his scientific method cannot demonstrate supernaturalism, he rejects all references to such in Scripture. This includes miracles, the incarnation of Jesus Christ, the resurrection, prophecy, and eschatology.

Interacting with Scripture

The interpreter should first view a passage in terms of its historical and cultural setting, the intent of the author for his original audience, and the message they likely would have derived from it. This guards against the interpreter's reading his own desires and viewpoints into the text, and he may then apply the message to himself and to the people of his day.

The interpreter should allow the text to modify and to mold his own preunderstandings, prejudices, and presuppositions. This is difficult but not impossible. He cannot remain so detached in his examination of the text as to remain aloof from it; he rather allows the text to examine him as he has examined it. Such an approach allows the message of God's Word to be heard afresh in each person of every generation. Each person's background becomes a door through which the text is approached, not a screen through which the text is altered. The text is primary. Thiselton observes that the interpreter is not merely to support an existing understanding of the text but is to go "onwards *beyond* his own existing horizons, so that the text addresses and judges him *anew*."[45] The truth has mankind as its object, but it is difficult to understand how the text can transform man before man translates and understands it. Although there may be a subtle interaction continually going on between the text and the person, change cannot come before some sort of understanding takes place. The text helps one to understand present experience. Understanding comes through the language of the text, but understanding by its very nature takes place at different levels.

Thiselton states the ideal: the interpreter is not merely an active subject who is scrutinizing passive text, but the text speaks to him as its object, molding his questions. "The notion of the hermeneutical circle is not, then, a sell-out to man-centered relativism, but a way of describing

---

45. A. C. Thiselton, "The New Hermeneutic," in *New Testament Interpretation* ed. I. H. Marshall (Grand Rapids: Eerdmans, 1977), pp. 308–333.

the process of understanding and interpretation of text."[46] Moreover, Thiselton adds, "as one interacts with the text, there is a *continuous* dialogue of question and answer until his own continual horizons are creatively enlarged."[47]

In every step of exegesis, a spiritual attitude is helpful. In the land of Babylon, Ezra prepared his heart "to seek the law of the LORD and to do it and to teach in Israel statutes and judgments" (Ezra 7:10, KJV). Israel was to delight in Jehovah's law (Ps. 1:2, 19). The Old Testament prophets tell us that the people were slow to comprehend spiritual things. Paul says to Christians in Corinth that the natural man "does not receive the gifts of the spirit of God, for they are folly to him, and he is not able to understand them because they are spiritually discerned" (1 Cor. 2:14, RSV). This presents a dilemma; the Bible makes us spiritual, yet must we come to it already spiritual? We should keep in mind that some Christians in Corinth were carnal (1 Cor. 3:1). Whether or not we are Christians, we must come to the text with a mind that is seeking truth, for we get just about what we seek. "Because the carnal mind," Paul writes, "is enmity against God. . ." (Rom. 8:7, KJV). Jesus says, "For every one that doeth evil hateth the light," and comes not to the light "lest his deeds should be reproved" (John 3:20, KJV). Evildoers avoid truth. The Christian is inhabited by God, Christ, and the Holy Spirit (John 14:23, Acts 5:32) and comes to have the mind of the Spirit (Rom. 8:6). He comes to know the things of God by diligent study of what the Spirit of God has revealed (1 Cor. 2:7–13).[48] The Christian should continually examine his commitments and attitudes and become personally involved with the claim of the biblical text upon his life.

Summary

There are certain tensions that arise in a study of attitudes and presuppositions as they relate to biblical interpretation:

What is the difference between a presupposition and a belief?

When one makes an assumption, does that mean that there is no evidence to support it?

When one gains knowledge by faith, does this mean that there is no evidence for that faith?

How does one know that his attitudes are not serving as a screen through which he reads the text?

How does one become involved in the text and yet not edit or screen it?

How does he ask the appropriate questions of the text in order to gain the intended message?

46. Ibid., p. 327.
47. Ibid., p. 328.
48. Terry, pp. 156–58.

Since all people have different backgrounds and have been conditioned differently, will they not ask different questions of the text?

How does this affect unity in the church?

How do different levels of understanding of truth affect unity?

How does one know that he has adequate tools for correct exegesis?

Perhaps all of these questions simply indicate the need for humility when examining Scripture. One should recognize the need for continued scholarship and continued search of the Scriptures. There surely is a place in the church for both experts in exegesis and for others who do not have extensive tools but can utilize the resources that are available to them. All can interact with the text and allow it to mold their lives. If people submit themselves to the message of the text, God can guide their lives and make them useful servants. That is the real reason for exegesis.

4

Identifying the Pericope and Its Context

Raymond C. Kelcy

Identification of the pericope and its context are hermeneutical matters that must be considered in any discussion of scriptural exegesis. A dictionary definition of *pericope* is "a short passage, section, or paragraph in a writing." The same dictionary recalls that the *Edinburgh Review* in 1884 and Lightfoot in an 1889 essay had referred to the passage concerning the woman taken in adultery as a "pericope."[1] The word is derived from two Greek words: *peri* ("around") and *kope* ("cutting")—hence, a "cutting around," or the marking out of a section. In this study the word is used to denote a section of Scripture that is a unit within itself. "Context" is from the Latin *con* ("together") and *textus* ("woven") denoting "that which is woven together." When applied to a writing, it refers to the connection of thought that the passage bears to the larger discussion of which it is a part.

Identification of the pericope and its context prepares the way for one of the most fruitful procedures in Bible study. First, such identification enables the student to make a thorough study of a unit of Scripture for his own edification. It is apparent that a study of a complete section in the light of its setting is more edifying than a study of words or sentences taken at random from various books. Second, identification of a pericope and its context prepares the way for a procedure that can be fruitful insofar as enabling the student to communicate with others. He who wishes to impart knowledge to others may be either a teacher of a small group or a preacher who speaks to thousands. In either case, dealing with

1. *The Oxford English Dictionary*, Vol. 7 (Oxford: Clarendon, 1933), p. 695.

a complete unit of Scripture in connection with its context will be effective. Dealing with a pericope and its context is a must for the preacher who would do expository preaching, the kind of preaching called by Ramm "the crowning method of preaching."[2] The preacher who uses the correct principles of hermeneutics and does a correct exegesis of a section of Scripture—and then explains, illustrates, and applies that passage to his audience—is doing expository preaching.

Identifying the Pericope

How may a pericope be identified? This is very important but is sometimes quite an easy procedure.

The identification of a passage as a complete unit is somewhat arbitrary. For example, 1 Corinthians 13 may be considered a unit, being a discussion of love. However, the chapter may be subdivided so that smaller complete sections are formed. Verses 1–3 constitute a discussion of the supremacy of love; verses 4–7 form a section on the behavior of love; verses 8–13 are a section on the exalted nature of love. Any one of these sections could be used for a lesson or a sermon. Likewise, the Beatitudes of Matthew 5:3–10 constitute a pericope that could be used as a study unit. However, any one of the Beatitudes may be taken as a pericope and used for an entire lesson. Again, the series of parables of Matthew 13:3–52 could well be treated as a complete section with some such title as "The Nature of the Kingdom as Taught in Parables." However, each parable may be considered a pericope, and the student may wish to deal with each as a separate section.

The student will derive great benefit from diligent practice in reading the Bible and making his own identifications. Ability in accurate demarcation of pericopes will increase with practice. As one reads, such pericopes as the following will be obvious: Cleansing the Temple (John 2:13–22); Discourse with the Samaritan Woman (John 4:4–26); The Baptism of Jesus (Matt. 3:13–17); The Temptation of Jesus (Matt. 4:1–11). Identification of pericopes in the epistles will not be so easy, but that skill, too, can be acquired. Pericopes such as the following will soon become apparent: Abraham's Justification by Faith (Rom. 4:1–25); The Christian's Relationship to Sin (Rom. 6:1–14); The Christian and Government (Rom. 13:1–7); Factions in the Church (1 Cor. 1:10–17); The Christian Soldier (Eph. 6:10–18). After identifying pericopes in the manner illustrated, the student will find profit and pleasure in comparing the results of his study with the works of others.

There are many Bibles that contain helpful outlines and notes. Some have brief headings at the top of the page. Others have a more thorough

---

2. B. Ramm, *Protestant Biblical Interpretation* (Boston: W. A. Wilde, 1956), p. 89.

breakdown. Some Bibles have outlines within chapters, for example: The Lord's Supper (1 Cor. 11:17–34); Spiritual Gifts (1 Cor. 12:1–11); One Body and Many Parts (1 Cor. 12:12–21). Helps of this kind are available in a variety of versions of the Bible.

Commentaries are another source with which comparisons may be made. Although the student will find some variation among commentaries as to exact divisions, in general he will find substantial agreement. From a one-volume commentary on the entire Bible the following illustrations are taken: The Death of John (Matt. 14:1–12); Feeding the Five Thousand (Matt. 14:13–21); Walking on the Water (Matt. 14:22–36). In the commentary from which these examples are taken, the divisions are set off in a style that makes the sections stand out in a prominent way.[3]

In a study of the Gospels the student will find helpful a work on the "harmony" of the Gospels. The following examples of pericope divisions are taken from one such standard work: Prologue of John's Gospel (John 1:1–18); Annunciation to Mary (Luke 1:26–38); The Parables by the Sea (Matt. 13:1–53); The Stilling of the Tempest (Luke 8:22–25).[4]

The Expositor's Bible is a commentary on the entire Bible and is written in an expository style. The expositions are presented according to pericopes rather than as a verse-by-verse treatment.[5] Following are examples of the way in which the text is divided: The Way, the Truth, and the Life (John 14:5–7); The Father Seen in Christ (John 14:8–21); The Bequest of Peace (John 14:22–31); The Vine and the Branches (John 14:31–15:12).

Alexander Maclaren's *Expositions of Holy Scripture*[6] is a multivolume set that provides the student with examples of pericope division as well as outstanding material for expository treatment of Scripture. Maclaren at times breaks the material into shorter sections than most writers do, but this will be no hindrance to the student who wishes to extend the material into longer pericopes. Following are some samples of Maclaren's method of division: The Growth and Power of Sin (Gen. 4:3–16); The Saint Among Sinners (Gen. 6:9–22); An Example of Faith (Gen. 12:1–9); The Importance of a Choice (Gen. 13:1–13); Afraid of Giants (Num. 13:17–33).

Although there is an abundance of helpful materials for identifying the pericope, it should be repeated that the student will receive more profit and satisfaction if he makes his own decisions about divisions of sections before looking at what has been done by others. After he has done his own

3. *The New Bible Commentary*, edited by F. Davidson (Grand Rapids: Eerdmans, 1956).

4. W. A. Stevens and E. D. Burton, *A Harmony of the Gospels* (New York: Scribner's, 1932).

5. Edited by W. R. Nicoll (Grand Rapids: Eerdmans, 1947). The set combines the labors of a remarkable group. Among the writers are M. Dods, F. W. Farrar, A. Maclaren, H. C. G. Moule, J. Denney.

6. A. Maclaren, *Expositions of Holy Scripture* (New York: George H. Doran, n.d.).

work, he will do well to look at what others have done. If he finds an arrangement that is superior to his own, he will be glad to make use of it.

Identifying the Context

How may the context, the scriptural setting, of a pericope be identified? The matter of ascertaining the context is vital to an understanding of the passage. Here, too, the procedure is not necessarily complicated and, as is true of other practices, is one in which the student gains in proficiency as he pursues the task.

In identifying the context, the student should first read the pericope thoroughly and study it until he is familiar with its basic thrust. He will locate the context by careful reading of the material that precedes and the material that follows. There is no way to predict how much material he will need to read, for the amount will vary with each case. Illustrations will be helpful in demonstrating the procedure involved in locating the context.

1 Corinthians 13. Paul's famous discussion of love may be considered a pericope. Paul first shows the importance of love by contrasting it with spiritual gifts such as tongues, prophecy, and so on. Next Paul turns to a discussion of the behavior of love, showing that love does not seek its own, does not envy, does not keep account of evil, and so on. He shows that love is longsuffering, and it endures all things and is kind. Near the end of the chapter, Paul shows that love transcends in importance such things as spiritual gifts, faith, and hope. Spiritual gifts such as knowledge and prophecy will fail, but love abides. One does not have to read long in the preceding and following chapters to see that Paul's discussion of love is related to his discussion of spiritual gifts. The situation at Corinth was apparently one in which some of the church members were envious of those with certain spiritual gifts. Others were puffed up because of having special gifts; some were placing too high a priority on such gifts; and there was confusion in the assemblies in which spiritual gifts were employed. Paul discusses spiritual gifts, promises to show to his readers "a most excellent way," and then proceeds to a discussion of love. It now becomes apparent why Paul stressed the supremacy of love over spiritual gifts and why he gave emphasis to the wonderful, surpassing characteristics of love!

Luke 15:3–32. As one studies this pericope—the passage concerning the lost sheep, the lost coin, and the prodigal son—he will find the clue to what Jesus sought to accomplish by reading the first two verses of the chapter. There Luke tells about the publicans and sinners coming near Jesus to hear him. The scribes and the Pharisees had found fault because Jesus associated with sinners and ate with them. It is clear that Jesus related the parables in which God's attitude toward the lost is emphasized in reply to the charges of these murmurers.

Luke 10:30–35. The parable of the Samaritan, becomes clear as to meaning when the conversation of Jesus with the lawyer is considered (vv. 25–29). Jesus gives the parable after the lawyer asks, "Who is my neighbor?" After he had told the parable, Jesus asked him who, in the parable, was a neighbor. The train of thought is seen to flow into the pericope, through the pericope, and away from the pericope.

Matthew 18:23–34. What is known as the parable of the unmerciful servant is another instance in which the thought flows into, through, and away from the pericope. The preceding material shows that Peter had raised the question about forgiveness (v. 21). At the end of the parable, Jesus says that God will not forgive the unforgiving. The idea of forgiveness can be seen permeating both the pericope and the context.

1 Corinthians 5:6–8. Paul teaches here that a little leaven will leaven the entire lump. He says that Christ is the Christian's Passover and urges that the feast be kept with the unleavened bread of sincerity and truth, not with old leaven. The context enables one to understand that Paul is speaking relative to the incestuous person over whose case the church at Corinth had not mourned (vv. 1–5). He is reminding his readers that toleration of such impurity in their midst will tend to corrupt the whole body. Paul's discussion, both before and after the pericope under study, aids greatly toward an understanding of his intention in the passage.

Galatians 4:31. At times the writer states the conclusion he reaches from what he has said. Paul often does this with the word *so* or the word *therefore.* An example is his statement in this pericope: "So then, brethren, we are not children of a bondwoman, but of the free woman" (NASB). This conclusion comes after Paul has recalled the details concerning Abraham, Sarah and Hagar, Isaac and Ishmael, and after he has shown that these persons and their actions have a figurative significance for Christians (vv. 22–30). He shows that Hagar and Ishmael were cast out and declares that the son of the handmaid will not inherit with the son of the free woman. When he closes with "so then," the readers must be aware of the significance of his teaching.

Philippians 2:6–11. Here, in Paul's great Christological passage, he teaches the humiliation and the consequent exaltation of Christ, and it becomes clear as to its practical import when the context is noted. In the preceding material (vv. 1–5), Paul pleads with Christians to be united, to have the good of others in mind, to have the mind of Christ. Then he goes on to discuss the mind of Christ, showing that Christ was willing to be abased and to take the form of a servant. It becomes clear that "the mind of Christ" that Christians are to have is a mind that is willing to forego personal position in order to be effective servants of others.

Hebrews 2:1–4. The pericope concerning the "great salvation" illustrates how a passage receives additional light from what precedes and what follows. Both contexts focus the attention upon angels. The writer discusses at length the superiority of Christ over angels. The thrust of the passage under study is that the readers should consider the fact that if men of old did not escape when they transgressed the word spoken by angels, one could not expect to escape if he neglects the great salvation that was first spoken by Christ. The word *therefore* calls the attention of the readers back to the contrast between Jesus and angels.

Luke 12:16–20. The pericope of the rich fool is another passage illustrating the contribution made by the material that precedes and follows. Jesus had warned about the need for being on guard against all sorts of greed; he had emphasized that one's life does not consist of the things he has (v. 15). After relating the parable, Jesus makes the application by saying that it is this way with those who are rich toward themselves and not toward God. The pericope with context thus has a continuity of thought. The ideas of materialism and covetousness flow throughout the whole.

Isolated Passages

While there are many passages in which the context affords great help, there are others for which no such help may be found. Mickelson points out that in certain sections of the Bible there are various sorts of terse statements for which the reader will receive little or no help from that which precedes or that which follows. Mickelson says that "much of Proverbs and Ecclesiastes consists of individual units which are complete in themselves." He suggests that in such cases parallels from other places may shed some light.[7] Regarding the same matter, Terry comments:

> There are portions of Scripture in the exposition of which we are not to look for help in the context or scope. The Book of Proverbs, for example, is composed of numerous separate aphorisms, many of which have no necessary connection with each other. . . . Several parts of the Book of Ecclesiastes consist of proverbs, soliloquies, and exhortations, which appear to have no vital relation to each other. . . . The Gospels, also, contain some passages which it is impossible to explain as having any essential connection with either that which precedes or follows.[8]

Terry adds that with such isolated texts a comparison of parallel passages will prove helpful. First, parallels should be sought in the writings of the same author; then parallels may be sought from other writers.

7. A. B. Mickelson, *Interpreting the Bible* (Grand Rapids: Eerdmans, 1963), p. 112.
8. M. S. Terry, *Biblical Hermeneutics* (Grand Rapids: Zondervan, 1964), p. 221.

Remote Contexts

Emphasis has thus far been given to the immediate context, that is, the material immediately preceding and following the passage being studied. But there are other important contexts. The student—in addition to giving attention to the sentences, words, grammar and syntax of the pericope and examining the immediate context—should also consider the other areas of context, which may be designated "the remote context."

Scriptural Contexts

One important context to be considered is that of the entire book of Scripture in which the passage is found. For example, if one is dealing with a pericope in the Book of Acts, a knowledge of the entire book will be of great help. After the purpose and plan of the book have become apparent, it will be easy to see how the passage under study fits into this overall plan.

The student should also take into account the context of covenant. Under what covenant was the passage spoken? Although in many senses the Bible is a unity, there are significant differences between the religious system of the Mosaic covenant and that of the covenant of Christ. Passages written during the days of the temple ritual will naturally have a different overall context from those written during the Christian age.

Then there is a sense in which the entire Bible is a context unto itself. A passage of Scripture is to be understood in the light of all Scripture. This shows the significance of the oft-made statement to the effect that Scripture must interpret Scripture. Mickelson, after pointing out that the interpreter must know both the contents of the book containing the passage under study and the contents of other books that treat the same theme, goes ahead to say: "But even the best sources of parallels are not enough. The interpreter should know well the content of the whole Bible." He adds: "Sometimes the obvious is forgotten simply because it is so self-evident. One cannot properly handle context until he has a good grasp of Bible content."[9]

Cultural-Historical Context

The student must also give attention to the general cultural context. At times this is referred to as the "historical" context. When reference is made to the grammatical-historical method of hermeneutics, emphasis is on the fact that both the grammar of a passage and the history and culture of the time in which the passage was written must be understood. Ramm says: "Culture, in the anthropological sense, is all the ways and means, material and social, whereby a given people carry on their exis-

9. Mickelson, pp. 100–101.

tence."[10] G. H. Ensign adds that by the term *cultural*, the interpreter is led "to every feature of the writer in his social environment and the total conditions of his thought patterns. The interpreter will study the geography . . . the nations and tribal groups that are involved in the life of the author or the writing of the text." Ensign goes on to point out the importance of understanding something about the domestic life of the times, the tools, implements, utensils, food, furniture, armies, military strategy, titles and roles of officials.[11] In order to understand what a passage means to men of today, one must first ascertain what it meant to those to whom it was first written. To do this it is often necessary to understand the history of the times and to be acquainted with such matters as marriage customs, legal matters, agricultural practices, and a variety of other items.

Sources for learning about the cultural context are plentiful. There are books which deal solely with the life and customs of Bible times. Commentaries furnish help. Introductory material in books such as "introductions" to Scripture, commentaries, and some Bibles are another fruitful source. Bible dictionaries and encyclopedias are also quite valuable in this field and are tools that should be in the library of every Bible student.

Benefits of Contextual Study

The benefits that come to a student from the study of passages in the light of their context are significant.

Contextual study of a passage brings an understanding of the underlying thought of the passage. Since a basic thought is expressed by a series of ideas, and since a study of the context enables the student to see the connection of thought as it goes into, through, and away from a passage, it follows that such a procedure enables him to grasp the thought that the writer had in mind. A study of a passage and its context brings an understanding of the end the writer had in view, the object of his writing. A knowledge of this will add a dimension to one's understanding of a passage.

Contextual study also enables the student to determine how a particular word is used in the pericope. Berkhof points out that a word can have but one fixed meaning in the connection where it is found. He says that neither the etymological nor the acquired meaning of a word is the important question to be determined. He maintains that the most important factor is the "particular sense in the connection" in which a word occurs. Berkhof calls attention to the various meanings of the word translated "flesh" *(sarx)* and shows what serious errors would result if the

10. Ramm, p. 5.
11. G. H. Ensign, *You Can Understand the Bible* (Joplin, Mo: College Press, 1978), pp. 201–202.

interpreter were not careful to ascertain its meaning in each particular context.[12] In a similar vein, Terry calls attention to the various meanings of the word translated "spirit" *(pneuma)* and maintains that in each instance of its occurrence the context will aid in determining its meaning.[13] Ramm states: "Paul uses the word law *(nomos)* so flexibly that its particular meaning can be settled only by appeal to the context."[14]

Finally, contextual study produces a greater degree of faith in the student. A thorough study of a passage, along with a study of its context, is an exercise in which the student is dealing with the Word of God. As Mickelson says, "Faithful adherence to the context will create in the interpreter a greater appreciation for the authority of Scripture."[15] Such an increase of appreciation for Scripture, together with an increase of knowledge of Scripture, can be expected to bring about a salutary change of character. Ramm has remarked, "The goal of all interpretation is spiritual results in the listeners."[16]

Diligent study of the Scriptures whereby the student seriously considers passages in the light of their context will not only bring about a change in the character of the one who studies, but will also enable him to communicate more effectively with others. This is a challenging goal toward which to aim. It has well been said that "all theological endeavor serves as a preparation for the proclamation of the gospel, by means of which God himself intends to bring about living faith in Jesus Christ as Lord of the world and as Lord of His Church."[17]

12. L. Berkhof, *Principles of Biblical Interpretation* (Grand Rapids: Baker, 1975), pp. 74–75.

13. Terry, p. 182.

14. B. Ramm, "Hermeneutics," in *Baker's Dictionary of Practical Theology*, Ralph G. Turnbull, ed. (Grand Rapids: Baker, 1967), p. 18.

15. Mickelson, p. 113.

16. Ramm, *Protestant*, p. 88.

17. The substance of the thought is attributed to Augustine by O. Kaiser and W. G. Kümmel, *Exegetical Method*, translated by E. V. N. Goetchius (New York: Seabury, 1963), p. 9.

5

Diagraming and Sentence Analysis

F. Furman Kearley

The most important aspect of communication and understanding language is not simply understanding the meaning of individual words but rather understanding how each word relates to the other words in the sentence. In order to communicate effectively and understand what others have communicated, two things are essential. First, the speaker or writer must properly compose his statements in order that the words sustain the proper relationship to each other. Second, the hearer or reader must properly analyze the relation of each word to the others and of each sentence to the others. Failure on the part of either of these will cause a breakdown in communication. In the larger sense, of course, one must keep every sentence in relation to its overall context.

In most instances, speakers and writers in a native language adequately perform these two functions in order that communication may take place. However, many of the laughable incidents in life, numerous situation comedies, and much of what we call humor is based upon failure in one or both of these areas. As long as it results in humor, no harm is done. Tragically, however, inadequate communication in business—caused by a supervisor's failure to compose instructions properly or by workers' inability to understand instructions—has cost countless dollars in wasted time, squandered materials, and other areas. More tragic are the damages done in human relations because of the failure to use proper word and sentence analysis. Most tragic of all is the failure of humans to analyze correctly the right relation of words in the communications from God concerning spiritual matters. This failure is one of the key causes of division in Christendom.

A basic presupposition of this study is that God, through the Holy Spirit and the human agents he used to write the Bible, has properly composed every sentence and that the words do sustain the proper relationship one to another to convey God's true meaning. This author realizes that some who treat the Bible as human literature would reject this presupposition, and time and space at this point do not allow for an exploration of the evidences to support it. However, these evidences are contained in all of the studies related to the inspiration and inerrancy of God's Word.

Thus, since the Holy Scriptures have been composed properly, the failure in communication is on the part of man, who fails to analyze and understand the communication correctly. The purpose of studying word analysis, sentence structure, and diagraming is to help students of the Word be more effective and accurate in their understanding of the relation of individual words to other words, phrases, and clauses in a sentence in order to best understand it.

Word Analysis

Many think the first question to ask of a word is: "What does this word mean?" This is not true. The first and most important question to ask of a word is: "What is its function in this sentence?" The meaning of a word may change or vary slightly in its impact, depending upon its function in the sentence. For example, the word *rest* is defined differently and has a different impact when it is functioning as a noun than when it is functioning as a verb. In order to understand the word properly, one must know whether to define it as a verb or as a noun. Obviously, then, the analysis of words in a sentence must take place within the framework of the sentence itself.

Sentence Analysis

The first step in sentence analysis is to determine the function of each word in the sentence and, by this process, determine the part of speech of each word. This process is easy to accomplish if the sentence is a simple one. However, if the sentence contains modifying phrases and clauses, the process becomes more involved. In English four types of sentences can usually be identified. This parallels Hebrew and Greek, with the technical terminology varying extensively. One should not become bogged down in the terminology, but rather understand the concepts involved.

Types of Sentences

The four types of sentences are: (1) simple; (2) compound; (3) complex; (4) compound-complex. A basic sentence must contain a subject and a verb, but in imperative sentences especially, the subject ("you") may often be understood. Although the simple sentence consists of a subject and a verb, the verb may often take an object, and generally these main functioning words may take simple modifiers. From this point, obviously, the details of the terminology and classifications of grammar become extensive. It is not the purpose of this chapter to be a handbook on English or Greek grammar, but rather to outline for one who already understands grammar the basic process of careful sentence analysis. Some helpful English handbooks will be listed in the source section of this study.

The second type of sentence is the compound sentence. This involves two or more simple sentences joined together by coordinate conjunctions ("and," "but," and so on).

The third type of sentence is the complex sentence. This consists of a simple sentence plus one or more subordinate clauses, each of which must have a subject, a verb, and possibly an object with modifiers for one or more of these. In this type of sentence, one must determine whether a particular word is a subject or a verb and, if so, if it is the subject or verb of the main sentence or of one of the subordinate clauses. Then one must determine the relations of each word to other words or each phrase to other phrases, as well as the words of each clause to other words and to the sentence as a whole. This will be illustrated below.

The fourth type of sentence is the compound-complex sentence. This consists of two or more independent simple sentences joined by coordinate conjunctions, with the additional feature that one or more of these simple sentences has one or more subordinate clauses.

Thus, sentences may range from simple statements, such as "Jesus wept" (John 11:35) and "Rejoice always," (1 Thess. 5:16) to the very complex sentence found in Ephesians 1:3–14, which consists of twelve verses. Obviously, the first two examples are very simple to analyze. However, as one deals with the especially long and involved sentences in the Epistles of Paul, it becomes vital to do more careful sentence analysis and understand which words are modifying what and which phrases and clauses are modifying other parts of the sentence.

Systems of Sentence Analysis

There are several methods that may be employed for proper sentence analysis so as to understand the correct interrelation of words. Most of the time we analyze sentences automatically in our mind and do not think consciously about the process. However, for more involved statements and more serious purposes such as exegesis, it becomes necessary to be more careful and alert. This study will identify several systems for sentence analysis that will move from simple to extensive.

One may simply use the system of conscious mental analysis. This process involves pausing after each sentence read and asking: What is the

FIGURE 1 **Simple Sentence Analysis**

Notes:	Subject	Verb	
Text 1:	**God**	**rested.**	
Notes:	Subject	Verb	Direct Object
Text 2:	**God**	**made**	**everything.**
Notes:	Subject	Verb	Predicate
Text 3:	**God**	**is**	**love.**
Notes:	Subject	Verb	Direct Object
Text 4:	**God**	**made**	**man.**

subject of that sentence? What is the verb? Does the sentence have an object and what is it? Does the subject have modifiers and what are they? Does the verb have modifiers and what are they? Does the object have modifiers and what are they? Is the sentence simple, complex, compound, or compound-complex? Are there phrases in the sentence and what is their function? Are there clauses in the sentence and what is their function? Answers to these questions may be written down, as in Figure 1.

The student might consult the work by Barbara and Timothy Friberg titled *Analytical Greek New Testament.* This work has an excellent abbreviation system of notations concerning Greek grammatical analysis. It could be expanded and adapted for functional analysis as well.

One may progress to a circle- or box-analysis chart. Moving from the conscious mental phase of asking the questions and obtaining the answers in his mind, the analyst may list the book, chapter, and verse reference, and then proceed to ask the same questions, but this time schematically writing down the responses so he may meditate on them all together. One could simply draw a circle or box for the subject; to the right of that, a circle or box for the verb; and to the right of that, a circle or box for the object. Then one could place in these circles or boxes the words, phrases, or clauses that modify each one, as the case might be. Obviously, this system best lends itself to shorter, less involved sentences, whereas a passage such as Ephesians 1:3–14 would need to be laid out more formally and extensively. See Figure 2 for an illustration of how this process could be applied to Genesis 1:1.

This system can easily be expanded from simple sentences, as the above, to compound-complex sentences. One may also add notations, as in the verb box.

A third system one might use is called a verbal-analysis or a sentence-analysis chart. In this process one divides the paper into eight columns headed: (1) English word; (2) Greek or Hebrew word; (3) Greek or Hebrew root word; (4) grammatical analysis of Greek or Hebrew word; (5) part of

FIGURE 2 **Box or Circle Analysis Chart**

Passage: **Genesis 1:1—In the beginning God created the heavens and the earth.**

Subject Box	Verb Box	Object Box
God	**created** **In the beginning** (prepositional phrase functioning as adverb)	**the heavens and the earth.**

speech; (6) function of word in phrase or clause; (7) function of phrase or clause or word in the sentence; (8) meaning of the word. Obviously, these columns could be rearranged or expanded as needed. Column four, containing the grammatical analysis of the Greek or Hebrew word, involves identifying the person, number, tense, voice, and mood of Greek or Hebrew verbs; and the number, gender, and case for Greek or Hebrew nouns and adjectives. A detailed knowledge of Greek and Hebrew is necessary to do this properly and to interpret the significance of this analysis. However, tools are available to help the beginning student to go a long way in these areas. (These resources will be mentioned in a later section of this study.) See Figure 3 for a sample sentence-analysis chart for Colossians 3:19.

The fourth and most complete analysis system involves standard sentence diagraming. While diagraming systems have varied from time to time in the form taught at schools, and range from simple to extremely involved, most people are familiar with the basic elements of diagramming. See Figure 4 for a sample, and consult the sources listed below, for further guidance and illustrations.

The extensive diagram is the best and most complete system for sentence analysis. Many variations are used and taught, but all are basically the same. The most extensive known to this author is the one taught and used by John D. Grassmick in *Principles and Practice of Greek Exegesis*. Another good system is presented by William Sanford LaSor in *Handbook of New Testament Greek*. See Figure 4 for a sample.

Of course, the student may devise his own system of analysis, using some combination of the above methods, since in many instances only a few words or phrases might cause a problem. One might simply write in the margin of his study Bible, noting essential analysis facts that might not readily come to memory. However, for careful exegetical study, nothing is better than an extensive diagram that is developed along with a sentence-flow and thought-flow system of notation.

Figure 3 **Sentence Analysis Chart**

Passage: Colossians 3:19—Husbands, love your wives, and be not bitter against them.

English Word	Greek Word	Greek Root	Grammatical Analysis	Part of Speech	Function in Phrase	Function in Sentence	Meaning of Word
	hoi	ho,hē,to	voc. pl. masc.	Article adjective		adj. modifying husbands	the
Husbands	andres	anēr	voc. pl. masc. included in verb 2nd per. masc. pl.	noun		persons addressed or commanded	man or husband
(you)				pronoun		subject of verbs "love" and "be bitter"	you
love	agapate	agapaō	2nd. per. pl. pres. imper. act.	verb		verb	love
your	Tas	ho,hē,to	acc. pl. fem.	Article adjective		Adj. modifying wives	the
wives	gunaikas	gunē	acc. pl. fem.	noun		object of verb "love"	wife or woman
and	kai	kai	co-ordinate conj.	conj.		joins first clause with second clause	and
be bitter	pikrain- esthe	pikrainō	2nd per. pl. pres. imper. pass.	verb		verb	pass. - to be bitter, harsh
not	mē	mē	particle of negation	adverb		adv. modifying "be bitter, harsh"	not
toward	pros	pros	preposition	prep.	prep. controlling them	adverbial prep. phrase	to toward against
them	autas	autos	acc. pl. fem.	3rd per. pronoun	obj. of prep. pros (toward)	modifying "be bitter"	he, she, it

FIGURE 4 **Extensive Diagraming**

§30.6   *Sentence diagram.* There is nothing that will help us grasp the structure and
           sense of a passage like diagraming the sentence. In this Handbook, I have
           followed the system commonly taught in elementary English, except that I
           have adapted it to the typewriter so that all parts are typed horizontally. I have
           further tried to keep it simple, for a diagram needs to be simple to be clear.

§30.61   The *simple sentence* (§30.1) is basic to the diagram. With all modifiers re-
           moved, it forms a simple straight line.

§30.611   The verb in the predicate is the central element (§30.12). Note how the other
           elements are placed with reference to the verb.

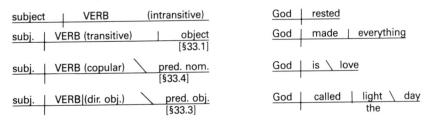

§30.6111   With a compound subject, compound predicate, or even a compound verb, the
           same basic diagram is used.

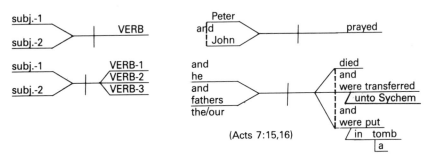

§30.6112   There obviously is no limit to the combinations that are theoretically possible,
           but the method of diagraming is the same.

Adapted from pp. B-137, 138 in *Handbook of New Testament Greek* by William Sanford LaSor (Grand
Rapids: Eerdmans, 1973).

Sources for Guidance and Study

The student may consult many sources for help in accomplishing effective word and sentence analysis and diagraming. Listed below are only a
few that have been found very helpful. These, in turn, will guide the
student to still others. One must first obtain a good working knowledge of
English grammar and syntax, and then progress to the grammar and
syntax of the biblical languages. The more knowledge one has in these,
the more accurate he can be in performing correct sentence analysis.

English Grammar and Handbooks

H. Ramsey Fowler, *The Little, Brown Handbook*. Boston: Little, Brown, 1980.

H. A. Gleason, Jr., *Linguistics and English Grammar*. New York: Holt, Rinehart and Winston, 1965.

Susan Emolyn Harmon, *Descriptive English Grammar*. Englewood Cliffs NJ: Prentice-Hall, 1950.

Samuel Jay Geyser and Paul M. Postal, *Beginning English Grammar*. New York: Harper & Row, 1976.

R. W. Pence and D. W. Emery, *A Grammar of Present Day English*. New York: Macmillan.

Greek Grammars (See Bibliography for Biblical Exegesis)

Hebrew Grammars (See Bibliography for Biblical Exegesis)

Greek Syntax and Diagraming

James A. Brooks and Carlton L. Winbery, *Syntax of New Testament Greek*. Washington, D.C.: University Press of America, 1979.

William D. Chamberlain, *An Exegetical Grammar of the Greek New Testament*. New York: Macmillan, 1961.

Barbara and Timothy Friberg, *Analytical Greek New Testament*. Grand Rapids: Baker, 1982.

Fritz Rienecker, *A Linguistic Key to the Greek New Testament* (two volumes). Grand Rapids: Zondervan, 1976, 1980.

Max Zerwick and Mary Grosvenor, *A Grammatical Analysis of the Greek New Testament* (two volumes). Rome: Biblical Institute Press, 1974, 1979.

Greek Diagraming

John D. Grassmick, *Principles and Practice of Greek Exegesis*. Dallas: Dallas Theological Seminary, 1974.

William Sanford LaSor, *Handbook of New Testament Greek*. Grand Rapids: Eerdmans, 1973.

Biblical Exegesis Handbooks

Gordon D. Fee, *New Testament Exegesis—A Handbook for Students and Pastors*. Philadelphia: Westminster, 1983. Note especially pages 60–83 for sentence analysis, sentence flow, and grammatical analysis.

Douglas Stuart, *Old Testament Exegesis*. Philadelphia: Westminster, 1980.

Conclusion

The student who will take the time, energy, and pain to master Hebrew and Greek, and to study God's Word carefully, slowly, painstakingly—including the use of sentence analysis or diagraming—will be richly rewarded in a deeper and more accurate understanding of the message of God's Word. The more students and teachers who will follow this careful, extensive process, the more the church will be strengthened by consistent unified teaching that will bring about greater unanimity and harmony among all believers. The world will be enriched as believers become more unified, for then the church can more readily convince the world concerning the truth about God and Christ. In knowing, understanding, and practicing God's great truths, there are incalculable rewards for all mankind.

6
Interpreting Figurative Language

Edward P. Myers

The Bible is God's revelation to man. The language of the Bible is varied, ranging from the rigidly literal to the highly figurative. Scripture encompasses a wide variety of classes of literature and language: history, letters, poetry, oration, allegory, parable, biography, romance, tragedy, drama, type, antitype, figure, symbol, and vision.

The Bible claims that its words are inspired of God (2 Tim. 3:16–17). If that claim is taken seriously, an individual is responsible for how he understands and interprets these words, since they give meaning and significance to life unlike any other writings today. A. B. Mickelsen points out that the task of exegesis is to find out the author's meaning for his first readers and then transmit that meaning to modern readers.[1] Because many people do not have a knowledge of Hebrew, Aramaic, and Greek—the languages in which the Bible was originally written—the task of exegesis begins with serious problems for English readers. First, English-speaking people often use biblical words but attach meanings to them not intended by the biblical writer. Second, in any living language, words change their meaning. "I do you to wit" does not mean today what it did in 1611. Third, words do not always mean the same thing every time they are used.[2] Context, not strict definition, is the final criterion for what a word means.

One of the greatest needs today is that correct principles of interpretation be used in sound biblical exegesis. The use of language involves an

1. A. B. Mickelsen, *Interpreting the Bible* (Grand Rapids: Eerdmans, 1963), pp. 3–5.

2. J. T. Willis, "Rewarding Bible Study," in *The World and Literature of the Old Testament*, ed. J. T. Willis (Austin, TX: Sweet, 1979), pp. 23–26.

understanding of the use of words and their meaning. All words have meaning and convey thoughts. Proper use of words allows one to be understood; improper word usage leads to difficulties in communication. Nowhere has there been more difficulty in the use of words than in the area of figurative language. Sometimes "figurative language" is spoken of as though it had no force or significance. One may say, "Oh, that's just figurative," as if this would weaken the meaning or suggest it had no meaning at all. Such is not the case. In fact, figurative language is usually used to add force or significance to what is being discussed.

There are both problems and advantages in using "figures of speech," a device common to all languages but especially to Oriental languages. It is a popular way of speaking and can be found in almost every book. The Bible is no exception. In fact, if all statements of the Bible were literal, it would destroy the beauty of the language. Try to express the Twenty-third Psalm without using figurative language! A figure of speech is a most powerful means of making an impression; it is a "word picture." To understand the Bible it is essential to know when language is literal and when it is figurative. There is a difference between something stated figuratively and something stated literally. Mickelsen observes: "By literal meaning, the writer refers to the usual or customary sense conveyed by words or expressions. By figurative meaning, the writer has in mind the representation of one concept in terms of another because the nature of the two things compared allows such an analogy to be drawn."[3]

Identifying Figurative Language

The question could properly be asked, "How can one recognize figurative language?" Some suggestions that might be helpful are as follows:

1. The sense in which the expression is used will usually indicate whether or not it is figurative. Expressions are to be understood literally unless the evident meaning forbids it. In the sentence, "The Lord is my shepherd," the word *shepherd* is obviously used figuratively.

2. An expression must be figurative when a literal meaning would involve an impossibility. For example, when Jesus said, "Let the dead bury their own dead" (Matt. 8:22) or "I am the vine, ye are the branches" (John 15:5), he was using language that would involve an impossibility if understood literally.

3. An expression is figurative if it requires what is ethically wrong or prohibits that which is right. For example, to have Jesus requiring one to literally amputate his hand or pluck out his eyes, as in the statement in Matthew 18:8–9, is to abuse the sense of figurative language.

3. Mickelsen, p. 179.

4. A passage is figurative if a literal view would conflict with another passage that is clearly understood. Thus there is no contradiction between "shall never die" (John 11:26) and "for as in Adam, all die" (1 Cor. 15:22). One is to be understood literally and the other figuratively or spiritually.

5. Some texts or their context will tell you they are figurative. In John 2:19, Jesus said, "Destroy this temple, and in three days I will raise it up." In verse 21 one is told that Jesus was not speaking of the literal temple but rather "the temple of his body."

6. Statements that are made to ridicule or mock are generally understood as figurative. When Jesus referred to Herod as a "fox;" he was not speaking of Herod literally, but used this language to refer to his craftiness.

7. Sometimes common sense will suggest that the language is figurative. For example, when Jesus was speaking with the woman at the well (John 4), he told her of the "living water" that one could drink and thereby never thirst again. He was not speaking of water from that well or any other literal well.

Some of these guidelines can be used to interpret both figurative and literal language. In analyzing biblical text, one must always consider the writer, the immediate context, and other clear teachings of Scripture. However, once language is determined to be figurative, it must then be interpreted according to the rules governing figurative language. To fail to make such a distinction is to fail to practice proper exegesis. E. D. Hirsch correctly points out that in order to understand games properly, there are two things necessary: (1) to know what game is being played, and (2) to know the rules of the game. Problems arise when someone questions what game is being played and when there is confusion over the rules of that game.[4]

Figures of Speech Found in the Bible

After having briefly expressed some introductory thoughts related to figurative language, we can now categorize and examine the figures of speech used in the Bible.

Simile. One of the most frequent figures of speech in the Bible is that of the simile. It occurs often and is usually easy to detect, because the action or relation that is compared is marked by the use of the word *like* or *as*. Comparison is a valuable source of knowledge and according to G. B. Caird "is the main road leading from the known to the unknown."[5]

4. E. D. Hirsch, *Validity in Interpretation* (New Haven: Yale University, 1960), p. 70.

5. G. B. Caird, *The Language and Imagery of the Bible* (Philadelphia: Westminster, 1980), p. 144

There are examples of similes used in both the Old Testament and New Testament. In Jeremiah 23:29, the prophet declares that God's word is "like fire" and "like a hammer" that breaks the rock in pieces. In Isaiah 53:6, the picture is that we are "like sheep." In Matthew 13:37, Jesus said that "the kingdom of heaven is like leaven." And in Matthew 23:27, our Lord referred to the scribes and Pharisees, saying they were "like unto whited sepulchres." Notice that the two subjects under discussion are kept separate. It is not that "the kingdom of heaven is" but rather that "the kingdom of heaven is *like*." This usage points to an aspect of similarity between one object and another.

While simile can be used effectively, it is possible for a comparison to fail. According to Caird, such failure occurs when (1) the speaker assumes what is to be known by the audience is unknown, and (2) when the two things compared are thought to be considered alike in every respect.[6]

Metaphor. A figure of speech closely related to the simile is that of the metaphor, in which one thing is said to be similar to another because of some resemblance. However, with a metaphor, there is no formal signal by use of words, as found with a simile in the use of "like" or "as." The simile gently says that "A" is *like* "B"; the metaphor says "A" *is* "B." The Old Testament has such examples as Genesis 49:9, where we find "Judah is a lion's whelp." In the New Testament, Jesus used a metaphor when he said, "Ye are the salt of the earth" (Matt. 5:13–16), and again in John 8:12, when he said, "I am the light of the world."

The metaphor is capable of multiple meanings. For example, "leaven" may be symbolic of good or bad influence (cf. Luke 13:20–21; 1 Cor. 5:6–7). "Water" is used with a variety of meanings: the source of life (Isa. 55:1); cleaning (Matt. 27:24); power (Amos 5:24); weakness (Josh. 7:5); or judgment (1 Peter 3:20). Decisions regarding which meaning is intended should be made in light of the context of each passage.

It is possible for a single metaphor to be used in two opposite or contradictory senses. The "wilderness" or "desert" may be the symbol of desolation, demonic power, and all that rebels against the authority of God (Isa. 13:20–22; 34:13–15; Luke 11:24; Lev. 16:7ff). And yet, writes Caird—because of its association with the exodus—it may also be symbolic of innocence, sincerity, freedom, and security under the providential care of God (Exod. 5:1; Jer. 2:1–2).[7]

Caird adds that metaphors are found in describing the activities of God. There are two types: anthropomorphism, which ascribes bodily members and physical movements to God; and anthropopathism, which ascribes human emotions and responses to God. According to Caird, there are degrees of low and high correspondence in classifying meta-

6. Ibid., p. 145.
7. Ibid., p. 149.

phors that speak about God. He makes distinctions between these degrees of correspondence in three areas of application. First, it provides a criterion for distinguishing between the nonliteral and the literal. Second, it has a bearing on distinguishing between the nature of a parable and an allegory. Third, it is useful in classifying metaphors that the Bible uses to speak about God.[8] Correspondence is especially useful to Caird in providing a classification of metaphors that the Bible uses about God. The degree of correspondence is low when the Bible compares God to a dry wadi (Jer. 15:18), a festering sore (Hos. 5:12), or a panther mauling its prey (Hos. 5:14). But the correspondence is higher when the image is drawn from nature in its higher and finer qualities: the security of the rock (Ps. 31:2–3) or the sun as the source of light and life (Ps. 84:11). Anthropomorphic metaphors provide a low correspondence when the metaphor is drawn from man's dealings with the subhuman world (potter, woodsman, shepherd—Jer. 18; Isa. 11; Ezek. 34). A higher correspondence is found with those drawn from human relationships (judge, father, king—Mal. 3:5; Isa. 11:2; Dan. 5:18).

The above discussions of the metaphor and the simile illustrate the distinct differences between the two. If the comparison is explicit, it is a simile. If it is implicit, it is a metaphor.

Metonymy. This device differs from simile and metaphor in that the comparison is made between two objects that are associated with each other through some common traits or characteristics. Metonymy involves substituting one person or thing for another person or thing that is associated with it, or the use of one word for another that it suggests. In a metonymy, the exchange is between two related nouns. For example, "parents" and "ancestors" are cited in place of their posterity or children. "Jacob and Israel" are used to denote the people of Israel (Amos 7:9). "David" refers to the dynasty descended from him (Ezek. 34:23). Scripture sometimes cites "Moses and the prophets" for their teaching (Luke 16:29). Or, "the cup" is mentioned by Jesus in his blessing when the obvious reference is to its contents (Matt. 26:27). This kind of language is used today when someone reports, "The White House says," when he means that the President has said such and such.

Synecdoche. Similar to a metonym is a synecdoche, a figure of speech where either a part is mentioned for the whole, or the whole for the part. In this device, one word receives something from another that is internally associated with it by the connection of two ideas. An individual may be used for a class, or a class for an individual. Similarly, a singular may be used for a plural, or a plural for a singular. For example, "bread" can be used to mean food, and "the army" can refer to a soldier in general.

---

8. Ibid., pp. 151ff.

Because of its closeness with metonymy, synecdoche is sometimes mentioned under that heading.

In Jeremiah 6:16, the plural is used for the singular. "Paths" (plural) denotes that which is right in the sight of God, and therefore could not have been different—the "good way" (singular) in which they were to walk. In Jeremiah 8:7, the singular is substituted for the plural ("stork" for "storks" and so on). In Isaiah 40:2, there is a definite put for an indefinite.

Hyperbole. This figure of speech is an overstatement or a conscious exaggeration by the writer to gain effect. As E. W. Bullinger observes, this is "when more is said than is literally meant."[9] When an author wants to represent something as greater or less or better or worse than it actually is to gain effect or make an impression on others, he uses hyperbole. Though it may often be expressed in the form of a simile, this device is a deliberate exaggeration. In Genesis 15:1–6, God said he would number Abram's seed more than the stars of the heavens. Such an account can only be understood as an exaggeration for an intended effect.

Personification. In this figure of speech, a thing, quality, or idea is represented as a person; personal form or character is attributed to an inanimate object. This is often found in Scripture, where intelligence, volition, and life are attributed to either inanimate objects or abstract ideas. This figure is employed when the absent are spoken of (or to) as if present, when the dead are spoken of (or to) as alive, or when anything inanimate is referred to as a person. For example, Isaiah speaks of Jerusalem and says, "Her gates will lament and mourn" (3:26); and dead people in the grave are represented as being moved or stirred (14:9–11). In Isaiah 24:23, the prophet speaks of the moon as being confounded and the sun ashamed. In fact, personification is used often by the prophet Isaiah. The Lord used this figure of speech in Matthew 6:34 when he said, "Be not therefore anxious for the morrow: for the morrow will be anxious for itself."

Irony. Simply stated, irony consists in saying one thing and intending the opposite. It is usually a sort of humor, ridicule, or light sarcasm both in tone and intent. Bullinger writes, "There are not too many examples of this in Scripture. Irony has too much of contempt in it to suit the pity which is rather the spirit of Scriptures."[10] One such example is found in Job 12:2, where Job responds to Zophar and says, "No doubt you are the people, and wisdom will die with you." It seems obvious that Job's language is that of irony, for he means just the opposite of what is being said. The prophet Elijah speaks ironically when he speaks to the false prophets

---

9. E. W. Bullinger, *Figures of Speech Used in the Bible* (London: Eyre and Spottiswoode, 1898; reprint ed., Grand Rapids: Baker, 1968), p. 423.

10. Ibid., p. 807.

of Baal to call upon their God and says, "Cry aloud, for he is a god!" (1 Kings 18:27). The thought is for them *not* to cry to their god, for he is really no God and will not hear them.

Quite similar to irony is sarcasm, and while it might be considered by some as a separate figure of speech, it is so closely related to irony that it is often considered simply as a severe irony. This involves the use of such keen, bitter, cutting words as those of Elijah in the above example. Or consider the words of sarcastic irony spoken to Jesus by the soldiers, "Hail, King of the Jews" (Matt. 27:29).

Apostrophe. Mickelsen explains this figure of speech: "In apostrophe words are addressed in an exclamatory tone to a thing regarded as a person (personification), or to an actual person."[11] It is not important whether or not the person or thing is present. In direct address or a speech, the speaker turns away from his immediate audience and addresses either the inanimate object or the person or persons who are the object of his discourse. Mickelsen observes that this is often noted when a person is thinking out loud, and the object of his thoughts is not physically present.[12] If one were conducting a funeral and stopped his sermon to address the dead, that would be apostrophe. In David's lament over Saul and Jonathan (2 Sam. 1:24–25), he suddenly turns and speaks to the daughters of Israel and then turns from these to address the dead Jonathan. In Psalm 2:10–12, after speaking of what God will do, he turns suddenly and addresses the kings and judges of the earth.

Litotes or Meiosis. Mickelson describes this device as figure used to declare an affirmative truth by using a negative.[13] Such is true in the statement of Jesus in Acts 1:5, where he says, "But you will be baptized with the Holy Spirit not many days hence." The phrase *not many days hence* obviously means "within a few days." A milder form of this occurs when a simple statement is used to heighten the action being described, or, when an understatement is used in order to increase the effect. According to Caird, the Hebrew people never discovered the emphatic use of understatement, and except for the case of "a drop of water" (Gen. 18:4), there is no use of litotes found in the Old Testament.[14]

Aposiopesis. This technique involves the sudden breaking off of a thought before it is completed. It occurs when a speaker or writer consciously suppresses what he is saying, either because he is strongly moved emotionally or because he wants to achieve a rhetorical effect. An example of this is when Moses prayed to the Lord on behalf of Israel and said,

11. Mickelsen, p. 188.
12. Ibid.
13. Ibid., p. 193.
14. Caird, p. 134.

"Yet now, if thou wilt forgive their sin—and if not, blot me, I pray thee, out of thy book which thou hast written" (Exod. 32:32, KJV).

Proverb. This familiar figure of speech is commonly known to all people and is recognized as a wise or moral lesson expressed in short, pithy statements. In the Bible, the Book of Proverbs is one of our greatest sources for this type of figurative speech. But proverbs are found throughout the Bible and are not to be thought of as limited to one book. Bullinger divides proverbs into three groups. There are (1) those that are quoted as being already in use as such (Gen. 10:9; Num. 21:27; 1 Sam. 10:12); (2) those that, though not quoted as such, were very probably already in use as proverbial expressions (Matt. 13:31–32; Gen. 22:17); and (3) those that appear for the first time in Scripture, but which, because of their fullness of meaning and their wide application, have since passed into general use as proverbial sayings (Job 28:18; Prov. 1:32; 6:6).[15]

Hendiadys. This figure of speech is the use of two words occurring together and joined by "and" to express a single idea. Bullinger refers to this as "two for one" and says that this is two words used, but one thing meant.[16] The two words are the same parts of speech (two nouns or two verbs) and are always joined by the word *and*. Such usage is found in Genesis 19:24: "Then the Lord rained upon Sodom and upon Gomorrah brimstone and fire from the Lord out of heaven." The phrase *brimstone and fire* is a hendiadys meaning "burning brimstone." In Jeremiah 22:3, the prophet speaks of God executing "judgment and righteousness," which would best be understood as God executing "righteous judgments." In both cases, two nouns are used instead of a noun plus modifying adjective.

Euphemism. Here, agreeable language is substituted for an expression that might be offensive. By "offensive" we do not mean vulgar in itself, but offensive to one's sensitivity. A euphemism changes the unpleasant to the pleasant. In 1 Samuel 24:3, one reads about Saul going into a cave "to cover his feet." Willis explains that this is a Hebrew idiom meaning "to have a bowel movement," and it does not mean "to take a nap."[17] Caird points out that these "taboos of delicacy" are euphemisms involving mostly the use of the word *feet* (Deut. 28:57; Judg. 3:24; 1 Sam. 24:3; Isa. 7:20; Ezek. 16:25).[18] He adds that some euphemisms may be classed as metonymy (e.g. "sleep" for "death," John 11:11).[19]

Allegory. Mickelsen notes that an allegory is generally understood as an extended metaphor[20] and is considered a longer figure of speech

15. Bullinger, p. 755–6.
16. Ibid., 657.
17. Willis, p. 31. Cf. also J. T. Willis, *First and Second Samuel* (Austin, TX: Sweet, 1982), p. 237 for further discussion of this Hebrew idiom.
18. Caird, p. 72.
19. Ibid., p. 136.
20. Mickelsen, p. 212.

involving a narrative that teaches some spiritual or moral truth. Allegories and parables are often confused. An allegory differs from a parable, for example, in that the latter keeps the story distinct from its interpretation or application, but an allegory intertwines the story and its meaning. An allegory will have several points of comparison, whereas the parable will usually have one main comparison. Allegories appear in both the Old Testament and New Testament and usually have explanations with them. In the Old Testament, Psalm 80 and Proverbs 5:15–18 make use of allegories. The New Testament contains such allegorical passages as Ephesians 6:11–17; Galatians 4:21–31; and John 10:1–16.

Caird reminds us that it is important to notice the big difference between allegory and allegorization. In an allegory, the author tells a story to convey a hidden meaning. It is correctly interpreted when that intended meaning is perceived. But allegorization occurs when we impose on a story certain hidden meanings that the author did not intend. This mental process takes place when we treat as allegory that which an author did not intend to be allegory.[21]

Parable. When we read a parable, we are reading one of the oldest and most common of all figures of speech. A parable is often referred to as an extended simile. It is a story by which something real in life is used as a means of presenting moral or spiritual truth. The actors in a parable are believable characters and do nothing that they could not do in real life. Caird notes that in the Gospels, "parable" is the designation given to five different types of sayings of Jesus: (1) *simple simile:* "the kingdom of heaven is like unto leaven, which a woman took, and hid in three measures of meal, till it was all leavened" (Matt. 13:33); Luke 13:20–21; (2) *simple metaphors:* "neither cast your pearls before the swine, lest haply they trample them under their feet, and turn and rend you" (Matt. 7:6); (3) *simple story:* the Laborers in the Vineyard (Matt. 20:1–16); (4) *metaphor story:* the Prodigal Son (Luke 15:11–32); (5) *example story:* the Good Samaritan; the Rich Fool; Dives and Lazarus; the Pharisee and the Publican (Luke 10:30–37; 12:17–21; 18:9–14).[22] Most of the parables of Jesus are not hard to identify, for the writers designate them as such. One of the earliest parables is that of Nathan speaking to David (2 Sam. 12:1–6), in which David condemned himself for his own sin.

Conclusion

God's revelation to man makes use of figurative languages as a means of arresting our minds in a way that simple narrative could never do. Figurative language contributes to a fullness of expression and richly mean-

---

21. Caird, p. 165.
22. Ibid., pp. 162–3.

ingful communication that challenges the imagination. Beyond any doubt, there is a place for the clear, precise sentence. But our minds are captivated by the uniqueness of a well-chosen figure of speech, perhaps no better illustrated than in Scripture.

Part Two

Old Testament Interpretation

7

The History of
Old Testament Interpretation

Timothy D. Hadley

This essay must be partially defined by what it *cannot* accomplish in the space available. First, it cannot give a full account of all important people, events, and ideas within the more than two-thousand–year history of Old Testament interpretation. Second, it cannot (regrettably) give adequate bibliography or citations to document fully the enormous range of literature that accompanies this topic. Finally, it cannot, except in the broadest terms, discuss critical arguments or philosophical presuppositions connected with the hermeneutical methods discussed. Within these limitations, the material covered will be both an adequate and stimulating introduction to the topic, as well as a convenient summary for more advanced scholars.

Early Interpretation of the Old Testament

The interpretation of the Old Testament is as old as the Old Testament itself. Within its pages, later writers were already interpreting earlier material. Jeremiah 31:29–30, interpreted in Ezekiel 18, is one example. In fact, Ezekiel's interpretation explains why the earlier statement is no longer operative in Israel.

Targums and Septuagint

All ancient versions (including the Syriac Peshitta) were part of ancient exegetical literature and reflected the hermeneutical trends of their times. According to rabbinic tradition, Nehemiah 8:7–8 relates the beginnings of the Aramaic Targums to the Old Testament. After the Babylonian exile, most Jews spoke Aramaic as their native tongue. It thus became the practice, at the weekly synagogue worship, to read the appointed Hebrew portion accompanied by an oral paraphrase into Aramaic. Gradually these paraphrases became more elaborate and expansive and tended to become fixed and traditional by the time they were committed to writing. By this process, many of the Targums preserve not only translation but also interpretation.

Although generally more faithful to the Hebrew text, the Septuagint (LXX, ca. 275 B.C.) also contained paraphrase and supplementary explanations. The witness of the LXX to early Old Testament interpretation is valuable, but the Palestinian Targums seem to preserve the earliest form of biblical exegesis.

Qumran

The scribes at Qumran used various methods of interpretation, but the best-known is probably the *midrash pesher*. *Pesher* means "interpretation," and the examples of this genre from Qumran are primarily commentaries on biblical books. At times *pesher* is simply a verse-by-verse commentary, but it often takes the form of a specialized, nonliteral interpretation. Such is the case with the *pesharim* of Nahum, Habakkuk, and Isaiah found there.

Qumran exegetes also used the full midrashic technique employed by contemporary rabbis, recasting the story of Scripture so that the interpretation blended with Scripture and became one. The best exemplar of this approach is the so-called Genesis Apocryphon (1QapGen). It is filled with additional explanations and interpretations that supplement the actual words of Scripture.

The New Testament

The Old Testament writings had an enormous and lasting effect on New Testament writers, and the New Testament reflects this on every page. There are over 1,600 Old Testament citations in the New and many more allusions. When the New Testament writers quoted the Old Testament, they usually quoted the LXX. The basic hermeneutical principle for New Testament writers is expressed by Paul in Romans 15:14: "Whatever was written in earlier times was written for our instruction." The New Testament writers regarded the Old Testament promises as being fulfilled in their times (cf. 1 Peter 1:10–12).

Since most New Testament writers were Jewish, they show the expected influence of Jewish rabbinic hermeneutical methods (see below for fuller discussion). Paul uses both *pesher* (1 Cor. 15:54–55) and allegory (Gal. 4). Some scholars find allegory in the Book of Hebrews as well. The *peshat* (simple meaning) is adduced in James 5:17 concerning Elijah. But by far the most common method used was typology. The Old Testament was viewed as a combination of typology and prophecy. The New Testament writers attempted to correlate events mentioned in the Old Testament with the age in which they lived. Examples are Adam and Christ (Rom. 5:12–21) and Melki-zedek and Christ (Heb. 7:1–17).

The results of these methods brought three primary emphases to New Testament interpretation: (1) Christology—Old Testament references to the Messiah were uniformly understood as referring to Jesus; (2) Ecclesiology—the New Testament church was now God's chosen people, the new Israel; (3) Ethics—the Old Testament moral law was adapted and expanded for Christian conduct.

Early Rabbinic Interpretation

New Testament writers and later Christian exegetes owed much to Jewish methods of interpretation. The process that culminated in the Jewish Talmud involved interpretive and analytical exegesis of the Old Testament from the first through the sixth centuries A.D. Since Jewish society had adopted "the Bible" (Hebrew Old Testament) as its fundamental charter, exegesis was required to correspond to every practical, apologetical, and doctrinal need of the community. Interpreters sought to uncover the timeless significance of Scripture by making it respond to contemporary issues. This led to the establishment of the "Oral Law," the result of the search for biblical bases for new laws and customs not mentioned in Scripture. Interpretation and exegesis were needed to forge a link between the Oral Law and the written Torah of Moses.

Rules for interpretation grew from Hillel's seven to Ishmael's thirteen (early second century) to Eliezer's thirty-two (mid-second century A.D.). The approach was to find the *peshaṭ* (simple meaning or plain sense) of a passage, and then to supplement the interpretation with *derash* (derived meaning; cf. *midrash*). *Peshaṭ* was not always slavishly literal, but *derash* allowed greater freedom for the interpreter.

The classical period of *midrash* (second century A.D.) saw the formation of two schools of exegesis: that of Ishmael, which was didactic and literal, and that of Akiba, which sought all possible meanings and was more liberal. This attitude applied primarily to the legal portions of the Torah. Nonlegal materials, even among conservatives, allowed for greater freedom and imagination. Unfortunately, the finished product often became not the Bible interpreted, but the Bible rewritten.

The PARDES method (Hebrew for "garden") was used to arrive at a fourfold interpretational scheme: P = *peshaṭ* (simple meaning); R = *remez* (implied meaning); D = *derash* (homiletical meaning); and S = *sod* (mystical, allegorical meaning). *Peshaṭ* and *derash* were the most popular and widely used methods, but the others, especially allegory, became more widely used during the Middle Ages.

Early Jewish and Christian interpreters were all strongly influenced by Philo of Alexandria (20 B.C.–A.D. 45), a contemporary of Jesus. Philo was an early advocate of plain, literal interpretation but came to be the leading example of the allegorical method. When Old Testament statements could not be understood literally, Philo drew theological, philosophical, and moral lessons from them by means of allegory. It is impossible to appreciate fully the far-reaching influence of Philo upon all early Old Testament interpreters.

Early Christian Interpretation

In the early centuries of the Christian era, the Old Testament was interpreted by Christian exegetes primarily as a book about Christ. The emphasis was on prophecy and fulfillment. Typological exegesis was applied at every point to Christ and the church, and I Clement and the writings of Justin illustrate these matters well. But it was Origen of Alexandria (185–254), influenced by Philo's allegorical emphasis, who exemplified a new dependence on allegory as the chief method of Old Testament interpretation. Origen taught that there were at least two deeper meanings, besides the literal meaning, to be found by use of allegory. Unfortunately, as with Jewish *midrash*, this procedure was open to abuse, and frequently the exegete read into the Bible what he wanted to find there.

Opposing Origen was the "school of Antioch," led by Theodore of Mopsuestia (d. 428). He protested the improper expansion of allegory and taught that "the narratives of events in olden times are not fictitious." He was even reluctant to find direct predictions of Christ in the Old Testament, although he did admit an underlying dual meaning through use of typology.

Despite the protests of Theodore and his colleagues, the allegorical method soon gained the upper hand. Christ was the theme of all Old Testament interpretation. Augustine's famous statement reflected exegetical motivation: "The New Testament is latent in the Old Testament, and the Old Testament is patent in the New Testament."

Exegesis in the Middle Ages

Numerous problems beset biblical interpretation during the Middle Ages.

Medieval Christian Interpretation

Besides the virtual canonization of the allegorical method, medieval Christian exegetes also faced the growing authority of the established church and its traditions. Vincent, an early opponent of Augustine, said, "Care is to be taken that we hold that which has always been believed everywhere, always, by everybody." This attitude inhibited free and open study. Lack of emphasis on the original languages and a growing dependence on translations brought about expected errors and confusions.

One influential scholar overcame these problems. Jerome (347–420) studied Hebrew with a rabbi and later moved to Jerusalem (385) to finish his revision of the Latin Scriptures. Jerome's primary exegetical thrust was literal/historical, with some spiritualizing. He moved strongly away from the fanciful allegorizing of Origen. His work, both in translation and exegesis, came to have lasting influence and value. The Vulgate became the Bible of the church for more than a thousand years and was *the* text in medieval universities.

Gregory the Great (d. 604) was known as a master of spiritual interpretation and wrote commentaries on Job, Ezekiel, and Kings. During the Carolingian Revival (ninth to eleventh centuries), Bible study was linked closely to monastic piety. Unfortunately, scientific exegesis based on sound philology was lacking in this atmosphere.

Closer to the Reformation the situation began to remedy itself somewhat. The school of St. Victor emphasized the study of Hebrew. A pupil, Andrew (d. 1175), studied Hebrew and relied on literal Jewish interpreters in his own exegesis. Nicholas of Lyra (d. 1349) also made frequent use of Jewish insights, especially from Rashi (see below).

Otherwise, allegory triumphed until the time of Luther, who insisted more on the simple, literal meaning of the text. The positive aspects of medieval Christian interpretation included a gradual move away from unrestrained allegory; increased interest in the study of Hebrew; and more stress on the original text and its literal meaning.

Medieval Jewish Interpretation

Before the Renaissance and Enlightenment, Jewish interpreters were laying foundations for a move away from Talmudic *midrash* to a greater reliance on the plain meanings of the text. *Derash* was still used, but was not always uninhibited. Many Jews believed in the principle that no verse of Scripture could lose its literal meaning. In other words, the *peshaṭ* would not be explained away by any *derash*, including allegory. Therefore *derash* was considered to be a legitimate second meaning.

Newer concerns came to characterize Jewish interpretation during the Middle Ages. Philosophical explanations, linguistic studies, and enriched homiletic exposition are a few examples. In the Eastern Mediterranean area, the Karaites, who held to the reading of the text and rejected rabbinic traditions, opposed the attempts by Rabbanites to reconcile philosophical thought with their tradition. The Karaites extended individual freedom in interpretation and disregarded traditional limitations.

Notable among Eastern Jews was Saadyah Gaon (882–942), who contributed greatly to proper interpretation by limiting metaphysical interpretation and insisting on more literal exegesis. Saadyah translated the Bible into Arabic and commented profusely on Bible passages in his writings.

In Spain, the emphasis was on philology, lexicography, grammar, and related matters. Jonah ibn Janah (ca. 1000) formulated the syntactic laws of biblical Hebrew. Abraham ibn Ezra (1092–1167), the greatest Spanish exegete, combined scientific investigation with traditional interpretation, insisting on simple meaning and opposing allegory when the plain sense of Scripture did not contradict reason (cf. his commentary on the Pentateuch). Ibn Ezra was well ahead of his time on matters concerning Literary Criticism of the Pentateuch and Isaiah. Also worthy of note is Judah Halevi (1086–1141), who sought to reconcile revelation with reason.

Maimonides, known as Rambam (Rabbi Moses ben Maimon, 1135–1204), was the outstanding philosopher of the age. His *Guide to the Perplexed* promoted reason, but also read Aristotelian metaphysics into Scripture. He felt that the true meaning of Scripture lay in philosophical truth.

In France, Rabbi Solomon ben Isaac (Rashi, 1040–1105) became the most influential medieval Jewish exegete. He commented on almost the entire Bible, and his writings exerted far-reaching influence all the way to Luther and beyond. His commentary on the Pentateuch became the first book to be printed in Italy and the first Pentateuchal commentary to be printed anywhere (1475). Rashi's forte was literal interpretation and refutation of Christological interpretations of many passages.

David Qimchi (1160–1235) commented on the Psalms and the Prophets, and was well known for grammatical and lexicographical studies.

Mainline medieval Jewish interpretation, with its renewed interest on more literal interpretation and underlying philological matters, laid the foundation for the beginnings of modern critical study of the Old Testament.

Modern Critical Methods

Early Predecessors

For the most part, literary-historical criticism of the Old Testament was not viable during the early and medieval periods because of the lack of freedom to investigate the Scriptures independent of established tradition. Notable exceptions were Jerome, who suggested that Deuteronomy was from the time of Josiah, and some Jewish exegetes (Rashi, Ibn Ezra), who anticipated later critical ideas in their writings.

The intellectual and scientific interests awakened by the Renaissance naturally led to increased scrutiny of the Bible, especially the Old Testament. The rationalism of Bacon and Descartes in the seventeenth century led to bold speculation about the origins of the earth and the biblical accounts of man's early history. Significantly, the eighteenth-century beginnings of modern biblical criticism arose from four nontheological sources. The Dutch lawyer Grotius (Huig de Groot, 1588–1679) assumed the right to study the Bible as one would study other works of literature. British philosopher Thomas Hobbes suggested in *Leviathan* (1668) that the books of Moses were written after Moses' time. Likewise, B. Spinoza, a Jewish philosopher, advanced the same ideas in his 1670 *Tractus Theologico-Politicus*, a work described as the forerunner to modern Old Testament introductions. Finally, there was a French court doctor, J. Astruc, whose 1753 work, *Conjectures . . .*, put forth the idea that the use of two divine names in Genesis (*Elohim* [E] and *Yahweh* [J]) indicated at least two authors. (The actual title, in French, was much longer. For purposes of simplicity, titles of works will be given in English translation; in most cases, the reader may assume that the original title was in the native language of the writer.) Astruc's work was the beginning of the modern source-critical study of the Old Testament.

Critical impetus was also coming from theological circles. In 1538, Jewish grammarian E. Levita challenged prevailing views of inspiration by showing that the vowel points and accents in the Masoretic Text were not original. French Catholic priest R. Simon provoked the anger of Protestants by suggesting (in *Critical History of the Old Testament*, 1678) that Moses did not write all of the Pentateuch and that the other historical books were products of late compilation and redaction. In this work, Simon produced what later became the pillars of Pentateuchal analysis: diversities of style, contradictions, and doublets. In addition to these scholars, the German Jewish exegete Moses Mendelssohn (1729–86), called the father of the Enlightenment among Jews, helped to initiate modern critical exegesis in his commentary on the Pentateuch.

The Modern Critical Period

All of these developments led to the inevitable flowering of a full-scale and intensive scrutiny of the Old Testament documents. J. G. Eichhorn began the process with his three-volume *Introduction to the Old Testament* (1780–83), which is considered the first modern introduction to the Old Testament. Eichhorn initiated the term *higher criticism* and is often called the father of Old Testament criticism. His major specific contribution was to extend the J and E sources to the entire Pentateuch.

After Eichhorn came the promotion of the Fragment Theory, which said that Genesis was composed of one basic source (E) and expanded by fragments of other sources. W. M. L. de Wette promoted this view in *Articles on Old Testament Introduction* (1806–07), but the idea was not original with him. Scottish priest A. Geddes, in his *Introduction to the Pentateuch and Joshua* (1792–97), had said that the Pentateuch was composed during the Solomonic era from many fragments. J. S. Vater (*Commentary on the Pentateuch*, 1802–05) introduced the ideas of Geddes into Germany, with the proposal that Genesis was composed of thirty-nine fragments and reached its final form during the Babylonian exile.

Then came the Supplement Theory, which stated that the Pentateuch was comprised of one basic document (E), supplemented by J. Major advocates of this view were H. Ewald (*The Composition of Genesis*, 1823), F. Bleek (who extended literary analysis to Joshua and used the term *Hexateuch*), and F. Delitzsch (*Commentary on Genesis*, 1852), who was somewhat more conservative than the others.

The inability of scholars to arrive at a consensus led to the epochal work of H. Hupfeld (*The Sources of Genesis*, 1853), who saw E as consisting of two sources: E^1, which he called the *Grundschrift* ("basic document"), and E^2, which resembled J. Hupfeld's E^1 was later to become known as P. He also reordered the documents E^1(P)-E^2-J-D, thus establishing the basis of the classical four-document theory.

Hupfeld was followed by K. H. Graf (*Historical Books of the Old Testament*, 1866), who dated the final form of P as exilic and divided it into two strata: historical material (early) and legal material (late). Graf's work set the stage for Wellhausen (thus the common designation, "Graf-Wellhausen hypothesis"), but the Dutch scholar A. Kuenen strengthened the theories of Graf by stating that P was a unit and was late (*The Religion of Israel*, 1869). He also reordered the documents in the J-E-D-P sequence that was to become the standard order of Wellhausen's proposal.

It was left to Julius Wellhausen to create the statement that came to be accepted as the standard in Old Testament criticism from his time until today. To say this is not to imply that Wellhausen was right, or that everyone then or now agreed with him. Rather, it is to recognize that his formulation became the departure point for all subsequent research into the problem of Pentateuchal origins. This in itself indicates the impact of his contribution.

In two major works (*The Composition of the Hexateuch*, 1876; *The History of Israel I*, 1878; later revised as *Prolegomena to the History of Israel*, 1883), Wellhausen restated the documentary theory of Pentateuchal (or Hexateuchal) composition, ordering the documents J-E-D-P. It was not so much original thinking that gained Wellhausen's views their acceptance as it was the systematic way in which he synthesized preceding theories into a coherent and seemingly plausible arrangement. Utilizing the prevailing intellectual climate of evolutionary theory (based on Darwin's *The Origin of Species*) and dialecticism (based on the writings of Hegel), Wellhausen proposed a view of Israel's history and religious development based on a slow evolutionistic rise from primitive animism to ethical monotheism. His was a true liberal approach: he rejected supernatural explanations of scriptural origins in favor of naturalistic and rationalistic evolutionary theories of history.

The basic documentary scheme proposed by Wellhausen was as follows: J, 850 B.C.; E, 750 B.C. (both combined by an editor/redactor into J/E, 650 B.C.); D, 621 B.C. (the law book upon which Josiah's reforms were based); and P, 500 B.C.—all united into final form by Ezra or some other redactor, 450 B.C. (all dates are approximate). This view proposed the five primary pillars upon which the four-document theory rested: (1) diversity of divine names indicates diversity of authors; (2) J, E, and P are separate documents; (3) J preceded E; (4) E had a separate origin from J; and (5) D is from the time of Josiah.

Thus Wellhausen proposed an understanding of Israel's religion and development that was totally different from what the Bible itself claimed. According to him, the documents that lay behind the text were not written in the times they described but much later. These documents were not "historical" (containing reliable facts), but were only a reflection of the times in which they were composed or edited.

It is easy to see how such a proposal would engender opposition from more conservative circles. Leaders of conservative opposition to documentary theories were scholars such as E. W. Hengstenberg, a German who defended the Mosaic authorship of the Pentateuch as early as the 1830s. Hengstenberg had an influence on C. F. Keil, who became the foremost conservative German biblical scholar in the last half of the nineteenth century. In America, W. H. Green, professor at Princeton, attacked Wellhausen's theories in two works: *The Unity of the Book of Genesis* and *The Higher Criticism of the Pentateuch* (both 1895–96). Others of note were J. Orr and J. A. Alexander.

Early Jewish opposition came primarily from two scholars: U. Cassuto, who proposed that variations in P were purposeful and did not represent different authors (*The Documentary Hypothesis*, 1941/1961), and Y. Kaufmann, whose massive works championed the view that Israel's religion had been monotheistic from the beginning and that P was the earliest, not the latest, document/source.

But many scholars did accept Wellhausen's ideas, and support gradually built from virtually the entire world of biblical scholarship. In England, W. R. Smith and S. R. Driver (*Introduction to the Literature of the Old Testament*, 1891—the classic British formulation of Wellhausenism) became known for their enthusiastic support of the new theories. Meanwhile, C. A. Briggs (*The Higher Criticism of the Pentateuch*, 1893) became the foremost champion in America.

Later scholars accepted the basic outlines of the documentary thesis but added additional documents. Numerous proposals include those of O. Eissfeldt (1922), who saw a Lay source (L) within J; J. Morgenstern (1927), who proposed a Kenite source (K) connected with the reforms of

Asa (1 Kings 15); and R. Pfeiffer, whose 1941 *Introduction to the Old Testament* found a source from Edom/Seir (S).

Problems with Classical Wellhausenism

Although Wellhausen's classic formulation of Pentateuchal origins was widely accepted, it was also recognized as being an imperfect system. Later scholars have come to increasing awareness of the faults of the Graf-Wellhausen theories, and in our time it is safe to say that few, if any, modern scholars accept Wellhausen's views without modification. This is not to say that only a few accept the basic idea that the Pentateuch was composed of materials edited by later redactors and was not written by Moses. Many scholars do hold this view.

However, conservative opposition and new discoveries have combined within the past hundred years to render Wellhausen's views *passé* in virtually every respect. The classical formulation of documentary theory is fraught with many problems, of which only a partial list can be discussed here.

First, the *a priori* rejection of supernatural explanations, combined with the obvious and consistent connection between classical higher critical theories and rationalistic philosophy, have caused many conservatives to reject the theory. This is not to say that conservatives are without presuppositions. Rather, it signals the rejection of a theory based upon presuppositions that are clearly antagonistic to a high view of inspiration. An unsuccessful attempt has been made (L. Perlitt, *Vatke und Wellhausen*, 1965) to minimize the supposed reliance of Wellhausen on Hegelian dialecticism.

Second, a view of the Bible that strips the historical material of reliability and objective factual value is, for the same reason, unacceptable to conservatives. Some way must be found to maintain the historicity of the documents, and Wellhausen clearly eliminated this as a viable consideration.

Third, many have rejected serious consideration of documentarianism because of the ridiculous extremes taken by some interpreters. Attempts to divide chapters, verses, and even clauses into different sources have strained credibility and harmed the critical cause. S. A. Kaufman has pointed out, concerning the Temple Scroll, that the attempt to reconstruct the specific sources of Pentateuchal composition is "a consummately fruitless endeavor." Kaufman believes that the Temple Scroll makes the source origin of the Pentateuch "probable." He does not deny that sources were behind the text, but only the possibility of ever reconstructing those sources through any type of literary analysis, other than in the "broadest outlines."

Fourth, more recent knowledge of the ancient Near East has brought new evidence to bear on matters affecting Wellhausen's proposals. Discoveries such as Ras Shamra (Ugarit, 1929) and other archeological contributions have shown, among other things, that the theory of Israel's evolutionary religious development is not valid, and that the narratives of the Hexateuch reflect genuine second-millennium B.C. historical, cultural, and compositional patterns. Leaders in the archeological study of Bible backgrounds were W. F. Albright, Nelson Glueck, and others whose work continues to bless biblical studies.

Fifth, it has now been conclusively shown that Wellhausen's theories imposed artificial and uncontrolled literary criteria on the ancient documents. Most notably, there is the article by Tsevat, who counsels, among other things, the elimination of "bold hypotheses" in biblical studies, which often seek the new and sensational at the expense of controllable evidence and methodology. Such matters as diverse names for God, change of author's viewpoint, and other literary concerns are shown by modern examples to be inappropriately applied by classical documentary analysis.

Sixth, proponents of documentary schemes have often been accused of selectively ignoring evidence that would corroborate biblical statements. Especially telling are the criticisms of Henry, Kitchen, and Yamauchi. For want of space, these matters cannot be discussed here. It is hoped that the interested reader will seek out the relevant articles in this volume's bibliography.

In summary, the classical formulation of documentary theories, as synthesized by Wellhausen and accepted by many others, is fraught with serious problems which mitigate its acceptance by conservative scholars. No evidence whatsoever from any external controllable source has ever been brought forward to verify any of the tenets of Wellhausenism. The theories remain theory—unproven and, many would say, unprovable.

Twentieth-Century Responses

In large measure, the failures of Wellhausenism led to the establishment of new approaches to the Old Testament during this century. These will be briefly summarized.

Form Criticism is a literary-sociological method of dealing with folk material that was previously transmitted orally. It deals with the oral, preliterary stage of the material now found in the text. Form Criticism seeks to delineate the "units of tradition" by the forms or genres in which they occur. This method was pioneered by J. and W. Grimm in working with secular folklore (from 1812 on). The scholar who introduced this method to biblical studies was H. Gunkel, who conceived, named, and applied almost all concepts now used by Old Testament form critics. Gunkel took a comparative-religions *(religionsgeschichte)* approach, and his *Legends of Genesis* (1901) marked a major advance in Pentateuchal studies. However, it was his *Commentary on the Psalms* (1933) that brought Form Criticism most forcefully to bear on biblical studies. Here he sought to understand the "life setting" (*Sitz im Leben*, now termed "matrix") that had produced the various psalm genres.

S. Mowinckel, a Norwegian scholar and pupil of Gunkel's, advanced the idea of an annual New Year festival where Yahweh was enthroned as king (*The Psalms in Israel's Worship*, 1962, translated from studies dating back to the 1920s). Mowinckel's contributions fit both in Form Criticism and in Traditio-Historical Criticism (see below).

Traditio-Historical Criticism is an approach used in the work of many Scandinavian scholars. Whereas Form Criticism sought to go behind the text to the life situation that produced the tradition, these oral-tradition critics dealt with the text as it stood, seeking to understand the process of oral transmission that led to the text. This approach assumed that most Old Testament materials were once transmitted orally and that very little of the material was committed to writing until long after its origin. This assumption is the major weakness of this approach. Bright has noted, "Writing was. . . known through the entire history of Israel, and it is unbelievable that the tradition did not in many cases attain a written form far earlier than [some scholars seem] to think." Besides the fact that there is no evidence for the kind of oral transmission proposed by this approach, many who utilized Traditio-Historical Criticism also assumed the nonhistorical nature of the texts.

Notable names among the oral-tradition school include I. Engnell (Swedish), whose major work, *The Old Testament: A Traditio-Historical Introduction* (1945), rejected the documentary hypothesis but assigned a major role to oral tradition in the formation of the Pentateuch (or Tetrateuch). Lamentably, this work was never translated into English, partly because Engnell himself intended to revise it and some of its conclusions, but his untimely death ended this possibility. Danish scholar J. Pedersen, known for sociological studies of the Old Testament, also played a role in the oral-tradition school. In England, S. H. Hooke (*Myth and Ritual*, 1933) led the myth-and-ritual school, which saw the Canaanite cults as a pattern for Old Testament worship, and later adapted some of Engnell's ideas concerning sacral kingship.

Redaction Criticism sought to discover how traditions were compiled, edited, and re-edited to reach their final form. By its nature it was similar to Wellhausen's approach, but without the dependence on hypothetical documents. German scholars G. von Rad (1901–71) and M. Noth (1902–68) pioneered redaction-critical work on the Pentateuch.

Canon Criticism concerns the nature, function, and authority of the canon in the community of faith. This relatively new approach was coined by J. Sanders in *Torah and Canon* (1972) and expanded by B. S. Childs in his weighty *Introduction to the Old Testament as Scripture* (1979). Although Childs does not think "canon criticism" is the appropriate term for his approach, others have applied it to his work, and his name has remained associated with it.

Biblical history has engaged numerous scholars who are concerned with historicity and historiography as related to the Old Testament. Especially worthy are A. Alt, who in his "The Origins of Israelite Law" (1934) delineated the two types of law—casuistic and apodictic—now universally recognized within the Old Testament and the ancient Near East. Alt contributed many other ideas to numerous Old Testament disciplines. M. Noth is known for *A History of Pentateuchal Traditions* (1948), *The History of Israel* (1950), and *The Deuteronomic History* (1980, but translated from much earlier works).

Biblical theology has been the focus of study of W. Eichrodt (1933), E. Jacob (1955), and especially G. von Rad (1957). More recently B. S. Childs has cogently addressed numerous concerns in *Biblical Theology in Crisis* (1970).

Sociological insights as applied to the Old Testament have been the special concern of N. Gottwald (*The Tribes of Yahweh . . .* , 1979), J. Pedersen (*Israel, Its Life and Culture*, 1926–40), and R. de Vaux. The specific interest in understanding the social dynamics of the people of ancient Israel has also incorporated insights from German sociologist Max Weber.

For lack of space, nothing can here be said about the numerous advances made in studies relating to the historical books, the Prophets, and the Writings. In many cases these studies have followed the general trends of Pentateuchal studies, long the beginning point for critical departures.

Conservative Approaches and Criticism

Conservatism is not a retreat into tradition but an appreciation for the fruits of honest and solidly based study. In the past, conservatives have damaged their cause by radically opposing any critical approach to the Bible. Happily, the more widely accepted conservative attitude today seems to be one of using any and all appropriate critical methods to learn as much as possible about the Old Testament. Conservative presuppositions regarding such matters as inspiration and inerrancy should control the methodologies used; but within this framework, conservative/evangelical scholars can gain much from many of the various critical approaches discussed above.

Within today's scholarly world at large, there is a growing appreciation for the trustworthiness of the biblical writings; a realization that the Pentateuch and other historical books contain old documents and authentic traditions; an appreciation for the pre-exilic nature of the Psalms and Wisdom literature; and an understanding that the prophets were the heirs, not the originators, of monotheistic tradition within Israel.

Henry summarizes the conservative approach toward criticism: (1) historical criticism and Christian concerns are not mutually exclusive; (2) the various critical approaches are never philosophically or theologically neutral and so must be "controlled" by conservative presuppositions to be of value; (3) biblical events acquire meaning from divinely inspired Scripture.

In other words, the conservative must be capable of dealing with the various critical approaches to the Old Testament. Not all methodologies are compatible with conservative-Christian presuppositions. The conservative presupposes the historical accuracy of narrative unless forced by objective evidence to see otherwise. Above all, he recognizes the fallibility of the exegete and does not set human conclusions above divinely revealed truth. In so doing, he will use the Old Testament profitably and will apply critical methodologies to the never-ending task of more fully understanding that which, next to Christ himself, is the supreme miracle of the ages—the very Word of God revealed to man.

8

Old Testament Textual Criticism

Don Shackelford

History of Textual Criticism

The critical text study of the Old Testament prior to the twentieth century was hampered by a paucity of ancient Hebrew manuscripts. The ancient practice of destroying defective or worn-out copies of the text left little material with which to work.

Prior to this century, the oldest and most important complete Old Testament manuscript for textual studies was the *Codex Leningradensis* (B19^A), which—according to its colophon—was the work of Aaron ben Moshe ben Asher. It was completed by A.D. 1008-9 and served as the basis of the third edition of *Biblia Hebraica*, edited by R. Kittel.

The *Codex Aleppo* of A.D. 980 was also the work of Aaron ben Asher. It was taken from Aleppo to Cairo about A.D. 1000, where it was conserved in the Sephardic synagogue. About 1948, one-fourth of it was destroyed by fire. The rest has since been brought to Jerusalem.

Codex Cairensis, a manuscript of the former and latter prophets by Moshe ben Asher and dated to about A.D. 895, was preserved by the Karaite communities of Jerusalem and Cairo.

Another important family of Old Testament texts is the *Ben Naphtali* group. The oldest exemplars are the *Codices Erfurtensis*, initially kept in the Prussian State Library in Erfurt.

At the beginning of the twentieth century, the oldest manuscript of any portion of the Old Testament was the *Nash Papyrus*, which is dated by F. E. Deist to the second century A.D.[1] but by W. F. Albright to the second

---

1. F. E. Deist, *Towards the Text of the Old Testament* (Pretoria, South Africa: D. R. Church, 1978), p. 81.

century B.C.[2] It was first published in 1903. Textual critics also had available for their use the various translations of Hebrew Scriptures into Latin, Greek, Syriac, and other languages. However, one can readily see that textual critics before this century were dealing with manuscripts much removed from the original autographs.

There have been two discoveries in particular which have enhanced textual studies in the twentieth century. First, in 1890, during the rebuilding of the synagogue at Cairo, a storeroom *(genizah)* was discovered with over 200,000 items of texts, fragments, and manuscripts. A *genizah* was a place for storing texts that were to be destroyed because they were no longer fit for use. Fortunately, this room in the Cairo synagogue had been walled up and forgotten over the years. Its treasure trove of manuscripts written in Hebrew, Aramaic, Arabic, Samaritan, and Greek have been the object of intense textual study in this century.

The second discovery that has provided much material for Textual Criticism was the discovery of the famous Dead Sea Scrolls from 1947 onwards. The Judean caves near Qumran have yielded what Albright characterizes as the greatest manuscript discoveries of modern times.[3] Perhaps the most important of these scrolls is that of Isaiah (1QIs[a]), which is a complete copy of the book and consists of fifty-four columns of writing on seventeen sheets of leather approximately twenty-four feet in total length. It dates to about the first century B.C.

Other scrolls and fragments of every book of the Old Testament except Esther have come from Qumran over the years. These all date from the time before the fall of Jerusalem in A.D. 70 and provide rich resources for Textual Criticism.

What Is Textual Criticism?

Because the term *criticism* seems to have negative connotations in our day, it is important to define what is meant by Textual Criticism. R. W. Klein gives the following definition: "Textual criticism is the discipline that tries to recover the original copy (autograph) of a piece of literature by comparing its available copies, all of which inevitably contain mistakes. For the Hebrew Bible this task is complicated by the special factor that almost all early manuscripts have disappeared in whole or in part."[4]

---

2. W. F. Albright, *From the Stone Age to Christianity* (Garden City, New York: Doubleday, 1957), p. 350. See also Albright's article, "A Biblical Fragment from the Maccabean Age: The Nash Papyrus," JBL 56 (1937):145–176.

3. J. C. Trever, *The Dead Sea Scrolls: A Personal Account* (Grand Rapids: Eerdmans, 1977), p. 79.

4. R. W. Klein, *Textual Criticism of the Old Testament* (Philadelphia: Fortress, 1974), p. vii.

F. E. Deist adds:

> In the sense which is appropriate here, *to criticize something* means "to evaluate it": "to judge its worth." Correspondingly, *criticism* means "evaluation" or "judgement of the worth of a text." But what is the *sort* of worth which textual criticism seeks to judge? It seeks to judge the accuracy with which a text has been handed down, passed on, or—as we will say— "transmitted."[5]

The process of Textual Criticism of the Old Testament is extremely complex due to its long period of transmission—from Moses to Malachi. Prior to the invention of the printing press, copying ancient manuscripts was a laborious process. Scribes were employed in manufacturing copies of texts for general use. In the ruins of Qumran, archeologists excavated a scriptorium that may be characteristic of many others in ancient times. Here, while a reader slowly enunciated the text, scribes copied it down by hand. It is obvious that errors would be made, even though many safeguards against them were practiced.

In our day, some textual critics are advocating the theory that it is impossible to recover the original text, or autograph. Due to their belief in the "documentary hypothesis," they have modified the aim of obtaining the original text. Ernest Würthwein so modifies the aim of Textual Criticism when he argues:

> This does not mean recovering the original wording of the sentences as they were first conceived, but the textual form of the Old Testament books when they attained their present shape and content and became canonical writings, i.e., in the fourth century B.C. or later, depending on the book. Even when the goal of textual criticism is defined in this way there should be no illusions about its attainability in detail.[6]

This is the approach that Deist takes in *Towards the Text of the Old Testament*. He states emphatically that "we reject the view that Textual Criticism should reconstruct the autographa."[7] He is influenced in this statement by his *a priori* assumption that the books of the Old Testament went through a long redactional process before achieving their present canonical status.[8] If the books of the Old Testament grew gradually, as is assumed by many modern scholars, any meaningful attempt to arrive at the text of the original autographs is impossible.

---

5. Deist,p.11
6. E. Würthwein, *The Text of the Old Testament*, 4th ed. (Grand Rapids: Eerdmans, 1979), p. 103.
7. Deist,p.251.
8. Ibid.,p.250.

If one does not accept the documentary thesis or its modifications, which have been propounded since the time of Wellhausen,[9] the task of Textual Criticism remains the recovery of the original autographs. It is to this task that conservative biblical scholars must dedicate their energies.

Causes of Textual Difficulties

It can be unsettling to the novice to think of errors in the biblical text. Anyone who holds a high view of the inspiration and reliability of the Bible is naturally cautious in his approach to textual studies. However, since for nearly three thousand years portions of the sacred text were copied by hand, it must be admitted that discrepancies could creep into the manuscripts. There are many studies of the types of errors that one might expect.[10]

Unintentional Errors

Most of the errors that appear in various manuscripts of the Old Testament may be classified as unintentional. Deist lists eight reasons for such errors: sound-alike words were confused; look-alike words were confused; consonants were switched; letters, words, or phrases were omitted; letters and words were written twice; incorrect word divisions were made; the consonantal text was misread; and marginal glosses were incorporated in the text.[11] These errors can generally be recognized and corrected rather easily by comparing the text with ancient manuscripts now available.

Intentional Changes

Deist also discusses another category of errors—those committed deliberately. He examines four types: simplifications of the text; linguistic emendations; emendations on religious or moral grounds; and emendations on theological grounds.[12]

It is obvious that caution is necessary in evaluating the textual evidence. One may easily let his own judgments or presuppositions cause him to suppose error where there is none. At the same time, it behooves any Bible scholar to look fairly at the textual evidence in the search for truth.

---

9. J. Wellhausen, *Prolegomena to the History of Ancient Israel* (New York: World, 1965).

10. Deist, pp. 240–259; Klein, pp. 62–84; Würthwein, pp. 105–110; B. J. Roberts, *The Old Testament Text and Versions* (Cardiff: University of Wales, 1951), pp. 92–100.

11. One may see examples of these in Deist, pp. 38–46.

12. Ibid., pp. 46–49.

Methodology of Textual Criticism

It is unfortunate that there is no satisfactory textual apparatus in the present-day printed Hebrew Bibles comparable to that found in critical editions of the Greek New Testament. Anyone who has attempted to use the apparatus of the *Biblia Hebraica* is painfully aware of its inadequacies. The *Biblica Hebraica Stuttgartensia* does offer some improvement, but Deist points out that it, too, has many deficiencies.[13]

The remaining part of this study will offer some suggestions as to the principles and practice of Textual Criticism as applied to the Old Testament.

Text-Critical Preliminaries

Since the textual critic seeks to arrive at the original reading of the text by comparing ancient manuscripts, he must begin by collecting for study the necessary textual materials, i.e., pertinent ancient manuscripts. The comparison will be made to the Masoretic Text, which has been handed down from the early centuries of the Christian era. It is the basis of the latest edition of the Hebrew Bible. The *Biblia Hebraica Stuttgartensia*, published between 1976 and 1977, provides one with a critical edition for comparative purposes.[14]

The next step is to compare all available ancient manuscripts to the Masoretic Text. Würthwein proposed the following relative order of importance of other manuscripts: Samaritan Pentateuch, Septuagint, Aquila, Symmachus, Theodotion, Syriac, Targums, Vulgate, Old Latin, Sahidic, Coptic, Ethiopic, Arabic, and Armenian.[15] This may be too simplistic an approach, but these versions are certainly important to Textual Criticism. It is obvious that this type of investigation requires the cooperation of a number of scholars in various disciplines.

Canons of Textual Criticism

G. L. Archer lists seven canons that will serve as a reliable guide to the textual critic as he arrives at intelligent choices of readings.[16]

Canon #1: The older reading is to be preferred.

Canon #2: The more difficult reading is to be preferred.

Canon #3: The shorter reading is to be preferred.

13. Ibid., pp. 95–96.

14. K. Elliger and W. Rudolph, eds., *Biblia Hebraica Stuttgartensia* (Stuttgart: Deutsche Bibelstiftung, 1976/77).

15. Würthwein, p. 112.

16. G. L. Archer, Jr., *A Survey of Old Testament Introduction* (Chicago: Moody, 1974), pp. 58–59.

Canon #4: The reading which best explains all the variants is to be preferred.

Canon #5: The reading with the widest geographical support is to be preferred.

Canon #6: The reading which most conforms to the style and diction of the author is to be preferred.

Canon #7: The reading which reflects no doctrinal bias is to be preferred.

The reader is urged to read the fuller explanation of each canon, as discussed by Archer in *A Survey of Old Testament Introduction*. It is obvious that subjectivism may easily enter into one's decisions when attempting to apply these canons to the troubling passages of Scripture. It is always necessary to examine one's motives and to seek to be as objective as possible in examining the evidence for variant readings.

Reaching Decisions

When one has gathered all possible evidence for the text and has applied as fairly as possible the canons listed above, it is still necessary to make decisions concerning the validity of a given reading. It is well at this point to summarize the methodology proposed by Würthwein.[17]

1. When a comparison of the Masoretic Text and other textual witnesses offers a text that concords and makes sense, one may assume that this is the original text. It is not admissible to reject this text and resort to emendation, as many critics have done. Theological presuppositions should not be allowed to displace the clear statements of Scripture!

2. When other witnesses to the text deviate from the Masoretic Text, so that there are variants, the Masoretic Text is to be followed unless one of the canons cited above shows clearly that the other witnesses are to be preferred.

3. When the Masoretic Text is doubtful or impossible on linguistic or contextual grounds and other witnesses offer a satisfactory reading, the text should be corrected. Even here, caution should be used because of the subjective nature of textual emendation.

4. When neither the Masoretic Text nor the other witnesses seem to make sense, one may resort to conjecture. But he should be humble enough to recognize it for what it is—conjecture!

Conclusions

In conclusion, I feel compelled to make the following personal statement. In the quarter of a century that I have read and studied the Hebrew

17. Würthwein, pp. 116–117.

and Aramaic Old Testament and the Greek New Testament, my faith in Christ and God has grown immeasurably. It has been a thrilling experience, and I am thankful to my teachers for their guidance in this enterprise. I am also indebted to the linguists and lexicographers of the past who have provided the basic tools of research. We have nothing to fear from the careful and accurate scrutiny of the text.

All are indebted to the Sopherim and Masoretes of ages past, who so carefully went about their work of copying and recopying the ancient scrolls. Perhaps Archer expresses this best:

> We should accord to the Masoretes the highest praise for their meticulous care in preserving so sedulously the consonantal text of the Sopherim which had been entrusted to them. They together with the Sopherim themselves gave the most diligent attention to accurate preservation of the Hebrew Scriptures that has ever been devoted to any ancient literature, secular or religious, in the history of human civilization. So conscientious were they in their stewardship of the holy text that they did not even venture to make the most obvious corrections, so far as the consonants were concerned, but left their *Vorlage* exactly as it was handed down to them. Because of their faithfulness, we have today a form of the Hebrew text which in all essentials duplicates the recension which was considered authoritative in the days of Christ and the apostles, if not a century earlier. . . . These bring us very close in all essentials to the original autographs themselves, and furnish us with an authentic record of God's revelation.[18]

18. Archer, p. 65.

9
Hebrew Word Studies
Hugo McCord, enlarged by Joel Elliott

Principles

In recent years, much research in the area of biblical semantics has utilized the findings, terminology, and methodology of modern linguistics. J. Barr's *The Semantics of Biblical Language* (1961) is probably the most influential work in this area, and it has also prompted similar research from other Bible scholars.

One article this writer has found extremely significant for this study was "Semantics and New Testament Interpretation" by A. C. Thiselton, in *New Testament Interpretation: Essays on Principles and Methods* (I. H. Marshall, ed., 1977). Although Thiselton is obviously concerned with New Testament application, he surveys semantic theory, as well as the particular contributions of individual linguists and their relevance for biblical studies.

Because of this revolution in biblical semantics, word study may seem to be an illegitimate approach. Great emphasis is placed on proper distinction between diachronic and synchronic linguistics. Diachronic linguistics is the study of language or a word from its historical evolution; synchronic linguistics is the "language-state," or, perhaps a language in current usage. According to Thiselton, synchronic linguistics must have priority, since this principle in particular strikes at etymologizing, and thus at word study as it is so often practiced.

Methodology

This study is aimed at developing a sound methodology for doing Hebrew word studies. In doing so, it seems helpful therefore to choose a word and use it to outline and illustrate the development of such methodology. The word chosen was *še'ōl*.

I. Identify the root word (and its cognates) and define the semantic field of the chosen word.
   A. How does one find the root word?
     1. Make an educated guess and look it up in Brown-Driver-Briggs (BDB) lexicon. (See III.B.)
     2. Look up the word in Koehler-Baumgartner (K-B) and read their views concerning the word's root. (See III.B.)
     3. Using a work such as G. M. Landes, *A Student's Vocabulary of Biblical Hebrew* (1961), look up the word in the index, which will refer one to the body of the book, where words are often placed under their root.
   B. This can be illustrated with *še'ōl*.
     1. BDB lists *še'ōl* under the hypothetical root *š'l*, "to ask, inquire," though they regard this association as doubtful. They explain the association with *š'l* as a "place of inquiry (reference to necromancy)." They also note that the word has been associated with *š'l*, from which is derived *šō'l*, "the hollow of the hand," which root would thus signify "hollow place." They observe that "most now refrain from positive etymology."
     2. K-B suggest the word may be from *š'h*, "to be extinguished, desolate."
     3. Landes places *še'ōl* under the root *š'h*.
   C. Often (as with *še'ōl*), the root cannot be positively identified. It should be noted also that discovering a word's root, even when it can be known, may be of minimal importance for discovering a word's meaning. Note the following quotes:
     1. E. A. Nida (JBL 91 (1972): 85): "Etymologies, whether arrived at by historical documentation or by comparative analysis, are all very interesting and may provide significant clues to meaning, but they are no guarantee whatsoever that the historical influence is a factor in the people's actual use of such linguistic units. Valid lexicography must depend in the ultimate analysis upon patterns of co-occurrence in actual discourse."
     2. J. Barr (*Semantics*, pp. 107, 109): "Etymology is not, and does not profess to be, a guide to the semantic value of words in their current usage, and such value has to be determined from the current usage and not from the derivation. . . . The main point is that the etymology of a word is not a statement about its meaning but about its history . . . ."

D. Probably more important than discovering the etymology of a word is to study the semantic field of a word (this is particularly true of *šᵉ'ōl*). This is done by observing words with opposite meanings and with similar meanings (opposition and synonymy). These are words that occur in paradigmatic relation to the word to be studied (i.e., "This is the relation between a word or linguistic unit and another such unit which is *not* present in the actual utterance, but which might have been chosen *in its place*" [from Thiselton, "Semantics," p. 83]).

For example, the root of *šᵉ'ōl* is debatable, but perhaps not too much attention should be given to etymology. One perhaps can deal more adequately with the semantic value of *šᵉ'ōl* by observing it in paradigmatic relationship with other words. Thus, *šᵉ'ōl* is parallel (synonymous) with *māwet* ("death," e.g., 2 Sam. 22:6 and Ps. 6:5, 18:5, 49:14); *'ăbaddôn* ("Abaddon, destruction," Ps. 26:6 and Prov. 15:11, 27:30); *šaḥat* ("pit," e.g., Ps. 16:10); *bôr* ("pit," e.g., Ps. 30:3). *šᵉ'ōl* is also used opposite *šāmayim* ("heaven," e.g., Job 11:8 and Ps. 139:18). Note the following from Nida, (JBL 91 (1972): 85): ". . . critical studies of meaning must be based primarily upon the analysis of related meanings of different words, not upon the different meanings of single words. Only by the study of related meanings of different lexical units within well-defined lexical domains can one really succeed in determining the significant common, diagnostic, and supplementary components of meaning."

II. Concordance Study
   A. The standard concordances are:
      1. S. Mandelkern, *Veteris Testamenti Concordantiae*, 2 vols., 1955.
      2. G. Lisowsky, *Konkordanz zum hebräischen Alten Testament*, 1958.
      3. (George Wigram), *The Englishman's Hebrew and Chaldee Concordance*, 5th ed., 1890.
   B. Mandelkern's concordance is considered the most comprehensive, while Lisowsky's is somewhat easier to use. A good method for some is to use *Englishman's*, with Lisowsky or Mandelkern handy for quick reference to Hebrew (*Englishman's* works from Hebrew to English).
   C. What one looks for in a thorough concordance study is the semantic range of a word. Concordance study was touched on in I. D. above. One should study the word for its *syntagmatic* and *paradigmatic* relations. Syntagmatic relationship has to do with how a word is joined together with other words in a context. For example, in the phrase "a crown of thorns," the word *crown* stands in syntagmatic relationship to "a" and "of

thorns," which establish the meaning of "crown" (from Thiselton, "Semantics," p. 82).

D. To define a word in a given context, one should observe how the word is used elsewhere by the same author, subsequently moving to consider the usage by other authors. For Old Testament study, one should be aware of possible chronological differences (e.g., between the Pentateuch and Prophets) that may affect meaning. One should also consider the genre of a given context (e.g., narrative or poetry).

E. One should be careful not to do what J. Barr calls "illegitimate totality transfer" (*Semantics*, p. 218). That is, "when the semantic value of a word as it occurs in *one context* is added to its semantic value in *another context*; and the process is continued until the *sum* of these semantic values is then *read into a particular case*" (Thiselton, "Semantics," p. 84).

F. Ideally, one should then study the word in extra-biblical Hebrew. Tools will be discussed under III.

III. Lexical Study

A. The standard lexicons for biblical Hebrew are:
1. Brown-Driver-Briggs (BDB).
2. Koehler-Baumgartner (K-B).
3. W. L. Holladay, *A Concise Hebrew and Aramaic Lexicon of the Old Testament*, 1971.

B. BDB is rather old and thus does not make full use of relevant twentieth-century archeological finds. On the other hand, K-B does make full use of cognate Semitic languages, and it is considered now to be the standard. Also, BDB lists all words under roots, which quite often involves hypothetical and dubious roots. K-B lists all words alphabetically. Holladay's lexicon is an English work based on the second edition of K-B (German and English), and on what was completed of the third edition (German only). It does not, however, contain references to cognates in other Semitic languages (see D. Stuart, *Old Testament Exegesis*, 1980, p. 120f).

The lexicon allows observation of a word in various contexts with its varied meanings. A typical lexical entry can also be helpful in defining semantic fields. For example, under the entry "*rûaḥ*," BDB breaks the word down into different nuances of meaning. Thus, (4) "spirit of the living" is very similar to some usages of *nephesh*; (6) *rûaḥ* is defined as "seat or organ of mental acts," suggesting synonymy with *lebh*, and so on.

C. Non-biblical Hebrew

    1. The basic dictionary of the Targumim, Mishnaic, Talmudic, and Midrashic Hebrew is M. Jastrow's *A Dictionary of the Targumim, the Talmud Babli and Yerushalmi, and the Midrashic Literature* (2 vols., 2nd ed., 1926).

    2. At least one concordance of the Qumran texts is available: K. G. Kuhn, ed., *Konkordanz zu den Qumrantexten* (Gottingen, 1960).

    3. Inscriptions will be considered in IV.D.

IV. Cognate Semitic Languages

  A. Because of the limited literature of classical Hebrew, the student of the Old Testament is quite often dependent upon cognate Semitic languages to help define a biblical Hebrew word.

  B. There are usually three divisions made in the list of Semitic languages. The listing below is from C. U. Wolf's "Semite" in *The Interpreter's Dictionary of the Bible* (1962, 4:269):

    1. Eastern—Akkadian (Babylonian and Assyrian)

    2. Northwestern—Aramaic, Syriac, Samaritan, Palmyrene, Nabatean, Canaanite, Phoenician, Moabite, Hebrew, (Amorite)

    3. Southern—Arabic, Sabean, Minean, Ethiopic, (Amharic) Note: It is a matter of debate where Ugaritic fits in, although it is often regarded under the Northwestern Semitic languages.

  C. For Akkadian, there are two standard works:

    1. I. J. Gelb, B. Landsberger, A. L. Oppenheim, E. Reiner, eds. *The Assyrian Dictionary*, 1964ff.

    2. W. von Soden, *Akkadisches Handwörterbuch*, 1965.

  D. For inscriptions:

    1. C. F. Jean and J. Hoftijzer, *Dictionnaire des inscriptions sémitiques de l'Ouest*, 1965.

    2. J. C. L. Gibson, *Textbook of Syrian Semitic Inscriptions: Vol. I, Hebrew and Moabite Inscriptions; Vol. II, Aramaic Inscriptions; Vol. III, Phoenician Inscriptions;* 1971, 1975, 1982.

    3. W. Aufrecht and J. C. Hurd, *A Synoptic Concordance of Aramaic Inscriptions*, 1975.

    4. M. Donner and W. Röllig, *Kanaanäische und aramäische Inschriften*, 1962–64.

  E. For other Semitic languages:

    1. J. Aisleitner, *Wörterbuch der ugaritischen Sprache*, 4th ed., 1974.

    2. R. Tomback, *A Comparative Semitic Lexicon of the Phoenician and Punic Languages*, 1978.

V. Early Translations

A. For a thorough word study, it is significant to know how a given word was translated by the early versions. Most relevant are those versions that are based primarily on the Hebrew text:

1. Septuagint—The major source is Hatch and Redpath, *A Concordance to the Septuagint* (2 vols., 1954). Extremely helpful for Hebrew word studies is E. C. Dos Santos, *An Expanded Hebrew Index for the Hatch-Redpath Concordance* (n.d.). The standard dictionary is Liddell-Scott, *A Greek-English Lexicon* (9th ed., 1940).

2. Although there are several Greek translations known, the only other one really accessible is that of Aquila. Besides Hatch and Redpath, see J. Rieder and N. Turner, *An Index to Aquila* (1966).

3. For the Aramaic Targums, see M. Jastrow's dictionary (cf. III.C.1.).

B. Also of significance is the Vulgate, as it was translated by Jerome from the Hebrew (ca. 390–405). K-B often give the Vulgate translation at the beginning of an entry. Lisowsky's concordance gives German, English, and Latin equivalents to each word.

VI. New Testament Translation Equivalents

A. Finding how the New Testament translates a particular word is not always easy. One might begin by comparing the Septuagint translation of a word with the Hebrew text, then consult an index of New Testament quotations and allusions (such as the one found in the back of the Nestle-Aland, *Novum Testamentum Graece*, 26th ed., pp. 739–775) to find if and where the New Testament uses the particular passage in which the word occurs. After consultation of Hatch and Redpath, the Septuagint translation may key one in to the usual Greek translation of a Hebrew word. In that case, one might then consult the standard Greek lexicons and concordances.

B. Some Greek lexicons give significant information concerning the Hebrew background of a particular word. For example, under the entry *"ḥạdēs"* in Abbott-Smith's *A Manual Greek Lexicon of the New Testament* (3rd. ed., 1937), it is noted that *ḥạdēs* is the usual LXX translation of *šeʾōl*. An older lexicon like Thayer's *A Greek-English Lexicon of the New Testament* (1889) gives much the same information.

C. An extremely important source for Hebrew word studies is the ten-volume Kittel-Friedrich *Theological Dictionary of the New Testament*. Volume 10 is the index volume and contains, among other things, an index of Hebrew and Aramaic words. Under the word *šᵉ'ōl*, the reader is referred to volume 1, pages 146–148, which is J. Jeremias's article on *hadēs*. Jeremias's first section discusses the Old Testament background of *šᵉ'ōl*. Also of importance is Botterwick-Ringgren's *Theological Dictionary of the Old Testament* (1974ff) although only four volumes have been completed.

D. Unfortunately, most Greek lexical sources do not note whenever a New Testament passage is a quotation of, or allusion to, an Old Testament passage. However, once a particular Greek word has been identified as the usual translation of a Hebrew word (as *hadēs* is for *šᵉ'ōl*), Moulton-Geden's *A Concordance to the Greek Testament* (3rd ed., 1926) can be consulted. Thus, under the word *hadēs*, Moulton-Geden note that Acts 2:27 is a direct quotation of Psalms 16:10.

VII. Other references to discussions of a given word in early Jewish and Christian sources:

A. For early Jewish literature, the primary source is Jastrow's dictionary (see III.C.1.). For the English reader, the index of a good edition of the Talmud might be consulted (e.g., *The Babylonian Talmud*, London: Soncino, 1948). Herbert Danby's edition of the Mishnah also has a good index. In addition, for particular New Testament passages, one might consult H. L. Strack and P. Billerbeck, *Kommentar zum Neuen Testament aus Talmud und Midrasch* (5 vols., Munchen, 1926).

B. For Jewish literature in Greek—such as Josephus and Philo—Liddell-Scott's *A Greek-English Lexicon* should be consulted under key words (e.g., *hadēs*) as well as the indices of good editions (such as *The Loeb Classical Library*). For Josephus, also seek K. G. Rengstorf, ed., *A Complete Concordance to Flavius Josephus* (3 vols. ready, 1973ff).

C. For Christian literature outside the New Testament, the best and most exhaustive source is G. W. H. Lampe, ed., *A Patristic Greek Lexicon* (1971).

VIII. Modern Critical Works

A. Finally, the word(s) should be studied in modern critical sources, which include the latest dictionaries and commentaries, as well as important articles and monographs.

B. For a complete list of possible sources, one should consult such works as S. B. Marrow, *Basic Tools for Biblical Exegesis* (Rome, 1976); F. W. Danker, *Multi-purpose Tools for Bible Study* (St. Louis, 1970); and D. Stuart, *Old Testament Exegesis* (Philadelphia, 1980).

C. In addition to the bibliographical references above, the student should attempt to consult the following sources:
1. *The Interpreter's Dictionary of the Bible.*
2. *Anchor Bible* (Doubleday).
3. *Hermeneia* commentary series (Fortress).

Practice

Hebrew word studies are no different from word studies in any other language. However, in Hebrew one learns early that nearly every word (of which 8,198 have been counted in the Hebrew Bible) is derived from a tri-letter root (of which some 1,860 have been listed).[1] Immediately, then, when inquiry is made as to a word's meaning, the first reaction is to search for the root from which the word is derived. If that root is readily found, the researcher, in order to determine how authorities define the word, will begin examining as many lexicons as possible.

For example, the Hebrew word *she'ol*, appearing sixty-five times in the Old Testament, is apparently derived from the verb *sha'al*.

The Lexicons

For *sha'al*, Gesenius assigned two meanings: (1) "to ask" and (2) "to excavate" (equal to *sha'al*). His translator, Tregelles, remarked that in the Gesenius *Thesaurus*, the primary meaning is "to dig" or "to excavate." Gesenius then defined *she'ol* as "a subterranean place, full of thick darkness," and he summarized: "I think that I have lighted on the true etymology of the word. For I have no doubt that *she'ol* is for *she'ol*."[2]

She'ol *in the Old Testament*

Literalness. Whether *she'ol* is derived from *sha'al* ("to ask," cf. Prov. 27:20; 30:15–16; Hab. 2:5) or from *sha'al* ("to dig," cf. Amos 9:2), the literal meaning appears to be a "hollow place," a "cavity," a "cavern." Thus Jonah, in the fish's stomach, described himself as in "the belly of *she'ol*" (Jonah 2:1–3 [1:17–2:2, Eng]). Likewise, when the ground split under the feet of Korah and his company, they sank into a fissure of the earth called "*she'ol*" (Num. 16:30–33). This *she'ol* became their grave.

The word *she'ol* came to be a synonym for the tomb.[3] *She'ol* is associated with death, destruction, dust, worms, corruption, darkness, silence, and the pit. Since the deceased are there, it is the opposite of "the land of

---

1. R. B. Girdlestone, *Synonyms of the Old Testament* (Grand Rapids: Eerdmans, 1951; reprint 2nd ed., 1897), p. 5.

2. Other lexicons (Brown-Driver-Briggs, Davidson, Davies, Harkavy, Koehler-Baumgartner) give corroborative but no differing information.

3. Gen. 37:35; 42:38; 44:29, 31; Ps. 88:4–6 [3–5,Eng.].

the living."[4] Characterized as a place of hiding and of rest, yet in it is no memory, no work, no consciousness, no planning, no knowledge, and no wisdom (Eccles. 9:10). Into *she'ol* go the bodies of beasts and of human beings, and the humans include both the righteous and the unrighteous.[5] From *she'ol* there is no exit until the heavens are no more (Job 7:9; 14:10–13). When one remembers that the word "soul" (*nephesh*) is at times rightly translated as a dead body, the incongruity of a righteous disembodied spirit's being in as repulsive a place as *she'ol* disappears.[6]

Apparently the King James translators thought that often *she'ol* referred to "the hell of fire" (Matt. 5:22), for they translated it as "hell" thirty-one times. But "nowhere in the Old Testament is the abode of the dead regarded as a place of punishment or torment."[7] "Not in a single passage" is *she'ol* used "in the sense of the place of punishment after the resurrection."[8] Instead, all that is pictured is "a typical Palestinian tomb, dark, dusty, with mingled bones and where 'this poor lisping stammering tongue lies silent in the grave.'"[9]

Metaphor. From its literal meaning, the word *she'ol* passed into a representation of the lowest place as opposed to the highest (Deut. 32:22; Isa. 44:23; Job 11:8). Also, figuratively, the word meant a place of degradation and disgrace (Isa. 57:9). Further, a metaphorical usage is found in the picture of a real estate compound enclosed by bars, locked by gates, and containing a house and a bed (Job 17:13, 16; Ps. 139:8; Isa. 38:10).

Personification. Beyond the metaphorical usage, Old Testament writers sometimes made *She'ol* a living thing (and so for the first time in this study the word is capitalized). Strangely, that which is associated with everything that is the opposite of life is by a bold figure presented as an animated "insatiable monster,"[10] or "a demon with wide-open throat or gaping jaws."[11] In this personification, Death has come alive. His hand is

4. Ps. 6:6 [5,Eng.]; 31:18 [17,Eng.]; Job 11:8; 14:13; 17:13–16; 24:20; 26:6; Isa. 38:11, 17–18; Ezek. 31:15–16; Eccles 9:10. The *repa'im* (etymologically, the *weak* or *feeble*) came to denote the dead ones in *she'ol* (Isa. 14:9; 26:14, 19; Prov. 2:18; 9:18; 21:16; Ps. 88:11 [10,Eng.].

5. Eccles. 3:19–20; Gen. 37:55; Job 24:19; Ps. 31:18 [17,Eng.]; 49:11–16 [10–15,Eng.].

6. Num. 5:2; 6:6; 9:6,7,10; 19:11, 13. In reference to Ps. 16:10, Girdlestone wrote that some are of the "opinion that it should be translated, 'Thou shalt not leave my dead body in the grave.' That the word *nephesh*, soul, may sometimes be translated 'dead body' is true . . . and that the word *hades* is often translated *grave* we have also seen to be true" (*Synonyms*, p. 283).

7. G. A. Buttrick, ed. et al., *The Interpreter's Dictionary of the Bible*, 4 vols. (Nashville: Abingdon, 1962), 1:787f.

8. Girdlestone, p. 283.

9. R. Harris, ed. et al., *Theological Wordbook of the Old Testament*, 2 vols. (Chicago: Moody, 1980), 2: 893.

10. F. Brown, S. R. Driver, and C. A. Briggs, *A Hebrew and English Lexicon of the Old Testament* (Oxford: Clarendon, 1907), p. 983.

11. Buttrick, 1: 787f.

strong and he carries cords or ropes. His prey trembles. *She'ol* swallows his victims. He is able to talk, and he can be spoken to, even challenged, "O *She'ol*, where is your destruction?"[12]

Furthermore, in vivid personalization, corpses put their swords under their heads, and are pictured as speaking (Ezek. 32:21, 27). An animated *She'ol* stirs up the dead ones (kings and princes) to greet a newcomer, the king of Babylon, and they shout taunts to that once-proud monarch: "Have you also become as weak as we? Have you become like us? Your pomp has been brought down to *She'ol*, the noise of your viols; the worm has been spread under you and the worms cover you" (Isa. 14:9–11).

So living and conscious do Old Testament writers personify *She'ol* that many authorities have been misled into making the language literal. As a result they see *She'ol* as a state in which people outside their bodies are half awake, partially conscious, existing in a dismal, shadowy waiting place. "The Israelite conception," wrote one scholar, is that "the 'shade' of the living man separates from the body and takes up its abode in *She'ol*," lacking "everything which . . . could be called life."[13] Gesenius held that people in *She'ol* are "void of blood and animal life . . . therefore weak and languid like a sick person . . . but not devoid of powers of mind, such as memory." Brown-Driver-Briggs concluded that *She'ol* is "dark, gloomy, without return . . . all being alike." Orr wrote that existence in *She'ol* is ". . . feeble, inert, shadowy, devoid of living interests . . . a slumbrous semi-consciousness and enfeebled existence from which in a partial way the spirit might temporarily be aroused."[14]

Some scholars put all disembodied spirits, both the righteous and the wicked, into a dark, gloomy halfway house. They make the end of a righteous person's life anticlimactic and miserable. If the theory of those scholars is true, the end is not better than the beginning (Eccles. 7:8). If there is no distinction at the time of death between the righteous and wicked, futile would be the prayer, "Let me die the death of the upright, and let my last end be like his" (Num. 23:10). But a man of faith did not see in front of him a murky interim realm of shadows and semi-consciousness, for he believed that "the path of the just is as a shining light that shines more and more to the perfect day" (Prov. 4:18). His anticipation, ever bright and vibrant and cheerful, was set forth in an aphorism: "In the path of the righteous is life, and in its way there is no death" (Prov. 12:28).

12. Num. 16:32; Ps. 49:16 [15,Eng.]; 89:49 [48,Eng.]; 141; 7; Prov. 1:12; 30:15–16; Isa. 5:14; 28:15, 18; Hos. 13:14; Hab. 2:5

13. *The New Schaff-Herzog Encyclopedia of Religious Knowledge*, S. M. Jackson, ed. et. al., 13 vols. (Grand Rapids: Baker, 1949), s.v. "Hades," 5:109, by G. Dalman.

14. *The International Standard Bible Encyclopaedia* [ISBE], J. Orr., ed. et. al., 5 vols. (Grand Rapids: Eerdmans, 1946), s.v. "Eschatology of the Old Testament," 2: 974, and "Sheol," 4: 2761, by J. Orr.

In the New Testament She'ol Becomes Haides

Literalness. Almost uniformly (sixty-one times out of sixty-five) the Septuagint translated *she'ol* by *haides* (literally, the "not seen," *a* + *idein*, *hades*). Thayer, describing hades as a dark and dismal place, defined it as "the common receptacle of disembodied spirits," citing Luke 16:23 and Acts 2:27, 31 as supporting his opinion. True it is that Luke 16:23 does place the disembodied spirit of the rich man in a hades of fiery torment, but that citation does not put the spirit of Lazarus in hades. The distinction in Luke 16:22–23 "is not between 'the bosom of Abraham' and another place, as both included in Hades, but between 'the bosom of Abraham' and Hades as antithetical and exclusive."[15] Although the passage in Luke does make hades a receptacle for unrighteous spirits, it does not put righteous disembodied spirits into hades or a subdivision of it.

On the surface, Thayer's citation of Acts 2:27, 31, as proving that hades is a receptacle for a righteous disembodied spirit, appears justified. This is true because an important usage of "soul" (*psuche*) is to mean a conscious disembodied spirit (Rev. 6:9). But in hades (*she'ol*) there is "no work, nor device, nor knowledge, nor wisdom" (Eccles. 9:10). To that place a conscious soul could not go.

It has already been indicated in this study that in some contexts "soul" (*nephesh*) is rightly rendered "a dead body." In context, Acts 2:27, 31 puts Jesus' soul in hades. If hades is a literal tomb and if the soul spoken of was Jesus' fleshly body, then Acts 2:27, 31 does not put a righteous disembodied spirit in hades. On the contrary, it merely puts Jesus' corpse in Joseph's sepulchre. The parallelism in the passage supports such an interpretation, for "soul" is equated with "flesh," and "hades" is equated with "corruption": " . . . you will not abandon my soul in hades, neither will you give your holy one to see corruption. . . . neither was he abandoned in hades, nor did his flesh see corruption."

Normally, hades (as *she'ol*) is the tomb. Except as an escape from misery (as a place where a physical body is hidden and at rest, Job 14:13; 17:16), nothing pleasant biblically is spoken of hades. It is always a place from which deliverance would be a blessing.[16] Therefore, it does not appear reasonable that Jesus' soul as a conscious disembodied spirit went to hades. But it is clear that his soul as a dead body did go to a literal hades, a tomb, and likewise it is clear that his flesh saw no corruption.[17]

---

15. Ibid., s.v. "Hades," 2: 1314, by G. Vos.

16. Ps. 16:10; 30:4 [3,Eng.]; 49:16 [15,Eng.]; 86:13; Prov. 23:14.

17. "David . . . saw corruption; but [Jesus] whom God raised did not see corruption" (Acts 13:36–37). Some scholars allege that Luke mistranslated the *shahath* of Ps. 16:10, saying he should have written "pit" instead of "corruption." Gesenius and Brown-Driver-Briggs joined in that indictment of Luke. Davies listed the possibility of the word "pit," but he said the probability is in favor of the word "corruption." Davidson did not list "pit" as a possibility, restricting his translation to "corruption,

Thus, to this writer, Thayer's use of Acts 2:37, 31, as establishing hades as a receptacle for a righteous disembodied spirit, is in error. In the New Testament, two clear and different literal meanings of "hades" appear: the grave for fleshly bodies and a place of torment for wicked disembodied spirits.

Metaphor. The previous section set forth two literal meanings of "hades." Beyond the literal usages, Jesus appropriated a figurative significance from Isaiah. As Babylon's boasting king had affected ascent "into heaven . . . above the stars of God," and would be cast down to *she'ol* (Isa. 14:4, 12–15), in like manner proud Capernaum would fall: "You Capernaum, are you not lifted up to heaven? To hades you will go down" (Matt. 11:23; Luke 10:15). Apparently more than a graveyard destiny (a literal hades) inheres in Jesus' condemnation: "hades" in this language is degradation and embarrassment. Thayer classified Jesus' use of "hades" as metaphorical in the reference to Capernaum's being "thrust down into the depth of misery and disgrace."

A second metaphorical use of the word *hades* is in the grave's being pictured as a building with gates and a lock: the "gates of hades" (Matt. 16:18, cf. Job 38:17, "gates of death") would not prevent Jesus' building his *ekklesia*. He knew that after his walking unassisted from the cemetery he would have "the keys of death and of hades" (Rev. 1:18).

Personification. The final figurative use of the word *hades* is in its being pictured as a living creature. In the writing of the word hades in the two literal meanings discussed above, and in the writing of the letters to set forth the two metaphorical uses, capitalization would not be expected. But in the personalization of Hades as a living being, capitalization becomes proper.

As *She'ol*, a synonym for Death, is personalized by Isaiah (28:15) and by Hosea (13:14), so Hades, a synonym for Death, is personalized by Paul (1 Cor. 15:55) and by John (Rev. 6:8; 20:13–14).[18]

Non-Biblical Meanings

Whereas the Bible nowhere puts the disembodied spirit of a righteous man in hades, apocalytic literature listed four areas, "two for the right-

---

puridity." Actually, if Luke had used "pit" he would have contradicted history, for Jesus' flesh did see the pit. Luke's use of "corruption" is thus justified both by the lexicons of Davies and Davidson and also by the historical fact. Corroborative also is the fact that the Septuagint used *diapthora*, and the Vulgate *corruptio*.

18. The omission of the word *haides* from the Aland-Black-Metzger-Wikgren Greek New Testament in I Cor 15:55 was done with "some degree of doubt." The antecedent of I Cor 15:55 in Hosea 13:14 has *haides* in the LXX and *she'ol* in the Hebrew. As far as the thrust of this study is concerned, its omission or inclusion is immaterial. This is true because the personalized use of *Haides* (even if not in I Cor. 15:55) in Rev. 6:8; 20:13–14 is indubitable.

eous, and two for the wicked."[19] Post-biblical Judaism held to two compartments in hades, one for the righteous and one for the wicked. Josephus described hades as "a place of custody for souls," and continued:

> In this region there is a certain place set apart, as a *lake of unquenchable fire* . . . into which no one has yet been cast. The just . . . are now indeed confined in Hades, but not in the same place wherein the unjust are confined. . . . This place we call *The Bosom of Abraham*. It is on the right hand beyond the entrance gate, while the unjust are on the left hand, close to hell's "hot vapour," but they see, beyond a chaos (deep and impassable and large and fixed), the just.[20]

One scholar has observed that the double-compartment theory is received by a large portion of the nominal Christian Church, and "it forms the foundation of the Roman Catholic doctrine of Purgatory, for which there would be no ground but for this interpretation of the word *hades*."[21] He further observed that the "upper part" of hades, "the region of the blessed," was called Paradise, while beneath was Tartarus, "in which the souls of the wicked were subjected to punishment."

Among the Greeks and Romans the region of the blessed souls was called the Elysian Fields (*Elusia Pedia*).[22] Concerning the two-compartment conjecture, another scholar was cautious: "This conception should not be rashly transferred to the New Testament."[23] Textually, the only way the idea of a compartmentalized hades can be found in the New Testament is by an arbitrary transfer. In this writer's opinion, it would have to be by eisegesis, not exegesis.

Conclusions

This study leads to three conclusions:

1. Greek and Roman mythology, as well as post-biblical Judaism, pictured a *haides* (and so, a *she'ol*) not found in either the Old Testament or the New.

---

19. *The Book of Enoch*, 21, 1–13, cited by J. Orr, "Eschatology of the Old Testament," ISBE 2: 974; cf. also G. Vos, "Hades," 2: 1314f.

20. F. Josephus, "Hades," *The Life and Works of Flavius Josephus*, W. Whiston, tr. (Philadelphia: The John C. Winston Co., n.d.), pp. 901–903. (Most scholars reject this as an authentic work of Josephus.)

21. *Bible Encyclopaedia*, S. Fallows ed. et al., 2 vols. (Chicago: Howard-Severance, 1902), 1: 747–748.

22. *Webster's Third New International Dictionary*, P. Babcock Gove, ed. in chief (Springfield, MA: G&C Merriam, 1971), s.v. "Hades," and *The Classic Greek Dictionary* (New York: Hinds & Noble, n.d.), s.v. "Elusion."

23. ISBE, s.v. "Hades," 2: 1314f., by G. Vos.

FIGURE 1 **The Living and the Deceased**

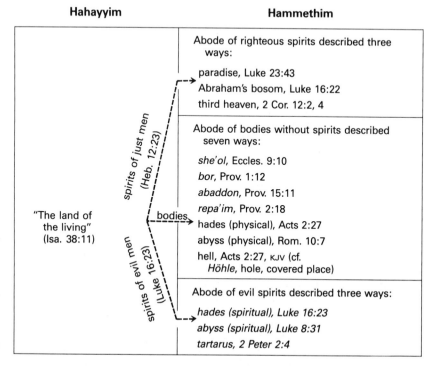

2. The Old Testament and New Testament are a unit in three uses of the word *she'ol* (and so, *haides*), namely, a literal, a metaphorical, and a personalized significance.

3. Whereas both the Old and New Testaments portray hades as a literal grave, the New Testament in addition portrays hades as an internment area for unrighteous disembodied spirits.

The relation between the biblical meanings of *she'ol* and associated words is seen in Figure 1.

10

Interpreting Hebrew Syntax

John T. Willis

Syntax is the arrangement of words in a sentence to show their mutual relationship. It is the single most important aspect of the study of any language, because a word has no meaning isolated from a context, and people do not think disconnected words, but expressions, clauses, and sentences. The word *name* (Hebrew *šēm*) illustrates this point. It can mean a proper name given to a person (Gen. 3:20) or place (Num. 11:3). But it can also mean "reputation" (Prov. 22:1) or function as a substitute for the person himself, so that "Holy and terrible is his [i.e., God's] name!" (Ps. 111:9) actually means "Holy and terrible is he!" Then there are whole expressions that contain the word name. For example, to "walk in the name of God [or a foreign god]" (Mic. 4:5) suggests something like living according to the will of, or in submission to the authority of, that deity, and to "call on the name of the Lord" (Ps. 116:4, 13, 17) means to seek the Lord's help, depend on him, and give him all the glory for salvation and blessing. The purpose of this article is to sketch major characteristics of Hebrew syntax, then to show how a knowledge of certain principles of Hebrew syntax aids in the interpretation of Old Testament passages.

Major Characteristics of Hebrew Syntax

Hebrew phrases and sentences lend themselves to a variety of interpretations because the Hebrew language is much less precise than Greek or Latin. For example, there are no tenses in Hebrew. Both the perfect and imperfect may be past, present, or future.[1] Hebrew has no subjunctive mode. The imperative is not used with a negative particle.

The parts of speech that occur in Hebrew are the verb, the noun, the pronoun, the adjective, the adverb, the conjunction, and the preposition. The verb has perfect, imperfect, participial, imperative, infinitive absolute, and infinitive construct forms. The noun and adjective may take suffixes, which function like a possessive pronoun and may be subject or object. Pronouns belong to personal, demonstrative, interrogative, and relative categories.

There are verbal and nominal sentences in Hebrew. The three parts of the common verbal sentence are *verb—subject* (with its modifiers)—*object* (with its modifiers). The nominal sentence consists of only two parts: *subject—predicate*. By and large, Hebrew omits the verb "to be" in the present. The article *(ha)* is attached directly to the word with which it is associated, while the definite direct object is preceded by the sign *'et.* There are comparatively few subordinating conjunctions marking adverbial clauses.

Different scholars identify and define various types of sentences in the Hebrew Old Testament. The list given by Davidson is longer than usual, but provides thought-provoking suggestions that promote specificity: interjectional, affirmative, interrogative, negative, conditional, optative, conjunctive, circumstantial, relative, temporal, subject and object, causal, final, consequential, comparative, disjunctive, restrictive, exceptive, and so forth.[2]

Hebrew poetry varies considerably from the patterns of Hebrew prose because of the tendency of poetic parallelism to balance the corresponding lines. A great deal of vocabulary in poetry differs from that found in prose. Poetry frequently uses longer forms of prepositions, the endings -*î* and -*ô* in nouns, longer forms of pronominal suffixes, and the masculine plural form -*în*. It employs the article, relative pronoun, and sign of the accusative, *'et,* much less than prose. The construct often appears before prepositions. Generally speaking, Hebrew poetry is very abbreviated, thus requiring a great deal of interpretation.

Using Certain Principles of Hebrew Syntax in Interpretation

A knowledge of the principles of Hebrew syntax is of great aid in interpreting Old Testament texts correctly. Limitations of space permit only a few select examples in this article. These may be divided into four large categories.

---

1. See the discussion (with examples) of W. R. Harper, *Elements of Hebrew Syntax* (New York: Scribner's, 1888), pp. 51–64.
2. A. B. Davidson, *Hebrew Syntax*, 3rd ed. (Edinburgh: T & T Clark, 1942 reprint), pp. 162–203.

Verb Forms

As in most languages, the various forms of the verb are very important in Hebrew. There is much debate among scholars as to whether or not the perfect and imperfect represent tense forms. S. R. Driver and others contend that they denote aspects, i.e., the perfect connotes completed action and the imperfect indicates incompleted action.[3] On the other hand, Blake contends that the imperfect was originally an omnitemporal form, which developed into a way of expressing present-progressive past-future-modal ideas while not totally abandoning past meaning—whereas the perfect was originally a predicate-adjective form with present meaning, which developed into the common expression of past time while retaining the present sense in some cases.[4] Be this as it may, all scholars agree that in specific contexts both the perfect and the imperfect may refer to past, present, or future time. Thus God can say to Abraham (literally), "to your descendants I *gave* [*have given*, Hebrew *nātattî*] this land" (Gen. 15:18), or "all the land which you are seeing [looking at], to you I *will give* it [Hebrew *'ettᵉnennāh*] and to your descendants for ever" (Gen. 13:15; cf. 12:7). Further, even before Joshua and the Israelites cross the Jordan to the west to begin the conquest, God instructs Joshua to go "into the land which I *am giving* [Hebrew *nōtēn*] to them" (Josh. 1:2). In all three instances, the point of reference shows that, as far as *time* is concerned, the perfect, imperfect, and participle all point to the *future*, so that all three of these statements mean "I *will give* you the land." Scholars also debate as to whether a *wᵉ (and)* before a perfect should be conceived as converting it into an imperfect, or a *wa* before an imperfect as converting it into a perfect.[5] In either case, these forms ordinarily fit the temporal and contextual circumstance of the verb form preceding the *waw.*

In numerous cases, the context demands that a perfect be translated as a pluperfect or a future perfect (there is no pluperfect or future perfect verb form in Hebrew as there is in Greek). Thus, the perfect in 1 Samuel 28:3 *(mēt)* must mean "and Samuel *had died*" (see RSV), because the ac-

---

3. S. R. Driver, *A Treatise on the Use of the Tenses in Hebrew* Third edition (Oxford: Clarendon, 1892). So also H. Ewald, *Syntax of the Hebrew Language of the Old Testament.* Translated by J. Kennedy (Edinburgh: T & T Clark, 1881), pp. 1–15; see further C. F. Burney, "A Fresh Examination of the Current Theory of the Hebrew Tenses," *JTS* 20 (1918/1919): 200–214.

4. F. R. Blake, *A Resurvey of Hebrew Tenses. Scripta Pontificii Instituti Biblici,* 103 (Rome: Pontificium Institutum Biblicum, 1951).

5. Davidson, pp. 70–86; and Blake, pp. 44–53, 57 prefer to speak of the *waw-conversive,* while Harper, pp. 68–81; and J. W. Watts, *A Survey of Syntax in the Hebrew Old Testament* (Grand Rapids: Eerdmans, 1964), pp. 103–117, favor the use of *waw-conjunctive* with the perfect and *waw-consecutive* with the imperfect. A. Sperber, "Hebrew Grammar: A New Approach," *JBL* 62 (1943): 195–199, avoids both of these categorizations.

count of his death had already been recorded in 25:1. Again, the perfect in Isaiah 4:4 *(rāhaṣ)* must mean "And he who is left in Zion and remains in Jerusalem will be called holy, every one who has been recorded for life in Jerusalem, when the Lord *shall have washed away* the filth of the daughters of Zion . . ." (Isa. 4:3–4, RSV; italics added).

The use of the perfect in prophetic literature causes serious problems for the interpreter, since it may be understood as either a simple statement of the past or a "prophetic perfect" predicting the future. For example, the opinion of some scholars is that the perfect verb forms in Isaiah 9:6 should be translated "for a child *shall be* born to us, a son *shall be* given to us," referring to the coming Messiah; while the opinion of others is that it should be rendered "for a child *has been born* to us, a son *has been given* to us," referring to a royal child who has been born recently or to a king who has just taken the throne. Syntactically, either view is possible.

In all Hebrew binyans (something like conjugations) except the hiphil (causative), the jussive has the same form as the imperfect, third masculine or feminine singular or third person plural. Consequently, it is impossible to know what the intended nuance is in many passages. One example occurs in 1 Samuel 1:17, which has the verb form *yittēn*. This may be an imperfect: "Go in peace, and the God of Israel *will grant* your petition," or a jussive: "Go in peace, and *may* the God of Israel *grant* your petition."

The imperfect is often used to describe actions or activities that were customary or repeated. This must be determined by the context. It is usually necessary to insert words into the text to communicate the sense into English accurately. In describing the annual pilgrimage that Elkanah and his two wives took to Shiloh, the author of 1 Samuel 1:7 writes (literally), "and thus *it will be done* (reading *yēʻāśeh*) year by year." But the context shows that this must mean "and thus *it was done customarily* [*regularly*] year by year."

Since Hebrew does not have a subjunctive mood such as found in Greek, a subjunctive meaning must be determined by the context. Sometimes the subjunctive may be contrary to fact, in which case it is usually expressed by *lû* or *lûlē*, with the perfect in the protasis and the perfect in the apodosis. One example appears in Isaiah 1:9:

"If the Lord of hosts/*had* not *left* us a few survivors,/we *should have been* like Sodom,/and *become* like Gomorrah" (RSV, italics added).

The subjunctive may also raise the possibility of something happening (the potential subjunctive). In this case the imperfect is used. It seems likely that Isaiah 1:18 is to be explained in this way: ". . . though your sins are like scarlet,/they *may become* white as snow."

The so-called infinitive absolute poses a major problem for interpreting the Hebrew language.[6] When it appears *before* a finite verb it carries

6. See A. E. Cowley, editor, *Gesenius' Hebrew Grammar*. Second English Edition,

the idea "surely, certainly, indeed," as in Genesis 2:17 (RSV): "but of the tree of the knowledge of good and evil you shall not eat, for in the day that you eat of it you shall *surely* die" (Hebrew *môt tāmût*, literally "dying thou shalt die"). When it is used *after* a finite verb it ordinarily means "continually, utterly, prevalently," and the like. So the Lord tells Isaiah concerning those to whom he will preach:

> Go thou and say thou to this people
> Hear ye *continually* [literally "hearing"] and ye shall not understand;
> and see ye *continually* [literally "seeing"] and ye shall not perceive.

But in addition to these two main usages of the infinite absolute, it can also replace virtually every type of verb form. For example, it appears for the perfect in Haggai 1:9 (literally): "*looking* [Hebrew *pānōh*] for much, and behold little," that is, "you looked for much and behold there was little." Again, it is used for the imperfect in Isaiah 5:5 (literally): "*Removing* [Hebrew *hāsēr*] its hedge, and it shall be devoured;/*breaking down* [*pārōs*] its wall, and it shall be trampled down."

The context shows that "I" (referring to the Lord) is the subject, so that the meaning is "*I will remove* its hedge [etc.]." The infinitive absolute is also used for the imperative, as in Deuteronomy 5:12 (literally): "Remembering [Hebrew *šāmôr*] the Sabbath Day to keep it holy."

Conditional Sentences

There are basically four types of conditional sentences in Hebrew.[7]

1. In one type the condition is assumed as fulfilled. This is the case when God says to David concerning Solomon, "*When* he commits iniquity, I will chasten him" (2 Sam. 7:14). There is no question that Solomon will commit iniquity; the Lord assumes that he will.

2. The condition of a second type of conditional sentence is contrary to fact, presupposing that the statement is impossible of realization. Manoah's wife reasons, "*If* the Lord *had meant* to kill us [implying the thought, but he did not], he would not have accepted a burnt offering and a cereal offering at our hands" (Judg. 13:23).

3. In a third type of conditional sentence, the condition is more probable; that is, it is possible but uncertain. In Isaiah 1:19–20, God says to the Jews:

edited and enlarged by E. Kautzsch (Oxford: Clarendon, 1952 reprint), § 113, pp. 339–347; P. Paul Joüon, S. J., *Grammaire de l'Hébreu Biblique* (Rome: Institut Biblique Pontifical, 1923 [1965 edition]), § 123, pp. 347–358.

7. See Davidson, pp. 175–182; C. Brockelmann, *Grundriss der vergleichenden Grammatik der Semitischen Sprachen: II. Syntax* (Hildesheim: Georg Olms Verlagsbuchhandlung, 1961 [first published in 1913]), §§ 419–454, pp. 635–662; Watts, pp. 133–142.

> *If you are willing* and obedient,
>   you shall eat the good of the land;
> But *if you refuse* and rebel,
>   you shall be devoured by the sword [RSV, italics added].

It is certainly possible that they can repent and obey God, but it remains to be seen whether they will choose to do so.

4. A fourth kind of conditional sentence presents the condition as less probable; that is, both the possibility and actuality of the condition are questioned. So God says to Abram, "If a man *could* count the dust of the earth [implying that this is highly unlikely], your descendants also can be counted" (Gen. 13:16).

The Construct State

A very common syntactical phenomenon in Hebrew is the use of a noun or adjective in the construct state (the *nomen regens*, or governing word) followed by a noun, adjective, pronoun, or clause in the genitive (the *nomen rectum*, or governed word).[8] The translator and interpreter must be very careful in rendering this type of expression into English (or any modern language, for that matter), because it has such a wide variety of meanings. A few examples may be cited here:

1. The second part of the expression may be a *subjective genitive*, that is, the person or thing named is the subject of the action. Thus "the wisdom of Solomon" (1 Kings 4:30) is the wisdom that Solomon had; "the food of the governor" (Neh. 5:14) is the food that the governor supplied, and so on.

2. The second part of the phrase may be an *objective genitive*, that is, the person or thing named is the object of the action. Accordingly, "the mourning of an only son" (Amos 8:10) is mourning for (over) an only son, "vengeance of his [i.e., the Lord's] temple" (Jer. 50:28) is vengeance for what had been done to his temple, and so on.

3. The construct form occurs frequently with an *adjectival sense*, because the Hebrew language does not lend itself to the use of adjectives to the extent that other languages do. In this case, the word in the genitive connotes attribute or quality. So "the place of holiness" (Lev. 10:17) is the holy place or sanctuary; "balances of righteousness" (Lev. 19:36) are just (or accurate) balances; "the spirit of thy holiness" (Ps. 51:11) is thy holy spirit; "wrestlings of God" (Gen. 30:8) are divine (mighty, powerful) wres-

---

8. See W. M. Philippi, *Wesen and Ursprung des Status constructus im Hebräischen: Ein Beitrag zur Nominalflexion im Semitischen überhaupt* (Weimar: 1871); Ewald, pp. 77–102; Davidson, pp. 30–39; Joüon, § 129, pp. 385–393; Sperber, pp. 209–226; Brockelmann, §§ 154–167, pp. 229–246. For an interesting treatment of the genitive in the NT, see H. K. Moulton, "Of," BT 19 (1968): 18–25.

tlings; "wind of God" (Gen. 1:2) is divine (mighty, powerful) wind; and so on.

Certain words—such as "man," "woman," "son," "daughter," "owner, possessor" (Hebrew *ba'al*)—are used very often in such clauses. Thus "a man of words" (Exod. 4:10) is an eloquent man or a good speaker; "a man of death" (1 Kings 2:26; cf. "sons of death," 1 Sam 26:16) is one who deserves to die; a "son of worthlessness" (Hebrew *beliya'al* [KJV "Belial"], 1 Sam. 25:17; cf. 2:12; "daughter of worthlessness," 1:16) is a worthless, base, ill-natured person; a "son of ninety-eight years" (1 Sam. 4:15) is a person ninety-eight years of age; an "owner of soul" (Prov. 23:2) is one who has a big appetite; "possessors of a covenant" (Gen. 14:13) are allies; "sons of the prophets" (2 Kings 2:3) are prophets; and "a son of man" (Ps. 8:4) is a man.

4. Other genitival expressions must be taken as *appositional*. For example, "the land of Canaan" (Num. 34:2) means the land which is Canaan, and "daughter of Zion" (Isa. 1:8) means daughter, namely Zion.[9]

Ways of Expressing Emphasis

Frequently, modern translations of the Old Testament, including those rendered into English, obscure the emphasis expressed in the Hebrew text.[10] The Hebrew language employs several means of showing emphasis.

First, the biblical speaker or writer may vary from the common Hebrew word order of verb—subject (with its modifiers)—object (with its modifiers). For example, in Isaiah 1:2 the direct object "sons" is in first place in the sentence, showing that the Lord intended to place emphasis on the Judeans being his *sons*. The shocking truth is that it is not foreigners but God's own *sons* who have rebelled against their father. Again, Isaiah urges the Jews not to fear Pekah and Rezin, then by way of contrast cries out, "*the Lord of hosts, him* you shall sanctify" (Isa. 8:13), that is, they must sanctify or fear *the Lord alone* and none other.

Second, the biblical author may use repetition to denote emphasis. At Isaiah's call, he heard the seraphim declaring, "Holy, holy, holy is the LORD of hosts . . ." (Isa. 6:3, RSV). When the Lord sent down fire from heaven to consume the sacrifice that Elijah had prepared, the people of Israel cried out, "The LORD, he is God; the LORD, he is God" (1 Kings 18:39, RSV); in other words, they finally acknowledged the important truth that Yahweh and not Baal was truly God.

Third, the biblical spokesman may use the personal pronoun, even when this is unnecessary, because the pronoun is already clear in the verb

---

9. On this expression, see W. F. Stinespring, "Zion, Daughter of," *The Interpreter's Dictionary of the Bible: Supplementary Volume* (Nashville: Abingdon, 1976), p. 985.
10. See the excellent treatment in Davidson, pp. 158–173.

form. Accordingly, when the Israelites urge Gideon to become king over them, he replies emphatically, "*I* [Hebrew *'anî*] will not rule over you" (Judg. 8:23). Each of the four servants who came to Job to tell him about the calamities that had befallen him says, "*I alone* [Hebrew *raq 'anî lᵉbaddî*] have escaped to tell you" (Job 1:15–17, 19).

Finally, the Hebrew pronouns *hû'* ("he"), *hî* ("she"), and *'ēlleh* ("they") are used frequently to express emphasis. For example, when Ahaz rejects the Lord's offer that he choose a sign to convince him to trust in the Lord rather than in Tiglath-pileser III of Assyria, Isaiah declares, "the Lord, he, will give you a sign" (Isa. 7:14), that is, the Lord *himself* will give you a sign. Again, in the Lord's prohibition against eating blood, he explains, "for the blood, it, makes atonement" (Lev. 17:11), that is, the blood *itself* makes atonement.

The study of the syntax of any language is a large task and never ceases throughout one's lifetime. That Brockelmann wrote over seven hundred pages on the syntax of Semitic languages is evidence enough of the scope of such an undertaking. The present article is a modest attempt to point the reader to a few aspects of this area of investigation.

11

The Contributions of Archeology to Old Testament Interpretation

John McRay

Archeology is a rapidly developing science. Its potential for significant contribution to the interpretation of the Bible is already well established, and the future is bright for the discipline. There is much that remains to be done in Palestinian archeology; in fact, the available evidence has only begun to be tapped.[1]

Paul Lapp estimated in 1963 that of a total of five thousand sites in Palestine, there had been excavations at about one hundred and fifty, including only twenty-six major excavations. Of the more than five thousand mounds located in Iraq, ancient Babylonia, and Assyria, Beek's *Atlas of Mesopotamia* (1962) shows less than thirty major excavations, less than one percent of the total sites.[2] Yet W. F. Albright feared as a boy that all the mounds would be excavated by the time he was grown! Little more than ten percent of the 500,000 cuneiform tablets found in Mesopotamia had been published when another seventeen thousand were found in 1974 and 1975 at Tel Mardikh (Ebla).[3] Philip King is right: "Archeology has just begun to make its real contribution to biblical studies."[4] Even though there has been a virtual explosion in the number of excavations being conducted in the past twenty-five years, we have little hope of doing more

---

1. E. M. Yamauchi, "Stones, Scripts, and Scholars," CT (Feb. 14, 1969): 8ff.
2. M. A. Beek, *Atlas of Mesopotamia*, ed. H. H. Rowley, trans. D. R. Walsh (New York: Nelson, 1962).
3. P. Matthiae, *Ebla: An Empire Rediscovered* (Garden City: Doubleday, 1981); G. Pettinato, *The Archives of Ebla* (Garden City: Doubleday, 1981).
4. P. King, "The Contribution of Archeology to Biblical Studies," CBQ 45 (1983): 16.

than touching the fringe of the garment. Yigael Yadin estimated that at the rate of his normal excavation progress at Hazor in Galilee, it would take eight thousand years to excavate the site thoroughly! Hazor covers about two hundred acres in its upper and lower sections. How long would it take for a thorough excavation of the eight thousand acres of Caesarea Maritima? I have been working there since 1972 and estimate that we have dug less than five acres.

Scientific Advances in Archeology

Modern technology is having its impact on the science of archeology and promises to make the process of excavation both faster and more efficient. The last two decades have seen the use of many advanced scientific techniques in the field: ground and aerial photogrammetry, magnetometers and resistivity instruments, laser-guided and computerized transits, microfiche libraries in the field, computers, infrared photography, neutron activation analysis of pottery, thin-section and petrographic analysis of temper and clay, thermoluminescence, flotation of pollen samples, settlement pattern analysis, and the use of specialists such as cultural anthropologists, paleoethnobotanists, civil engineers, draftsmen, architects, surveyors, numismatists, and even medical and dental students.[5]

Even though these advancements are beneficial and welcome by all who work in the discipline, one should remember the cautionary remarks of D. Lance that "it is very easy to become entangled in the technical expertise in archeological disciplines and forget the origin of the quest."[6] It must not be forgotten that the methodology exists for the purpose of making possible the descriptive analysis and is not an end in itself. Although scientific excavation provides the basis for the art of historical reconstruction, both art and science are present in any attempt to explore man's past through his material remains. The cart must not get before the horse. At the same time, the art of historical reconstruction must be based on the best and most accurate scientifically obtained data.

Is Biblical Archeology a Valid Discipline?

A more precise question concerns biblical interpretation as it arises out of the continually changing methodology. What can be learned about

5. See J. Sauer, "Prospects for Archeology in Jordan and Syria," BA 45 (1982): 73–84; W. Dever, "The Impact of the 'New Archeology" on Syro-Palestinian Archeology," BASOR 242 (1981); 15–29, and "Archeological Method in Israel: A Continuing Revolution," BA 43 (1980): 41–48; F. M. Cross, "W. F. Albright's View of Biblical Archeology and its Methodology," BA 36 (1973): 2–5.
6. D. Lance, "American Biblical Archeology in Perspective," BA 45 (1982); 100.

the interpretation of the Old Testament from the rapidly developing science of Syro-Palestinian archeology?[7] The recent animated discussions on the question of whether "biblical archeology" is a pursuit independent of Syro-Palestinian archeology puts the matter of how one uses archeology in interpreting the Old Testament squarely on the line. Until 1981 it was common to read statements such as that of D. Ussishkin's with little or no anticipation of rebuttal: ". . . the biblical descriptions corroborate the archeological data recovered in the excavations, throw light on them, and help in their dating and interpretation; and conversely, the archeological remains illustrate the biblical text and help to clarify the obscure parts."[8] The whole tradition of the Albright-Wright-Glueck school lay behind this approach to the Bible and archeology.[9]

Since 1981, however, William Dever has argued that there is no such thing as "biblical archeology" and that the term should be abandoned. He insists that the interpretation of the Old Testament is independent of the archeological enterprises in Syria and Palestine and should not be regarded as a scientific discipline within itself, as conceived by the Albright school.[10] The gauntlet thus laid down has been picked up by D. Lance, E. Campbell, and H. Shanks, among others, who argue that there is a historical and intrinsic connection between archeology and the Bible.[11] Most of the early archeologists who worked in the field were biblical exegetes who were motivated by their exegetical needs to involve themselves in the excavation of the Holy Land. It is a moot question whether their motivations biased their work any more than Schliemann's did his at Troy, for example. That competent research in Syro-Palestinian archeology can be done by men with biblical interests is clearly demonstrated today in the work of S. Horn and L. Geraty at Heshbon; J. Callaway at Ai; Y. Aharoni at Beersheba; Y. Yadin at Hazor, Megiddo, and Masada; and a host of others. Dever would contend, however, that Syro-Palestinian

7. Frank Crüsemann, "Alttestamentliche Exegese und Archäologie," ZAW 91 (1979), 177–193.

8. D. Ussishkin, "King Solomon's Palaces," BA 36 (1973): 78.

9. Cross (note 5).

10. W. Dever, "Retrospects and Prospects in Biblical and Syro-Palestinian Archeology," BA 45 (1982): 103–107; "Biblical Archeology or the Archeology of Syria Palestine?" Christian News from Israel 22 (1972): 21–23; "Archeological Method," BA 43 (1980): 41–48; "Syro-Palestinian and Biblical Archeology ca. 1945–1980," The Hebrew Bible and Its Modern Interpreters, ed. D. A. Knight & G. M. Tucker (Philadelphia: Westminster, 1982); "What Archeology Can Contribute to an Understanding of the Bible," BArRev 8 (1981): 40–41; P. Lapp, Biblical Archeology and History (World Publishing, 1969), p. 66.

11. H. Shanks, "Should the Term 'Biblical Archeology' Be Abandoned?" BArRev 7 (1981): 54–57; D. Lance, "American Biblical Archeology in Perspective," BA 45 (1982): 97–101; The Old Testament and the Archeologist (Philadelphia: Fortress, 1981), see last chapter.

archeology has become such a highly specialized and technical science and has accumulated such a mass of evidence that even a W. F. Albright would not be able to keep abreast of it without becoming a professional archeologist. In fact, Albright once complained that he had to keep up with some aspects of archeology through reports in the *London Times*! The job can no longer be done by those whose sole expertise is in biblical studies, regardless of how dedicated or unbiased they may be. The debate will not soon end, however, because it is only part of a larger trend to reevaluate much that has been done by Albright and others of the previous generation.

We see this mood, for example, in statements such as A. Rainey's: "The 'positivism' of the Albright School . . . is, in practice, based more on personal opinions than on actual finds."[12] Thus, M. Miller writes: "Albright was inclined at the same time to overinterpret archeological data and to exaggerate the relevance of archeology for confirmation and clarifying the 'essential historicity' of the biblical traditions."[13] More cautious is the comment of M. Aharoni in her preface to Y. Aharoni's recently published posthumous volume: "Since Albright wrote his book, there have been many new discoveries about every period treated and methods of research have been greatly refined."[14]

The Search for New Directions

With the relatively recent deaths of many giants in the field of archeology—W. F. Albright, P. Lapp, N. Glueck, G. E. Wright, R. de Vaux, Y. Aharoni, and K. Kenyon[15]—there is what D. Lance calls a "present sense of loss of direction in biblical archeology."[16] This has been accompanied by what Lance sees as "the end of that era of Biblical theology which confidently spoke of the acts of God in history, that is, in the history available to the historian and the archeologist," as well as the information explosion. All three of these developments have stirred the foundations of modern archeology and caused major changes in the interpretation of excavated data. As A. Rainey writes: "The new sources, mainly epigraphic, such as the hieroglyphic and cuneiform texts, have opened new vistas for further toponymic research."[17] Wright spoke of "the arche-

---

12. A. Rainey, "Historical Geography—the Link Between Historical and Archeological Interpretation," BA 45 (1982): 220.

13. M. Miller, "W. F. Albright and Historical Reconstruction," BA 42 (1979): 42. See also W. Dever and S. Richard, "A Re-evaluation of Tell Beit Mirsim Stratum J," BASOR 226 (1977): 1–14; J. Callaway, BArRev (1982): 12. See also BA 36 (1973): 2–5.

14. M. Aharoni, preface to Y. Aharoni, *The Archeology of the Land of Israel*, trans. A. Rainey (Philadelphia: Westminster, 1982), p. xv.

15. P. Moorey, "Kathleen Kenyon and Palestinian Archeology," PEQ (1979): 3–10.

16. D. Lance, Op. cit., 97ff.

17. A. Rainey, "The Toponymics of Eretz-Israel," BASOR 231 (1978): 1–18.

ological revolution in Old Testament studies," in both epigraphic and non-epigraphic materials.[18] Space will permit only a selective look at some of the major reassessments currently being made in the interpretation of the Old Testament due to archeological discoveries.

Exodus and the Conquest of Palestine

The rejection of Wellhausen's evolutionary approach to the history of Israel has led to reevaluations of Israelite historiography.[19] The revision of John Bright's *History of Israel* demonstrates that a "veritable chaos of conflicting opinions" now exists about the premonarchic period of Israel's history.[20] Norman Gottwald denies that the Israelites came into Canaan by a militaristic conquest, arguing rather that they constituted a heterogeneous collection of social groups living in the Canaanite society itself.[21] A similar conclusion was reached by Boling in his commentary on Joshua and Judges. He argues that the "conquest" of Palestine was really nothing more than a sociological upheaval, most likely economically based, among people who already lived within the land—at best a civil war, not an invasion.[22] He suggests that the stratigraphic evidence based on ceramic typology, indicating the destruction of major sites in Palestine, has not been proven to belong to the Late Bronze Period (the time of Joshua)[23]; and more recent techniques, including settlement pattern analysis, have tended to indicate a possible migration pattern from north to south and from west to east rather than vice versa.[24] The view is shared by Miller, who insists that "contrary to Albright's claims, archeology does

---

18. G. E. Wright, "Biblical Archeology Today," in *New Directions in Biblical Archeology*, ed. D. N. Freedman and J. Greenfield (Garden City: Doubleday, 1969).

19. J. J. M. Roberts, "Myth Versus History," CBQ 38 (1976): 1–13; Z. Kallai, "Judah and Israel: A Study in Israelite Historiography," IEJ 28 (1978): 251ff; J. M. Miller, *The Old Testament and the Historian* (Philadelphia: Fortress, 1982); H. D. Lance, *The Old Testament and the Archeologist*, (Philadelphia: Fortress, 1981).

20. J. Bright, *A History of Israel* (Philadelphia: Westminster, 3rd ed., 1981), p. 15.

21. N. Gottwald, *The Tribes of Yahweh: A Sociology of the Religion of Liberated Israel 1250–1050 BCE* (Maryknoll, NY: Orbis, 1979). L. Stager holds a similar view, arguing that the Israelites were not desert nomads but agriculturists who left the disintegrating city states and resettled in the highland frontiers: *Highland Villages and Early Israel* (Chicago: University of Chicago, 1983); see the summary of approaches in Y. Aharoni, *The Land of the Bible*, (Philadelphia: Westminster, 1966), pp. 174ff; also see J. M. Miller in note 25 below.

22. R. Boling, Anchor Bible Series, (Garden City: Doubleday, 1975 & 1982). Similarly B. Mazar, "The Early Israelite Settlement in the Hill Country," BASOR 241 (1981): 76.

23. J. M. Miller argues that of 13 cities excavated (Arad, Hormah, Heshbon, Jericho, Ai, Gibeon, Jerusalem, Jarmuth, Lachish, Hebron, Debir, Hazor, and Bethel) only two, Lachish and Hazor, can be put easily into the 13th century: BA 42 (1979): 39.

24. J. Callaway, BArRev 8 (1982): 12

not provide determinative evidence for dating and/or clarifying the process by which the Israelites gained possession of Canaan."[25]

Recently, Aharoni put forward a view that is a restatement of the Noth-Alt view, argued from an archeological rather than literary perspective. Aharoni suggested that the "conquest" took about two hundred years to achieve.[26] Both Aharoni and Weippert hold to a dual conquest—an early one reflected in Joshua and a later one reflected in Judges.[27]

The impact of archeology has also been felt on the interpretation of the date of the exodus. Debate had previously centered around the choice of a mid-fifteenth- or an early-thirteenth-century date. Archeological dating has tended to indicate a late date, whereas the biblical material points to an earlier one. The discussions are well known. A recent contribution to the debate, however, has been made by John Bimson, whose controversial work[28] has argued that neither the archeological nor the biblical evidence militates against an early date. However, the selectivity with which he handles archeological data has limited the influence of his book among archeologists.[29] Aharoni was quite sure that the biblical account of the conquest of Palestine portrays a situation in the land that actually existed in the Middle Bronze rather than in the Late Bronze Age, the latter having no evidence of existence in the Negeb (Southern Palestine). He writes: "Thus the biblical tradition preserves a faithful description of the geographical-historical situation as it was some three hundred years or more prior to the Israelite conquest," i.e., in the Middle Bronze Age.[30] He dates the "conquest" to two phases of activity in the second half of the fourteenth century and the second half of the thirteenth century.[31] A previous attack on Arad and Hormah was made by some Israelites in the Middle Bronze Period. Although R. Cohen, after five seasons of excavations at Ein el-Qudeirat in the Negeb, failed to find anything earlier than the tenth century B.C., the time of King Solomon, he leaves open the question as to

25. M. Miller, "Archeology and the Israelite Conquest of Canaan," PEQ 109 (1977): 87–93; BA 42 (1979): 38f.; "The Israelite Occupation of Canaan," *Israelite and Judean History*, eds. J. H. Hayes and J. M. Miller (Philadelphia: Westminster, 1977), pp. 213–84.

26. Y. Aharoni, pp. 153–80. See also Yadin's critique of this view in "Is the Biblical Account of the Israelite Conquest of Canaan Historically Reliable?" BArRev 8 (1982); "The Israelite Occupation of Canaan," BArRev 8 (1982): 14–23.

27. M. Weippert, *The Settlement of the Israelite Tribes in Palestine: A Critical Survey of the Recent Scholarly Debate* (Naperville: Allenson, 1971).

28. J. Bimson, *Redating the Exodus and Conquest*, JSOT Supplement Series #5, (Sheffield, England: JSOT, 1978).

29. See Callaway's negative interview of the book in BA 44 (1981): 252.

30. Y. Aharoni, "Nothing Early and Nothing Late: Re-writing Israel's Conquest," BA 39 (1976): 73.

31. See note 26 above, esp. BArRev 8 (1982): 19.

whether the earlier materials are there and still unexcavated.[32] The basic problem seems to be that the materials excavated in the Negeb, those in the valleys of Palestine, and those in the hill country all seem to point to different dates for occupational levels of the Israelites. Thus many scholars are opting for a gradual takeover of the land, beginning with some sort of violence and progressing in time to a more socio-economic upheaval of an internal nature. Even Yadin seems to lean in this direction, dating a wave of destruction at Hazor by Israelites in the thirteenth century (as indicated by Mycenean III B pottery). Jericho may have been attacked as early as the fourteenth century. Then the Israelite nomads "slowly but surely moved into the next phase in Israel's history, the sedentary settlement of the tribes . . . ."[33]

A restatement of the early date of the exodus and conquest has come forth recently, not by a fundamentalist scholar, but by a leading Egyptologist—Hans Goedicke, chairman of the department of Near Eastern Studies at Johns Hopkins University. He dates the exodus precisely to the spring of 1477 B.C., when Thera/Santorini was blown apart by a volcano, which caused tidal waves that swept the Egyptians away at the Red Sea. Conservatives will not be happy, however, with Goedicke's rejection of the Bible as descriptive historiography. Reflections on his views appear in two successive issues of the *Biblical Archeology Review*.[34] The early date has been freshly argued by E. Merrill, with the twist that the dates of destruction levels of excavated cities in Palestine are irrelevant to the date of the conquest because the biblical record does not indicate a massive devastation by the Israelites.[35] The policy of Joshua, he argues, was to conquer but not destroy the cities. There were few exceptions to this rule. The invading Israelites simply reused the conquered cities as they captured them. Joshua 11:13 indicates that the burning of Hazor was exceptional. Merrill's views will not be accepted by most archeologists, but they merit systematic and reasoned examination.

32. R. Cohen, "Did I Excavate Kadesh Barnea?" BArRev 7 (1981): 33; "Excavations at Kadesh Barnea," BA 44 (1981): 93–107. See also C. Meyers, "Kadesh Barnea: Judah's Last Outpost," BA 39 (1976): 148–51. See similarly V. Fritz, "The Israelite Conquest in the Light of Recent Excavations at Khirbet el-Meshash," BASOR 241 (1981): 70–71.

33. Y. Yadin, *BArRev* 8 (1982): 18, 22.

34. H. Shanks, "The Exodus and the Crossing of the Red Sea According to Hans Goedicke," BArRev 7 (1981): 42–50; C. Krahmalkov, "A Critique of Professor Goedicke's Exodus Theories," Ibid.: 51–54; "How Not to Create a History of the Exodus—A Critique of Professor Goedicke's Theories," BArRev 7 (1981): 46–53. See also H. Shanks, "In Defense of Hans Goedicke," BArRev 8 (1982): 48–52.

35. E. Merril, "Palestinian Archeology and the Date of the Conquest: Do Tells Tell Tales?" GTJ, 3 (1982): 107–21. On the early date see also L. J. Wood, "The Date of the Exodus," *New Perspectives on the Old Testament*, ed. J. B. Payne (Waco: Word, 1970). The issue is left open by D. Wiseman in his *Archeology and the Bible* (Grand Rapids: Zondervan, 1979), p. 22.

It may thus be seen that archeology has not been able to settle the problem of interpreting the biblical evidence concerning the time of the exodus and the conquest of Palestine.

The Patriarchal Period

Reassessment of the earlier Patriarchal Period has also been stimulated by archeological discovery. The well-known views of Albright, Wright, Glueck, and others—that the period is to be identified with the Middle Bronze Age—have been rejected by Dever[36] and by some who deny even the historicity of the stories in Genesis. Prominent among these are T. L. Thompson[37] and J. Van Seters.[38] Many who hold to the historicity of the patriarchs are prone now to move them into the Early Bronze Age culture.[39] Noel Freedman, on the basis of the spectacular finds at Ebla in Syria, is prominent among those who see Syria, rather than Mesopotamia, as the milieu of the patriarchs in this earlier period.[40] Freedman argues that Van Seters and Thompson are not only looking in the wrong millennium for Abraham, but they may also be looking in the wrong place. The finds at Ebla mention a nearby city named Ur in the territory of Haran, a location defended by C. Gordon from the biblical text independent of the recent archeological data.[41] The sensationalism generated by the suggested connection between Ebla and the Bible has subsided considerably with the entry of politics into the discussions and the consequent changes made in the epigraphical staff of the excavation.[42] Petinatto found the mention of Sodom and Gomorrah[43] in the Ebla tablets but the new epigrapher who replaced him, Alfonso Archi, has

36. W. Dever, *IDB Supplementary Volume*, ed. K. Crim (Nashville: Abingdon, 1976), p. 46; "Palestine in the Second Millennium BCE: The Patriarchal Traditions," *Israelite and Judean History*, eds. J. H. Hayes and J. M. Miller, pp. 70–120.

37. T. L. Thompson, *The Historicity of the Patriarchal Narratives* (New York: De Gruyter, 1974), p. 9. See the interesting overview by John Huesman, "Archeology and Early Israel: The Scene Today," CBQ 37 (1975): 1–16.

38. J. Van Seters, *Abraham in History and Tradition* (New Haven: Yale Univ., 1975).

39. The end of the EB Period (2200 B.C.) is being moved downward by some archeologists to 2000. See the articles by S. Richard and W. Dever in BASOR 237 (1980): 5–64.

40. N. Freedman, "A City Beneath the Sands," *Science Year: The World Book Science Annual* (1978), p. 194; "The Real Story of the Ebla Tablets, Ebla and the Cities of the Plain," BA 41 (1978): 143–164.

41. C. Gordon, "Where is Abraham's Ur?" BArRev 3 (1977): 20ff. But see J. Muhly, "Ur and Jerusalem Not Mentioned in Ebla Tablets Say Ebla Expedition Scholars," BArRev 9 (1983): 74–75.

42. BArRev 5 (1979): 36–50; BArRev 4 (1978): 2ff; BArRev 4 (1978): 4ff; BA 39 (1976): 44ff; *Nat. Geog.* 154 (1978): 730–759. P. Matthiae, *Ebla;* G. Pettinato, *Archives of Ebla;* R. Briggs, "The Ebla Tablets," BA 43 (1980): 76–88; A. Archi, "Further Concerning Ebla and the Bible," BA 44 (1981): 145–154.

43. Freedman, BA 41 (1978): 148ff.

rejected the claim of Petinatto and finds no tablet with those names on it.[44] A condensed summary of the current status of the location of the cities may be found in a 1981 article by W. van Hattem.[45] Space will not permit the discussion of all the reassessments of Old Testament sites, in terms of both dates and locations, prompted by archeological excavation; e.g., Megiddo,[46] Beth Shan,[47] Ai,[48] Beersheba,[49] Dan,[50] and Jerusalem, to mention only a few.

Jerusalem

Special mention of Jerusalem is appropriate, and excavations have been progressing continuously there since the late sixties. Mazar thoroughly dug the area around the western ("wailing") wall and below the southern wall of the city but found no remains of the period of Solomon (Iron I).[51] This was a disappointment, but bits of evidence of the period have recently come to light. Yigal Shiloh's work on Mount Ophel, the southern extension of the mount on which the temple stood, has caused a reevaluation of Kenyon's conclusions, by indicating that the wall she identified as Nehemiah's was not built into the houses destroyed by Nebuchadnezzar in the 587 B.C. invasion[52] but rather ran twenty-one feet further underneath them and is therefore from an earlier period, dating to the tenth century and probably built by Solomon.[53] Its lower levels had a "skin" of beaten earth *(terra pisee)*, making ineffective the use of a battering ram against it.[54]

44. Alfonso Archi, BA 44 (1981): 151–52.

45. W. van Hattem, "Once Again Sodom and Gomorrah," BA 44 (1981): 87–92.

46. Y. Aharoni, "The Building Activities of David and Solomon," IEJ (1974): 13ff.; W. Shea, "The Conquests of Sharuhen and Megiddo Reconsidered," IEJ (1979): 1ff.; D. Ussishkin, "Was the Solomonic City Gate at Megiddo Built by King Solomon?" BASOR 239 (1980): 1–18; Rejoinder by Yadin, Ibid.: 19–23: Y. Yadin, "Megiddo of the Kings of Israel," BA 33 (1970): 66–96.

47. S. Geva, "A Reassessment of the Chronology of Beth Shan Strata V and IV," IEJ (1979): 6ff.

48. J. Callaway, "Excavating Ai (Et Tell): 1964–72," BA 39 (1976): 18–30.

49. M. Fowler, "The Excavation of Tell Beersheba and the Biblical Record," PEQ (1982): 7–11. Y. Yadin, "Beersheba: The High Place Destroyed by King Josiah," BASOR 222 (1976): 5–17; Z. Herzog, et al., "The Stratigraphy at Beersheba and the Location of the Sanctuary," BASOR 225 (1977): 49–58; Z. Herzog, "Beersheba of the Patriarchs," BArRev 6 (1980): 12–28.

50. A. Biran, "Tell Dan," BA 37 (1974): 26–51; "Two Discoveries at Tel Dan," IEJ 30 (1980): 89–98.

51. B. Mazar, *The Mountain of the Lord* (New York: Doubleday, 1975).

52. On the period see E. Stern, "Israel at the Close of the Period of the Monarchy: An Archeological Survey," BA 38 (1975): 26–54.

53. Y. Shiloh, "The City of David Archeological Project the Third Season, 1980," BA 44 (1981): 161–170. See also "Digging in the City of David," BArRev 5 (1979), 44.

54. H. Shanks, "New York Times Misrepresents Major Jerusalem Discovery," BArRev 7 (1981): 40–43.

Exciting new developments on the temple mount have been recently announced by A. Kaufman, who presents convincing evidence that he has identified part of the rock foundation of the temple of Solomon lying immediately north of the present Dome of the Rock.[55] The rock cuttings coincide with the 42.8-centimeter cubit used in the construction of the first temple (Solomon's)[56] and line up due west of the Golden Gate. In addition, J. Fleming has just announced his accidental 1969 discovery of a gate lying beneath the Golden Gate.[57] He makes a strong case for the lower gate's date as Solomonic, connecting with portions of the eastern wall currently visible above the ground that date prior to the Herodian stones in the southern extension of the eastern wall at the pinnacle. In another area of excavation "a corner of a monumental structure from the first temple period" has been found, but not yet identified, in the area south of the present southern wall.[58] (Also relative to the time of Solomon and David, debate continued between Yadin and Aharoni [until the recent death of the latter] about the gates and palaces at Megiddo and Beersheba.)[59]

Another instance of the reassessment going on in archeological circles relative to the Old Testament and Jerusalem is the recent rejection of Kenyon's identification of the earthen mass on the east slope of Mount Ophel as the "millo" that David built (2 Sam. 5:9) while expanding the city. Lawrence Stager of Chicago's Oriental Institute has argued rather that these are the Kidron terraces referred to in 2 Kings 23:4 in connection with the reforms of King Josiah.[60] Stager has been doing extensive research on agriculture, particularly the irrigation methods in Israelite villages in southern Palestine from the Iron Age. (I participated in one of these projects in the Buqeia area between Jerusalem and the Dead Sea in 1972.) This approach is a part of the "new archeology" and promises to provide valuable data for understanding the everyday life of the ancients.

It is now clear that Jerusalem expanded westward beyond Mount Ophel to the slopes of modern Mount Zion in the days of Hezekiah, and we have "our first definite evidence for a walled Israelite settlement on the western hill" of Jerusalem.[61] The evidence consists of a segment of the

55. A. Kaufman, "Where the Ancient Temple of Jerusalem Stood," BArRev 9 (1983). See also "New Light on the Ancient Temple of Jerusalem, *Christian News From Israel* 27 (1979): 54–58.

56. Cuttings from the Second Temple (using 43.7 cm. cubits) were also found.

57. J. Fleming, "The Undiscovered Gate Beneath Jerusalem's Golden Gate," BArRev 9 (1983): 24–37.

58. R. Gonen, "Keeping Jerusalem's Past Alive," BArRev 7 (1981): 22.

59. Y. Aharoni, IEJ 24 (1974): 13–16. See the literature on the exchange cited in note 2. See also Yadin, BA 33 (1970): 66–96; "Hazor, 1968–1969: BA 32 (1969): 50–70.

60. L. Stager, "The Archeology of the East Slope of Jerusalem and the Terraces of the Kidron," JNES 41 (1982); 111–21.

61. N. Avigad, "Excavations in the Jewish Quarter of the Old City, 1969–1971," in

wall excavated by Avigad, which he dates to the time of Hezekiah. The area just outside the wall to the west has been dug by Magen Broshi, who finds that it was settled in this period even though unprotected by a wall.[62]

"Yahweh" and Archeology

An appropriate place to close this very selective illustration of archeology's contribution to Old Testament studies is with the mention of the recently discovered divine name of God, Yahweh, found in the excavations on the eastern slopes of the hill west of the Hinnom Valley and immediately adjacent to the St. Andrew Church.[63] This is the first time that the tetragrammeton has been found in Jerusalem, although it has appeared in other places.[64] It appeared on a silver amulet of less than four inches in length when unrolled. The unusual treatment of the written name of Yahweh in Jewish and Christian Bibles is discussed by G. Howard in an important article in the *Journal of Biblical Literature*.[65]

Conclusion

Much more could be said, but the foregoing examples will perhaps indicate the potential of archeology to illuminate the Old Testament. It would be appropriate in this *festschrift* to Jack P. Lewis to close by recalling his remarks in a proposal to the American Schools of Oriental Research for the 1983–84 year at the Albright Institute in Jerusalem:

> Persuaded that the primary function of archeology in biblical studies is that of illustration, the author will attempt to avoid the fallacy of the apologist who claims more than the evidence allows on the one side and

---

Jerusalem Revealed, ed. Y. Yadin, (Jerusalem: Israel Exploration Society, 1975), p. 43. See also H. Geva, "The Western Boundary of Jerusalem at the End of the Monarchy," IEJ (1979): 85ff.; M. Broshi, "The Expansion of Jerusalem in the Reigns of Hezekiah and Manasseh," IEJ 24 (1974): 21–26. See also R. Grafman, "Nehemiah's Broad Wall," IEJ 24 (1974): 50ff.

62. See note 61 for Avigad. M. Broshi, "Excavations on Mt. Zion 1971–1972," IEJ (1976): 81ff.

63. G. Barkay, "The Divine Name Found in Jerusalem," BArRev 9 (1983): 14–19.

64. W. Brownlee, "The Ineffable Name of God," BASOR 226 (1977): 1–14. P. Miller, "El, The Creator of Earth," BASOR 239 (1980): 43–46; Z. Meshel and C. Meyers, "The Name of God in the Wilderness of Zin," BA 39 (1976): 6–10; Z. Meshel, "Did Yahweh Have a Consort?" BArRev 5 (1979): 24–35. W. Dever, "Recent Archeological Confirmation of the Cult of Asherah in Ancient Israel," *Hebrew Studies* 23 (1982); J. Emerton, "New Light on Israelite Religion: The Implications of the Inscription from Kuntillet 'Ajrud,'" ZAW 94 (1982): 2–20.

65. G. Howard, "The Tetragram and the New Testament," JBL 96 (1977): 63–83. A popular condensation of this appears in BArRev 4 (1978): 12–14, "The Name of God in the New Testament."

that of the extremist on the other side who sees every similarity between biblical material and near-eastern material as evidence of borrowing.[66]

Professor Lewis's published work is evidence of his commitment to this perspective of archeology's relevance to biblical studies.[67]

66. Unpublished.

67. J. P. Lewis, *Archeological Backgrounds to Bible People* (Grand Rapids: Baker, 1981). This was published earlier under the title *Historical Backgrounds of Bible History*, 1971. *Archeology and the Bible* (Biblical Research Press, 1975).

12

Interpreting Poetic Literature in the Bible

Clyde M. Miller

Since two-fifths of the Old Testament is written in poetry, it is extremely important that biblical poetry be properly understood. Even the scattered poetic passages in the New Testament follow Semitic forms, so the principles for interpreting Hebrew poetry apply to both Testaments.

When properly studied, biblical poetry is rich in spiritual insight. It is uplifting to the emotions, instructive to the intellect, and directive to the will of man. Most of the general rules for biblical interpretation apply to all the Scriptures for prose and poetry alike. Only the special rules which apply to poetry will be discussed here.

Historical Background and Basic Scholarship

A brief study of the history of the interpretation of biblical poetry will be helpful in formulating principles of study. Robert Lowth is universally acclaimed as the first person to present a systematic treatment of the formal elements of Hebrew poetry. His lectures on Hebrew poetry, which appeared in print in 1753, and his more extended studies in Isaiah (1778) have become classics. Lowth's exposition of the parallelistic structure of Hebrew poetry has been generally accepted by subsequent students. He also revealed that poetry is much more extensive in the Old Testament than had been formerly understood.

George Buchanan Gray refined and extended Lowth's work and developed a positive science for the study of Hebrew poetry. His book *The Forms of Hebrew Poetry*, first published in 1915, was reproduced in 1972.[1]

---

1. G. B. Gray, *The Forms of Hebrew Poetry* (New York: Ktav, 1972).

This monumental work, along with a *Prolegomenon* (Introduction) by David Noel Freedman, contains an excellent annotated bibliography from 1915 to 1972. Freedman makes some very important modifications of Gray's studies.

Two additional works have built upon these earlier studies to great advantage. One is the two-volume work (now available under one cover) by Sigmund Mowinckel, *The Psalms in Israel's Worship,* first published in 1962 by Basil Blackwell of Oxford and reprinted in 1967 by Abingdon of Nashville. Structural, historical, theological, and redactional criticisms are intermixed, and one must sift out the studies on poetic form from the vast array of related but divergent studies. Mowinckel is often considered radical in his theological presuppositions, but his book is extremely valuable for the study of psalm types. Hermann Gunkel, Mowinckel's teacher, has also done extensive work on the Psalms. In 1967, Fortress Press published his work, *The Psalms: A Form-Critical Introduction* (translated by T. H. Horner, with an introduction by J. Muilenberg). This fifty-one page paperback provides an excellent study of the structural content of the Book of Psalms.

For additional studies in Hebrew poetry, see *The Living Word Commentary on the Old Testament,* edited by J. T. Willis.[2] Critical commentaries on the Psalms, Prophets, and Wisdom literature of the Old Testament often provide excellent treatments of the poetic forms. Bible dictionaries and encyclopedias can also be helpful on this topic.

Gray, Lowth, and Freedman

In the introductory chapter of *The Forms of Hebrew Poetry,* Gray criticizes the translators of the English Revised Version of 1885 for failing to utilize Lowth's work to write the poetry of the Scriptures in poetic lines.[3] The King James and earlier English versions failed to distinguish between prose and poetry because their publication preceded the scientific study of Hebrew poetry. The American Standard Version of 1901, produced by the American members of the committee for the English Revised Version, likewise fails to translate most of the poetry in the Prophets and Wisdom books as such. All subsequent English versions, including the New King James Version of 1982, present the poetry in verse form.

Since the ancient Hebrew scribes filled up all available space on a manuscript, there was no indication of the ends of poetic lines. Because of this practice, the poetic lines are sometimes difficult to determine, and modern translations sometimes differ. A comparison of several translations of Psalm 8:1b–2 will illustrate the problem. However, overall, this is

---

2. J. T. Willis, ed., *The Living Word Commentary on the Old Testament* (Austin, TX: Sweet, 1979), vol. 1, pp. 200–204; vol. 2, pp. 13–38.

3. Gray, p. 7.

actually a minor problem, for the flow of thought and the structure of parallel members usually reveal the lines of poetry. The first suggestion to readers is to study biblical poetry from Bible versions that print it as poetry. A study of the original language is also most rewarding in understanding biblical poetic literature.

Gray also warns against making comparisons between medieval Jewish poetry and the poetry of the Old Testament.[4] Medieval Jewish verse bears little resemblance to the poetry of the Old Testament. One important difference is that biblical poetry makes no effort at rhyming, but medieval Jewish poetry borrowed this element from Arabic and Syriac verse. The theories of medieval Jewish poets about biblical poetry should be regarded as antiquarian, for the ancient art of Hebrew poetry had become a lost art by that time.

Direct testimony of Jews who lived while poetry similar to that in the Old Testament was being written is very scant. Philo of Alexandria asserts that Moses was taught "the whole theory of rhythm, harmony, and metre" by the Egyptians (De Vita Moses 1.5). He makes no effort to demonstrate the use of these elements in the Pentateuch. Josephus makes three statements about biblical poetry. He describes the songs of Moses in Exodus 15 and Deuteronomy 32 as composed in hexameter verse (Antiquities ii. 16. 4; iv. 8. 44) and says that David "composed songs and hymns in various metres, making some trimetrical, others pentametrical" (Antiquities vii. 12. 3). References to patristic writers are unclear and sparse.[5] Hence, scientific study of poetry in the Bible must rely upon relatively recent works, written over the last two centuries.

Ibn Ezra (1093–1168) advanced the understanding of Hebrew poetry by emphasizing the importance of recognizing synonymous parallel terms in two lines of poetry, which he says means that in the second line the poet was simply perfecting the form of his poetry.[6] Perhaps the modern understanding—that we have here "repetition for emphasis"—is much better stated, but Ibn Ezra did the favor of turning exegetes away from their search for some hidden meaning in every term or every line of poetry.[7]

One of the greatest values of recognizing synonymous parallelism is to realize that the second line of poetry does not necessarily advance the thought, but rather emphasizes it.

Gray also cites references from the Apocrypha and Pseudepigrapha that indicate that parallelism was a major feature of Hebrew poetry

---

4. Ibid., pp. 8–9.
5. Ibid., pp. 1–17.
6. Ibid., p. 18.
7. Ibid., pp. 18–19.

through the second century of the Christian era.[8] He believes that this is not true of later Jewish poetry.

Lowth set forth the phrase *parallelismus membrorum*, which has been reduced to "parallelism" in English. This term generally represents two lines with parallel members. Lowth's subdivisions into synonymous, antithetic, and synthetic parallelisms are almost univerally accepted today. The major problem of interpretation is in connection with synthetic parallelism. When synonymous or antithetic terms are employed in the two lines of poetry, identification is easy. But when the second line adds something to the first, a variety of subdivisions may be necessary to include all the variant forms. These varied forms have all been subsumed under the term *synthetic*. (The varied subdivisions will be discussed below.) The major problem is with those passages in which the context suggests that poetry is intended, though the second line contains nothing parallel to the first. Psalm 2:6 is a case in point. The passage reads like a prosaic statement. Only the rhythm and context suggest that it is poetry. Lowth, therefore, doubted whether parallelism was the main distinguishing characteristic of Hebrew poetry, or whether rhythm or a metrical principle might be a greater distinguishing mark between prose and poetry. However, he considered the metrical "principle undiscovered and probably undiscoverable."[9] This problem caused Gray to realize the necessity for a restatement of parallelism, which he proceeded to set forth.

For Gray, the basic difference between prose and poetry is the way a thought is developed.[10] Prose develops the thought in a continuous straight line, although there may be circumstantial clauses inserted to explain certain contingencies. Poetry develops the thought along two parallel lines.[11]

One of Gray's most valuable contributions to the understanding of parallelism is the recognition and demonstration of the difference between complete and incomplete parallelism. In complete parallelism, a term in the second line corresponds to each significant term in the first line. Incomplete parallelism has one or more terms in the second line corresponding to the first line, but one or more terms or phrases from the first line must be carried over in thought to the second line.[12] Examples illustrating the variations in these two groups are given by Gray[13] but are too numerous to be set forth here. A few simple forms will be presented later in this article.

---

8. Ibid., pp. 20–33.
9. Ibid., p. 52.
10. Ibid.
11. Ibid., p. 54.
12. Ibid., p. 59.
13. Ibid., p. 54–78.

Building upon the labors of Lowth and Budde, Gray discussed rhythm as illustrated in Lamentations 1–4, in contrast to chapter 5.[14] This is an excellent discussion of the *kinah* (lament) form so prevalent in Psalms. The style is patterned after what would naturally be followed by one articulating the deep distress of his soul. Short, unadorned phrases are employed. Budde advanced Lowth's work in that he further analyzed the *kinah* form to show that the period (often corresponding to the English colon or semicolon) breaks up the passage into two unequal parts, the longer part usually preceding the shorter, although the shorter may occur first. The many variations cannot be discussed in this brief treatise. Gray's conclusion to this discussion is valuable: rhythm may have naturally developed out of the parallelism of the lines of poetry. Brevity of expression and repetition for emphasis caused the poet to go just so far in stating an idea; he then repeated himself more or less by employing corresponding terms. This parallelistic style would naturally result in a rhythmic pattern, although the ascertainable rhythmic patterns are as variable as the parallelistic ones. Sometimes there is no discernible correspondence between the parallelistic and rhythmic patterns. An independent desire for rhythm may have grown out of this accident of the parallelistic form.[15] In chapters four and five, Gray discusses the elements and varieties of Hebrew rhythm.[16] He recognized that modern biblical interpreters, having often failed to acknowledge the natural variations in rhythm, have been all too quick to assign diverse authorship to a book or poem on the basis of the variations in rhythm.[17] Little attention to the study of metrical rhythm will be given in this essay, since such a study contributes little to understanding the message of biblical poetry.

Freedman, in his *Prolegomenon* to Gray's work, makes three suggestions, which should characterize future research on Hebrew poetry. He first summarizes Gray's distinctions between "balancing rhythm" and "echoing rhythm." If the second line is shorter in rhythmic elements than the first, the phrase *echoing rhythm* is employed.[18] Gray had proposed three criteria for determining which kind of rhythm is employed. The first is that all syllables be counted; the second is that the metrical values be counted, weighing long and short syllables; and the third is based on the number of stressed words or syllables in each subsection. Freedman believes that Gray should have reexamined the first two possibilities more thoroughly. However, most studies today continue to follow Gray in his suggestion that only the stressed syllables count in determining Hebrew

14. Ibid., pp. 87–120.
15. Ibid., pp. 112–113.
16. Ibid., pp. 123–197.
17. Ibid., pp. 200–240.
18. D. N. Freedman, Prolegomenon to Gray, p. xvii (referring to p. 133).

rhythm. As to whether particles and secondary accents be included Freedman believes these questions need to be considered further.[19] Second, Freedman believes Gray relied too heavily on the parallelistic structure to determine the rhythmic pattern of some difficult passages.[20] Finally, Freedman feels even stronger than Gray that strophe or stanza arrangement is not a major feature of Hebrew poetry, and that this element has been overemphasized to the detriment of the original form of the poem. Alphabetic arrangement and refrains help determine paragraphs in some poems (Lam. 3; Ps. 119), but most efforts to ascertain the stanza arrangement are uncertain and unfruitful. Most modern English versions of the Bible leave a blank space between lines to designate stanza or paragraph divisions. Sometimes the different versions reveal varied judgments on the part of the translators, as in Psalm 1.

Freedman concurs with Lowth (in disagreement with Gray) that the constant in Hebrew poetry is rhythm and that parallelism may either be used to complement rhythm or may be abandoned in other cases, where rhythm stands on its own. The distinguishing characteristic of poetry as opposed to prose, for both Freedman and Lowth, is rhythm.[21] In our judgment, the overtreatment of Hebrew rhythmic patterns can be as harmful to the devotional and instructional use of biblical poetry as to ignore this study altogether. The ICC commentary by Briggs and the Anchor Bible commentary by Dahood on Psalms are guilty of such overtreatment.

Gunkel and Mowinckel: The Psalms

At the turn of the century, H. Gunkel brought a new impetus to Old Testament studies with his introduction of Form Criticism.[22] Mowinckel, Gunkel's student, refined and developed his teacher's methodology. In the second and third decades of the twentieth century, Gunkel and Mowinckel were making their mark on Psalms studies. Since the translation of their works into English in 1962 and 1967, they have had tremendous influence on English-speaking students of Psalms. Although one may not accept all their conclusions in regard to Historical Criticism, a close study of these works can be helpful to the serious student of biblical poetry. The basic difference between Gunkel and Mowinckel is that the former believes that most of the psalms, although originally written in cultic settings, have been "democratized" for use by the individual in private devotion. On the other hand, Mowinckel insists that practically all were written for a particular cultic occasion and continued to be so used.

19. Ibid., p. xviii.
20. Ibid., p. xix.
21. Ibid., p. xxvi.
22. See J. H. Hayes, *An Introduction to Old Testament Study* (Nashville: Abingdon, 1979), pp. 123–154.

Gunkel's and Mowinckel's treatments of the literary and poetic forms are much the same.

Gunkel's classification of the psalms into types was a great step forward. While individual interpreters will differ on the social or cultic setting of some of these psalms,[23] the categorizations are useful tools for further study.[24] Gunkel also postulates that several individual psalms were later adapted for community use. He suggests that this type of psalm was most popular in post-exilic days.[25] Briefly stated, psalms may be classified as follows:

1. *Hymns* praise God in a general way for his works of creation and providence (cf. Ps. 104, 105, 106).

2. *Psalms of thanksgiving* thank God for deliverance from some recent trouble, although the specification is not always clear to the modern student (cf. Ps. 107, 138).

3. *Laments* complain over present circumstances and pray for deliverance (cf. Ps. 38, 51, 60, 130).

4. *Didactic psalms* (sometimes called *wisdom psalms*) are addressed to fellow-Israelites for their admonishment and encouragement (cf. Ps. 1, 14, 37, 49).

5. *Royal psalms* are not separate literary types, but their content pertains to the fortunes of the king and eventually of the nation (cf. Ps. 2, 18, 20, 21, 72, 89, 101, 110, 132, 144).

Some scholars find an additional category of *psalms of trust and confidence* (cf. Ps. 11, 17, 23, 27, 62, 63, 131), while other subsume these under categories of praise or thanksgiving or lament and petition. Some of the psalms have mixed characteristics and are difficult to classify. It is frequently impossible to determine the historical situation out of which a particular psalm was written or to discern its particular cultic setting. Mowinckel's work suggests the trend of much modern interpretation, but his conclusions are far from certain. For instance, the New Year's Renewal Festival, which permeates Mowinckel's thinking, cannot be demonstrated in the particulars that Mowinckel attaches to it. No such festival is clearly revealed anywhere in the Old Testament.

The Principles of Parallelism

A brief delineation of the forms of parallelism may be helpful. Synonymous parallelism employs two lines of poetry that say the same thing by using similar expressions. In complete parallelism, the key words may be synonymous (cf. Ps. 24:1) or complementary (cf. Ps. 19:2). In in-

---

23. Ibid. (cf pp. 5–25).
24. Ibid., pp. 30–39.
25. Ibid., pp. 26–29. For a study of the content and form of these psalm types, see T. Ash, *Living Word Commentary on the Old Testament* (Austin, TX: Sweet, 1979), vol. 10, pp. 21–28; also C. M. Miller, vol. 1, pp. 200–212.

complete parallelism, the verbal phrase is frequently omitted in the second line, but is understood as carried over from the first line (cf. Ps. 72:2). In antithetic parallelism, the second line uses terms in contrast to those in the first line (cf. Ps. 20:8).

Synthetic parallelism has several subdivisions. The following are usually sufficient for general study. In completion parallelism, the second line merely completes the thought of the first line (cf. Ps. 2:6). This is more a parallelism of rhythm than of thought. Comparison parallelism shows a difference in degree (cf. Ps. 84:10), and some call this progressive parallelism. Or the second line may state a reason for what was said in the first line (cf. Ps. 130:4). In stairlike (climactic, step) parallelism, part of the preceding line is repeated in the second, and then an additional thought is stated (cf. Ps. 29:1). Emblematic parallelism employs a figure of speech to illustrate in one line what is stated literally in the other (cf. Ps. 103:11). The parallelism may be inverted in the a-b-b-a pattern, so that the syntax of the first line is reversed in the second (cf. Ps. 91:14).

All of the above examples involve internal parallelism in which only two lines of poetry are compared. Sometimes one confronts the climactic triplet, in which three lines of poetry form a unit, and there may be any number of internal relationships within the passage (cf. Ps. 29:3, 9). In external parallelism, two or more couplets form a unit of thought. These may take the form of synonymous parallelism in which all four lines are synonymous (cf. Ps. 18:4, 5). Or the first couplet may be antithetic to the second (cf. Ps. 37:10, 11). Or it may take the a-c-b-d pattern, in which the first and third lines correspond, and the second and fourth lines correspond (cf. Ps. 44:2, RSV, NIV). The second couplet may be synthetic to the first; that is, it adds something to the thought of the first couplet (cf. Ps. 44:20, 21). Or it may follow the a-b-b-a pattern, in which the first and fourth lines correspond, and the second and third lines correspond (cf. Ps. 137:5, 6). More technical divisions of parallelistic structure could be made, but these are basic and usually suffice for most studies.

Gevirtz and Gevirtz: Early Biblical Poems

A sober and able treatment of early poems found in the Bible is found in Morris and Fannie Gevirtz's *Patterns in the Early Poetry of Israel: Studies in Ancient Oriental Civilization*, No. 32. One example must suffice to illustrate the careful way the poetic form is related to biblical interpretation. In 1 Samuel 18:7, the text reads:

> Saul has slain his thousands,
> and David his ten thousands.

This statement has often been misinterpreted to indicate that the women in their song were making a distinction between the military prowess of

David and Saul and that this contributed to Saul's jealousy of David. But the Gevirtz study[26] shows that Saul and David are parallel terms of leaders in Israel and that the numerals are fixed word pairs often used elsewhere without any discriminatory intent (cf. Mic. 6:7; Ps. 91:7; Dan. 7:10). Examples are given of several Ugaritic passages that use the same two numerals in word pairs as synonymously parallel. It is also suggested that the historical setting in which the passage is found in the Book of Samuel indicates how the author of Samuel employed the passage to exalt David, but the authors feel that this was not the original intent of the women. This consideration leads to other suggestions for the study of brief psalm passages in the context of historical narrative. The poems may be modified in meaning by virtue of their new context. For instance, note how parts of Psalms 105, 96, and 106 are employed in 1 Chronicles 16:8–34 to form a liturgy of which they originally had no part.

Guidelines for Interpreting Biblical Poetry

On the basis of the present state of studies in biblical poetry, the following principles can be set forth to enable the student to make the best use of this literature.

First, one should not attempt to interpret biblical poetry along the same straight-line method as one would interpret prose narrative. Recognition of parallelistic structure should cause one to think in terms of pairs of lines, or pairs of couplets, or in some cases (as in the Prophets and occasionally elsewhere) of more extended units of thought. Repetition, contrast, and the linking together of small units of thought to form a complete whole are characteristic of biblical poetry. The student should give careful attention to discerning the units of thought and their relationship to the whole.

Second, attention should be given to the type of poem in a given case. Such consideration will frequently reveal the central purpose of the poem and in turn will indicate the proper application of the message to one's own life situation.

Third, linguistic studies in biblical poetry can be very profitable. Words, like people, are known by the company they keep. Pairs of words frequently used in parallel as synonyms, complements, or contrasts reveal their shades of meaning in company with each other. Patterns of thought can frequently be derived from such studies. Poetic words often take on a richness of meaning that the same words might not sustain in prose.

26. M. and F. Gevirtz, *Patterns in the Early Poetry of Israel: Studies in Ancient Oriental Civilization*, No. 32 (Chicago: University of Chicago, 1963), pp. 16–17.

Fourth, allowance should be made for the richness of figurative language in poetry. Figures of speech are common throughout the Bible, but they are much more subtle in poetry. Because poetry has the tendency to be cryptic and elliptical, greater care should be exercised in interpreting its figures of speech. Here again, thorough understanding of parallelistic structure can serve as a guide and safeguard.[27] Since one primary tendency of a poet is to use vivid, exaggerated language, it may not be possible to apply the same strict literal interpretation to biblical poetry that can be used with some legal precepts or historical narrative.

Fifth, the historical and cultic setting of the poem should be studied, although this is often extremely difficult to ascertain. Historical allusions or notations may suggest whether a psalm is pre-exilic, exilic, or post-exilic. Stereotyped expressions such as "deliver us from among the nations" or "we have been gathered from among the nations" may be helpful. The cultic setting is frequently even more difficult to determine than the historical setting. Is the poem personal or community in its outreach? What is the community poem or book intended to accomplish in Israel's faith and practice? Often, just considering these questions intelligently provides the answers.

Sixth, the poetry of the Bible should be studied in harmony with the total context of biblical teaching. Strange interpretations should not be imposed upon biblical poetry so as to force it to contradict other plain Scriptures.

The careful study of biblical poetry is perhaps the most challenging and rewarding pursuit in which the earnest Bible student can engage. Man's love for God and the good way of life, his yearnings and his satisfactions, his defeats and his triumphs, his frustrations and his hopes, are all adequately treated in biblical poetry. Since some of the greatest lessons on the love of God for man are found in the poetic literature of the Bible, one's spiritual life is enriched and fortified through meditation upon these great truths.

27. For the usual figures of speech used in the Bible, see *The Living Word Commentary on the Old Testament*, vol. 1, pp. 28–32.

13

Sample Interpretation from Extra-biblical Sources

The Nuzi Material and the Patriarchal Narratives

Charles F. Myer, Jr.

The expansion of knowledge in the biblical field has been assisted by archeological discoveries that have broadened the base of data pertaining to the people and places of the Bible.[1] While the relative value of the discoveries and the relevance of the material will always be debated, it is a worthwhile endeavor to pause within the polemics of the protagonists and evaluate what has been done. The purpose of this paper is to assess one geographical facet and examine a few of the arguments that have been made by both the opponents and proponents of the utilization of the Nuzi material for biblical study. In this paper the application of the Nuzi material is restricted to the patriarchal narratives.

The study will be developed in the following sequence. The first section deals with the provenance of the Nuzi material; the second section discusses the response of the scholarly world to the material and its relevance to the patriarchal narratives; the third section discusses four issues that are exemplars of challenge raised by students of the first-generation scholars of Nuzi; and the last section of the study summarizes the present state of the inquiry and concludes with an observation about the intellectual process of the Nuzi project and an expectation of other scholarly endeavors.

---

1. Cf. G. E. Wright, "The Archaeology of Palestine" in *The Bible and the Ancient Near East*, ed. G. E. Wright (Garden City: Doubleday, 1965), pp. 85–139.

Provenance of the Nuzi Material

The cuneiform tablets that provide the Nuzi data emanate from three archeological sites. The primary source of the tablets is Yoghlan Tepe (also called Yolghan and Yorgan Tepe), which is a hundred and fifty air miles north of Baghdad and ten miles southwest of modern Kirkuk, near the foothills of southern Kurdistan in northeastern Iraq. This site was excavated by a joint expedition of the American School of Oriental Research in Baghdad and Harvard University during the years 1925–31.[2]

A small collection of tablets was found at Arrapkha,[3] which is modern Kirkuk. An earlier effort to excavate at this site was abandoned for fear of damaging a part of the modern city.

In the late sixties a third site was excavated at Tell al Fakhar, which is located forty-five kilometers southwest of Kirkuk on the road connecting Kirkuk with the east bank of the Tigris. The site was identified as the ancient Kurruhanni.[4] The Tell is 200 meters long, 135 meters wide, and 4.5 meters high. The decision to dig at this site was made after some children found some inscribed tablets at this locale. The excavation started in October 1967 and concluded in January 1968. Two occupational levels were unearthed: Level 1 contained three buildings, and Level II revealed a large complex of seventeen rooms. The rooms were floored with ceramic tile, and the walls were painted with a blue-green substance, which resulted in the complex being called "The Green Palace." The excavators found a heap of thirty-four skeletons, which suggests an abnormal demise for the inhabitants of the palace. Since there was an abundance of ash in the stratum, it was presumed that there was an invasion of some type that resulted in the death of the defenders and the burning of the complex. There were approximately eight hundred tablets found in various rooms of the palace. The tablets were land leases, business contracts, land purchases, and adoption records, all of which were analogous to the ones found at the other two sites.

---

2. For a detailed account of the expeditions cf. R.F.S. Starr, see *Nuzi: Report on the Excavations at Yorgan Tepe Near Kirkuk Iraq Conducted by Harvard University in Conjunction with the American Schools of Oriental Research and the University Museum of Philadelphia 1927–1931*, 2 vols. (Cambridge, MA: 1937, 1939). For a dichotomous listing of the published texts see B. L. Eichler, "Indenture at Nuzi," *Yale Near Eastern Researches 5*, ed. W. W. Hallo, J. J. Finklestein, W. K. Simpson (New Haven: Yale University, 1973), pp. 5, 6 n. 22.

3. Cf. E. Chiera, "Report of the Professor in Charge of The School in Bagdad," *BASOR* 20 (1925): 19–25.

4. A. Fadhil in his unpublished MA thesis, *Rechtsurkunden und Administrative Texte Aus Kurruhanni* (Heidelberg: 1972), refutes the identification of Al-Fakhar as Arwe. For a brief discussion of the site cf. F. El-Wailly, "Tell al-Fakhar," *Sumer* 23 (1967). There is an extensive discussion of the site in Y. A. Al-Khelesi, "Tell al Fakhar (Kurruhanni) a dimtu settlement": Excavation report, *Assur* 1 (1977), pp. 81–122.

Concomitant with the publishing of the Nuzi material, there arose a discussion about the proper spelling of the word *Nuzi*.[5] It appeared in print both as *Nuzi* and *Nuzu*.[6] Gordon gave an explanation based on the principle of the Akkadian three-case system—nominative -*u*, genitive -*i*, and accusative -*a*. His conclusion was that Nuzi is the genitive of the nominative Nuzu and the form should be normalized to Nuzu.[7] Goetze propounded the same normalization based on the genitive, but his methodology was based on Hurrian rather than Akkadian morphology.[8]

Speiser consistently maintained that Nuzi was the nominative form of the word. He acknowledged that the scribes had been trained to write Akkadian, but he reminded his linguistic opponents that the scribes were Hurrian and their native language characteristics would emerge. Speiser, who wrote a Hurrian grammar,[9] stated that Hurrian nouns end in -*a* and in -*i* or -*e*. Nouns ending in -*a* deal with primary concepts; and nouns ending in -*i* or -*e* are related to what the Hurrians considered to be secondary concepts. Based on his study of the Hurrian language, he concluded that etymologically the primary form would be *Nuzu* and the secondary form would be *Nuzi* or *Nuze* in the nominative case.

Relevance of the Nuzi Material

Since, from a geographical perspective, Nuzi is on the periphery of Palestine, one could legitimately raise the question as to why this one remote area might make a significant contribution to understanding the patriarchal narratives. Albright,[10] Speiser,[11] and Gordon[12] were three leading scholars who believed that the Nuzi material had great relevance to the biblical material. It was noted that these narratives attest to the fact that the patriarchs lived in the area of Haran in the middle Euphrates Valley before their migration to Palestine, and in subsequent times contact was maintained with that area. The region was heavily populated by the Hurrians, who were making great strides politically and culturally. In

5. The most common spelling among scholars is *Nuzi* and that spelling is used in this paper.

6. Speiser discussed the issue in this "Nuzi or Nuzu," JAOS 75 (1955): 52–55.

7. His position is stated in "The Dialect of the Nuzi Tablets," Or 7 (1938): 32–63.

8. A. Goetze's review of E. R. Lacheman, *Joint Expedition with the Iraq Museum at Nuzi: Miscellaneous Texts in Language* (1940), p. 171.

9. E. A. Speiser, *Introduction to Hurrian* (New Haven: ASOR, 1941).

10. Notice his summary statement in *From The Stone Age to Christianity* (Garden City: Doubleday, 1957), p. 237.

11. This view is clearly reflected in his commentary on "Genesis" in *The Anchor Bible*, ed. W. F. Albright and D. N. Freedman (Garden City: Doubleday, 1964). Hereafter *Genesis*.

12. C. H. Gordon, "Biblical Customs and the Nuzu Tablets," BA 3 (1940): 1–12, reprinted in BArRev 2 (1964): 21–33.

the political realm, the major achievement was the establishment of the Mitannian Empire, whose ruling class was made up of a small Indo-Aryan aristocracy and a large Hurrian nobility.[13] The empire was extended to the Mediterranean Sea on the west and to the land of Assyria on the east. Its capital was Washukanni, whose location has not been discovered. Eichler has observed that in the cultural realm the Hurrians made their major contribution by playing the role of "assimilators and disseminators of Mesopotamian civilization. Their eclecticism and cultural adaptability are vividly portrayed in the Nuzi documents which reflect the blending of native Hurrian traditions with assimilated elements in the fields of law, linguistics, religion, and art."[14]

It should be remembered that there is little contemporary material that has been excavated from the patriarchs' homeland in the middle Euphrates Valley, and one should be aware of Speiser's rationale for using the Nuzi material, namely, "the results obtained at Nuzi are valid, by *extension* [italics CFM] for the West Hurrians as well. It is in this roundabout way that the Nuzi records have a significant bearing on the patriarchal narrative of the Bible."[15] Not all scholars are willing to grant this extension.

To illustrate the way in which the Nuzi material has been helpful in solving some of the puzzles of the concepts and practices of the patriarchal narratives, Speiser listed six instances in which the Hurrian influence could be identified. The most impressive one, in Speiser's view, was Rachel's taking the teraphim or the house gods of her father, Laban (Gen. 31). The prior attempts to explain her behavior were futile until the proper data on family law were brought into the picture. The discovery of the tablets at Nuzi, Arraphka, and Kurruhanni now supply the needed information to understand this episode. In Hurrian society, property could pass to the husband of the daughter, but only under the circumstances that the father had made a formal presentation of the house gods to his son-in-law as an indication that the proper arrangements had been made. It was for this reason that Rachel was trying to make an irregular arrangement a legal one.

The second example of the applicability of the Nuzi material is found in trying to explain three pericopes (Gen. 12; 20; 26) in which the wife of a patriarch is introduced as his sister to a foreign potentate. The attempts to resolve the ethical implications have been many. With Nuzi material available, one now understands that the marital bonds were strength-

---

13. On the Hurrians' political expansion cf. W. W. Hallo and W. K. Simpson, *The Ancient Near East: A History* (New York, 1971), p. 110.

14. Eichler, "Indenture at Nuzi," 3–4.

15. E. A. Speiser, "Nuzi" in *IDB*, III, p. 573. It should be observed that Speiser considered Haran to be a part of that western Hurrian milieu.

ened in that society when the husband had not only taken a woman as his wife but had also adopted her as his sister. This provides an explanation for the behavior of Isaac and Abraham, who were acting on the basis of the mores of their society.

Another parallel is seen in the gift of a slave girl by Laban to each of his daughters as she married, and this practice is substantiated by the marriage contracts not only from Nuzi but from other neighboring societies who followed the same cultural guidelines.

The Nuzi documents also attest to the practice whereby an upper-class woman who was barren presented her husband with a slave girl as concubine, with the provision that the offspring would be treated as the heir of the wife. This phenomenon would explain Sarai's cryptic statement to Abraham (Gen. 16:2), "I shall obtain children by her."[16]

There was another incident in the patriarchal narratives in which the Nuzi material has shed additional light. In Genesis 27, Isaac begins a series of unusual events by a formulaic statement, "Now that I have grown old," which is attested in the society of Nuzi where birthright was not based on chronological seniority but rather on paternal decree. In spite of the ethical consideration of the parties involved, the setting of this pericope is analagous to the socio-juridical milieu of the Hurrian counterparts.

The last example that Speiser used to illustrate the relevance of the Nuzi material was the Habiru issue. The tablets supply a large number of personal names of the Habiru in a context that allows some speculation concerning ethnic origins. Examination reveals that a large number of the names of the Habiru at Nuzi had Akkadian origins, and a majority of the rest had Hurrian names. Another phenomenon discovered was that all of the Habiru, including the ones with Hurrian names, were considered to be foreigners. This caused Speiser to conclude that "what they have in common is not an ethnic or geographical classification but an inferior social status; their position throughout is that of underprivileged foreigners."[17] In summary, the term *Habiru* was applied to a class of people and was not an ethnic designation.

Gordon concurs with Speiser's general argumentation and succinctly states that the Nuzi materials "clear up some of our misunderstandings regarding the lives of Abraham, Isaac and Jacob, who wandered between Mesopotamia and Egypt in the first half of the second millennium B.C."[18]

---

16. Cf. his remarks in *Genesis*, pp. 117, 120.

17. Speiser, "Nuzi" in *IDB*, III, p. 574.

18. Gordon, "Biblical Customs," p. 2. For a broader discussion, cf. C. H. Gordon, *Before the Bible: Common Background of Greek and Hebrew Civilization* (London: Collins, 1962), p. 175. There is a later edition of this book with the title of subtitle above.

Four Issues as Exemplars of Challenge

The Habiru

Speiser believed that the Nuzi material would make a major contribution in clarifying the problem of the Habiru. After examining the data, he noted that there was a great deal of similarity between the careers of the Habiru and the Hurrians. There was also a parallel in the geographical range of the two groups. But at this juncture there would be a cessation of the similarities, for the Hurrians could always be recognized as an ethnic unity with discernible proper names, laws, customs, and culture. In contrast, a Habiru could not be identified unless he had been called specifically by that term of nomenclature. In some way the name came to denote the status of the group under consideration. In was clear that the Habiru did not enjoy the full civic rights of their respective communities and were definitely considered to be outsiders. Speiser concluded that "the best view seems to be that the Habiru consisted of bands of adventurers and soldiers of fortune."[19]

Moshe Greenberg, in an exhaustive study of the Habiru problem,[20] pointed out that the attempts for a solution are divided into two categories—one which sees the term as an appellative and the other which understands the term as a gentilic. From these two positions emerge four camps:

1. One group of scholars treats *Habiru* as an appellative and derives the term from the West Semitic *hbr*, meaning a "confederate" or an "ally."

2. A second group admits the possibility of connecting *Habiru* with *hbr* but emphasizes the connection to an early Hebrew clan related to Hebron. It is noted by this group that the Habiru mentioned in the El Amarna letters are associated with a Milki-el, just as the biblical record relates Heber and Malkiel as grandsons of Assher in Numbers 26:45 and Genesis 46:17.

3. A third group treats the Habiru as Kassites who were possibly serving as Elamite troops assigned to Palestine to look out for Babylonian interests there. This thesis is based on the Kassite personal names that were designated as Habiru, that is, *Harbishihu* and *Kudurra*.

4. The fourth group uses the depredation of the Habiru in the contemporary material to support the biblical record of a Hebrew invasion of Canaan.

Greenberg does a thorough job of research and warns the reader that the results have not always been positive. He notes early in his study that "it appears natural that further inquiry into the Habiru problem should

19. E. A. Speiser, "Ethnic Movements in the Near East in the Second Millennium B.C.," AASOR 13 (1931–32): 13–54.

20. M. Greenberg, "The Hab/piru," JAOS 39 (1955).

have been marked by growing caution."[21] There is a cautious spirit about the study, which suggests a reluctance on his part to advocate a view that would be an immediate solution to all the problems related to the Habiru issue.

In reference to the origin of the Habiru, Greenberg states that "it would seem reasonable to seek them in a time when an abnormally large element of indigent, propertyless foreigners might be expected to have been in Mesopotamia."[22] There is plausibility in the explanation of their move from Mesopotamia to coincide with the rapid spread of the Amorites into the eastern and central parts of the Fertile Crescent. This explanation would be chronologically valid as well, for it would posit itself in the ethnic movements that characterized the history of the ancient Near East in the second millennium B.C. At the end of this era, when the social conditions were more stable, one notices the disappearance of the Habiru and can assume that they blended in with the native population wherever they were and lost their designation as "the Habiru."

Greenberg seems to challenge his former mentor for reaching a conclusion that was based on such little evidence in the Nuzi material. In the cuneiform tablets, the place of origin for the Habiru is given, and without exception names of cities and countries are provided. Consequently:

> . . . no comparable evidence can be adduced for the view they were desert invaders—for that matter that they were invaders at all. It is as individuals and families that we find them moving from town to town; their groups are composed of many such individuals with no common place or origin discernible.[23]

While Greenberg suggests that at the present time there is no simple answer to the Habiru issue, he does make an interesting observation in one of his notes, which deals with the relationship of the Habiru and Ibri of the Bible. He notes that "once again a possible key to the puzzle may be a proper appreciation of the dual aspect of Abraham as socially an 'Apiru,' ethnically an 'ibri.'"[24] The solution to this problem must await further study.

The Teraphim

In the patriarchal narratives, the story of Rachel's appropriating the gods of her father, Laban, provides the *locus classicus* for Speiser's utilization of the Nuzi material for elucidation. While the biblical text gave the framework of an interesting story, it was the texts of Arrapkha and Nuzi

21. Ibid., p. 12.
22. Ibid., p. 88.
23. Ibid., p. 87.
24. Ibid., p. 94, n. 44.

that have supplied the details. According to Speiser, one can understand the story when one comprehends the social and juridical background of the family unit. With the appearance of the Nuzi material, one now sees that "in special circumstances property could pass to a daughter's husband but only if the father had handed over his house gods to his son-in-law as a formal token that the arrangement had proper sanction."[25]

This insight into the culture of Rachel's land provides the motive for her action and provides a key for solving some of the dilemmas which are raised by the text. Rachel was in a position to know the thinking of her father, and she was moving in conformity with the milieu of her home society. She was trying to circumvent the circumstances that would normally assign Jacob to a level of self-enslavement. Speiser notes: "That position would be altered if Jacob was recognized as an adopted son who married the master's daughter."[26]

Anne E. Draffkorn (now Kilmer) was one of the first to modify Speiser's explanation about the role of the teraphim in the household of Laban. In her study of "Ilani/Elohim"[27] she examines the Nuzi legal texts and concludes that the *ilani* were the source of legal decisions obtained by the use of the ordeal, and one finds a biblical parallel in the Covenant Code, which deals with the slave who chooses to stay with the master of the house. To formalize this decision, the slave is taken before the *elohim* and then to the door of the house, at which time his ear is pierced with an awl. In the Draffkorn article, two texts from Nuzi are examined and an additional function of the *ilani* postulated, namely, that the *ilani* are "the protectors of the family stake as a whole."[28] It would be undesirable to have property transferred to a foreign location where consequently it would no longer be under the aegis of the household gods. "It follows that the housegods symbolized the given family holdings as an integral unit."[29]

Another student of Speiser's, M. Greenberg, reexamines the data concerning Rachel's theft of the teraphim.[30] He traces the history of interpretation beginning with Josephus, whose explanation was "to have recourse to them to obtain pardon,"[31] to a more modern view that Rachel was eager to have the protection of the hearth gods away from home.[32]

25. Speiser, "Nuzi," *IBD* III, p. 574.

26. Speiser, *Genesis*, p. 250.

27. A. E. Draffkorn, "ILANI/ELOHIM," JBL 76 (1957): 216–224.

28. Ibid., p. 224.

29. Ibid.

30. M. Greenberg, "Another Look at Rachel's Theft of the Teraphim," JBL 81 (1962): 239–248.

31. F. Josephus, *The Works of Flavius Josephus*, Tr. W. Whiston (Philadelphia: McKay, n.d.), 62, Antiquities 1, 19, 8.

32. Cf. H. Gunkel, "Genesis," in *Göttingen Handkommentar Zum Alten Testament* (Göttingen: Vandenhoeck & Ruprecht, 1910), pp. 244.

Greenberg reviews both Speiser's and Draffkorn's positions and then provides an explanation of his own: "What is determined by bequeathal of the gods is not title to an inheritance share but rather who is to carry on as *paterfamilias*. That determination is separate from the matter of dividing up shares in the estate. . . ."[33]

The Wife-Sister Motif

There are three narratives in Genesis that contain essentially the same story: a patriarch visits a foreign land; the beauty of his wife captivates the local ruler's attention; the husband engages in a bit of subterfuge for reasons of self-interest; and he presents himself as his wife's brother. In Speiser's view,[34] attempts to give rational reasons for what appears to be unethical behavior were unfruitful in removing the dilemma until the discovery of the Nuzi material. The corpus of data showed that the Hurrian family structure was unique in contemporary society, and the texts provided the following information:

1. In Hurrian society the wife was attested as a sister.

2. Sistership could be transferred, and in one case the brother had ceded his own fraternal rights.

3. The status of sistership was based on the woman's choice, and she became a principal in the process.

4. Hurrian society established certain safeguards for the sister by drawing from the sphere of ritual practice.

There are several who have challenged this evaluation of the material, and another one of Speiser's students, A. Skaist, has questioned the validity of a basic tenet of his mentor's interpretation. In reference to the transferral of a sister status and the benefits that the woman would receive, Skaist's opinion is that it "was no more than any woman would have expected from her natural father or brother."[35]

In discussing the family structure, Skaist observes "the Hurrian family, and Nuzi is no exception to the rule that final jural authority over members of the family is vested in the father."[36] There was one situation in which *fratia potestas* would occur, but this was limited to instituting a marriage for a female orphan. In Skaist's opinion, this was not a vestige of an earlier age but rather the phenomenon developed in a patriarchal

---

33. Greenberg, "Another Look," p. 242.

34. Cf. E. A. Speiser, "The Wife-Sister Motif in the Patriarchal Narratives," in *Oriental and Biblical Studies*, ed. J. J. Finkelstein and M. Greenberg (Philadelphia: Univ. of Pennsylvania, 1967), pp. 62–82.

35. A. Skaist, "The Authority of the Brother at Arrapha and Nuzi" JAOS 89 (1969): 10–17. He is followed by Van Seters on this point. See note 39. For a fuller bibliography see B. L. Eichler's article in the *Finklestein Festschrift* (1977), pp. 45–49 and S. Greengus's article in HUCA 46 (1975): 5–31.

36. Ibid., p. 17.

society due to the absence of a patrilinial succession. The society of Arrapkha seems to have combined two institutions, namely, from "real sistership they took the mode of instituting the transaction and added it to the standard marital and *adoptiones in matrimonium* relationships." In essence he concludes there is no individual type of marriage which can be called "wife-sister marriage."[37]

Other scholars have challenged some of the Speiserian theses. Millar Burrows has questioned whether or not there was a change in the social status of the woman when she moved into the proposed wife-sister relationship.[38] Van Seters is concerned about the methodology used with the Nuzi data and has observed that it cannot "be shown that a woman involved in an *aḫatutu* act gained anything more than legal protection from the natural or adoptive brother . . . ."[39]

Abraham's Childlessness

In Speiser's treatment of Genesis 15:1–6, he notes in his commentary[40] that there are linguistic problems in verse 2 which are hopeless. But he does not despair, for there is found the approximate meaning of the clause in question in 3b, that is, since Abraham is without descendants, his property will pass on to a member of his household. In discussing the rest of the passage, Speiser notes that the linguistic interpretation he proposes is questionable, but "there can be little doubt, however, about the legal aspect of the passage." From this confident posture he explains that in Hurrian family law there are two types of heirs and no confusion between the two. One is a direct heir who is called an *aplu,* and the other is an indirect heir who is called an *ewuru* and who functions when there are no normal heirs within the family unit. It was in this role that Eliezer found himself in the story of Genesis 15. Speiser concludes his observation on Eliezer's status in this way: "Here then, is another instance of Hurrian customs which the patriarchs followed, but which tradition and its later expounders were bound to find perplexing."[41]

Albright, who was another proponent of the use of the Nuzi material for interpreting Genesis, found support in this text for his theory that Abraham was a great donkey caravaneer in the early second millennium.[42] His understanding of Eliezer's role was that of a money lender whom Abraham had adopted so he could be used for collateral for a loan in time of need for capital.

37. Ibid.
38. M. Burrows, *Israelite Marriage* (New Haven: AOS, 1938), p. 23.
39. J. A. Van Seters, *Abraham in History and Tradition* (New Haven: Yale Univ., 1975), p. 74.
40. Speiser, *Genesis*, p. 111.
41. *Ibid.,* p. 112.
42. Cf. W. F. Albright, "Abram the Hebrew," BASOR 163 (1961): 36–38.

As in other exemplars, several have objected to the way in which the Nuzi data has been handled. One critic has observed that here "is another example of rather undisciplined speculation about parallels with second millennium adoption practices mostly drawn from the Nuzi archives."[43] Thompson would remove this passage entirely from Nuzi influence by interpreting the pericope on the basis of a literary motif. From his perspective the key to proper understanding is seen in the pejorative stress in Abraham's concern about his servant Eliezer and in the flow of the narrative, which shows that the concern of Abraham is removed only by Yahweh's answer. Thompson sees in this pericope the anti-Damascan tendency that reflects the antagonism between Israel and the Arameans. He then observes that his is a "motif which fits well with other *Stammessagen* in the Patriarchal narratives."[44] In his opinion there is no connection between the Nuzi material and the incidents recorded in Genesis 15.

The Present State of Inquiry

Over fifty years have elapsed since the first archeological work was done at the site of Yoghlan Tepe, and Eichler has observed that "most of the Nuzi tables have now been published and the time is therefore appropriate for a systematic analysis of the Nuzi documents and for a testing of previously advanced interpretations."[45] In essence the utilization of the Nuzi material has followed this pattern. The first generation of scholars— Speiser, Gordon, and Albright—explained and dated the patriarchal narratives on the basis of the common legal practices they found in both sources of material. Subsequently, students of these scholars have challenged their mentors and in the opinion of some have "demolished the putative parallels one by one."[46]

The process of investigation continues, and scholars such as Van Seters want to expand the criteria to more than legal considerations. He contends, justifiably so, that "there is the matter on the one hand of dating the written form of the tradition and on the other of deciding on the antiquity of the traditional elements behind the written form."[47] He has proposed that an examination of the data should fall under three types of scrutiny:

43. Van Seters, p. 85.
44. T. L. Thompson, *The Historicity of the Patriarchal Narratives* (New York: de Gruyter, 1974), p. 204.
45. Eichler, pp. 5–6.
46. W. W. Hallo, "Biblical History in Its Near Eastern Setting: The Contextual Approach," in *Scripture in Context*, ed. C. D. Evans, W. W. Hallo, J. B. White (Pittsburgh: The Pickwick Press, 1980), p. 11. For a partial delineation, cf. K. A. Kitchen, *The Bible in Its World* (InterVarsity Press, 1979), esp. pp. 56–74.
47. Van Seters, p. 1.

(1) dating by cultural aspects, personal names, and place names; (2) dating by literary criticism of the tradition; and (3) dating by noting Israel's self-understanding as a people and the development of its own social and religious consciousness and concern.[48]

Hallo has made a plea for perspective in the heat of controversy for, as he affirms, there has been confrontation. However, this need not "imply uncritical equation: on the contrary the term confrontation is chosen deliberately to stress the need for critical evaluation of the two terms of the equation."[49] He notes that the challenge of younger scholars does not invalidate the whole attempt to draw parallels from the Bronze Age and to apply them to the patriarchal material, but rather "it invites a reconsideration of the term of the comparison."[50] In this context Hallo suggests that the biblical material should not be compared to archival data of the Hurrians in a remote spot of the Mitanni Empire, but should be compared to "the archival data of Palestine and against the literary formulation of the surrounding Near East."[51]

Others have been more severe in their evaluation of the relevance of the Nuzi material as reflected in the following statement: "It is now generally agreed that the Nuzi finds are of no direct relevance for the Old Testament."[52] In a similar vein another scholar states his view: "The value that the Nuzi texts have for the study of Genesis is extremely limited. Our survey has shown the practices at Nuzi to be relatively different from those presupposed by Genesis."[53]

In an attempt to ascertain the range of Nuzi studies in the last three decades, the author examined the bibliographic sections of *Orientalia* for this period. After perusing these entries one observes that the application of the Nuzi material to biblical study has not been pursued with much intensity.[54] Of all the scholars who are working on Nuzi material, E. R. Lacheman has been the most productive, and he has also been instrumental in furthering the interest of Nuzi in the studies of his students. Approximately one-third of the dissertations written on Nuzi in this thirty-year period have been done by Lacheman's students. The influence of Speiser can be seen in the slightly larger number of dissertations that have been produced at the University of Pennsylvania. In Germany the emphasis on

48. Ibid., p. 2.
49. Hallo "Biblical History," p. 11.
50. Ibid., p. 12.
51. Ibid.
52. R. Biggs, "The Ebla Tablets," BA (1980): 82.
53. Thompson, p. 295.
54. For a representative bibliography, cf. B. L. Eichler, "Nuzi" *IDBSup*, p. 636. Also cf. The Lacheman Festschrift, M. A. Morrison and D. I. Owen, ed. *Studies On The Civilization and Culture of Nuzi and the Hurrians* (Winona Lake, IN: Eisenbrauns, 1981).

Nuzi studies has been sustained by K. A. Deller and his students.[55] There have also been several dissertations produced at Dropsie University and at Harvard University. For the most part, the studies of these three decades have been scientific investigations with a very narrow perspective, for example, "Nuzi Real Estate Transactions" and "A Study of Occupations and Professions in the Amarna Period at Nuzi." There have been, however, some studies that have continued the comparative methodology in the study of Nuzi and its usefulness for biblical studies.[56]

Eichler has astutely observed that

> argument for re-evaluation of suggested parallels must thus be based either on the testing of previously advanced interpretation of the Nuzi data or on ascertaining the uniqueness of the Nuzi data within Mesopotamian sociolegal tradition. If an interpretation becomes untenable the parallel can no longer be drawn. If however, the interpretation is still valid, but the Nuzi data can be shown to be no longer uniquely Hurrian but rather reflect common Mesopotamian practice, the parallel is of less value in resolving historical and chronological issues of Biblical inquiry.[57]

In summary, the Nuzi process has reflected a pedagogical ideal, which Albright frequently proclaimed in his classroom lectures. Following the Hegelian model, he would state that the search for truth follows the path of Thesis-Antithesis-Synthesis. It appears that the treatment of the Nuzi material has followed and continues to follow these same parameters of investigation.

The first generation of scholars was willing to posit certain theses and did so with confidence and assurance. The second generation, taking the antithetic posture, gradually challenged the solutions that had been proposed. Now it is time for a reexamination of the data so that a meaningful synthesis can take place. It seems most unlikely that anyone would take the position that the end result of the Nuzi investigation has been totally counterproductive in the understanding of the patriarchal narrative. As a result of this project and others, there is now available more information with which to work, and this information is needed to broaden today's understanding of the recorded past. If all of the efforts put forth in the study of Nuzi material has pushed back the frontier of ignorance only one millimeter on the spectrum of human knowledge, it has been worthwhile.

55. For an extensive bibliography on Nuzi studies, cf. M. Dietrich, O. Loretz, and W. Mayer, *Nuzi-Bibliographie* in AOAT (1972).

56. Cf. note 54.

57. Eichler, "Nuzi" *IDBSup*, p. 635.

14

From Creation to Chaos
An Exegesis of Jeremiah 4:23–26

Jack W. Vancil

J eremiah began his prophetic work in 627 B.C., the thirteenth year of King Josiah (1:1–2; 25:3). The decades following his call were filled with momentous political and international events, the outcome of which was the deportation of the Jews to distant Babylon in 586. Jeremiah's preaching spanned this entire period, his words reflecting the tumultuous happenings that shook traditional theology and challenged Israel into new channels of redemptive hope. Since the general character of the Book of Jeremiah reveals a complexity of literary types and forms, scholars face problems in any systematic presentation of its contents. For example, it is difficult to locate many passages in their exact time frame and to present the precise historical background for the material. However, a part of the book covering the early years of Jeremiah's preaching is generally thought to include chapters 2–6.[1] This section gives a highly descriptive presentation of Israel's spiritual, social, and political condition during the critical years preceding the Babylonian exile. The underlying theme of these chapters is the idolatrous temper of the people and how their departure from Yahweh has led them to the brink of destruction. This theme is developed by a number of poetic images, each designed to intensify the serious trouble in which the nation now found itself. Much of the language in these chapters is outspokenly sexual: Israel is likened to a bride who has forgotten her vows, who has thrust aside all

1. For an excursus on Jeremiah 1–6 and an extensive bibliography, see J. M. Berridge, *Prophet, People, and the Word of Yahweh*, in Basic Studies of Theology, no. 4 (Zürich: EVZ-Verlag, 1970), pp. 73-88.

restraint and cast her lot with street prostitutes (2:1–4:2; 4:30, 31; 5:7–9).[2] Other metaphors making the same point about Israel's apostasy are scattered through this material: God is a "fountain of living waters" from whom the people have turned aside (2:13, cf. v. 18); Israel has turned into a "wild vine" (2:21); a "hot wind" from the desert will judge them (4:11, 12); Israel is a well of wickedness (6:7). Especially notable is the extensive metaphoric language describing the coming military expeditions that will bring destruction to the community of Israel (4:5–8; 13–17, 29; 5:6, 15–17; 6:1–6, 22–26).[3]

It is therefore quite clear, even from a brief survey of these early chapters, that circumstances in Israel were severe in the extreme. The prophet uses harsh rhetoric; he heaps up metaphors and images, mixing and interweaving them so that Israel might know that destruction is coming upon their land. The passage chosen for this exegesis is found within the heart of this early material, the somewhat difficult and elusive poem in 4:23–26.[4] A translation of this passage runs as follows:

> I looked to the earth, and behold, it was waste and void;
>   and to the heavens, and there was no light.
> I looked to the mountains, and behold, they were shaking
>   and all the hills were swaying to and fro.
> I looked, and behold, there was no man,
>   and all the birds of the sky had fluttered away.
> I looked, and behold, the fruitful land was a desert,
>   and all its cities were laid in ruins
>   before the face of the Lord, before his fierce anger.

The amazing, outstanding feature in this passage is the thought of the creation, the cosmos, returning to the primordial, chaotic void that existed before God brought order out of the deep (Gen. 1:1–2; cf. vv. 3–31).

---

2. R. P. Carroll makes a number of interesting comments on this subject; among them he says: "No analysis of prophetic poetry can be adequate which does not pay some attention to that aspect of prophetic language which may be called "bawdy." Bawdy language is a characteristic element in the Bible, and the prophets, being users of strong language and graphic metaphor, use it regularly. This is especially true of Hosea, Jeremiah, and in particular Ezekiel. In the cases of three prophets, the use of bawdy language arises out of the involvement of the community in the fertility cults of the local Canaanite religion." *From Chaos to Covenant* (New York: Crossroad, 1981), p. 61.

3. For some observations on the combination of the themes of love and war—how they are often linked in our "folk wisdom," see W. L. Holladay, *Jeremiah: Spokesman Out of Time* (Philadelphia: Pilgrim) p. 47

4. Holladay has called the poem, ". . . one of the most appalling in the Bible, and at the same time one of the most beautiful. It is very carefully put together, like a delicate piece of jewelry." Ibid., p. 52. And, B. Duhm says: "Das Bild ist so grandios wie unheimlich," *Das Buch Jeremiah* (Tübingen und Leipzig, 1901), p. 54.

Certain difficulties are raised by the presence of this poem in the book, and scholars have sought to understand, although with difficulty, the perspective presented by these words. Some treat the passage as an apocalyptic insertion that came from the post-exilic period.[5] Other scholars see it as a prophetic pronouncement that is set simply within the framework of history and uses vivid imagery to depict the coming destruction of Israel and her land.[6]

Assuming that the passage finds its origins in the early part of Jeremiah's prophetic career—and indeed came from the prophet himself—one must now seek to construct the context and historical circumstances that gave rise to the sentiments expressed in the poem.

As has already been pointed out, a large part of the material in these chapters deals with the subject of an invading army, a foe that would

5. Cf. J. P. Hyatt, "Jeremiah," *Interpreter's Bible*, vol. 5, p. 839. This conclusion is based on the fact that the language of cosmic destruction which is used here presents sentiments not found elsewhere in the book. Since apocalypticism arose in the post-exilic period, apparently under the influence of Persian religious thought (Zoroastrianism), we should not expect such ideas in pre-exilic prophetic literature. Apocalypticism may be defined as a belief in dualistic cosmic powers (e.g., Ormazd and Ahriman; God and Satan, etc.) which rule the universe. Associated with this belief is the belief in two distinct ages: the present evil age and the ultimate, future age wherein all evil will be overthrown and God will rule forever. Dualism and notions about the cosmic order are the major features; see G. R. Larue, *Ancient Myth and Modern Man* (Englewood Cliffs: Prentice-Hall, 1975), pp. 131–50; J. P. M. Van der Ploeg, "Eschatology in the Old Testament," in *The Witness of Tradition* (Leiden: Brill, 1972), pp. 89–99. The conclusion that our passage is in fact apocalyptic is a question of interpretation, the assumption being that Jeremiah would not have used such cosmic language as is found here. On the other hand, it may be regarded as not strange at all that a pre-exilic prophet might use such metaphoric symbolism. The theology of God as Creator and Sustainer of the universe was an important Hebrew concept from very early times. That a creation sustained by God might also, by his command, enter back into its uncreated state in an understandable concept in pre-exilic Israel; cf. B. Anderson, "The Earth is the Lord's," Int. 9 (1955): 3–20; D. J. A. Clines, "Theme in Genesis 1–11," *CBQ* 38 (1976): 483–507; W. L. Holladay, "Style, Irony, and Authenticity in Jeremiah," JBL 81 (1962): 47–48.

6. See J. Bright, AB 21 (Garden City: Doubleday, 1965), pp. 32–34; J. Skinner, *Prophecy and Religion* (Cambridge: University Press, 1936), pp. 49–51. Though acknowledging the difficulty of fitting some parts of Jeremiah within the prophetic pattern of Amos, Hosea, and Isaiah, Koehler maintains that ". . . the true note of the final judgment is lacking. Jeremiah's message, in spite of all its intimations of doom, refers to a political and not to an eschatological epoch and looks ultimately always toward healing, return and pardon. . . ." *Old Testament Theology* (Philadelphia: Westminster, 1956), p. 223. J. Lindblom states: "Thus it is not correct to say that this passage (Jer 4:23ff.) contains an eschatological or apocalyptic prophecy. As we have tried to show, the chaos picture serves to illustrate what is soon to happen in Judaea, not something that will happen in the world in the remote future. Thus there is no reason for denying the authenticity of the passage in question. It may very well be Jeremianic. . . .", *Prophecy in Ancient Israel* (Oxford: Blackwell, 1962), pp. 126–27.

cause great alarm and create havoc throughout the land. This foe is commonly known as the "enemy from the north."[7] The enemy has often been identified with the Scythians, a nomadic people from the region of the Caucasus, who were causing much turmoil in the Near East after about 630 B.C. They were, perhaps, the very enemy of which Jeremiah speaks in the early chapters.[8] It is clear, however, that this enemy finally turns out to be identified with the Babylonians in the later chapters of the book. It should be noted that the issue of an "enemy from the north" takes on great significance in biblical literature and has mythological as well as historical connotations.[9]

The passage spanning 4:23–26 is thus considered to be a portion of the total complex of material dealing with the catastrophe to come when the evil from the north enters the land. The imagery with which the prophet chooses to identify this condition of devastation is that of chaos.[10] This is not simply chaos in the sense of disorder and confusion. Rather, the picture is that of the eclipse of creation—the history of the world has been reversed, and all has returned to the primordial void.[11] This vision of chaos coming upon Israel is a parallel expression to the better-known Day of Yahweh motif, a concept usually implying national and political upheaval.[12]

In 4:23, Jeremiah looks on the earth and sees that it is "waste and void" (tōhû wābōhû). This is the same phrase used in Genesis 1:2, where the cosmos in its original formless condition is described, a time before God began the creative acts that brought order to the universe. Jeremiah, it seems, is drawing from this imagery in Genesis in order to portray the confusion that will come when the enemy out of the north enters the land.

---

7. Jer. 1:13–15; 4:6; 6:1; 6:22; 10:22; 13:20, etc.

8. See Skinner's chapter, "The Northern Peril," pp. 35–52; J. P. Hyatt, "The Peril from the North in Jeremiah," JBL 59 (1940): 499–513; O. Eissfeldt, The Old Testament, An Introduction, trans. Peter R. Ackroyd (New York: Harper & Row, 1972), pp. 358, 424.

9. On this subject see R. Ahroni, "The Gog Prophecy and the Book of Ezekiel," Hebrew Annual Review 1 (1977): 1–27; also cf. W. Brueggemann's The Land (Philadelphia: Fortress, 1977), pp. 111–12. B. S. Childs questions any pre-exilic mythical significance for the enemy from the north; he sees the chaos myth becoming confused with the historical enemy in the late Exilic and post-exilic period: "The Enemy from the North and the Chaos Tradition," JBL 78 (1959): 187–98.

10. See T. H. Gaster, IDB, vol. 1, p. 552; cf. F. M. Cornford, Plato's Cosmology (London: Routledge and Kegan Paul, 1966), pp. 197–210.

11. As a tradition, the chaos motif has extensive significance in the Old Testament. See Child's thoroughgoing treatment of the subject, "The Enemy from the North and the Chaos Tradition."

12. Cf. Isa. 13:9–13; Joel 1:15; 3:14–17; Amos 5:18–24; Obad. 15–16; Zeph. 1:14–18; cf. Bright, pp. 32–33. For a suggested relationship between Jer. 4:23–28 and the Day of the Lord motif, see V. Eppstein, "The Day of Yahweh in Jeremiah 4:23–28," JBL 87 (1968): 93–97.

Such metaphorical language would apparently have been very significant to Judah: the creation was regarded as a great blessing from God, that which should have been enjoyed by all creatures (e.g., Ps. 104; 148).[13] Now, however, this creation, the gift of God that was judged "good" by God's own pronouncement (Gen. 1:3, 10, 12, 18, 21, 25, 31) has reverted to its former state of chaos! Robert Carroll suggests that also present here is the

> . . . chaos of social relations marked by cheating and oppression [which] . . . characterize the oracles of Jeremiah. . . . Elements of internal chaos (psychological) appear at certain points in the sections of the so-called "confessions" (mostly in Jer. 11–20), so that even the prophet seems to inhabit an unstable (mental) world.[14]

There is probably a further symbolic significance in the thought of creation's return to chaos. Just as the earth was shaped and made from a primordial, chaotic state, Israel was taken from a position of no significance and created an elect people of Yahweh.[15] The God that made the world had also made Israel. In fact, the words of Deuteronomy 32:6, which relate the beginnings of Israel, carry the thoughts of the creation narrative in Genesis 1: "Is not he your father, who *created*[16] you, who *made* you and *established* you?" (italics, JWV).

The three verbs used here are of special interest. The word used for "created" (from *qānāh*) is not the same term used for "created" in Genesis

13. On the significance of the creation language used in Genesis, see C. Westermann, *Creation*, trans. J. J. Scullion (Philadelphia: Fortress, 1971); on the points made above, see especially pp. 60–65; W. Eichrodt, *Man in the Old Testament*, Studies in Biblical Theology 4, trans. K. and R. Gregor Smith (London: SCM, 1972), pp. 28–39. Cf. J. A. Soggin's remarks on the meaning of "good" (*ṭôb*), "God as Creator in the First Chapter of Genesis" in BibOr 29, Old Testament and Oriental Studies (Rome: Biblical Institute, 1975), p. 126.

14. Carroll, *From Chaos to Covenant*, p. 66.

15. Israel's election was specific and was to become a boon for the nations (e.g., Gen. 12:1–7; 18:18; 22:17–18; 26:4–5; 28:14; Num. 23:9; Deut. 32:12); however, the election is often viewed with a dubious and ironic note, e.g., the prophets: Amos 3:2; 6:1–7; 9:7; Hos. 12:3–4; Mic. 2:6–9; Isa. 1:2–3; Mic. 1:2–16; Cf. Ezek. 16:1–5. The election did not preclude that Israel might be condemned and punished: Isa. 5:26; 7:18–19; Hos. 10:10; Amos 6:14; Zeph. 1:7. Cf. Exod. 12:38 where a "mixed multitude" (a motley mob) accompanied Israel during the Exodus.

16. Here, the King James Version uses the word *bought*. The term *qānāh* often means "bought" in the Old Testament, but this verse seems to speak of God as the one who has "formed" or "created" Israel. This is consistent with the rest of the verse. This question arises also regarding the translation of the same term in Exod. 15:16; here, too, the idea of "creation" seems to be present. Cf. Ps. 139:19; "For thou didst form my inward parts. . . ." Also, Ps. 74:2 uses the verb: "Remember thy congregation, which thou has created of old, which thou hast redeemed to be the tribe of thy heritage!" Cf. N. C. Habel, "Yahweh, Maker of Heaven and Earth, A Study in Tradition Criticism," JBL 91 (1972): 321–37.

1:1 (which is from *bārā'*); however, it is synonymous with *bārā'* and is used in this sense in Genesis 14:19, 22, where God is addressed as "Maker of heaven and earth" *(qōnēh šāmayim wā'āres)*. The verb for "made" (from *'āsâ*) is the same word that is often used for God's creative activity (e.g., Gen. 1:31; 2:2; 3:1, etc.) and is similar to the verb *bārā'* used in Genesis 1:1. The next verb, "established" (from *kûn*), is used in the sense of "be set up," or "fixed," as a house upon pillars (Judg. 16:26, 29) or as the world itself (Ps. 93:1; 96:10; Isa. 45:18). In 2 Samuel 7:24, the verb is used of the creation of Israel: "Thou didst establish [from *kûn*] for thyself thy people Israel for thyself into a people forever." Thus these three verbs, sometimes used to speak of God's creation of the cosmos, are also used in connection with God's creation of Israel.

Returning to Deuteronomy 32, one notes another interesting feature in God's election of Israel. Verse 10 (RSV) reads:

> "He found him in a desert land,
>   and in the howling waste of the wilderness;
> he encircled him, he cared for him,
>   he kept him as the apple of his eye."

Here God is said to have taken Israel from the desert *(midbar)* and from a howling waste *(tōhū*, the same word for "waste" that is used in Gen. 1:2 and Jer. 4:23). A conceptual pattern seems apparent in these different passages. This concept of Israel's creation may therefore lie behind the thoughts of Jeremiah 4:23–26. Just as God had taken Israel and created it as he had created the cosmos; so now, having corrupted themselves, they must return to the empty void from which they came.[17]

Therefore, the overall theme of this poem is the reversal of the good fortune that Israel had enjoyed as God's created community. Whereas Yahweh had chosen, redeemed, and brought Israel out of Egypt, their rebellion now threatened them with nonexistence. The Judean state would collapse; exile would be their lot. Such a catastrophe was like the earth returning to the chaos that existed before God's creative acts had made the waste and void "good." Israel had been a people chosen out of chaos and yet made into an elect people before God. Jeremiah's focus is now on moving backward instead of forward; the symbols of retrogression portend ominous events. The Old Testament views the creation as a

17. Deut. 32:22 also contributes to this understanding: here the earth is to be devoured because of Israel's sin. This language sounds like the earth is returning to chaos—the earth does not exist!—the fire burns to Sheol (i.e., to the deepest parts of the earth) and the foundations of the mountains are set on fire. This portends a coming of absolute destruction. Though the imagery is different from Jer. 4:23–26, the overall effect is the same. An important observation that should be made is that the evil works of man (here Israel) can bring destruction upon the earth!

great and powerful ongoing fact of God's handiwork, and his ordering of its collapse would be the strongest kind of negative imagery.[18]

It is important to note the parallelism within verses 23–26. Four times Jeremiah says: "I looked," and four times he exclaims, "behold." He observes "the earth," "the heavens," "the mountains," and "the hills." Then the prophet moves from the larger view of creation to the realm of man; but he sees no man, and even the birds are not to be found; his fruitful land languishes and his cities lie in ruins. The way the poem is constructed reveals symmetry and parallelism of thought: both realms, that of nonlife and that of life, are in a complete state of dissolution.[19] The "waste and void" of the earth is accompanied by the absence of light in the heavens. This reminds one again of the thoughts expressed in Genesis. Light was the first of God's creative acts as he began shaping order out of chaos.[20] But the vision reveals to the prophet a condition that is the very opposite of what is said in Genesis 1:3. Without light, that which prevails is the picture expressed in Genesis 1:2: "And darkness was upon the face of the deep"; the world has returned to the primordial ocean.

Jeremiah has poetically recorded a visionary diminution of the earth and the heavens. These two realms of the cosmos are paralleled, forming a balance (v. 23). After this, the prophet's attention is drawn to "the mountains" and to "the hills" (v. 24). These two nouns also form a poetic balance between themselves as well as with "earth" and "heavens" (v. 23).[21] The shaking of the mountains and the hills implies the shaking of earth's foundations.[22]

18. See Clines, "Theme in Genesis 1–11"; U. Cassuto, *A Commentary on the Book of Genesis*, Pts. I and II (Jerusalem: Magnes Press, Hebrew University, 1972), Pt. I, pp. 301–7; Pt. II, pp. 48–55; L. R. Fisher, "From Chaos to Covenant," *Encounter* 26 (1965): 183–97; D. J. McCarthy, "Creation Motifs in Ancient Hebrew Poetry," CBQ 29 (1967): 87–100.

19. See W. L. Holladay's detailed analysis of poetic construction in Jeremiah and especially his section on 4:23–26, "The Recovery of Poetic Passages of Jeremiah," JBL 85 (1966): 401–35. He calls 4:23–26 "an entrée into the nature of poetic structure within the book of Jeremiah," p. 404.

20. Light as a religious symbol is found in many religious and philosophical systems; its presence signified unity and an orderly cosmos. See E. Cassirer, *The Philosophy of Symbolic Forms*, vol. 2 (New Haven: Yale University, 1955), pp. 96–99, 102, 244, 245. Cf. G. Scholem, ed., *Zohar, The Book of Splendor* (New York: Schocken, 1949), pp. 27–30.

21. See Holladay's analysis, "The Recovery of Poetic Passages of Jeremiah," pp. 404–5.

22. Cf. Ps. 97:5; Isa. 5:25; Mic. 1:4; Ezek. 38:20; Nah. 1:5. Mountains are presented as the result of God's creative power, Amos 4:13; Ps. 9:2; Prov. 8:25. He removes and shakes them at will, Judg. 5:5; Job 9:5; Ps. 46:2–3; Isa. 5:25; 42:15; 64:3. The mountains and hills figure prominently in ancient Near Eastern cosmogonies; see T. H. Gaster, *Thespis* (New York: Harper & Row, 1966), pp. 196–200; *Myth, Legend and Custom in the Old Testament*, vol. 2 (New York: Harper & Row, 1975), pp. 663–64; "Cosmogony," IDB, vol. I (Nashville: Abingdon, 1962), pp. 702-9.

When Jeremiah looks to the place where man should have been found, he finds that man has disappeared from the earth.[23] In the beginning, man had been the ultimate creature; with his creation a benison was expressed that summed up God's creation of the cosmos: "And behold, it was very good" (Gen. 1:31). Then the prophet notes that the "birds had fled away."[24] Why are the birds and no other forms of animal life mentioned?[25] Their singling out here may simply be due to the poetic balance within the lines: as man was found dwelling upon the earth, so the birds are seen everywhere flying through the heavens; they are very numerous, and their mere presence usually implies abundance. Even today, in Middle Eastern art, birds are often found in association with an idyllic context. The complete absence of birds, therefore, would signify that a catastrophe had occurred. This is a further description of what has already been said in verse 23. The earth and the heavens have passed back into the time of chaos. Their inhabitants are nowhere to be found. This picture is that of a great tragedy. Creation has failed.[26]

The last line of the vision continues with another image of creation in reverse. Jeremiah sees that the once-fruitful land is now a desert, and all the cities lie in ruins.[27] Though the entire earth and all the cities of the earth might seem to be the main perspective of these words, which would be in keeping with the three preceding verses, the thought of a desolate, empty land would certainly have had special significance for Israel. The importance of the land in Israel's thinking is a consistent theme throughout the Old Testament. Israel's conception of the special place that the land occupies starts with the promise God made to Abraham

---

23. Gen. 2:5 should be studied in connection with the Jeremiah vision. This verse speaks of the earth's emptiness and specifically that "there was no man to till the ground"; cf. Holladay's remarks, "The Recovery of Poetic Passages of Jeremiah," pp. 405–6.

24. This phrase occurs nowhere else except here and in 9:9. One of the arguments Holladay uses for establishing the authenticity of 4:23–26 is this verse's similarity to 9:9, "Style, Irony, and Authenticity in Jeremiah," p. 48.

25. Jeremiah speaks of birds in several other passages. They usually describe birds of prey: 9:10; 12:4; 15:3; 16:4; 19:7; 34:20; only 9:10 and 12:4 are similar to our passage. Cf. J. Muilenburg's comments, "The Terminology of Adversity in Jeremiah," in *Translating and Understanding the Old Testament*, eds. H. T. Frank and W. L. Reed (Nashville: Abingdon, 1970), pp. 44–45. In biblical and world literature, birds are often found in close association with people; cf. Ps. 84:1–3; Gaster, *Myth, Legend, and Custom in the Old Testament*, pp. 765–66.

26. Bright comments: "It is as if the earth had been 'uncreated,'" p. 33; cf. Clines's discussion of "A Creation—Uncreation—Re-creation Theme," in "Theme in Genesis 1–11," pp. 499–502.

27. See Holladay's tightly knit argument on the relationship of our passage (specifically 4:19–28; that which he calls the "second double interlude," the first is 4:9–12) to the total complex of material, especially 4:5–31, *Architecture of Jeremiah 1–20*, pp. 55–101.

(Gen. 12:1–7) and runs through much Old Testament material. The land of Canaan becomes Israel's inheritance from God and is the fulfillment of his promise to provide the "great nation" with its own land. To Israel, Canaan is referred to as "the land which Yahweh your God gives you for an inheritance" (Deut. 4:21, 38; 12:9; 15:4; 19:10; 20:16; 21:23; 24:4; 25:19; 26:1; Josh. 23:4). Israel's theological thinking was molded around these two historical facts of nationhood and ownership of land. The land was God's gift to the community. Von Waldow has observed a number of important features about Israel: the election; the land; and how the ceremony of the Feast of Weeks provided the creedal response whereby Israel's gift was offered with reminiscent thanksgiving for God's gift of the land to them. In von Waldow's words: "A gift of nature is returned for a gift of history. The God of nature and the God of history have become one."[28]

Even though Israel had inherited the land, the land belonged to God; he was the owner. Israel was only permitted to live in the land and should always remember: ". . . for you are strangers and sojourners with me" (Lev. 25:23, RSV). Israel's reception of this gift imposed upon them the responsibility of living justly and honorably as God's elect community. To act in pagan ways would "defile" the land, and the land would subsequently "vomit" them out (Lev. 18:24–30; 20:22).

A warning note is sounded in Israel's ears in Deuteronomy 6:10–15. The sermon here presented was intended to remind Israel that God had kept his promise by bringing them into "the land" and that he had also given them "great and goodly cities" (v. 10). Then the following verses stress how God had provided them with all the necessities for life; but, "Anxiety is expressed lest the great and sudden change to affluence might entice Israel into forgetting God."[29] Their new residence in the land of Canaan exposed the community to a great danger. Their failure to heed the words of the Deuteronomic injunctions is well evidenced by the prophetic material in the Book of Jeremiah. The days of the prophet saw the warnings of Leviticus and Deuteronomy go unheeded, and the dreaded conditions so feared in the Torah legislation were now an unmistakable and sure reality. One reads in Jeremiah 5:1 (RSV):

> Run to and fro through the streets of Jerusalem,
>   look and take note!
> Search her squares to see
>   if you can find a man,

28. H. E. von Waldow, "Israel and Her Land, Some Theological Considerations," in *Old Testament Studies*, Gettysburg Theological Studies IV (Philadelphia: Temple University, 1974), p. 497.

29. G. von Rad, *Deuteronomy, A Commentary* (Philadelphia: Westminster, 1966), p. 64.

> one who does justice
>   and seeks truth;
>   that I may pardon her.

Although the formulation of Jeremiah 4:23–26 seems to be broader and more inclusive than a narrow, limited reference to Israel and her land, one feels justified in concluding that the words are in fact a direct reference to Israel and the land of Canaan, Israel's own inheritance from God. The poem is showing that Israel had lost her status as the community of Yahweh. They had forfeited their created, redeemed position through their wicked ways, and they now must suffer the loss of their inherited land. The land would become desert and the cities be ruined places.

Jeremiah had already referred to the land at the beginning of a long discourse concerning Israel's evil ways (2:6–7, RSV):

> [Thus says the Lord]:
> "They did not say, 'Where is the LORD
>   who brought us up from the land of Egypt,
> who led us in the wilderness,
>   in the land of desert and pits,
> in a land of drought and deep darkness,
>   in a land that none passes through,
>   where no man dwells?'
> And I brought you into a plentiful land
>   to enjoy its fruits and its good things.
> But when you came in you defiled my land,
>   and made my heritage an abomination."

Walter Brueggemann has emphasized the central issue in this passage: "Who is to blame for loss of land, Yahweh or Israel?"[30] He observes that the rhetorical point of the verses shows that "Yahweh's action leaves the land fruitful and good. Israel's action leaves it defiled and abominable."[31] Then Brueggemann notes that four times the prophet speaks of the land as "negative land" (land of "Egypt," "darkness," "drought and deep darkness," "where none passes through") and two times as "positive land" (land of "abundance" and "my land"), and the climax, a chiasmus, is verse 7b: "You defiled *my land, my inheritance* you set to abomination."[32]

---

30. W. Brueggemann, "Israel's Sense of Place in Jeremiah," in *Rhetorical Criticism*, ed. J. J. Jackson and Martin Kessler (Pittsburgh: Pickwick, 1974), p. 151.
31. Ibid., p. 152.
32. Ibid.

Directly related to the poem of 4:23–26, Brueggemann states:

> The crisis of the years before and after 587 is placed in the drama of "salvation history" which is here presented, vss. 6–8, as a *history of land*. Israel's career with Yahweh is from place to place: from land of slavery to land of precariousness to land of well-being and now to abominable land.[33]

A loss of the land presented a crisis equally as severe as Israel's loss of its election status. What God had created has now been uncreated: the nation and the land of Israel are no more.[34]

The poem leaves the reader with the impression that the absolute end has come; there is no hope for Israel. It is, however, precisely at this point that one must note a major theological concern of all prophetic material: that mingled with the message of doom is also the proclamation of grace and hope. This is a paradoxical crux of much prophetic material. Every vestige of hope for Israel's saving itself is taken from them; the nation is left completely at the mercy of God, the Creator; and only he can bring creation out of chaos. Pursuing this theme is beyond the space available here, but the subject is amply developed in the Book of Jeremiah. The purpose of the chaos imagery of 4:23–26—although sounding ominous and leaving little room for a future—in fact, serves to clear the way for hope and redemption. The redemption theme of the Old Testament is to be compared with the creation theme. God's creative activity is a parallel thought with his redemptive activity.[35]

The powerful imagery of this poem leaves the reader with a realization that there can be only one possible answer. The only thing left is for God himself to act, for he alone can recreate Israel as he had created Israel at the beginning. Echoes of the grace of God are found even within these

---

33. Ibid., p. 153. Von Waldow says, "The promise and bestowal of the land constituted only one aspect in Israel's concept of the land. Here Israel was dealing with her past. But there was something more. When Israel received the gift of the land, a heavy responsibility was placed upon her. She was to do everything necessary to keep and maintain this gift and not to lose it." p. 503; See W. Brueggemann, *The Land*, pp. 90–150; P. Diepold, *Israel's Land* (Stuttgart: Verlag W. Kohlhammer, 1972), pp. 125–26.

34. Cf. the circumstances that led to the Flood. See Cassuto, *Commentary on Genesis*, I, II; W. Brueggemann, *Genesis* (Atlanta: John Knox, 1982), pp. 73–88; cf. M. Eliade, *Cosmos and History*, trans. W. R. Trask (New York: Harper & Row, 1959), pp. 51–91.

35. Cf. C. Stuhlmueller, "Creative Redemption in Deutero-Isaiah," in AnBib 43 (Rome: Biblical Institute, 1970): 193–237; L. R. Fisher, "From Chaos to Covenant," *Encounter* 26 (1965): 183–97; D. J. McCarthy, "Creation Motifs in Ancient Hebrew Poetry," CBQ 29 (1967): 87–100; N. C. Habel, "He Who Stretches Out the Heavens," CBQ 34 (1972): 417-30.

early doom chapters of Jeremiah. Redemption and creation are fused together in much Old Testament thought. Strong rhetorical language has been used in Jeremiah 4:23–26 to describe Israel's oncoming tragedy, but by the grace of God a reversal of chaos can occur. After the destruction of 586, God once more began his work of creation.

Part Three

New Testament Interpretation

15

The History of
New Testament Interpretation

Larry Chouinard

An historical perspective of New Testament interpretation acquaints the modern student with the exegetical methods of both ancient and modern times. The hermeneutic diversity of past and contemporary exegetes should alert the modern interpreter to the delicate task of responsible exegesis. Most exegetical techniques of the past have been hammered out on the anvil of cultural influences and heretical challenges. The history of interpretation is, in a meaningful way, the history of the church as it adjusted to new cultural settings and responded to the challenge of diversity within. While reactionary exegetical methods may win the contemporary debate, they often do so at the expense of the ancient author's intended meaning.

This historical survey of New Testament interpretation makes no attempt at an exhaustive treatment of the subject.[1] Only major trends will be isolated and the work of some of the most influential exegetes noted. Primarily, the concern will be with the conditions that led to the adoption of a particular exegetical method. It is easy to stand in critical judgment of an exegetical method far removed from the heat of the controversy or reactionary influences that conditioned its rise. Judgment of the past must be tempered with the realization that successive generations are also children of their own age. If one is to understand exegetical methods of the past and constructively evaluate current trends, he cannot close his eyes to conditioning factors that often contribute to one's method of interpreting the Bible.

---

1. See the Bibliography for Biblical Interpretation for detailed surveys in the field.

Early Christian Exegesis

Christianity began and took its initial shape in the context of first-century Judaism. The writers of the New Testament lived and thought within the categories of Jewish tradition. Until the middle of the second century, exegetical efforts centered in a reinterpretation of Jewish Scriptures. While the exegetical procedures of early Christians resembled those of contemporary Judaism, the authoritative interpretation of rabbinic leaders was replaced with a Christocentric perspective.[2] Moule isolates three main factors that controlled the Christian use of Scripture:

> First, pre-Christian Judaism (drawing partly on Gentile traditions) had already developed certain ways of interpreting scripture. Secondly, Jesus himself, during his ministry had used scripture with great originality, and yet with an understanding of traditional methods. And thirdly, the early Christians were conscious that the voice of inspired prophecy, long silent, had begun once more to be audible; and they therefore used both scripture and the memories and traditions of the words of Jesus with the creative freedom of the inspired.[3]

It is not within the scope of this paper to discuss the use of the Old Testament in the New. The subject is introduced merely to surface the basic Christological concerns that governed interpretation within the New Testament. The authoritative basis of interpretation differed from rabbinic schools, because the record of the acts of God in history had found its fulfillment in the person of Jesus.[4] The Evangelists did not invent this method of interpreting the Old Testament; they simply built on the example left by the historic Christ.

Both apostolic preaching and literary correspondence continued the Christocentric interpretation of the Old Testament. The polemic between church and synagogue necessitated an exegetical procedure and development that understood the Old Testament Christologically.[5] Alexander notes that even in the second century the Apostolic Fathers[6] largely "fol-

---

2. R. Longenecker, *Biblical Exegesis in the Apostolic Period*, (Grand Rapids: Eerdmans, 1975), p. 207.

3. C.F.D. Moule, *The Birth of the New Testament*, (London: A. and C. Black, 1962), p. 58.

4. D. E. Aune, "Early Christian Biblical Interpretation," EvQ 49 (1969): 93.

5. M. Black, "The Christological Use of the Old Testament in the New Testament" NTS 18 (1970): 1–14; E. E. Ellis, *Paul's Use of the Old Testament* (London: Oliver and Boyd, 1957), pp. 57–58. Ellis argues that the main source for Paul's messianic interpretations of the Old Testament are the principles and emphases received from the Apostolic tradition and his own exegesis of the Old Testament as a Christian.

6. The name 'Apostolic Fathers' appeared in the seventeenth century and was applied to eight of the earliest surviving Christian writings because it was thought that they had known the apostles. The eight writings consist of: Clement of Rome, the

low this New Testament exegetical pattern and remain like Paul, Christocentric and just to the historical sense."[7] While most early Christians stand close to Judaism in their literal interpretation of the Old Testament, their polemic with Orthodox Judaism often drove them to a kind of prooftexting based upon Christological concerns.[8]

Patristic Interpretation: Justin to Augustine

The church's encounter with Hellenistic culture necessitated an apologetic that would preserve Christianity's Jewish roots, as well as respond to Hellenistic reason. The problem was intensified by militant anti-Jewish groups who were willing to totally discard their Jewish heritage. R. P. C. Hanson observes that Marcion (140), for example, was driven by the primacy of literal exegesis and a thoroughgoing dualism to reject the Old Testament and parts of the New. Gnostic thinkers also embraced a cosmic dualism; but instead of straining it through the theology of Paul, they were the first to resort to an allegorization of the New Testament.[9]

While Marcion and the major Gnostic thinkers did not persuade the majority, the threat was serious enough to call for a response. Justin Martyr's (160) typological interpretation of the Old Testament was basically an attempt to preserve it for a Hellenistic church.[10] Allegory first appeared in Christian tradition as an apologetic by-product of the typological method of interpretation. Philo (20 B.C.–A.D. 40) had earlier used the method to blend Greek philosophy with Scripture and to overcome the difficulties he found in the Old Testament.[11] Orthodox church leaders did not initially deny the legitimate use of allegory. Robert M. Grant notes that apologists such as Irenaeus (175) charged the Gnostics

---

Didache, Ignatius of Antioch, Polycarp of Smyrna, Papias of Hierapolis, the Epistle of Barnabus, the Shepherd of Hermas, and the Epistle of Diognetus; see J. L. Gonzalez, *A History of Christian Thought*, vol. 1 (Nashville: Abingdon, 1970).

7. J. N. S. Alexander, "The Interpretation of Scripture in the Ante-Nicene Period," Int 12 (1958): 273.

8. For example, the *Epistle of Barnabas* resorted to a form of allegory in order to force Christian interpretations on the Old Testament text. In one instance, Barnabas found the Mosaic legislation on animals that do not chew the cud to be an exhortation to meditation.

9. R. P. C. Hanson, "Biblical Exegesis in the Early Church" *Cambridge History of the Bible*, ed. P. R. Ackroyd and C. F. Evans (Cambridge: Cambridge University, 1970) 1:416. (From now on found *CHB*.)

10. D. E. Aune, "Justin Martyr's Use of the Old Testament," JETS 9 (1966): 179–97. In the midst of some bizarre interpretations of the Old Testament, Justin still maintains a core of exegetical tradition which can be traced back to the New Testament itself. Farrar notes that the only book in the New Testament which Justin mentions by name is the Revelation of St. John; see F. W. Farrar, *History of Interpretation* (Grand Rapids: Baker, 1961), p. 172.

11. S. Sandmel, *Philo of Alexandria* (Oxford: Oxford University, 1979), p. 28.

with abusive allegorization because they ignored the context of passages and interpreted the "clear and obvious by the dark and obscure."[12] Hanson points out that "Christian writers only adopted the allegorization of the New Testament by way of defence, in order to extract orthodox doctrine from it."[13] To control the abuse of allegory, Irenaeus developed a standard of interpretation based upon an authoritarian "rule of faith." To Irenaeus the refutation of Gnosticism was primarily a practical and pastoral matter. By making the church the authoritative interpreter of Scripture, Gnostic exegetical efforts could be dismissed and Christians would not be misled by Gnostic speculations.[14] Tertullian (160–215), an admirer of Irenaeus, pushed the concept further by contending that not only do heretics misunderstand Scripture, they have no right to use or intepret it. With the "rule of faith" as an exegetical method, neither Irenaeus nor Tertullian was forced to make a choice between literal or allegorical exegesis.[15]

By the third century, allegory was developed and widely used by Christian theologians.[16] The first detailed analysis of allegorization was provided by Origen in his work *On First Principles*. According to Hanson, to understand Origen's exegetical method it must be remembered that he owes his entire bent of thought to Plato, from whom he derived "his whole tendency to see all tangible and temporary phenomena as mere ephemeral symbols of a deeper, permanent, invisible reality."[17] For Origen, allegory was a way to preserve the integrity of the Christian faith. A Platonist named Celsus (178) had already attacked what he conceived as immorality and triviality in Scripture. Origen was convinced that a literal reading of Scripture led one to conclude that Scripture contained "errors, contradictions, unreasonable elements, impossibilities, and even fictional elements."[18] The imperfections of the outward form of Scripture suggested to Origen the necessity for a deeper meaning that is distinct from and in addition to the obvious sense. Theoretically, Origen believed that the allegorical method could be checked by its conformity to church tradition or rule of faith.[19]

Not everyone shared Origen's enthusiasm for the allegorical method. The school of thought located in Antioch refused to subjugate historical

12. R. M. Grant, *A Short History of Interpretation of the Bible* (New York: Macmillan, 1948), pp. 71–72.

13. Hanson, *CHB* 1:416.

14. C. C. Richardson, ed., *Early Christian Fathers* (New York: Macmillan, 1979), pp. 343–44.

15. As a matter of fact both Irenaeus and Tertullian employed the literal, typological, and allegorical method of interpretation as it suited their purpose.

16. R. P. M. Hanson, *Allegory and Event* (London: SCM, 1959), p. 124.

17. Hanson, *Allegory and Event*, p. 361.

18. M. W. Holmes, "Origin and the Inerrancy of Scripture," JETS 24 (1981):227.

19. M. F. Wiles, "Origen as Biblical Scholar," *CHB* 1:488.

concerns to hidden spiritual meanings. The Antiochian school came into being partly as a reaction to the excesses of Alexandrian allegorism and also because of the strength of the Jewish environment in Antioch. Grant observes "that wherever the influence of the synagogue was felt by the Church, the interpretation of Scripture had a tendency toward literalism."[20] The leading exegetes of the literalist persuasion were Theodore of Mopsuestia (350–428) and John Chrysostom (350–407). The latter stressed an interpretation based on a historical development "that theologically unified the Bible as a whole."[21] While Chrysostom tied his interpretation of Scripture firmly to the historical sense, he "preferred a cautious typology as an exegetical method."[22] It must be admitted that both writers sacrificed their principles of exegesis time and again in order to support ecclesiastical tradition.

In the long run the allegorical method of Alexandria prevailed over the exegetical traditions of Antioch.[23] Augustine (354–430) is generally recognized as a bridge between the church and the Middle Ages. As a Neoplatonist, Augustine exalted the spiritual sense above the literal. But unlike the Alexandrians, Augustine accepted the historical truth of the letter as the basis for spiritual meaning. His background in Manichaeanism militated against a literal exegesis, which led to the charge of immorality in Scripture. He affirmed that only with the allegorical method could he intellectually accept the Christian faith.[24] Although with age Augustine diminished the allegorical element in his exegetical method, he never wholly abandoned it.[25] The influence of Augustine on exegesis in the Middle Ages was enormous. Not only did he formulate the fourfold method of interpreting Scripture, which was later an important element of medieval interpretation; his methodology also became a major springboard for the medieval theologians' insistence that the Bible could only be understood by means of ecclesiastical interpretation.[26]

Interpretation in the Middle Ages

R. W. Southern's informative work on the history of the church in the Middle Ages opens with the words: "The history of the Western Church in

20. Grant, *A Short History*, p. 89.

21. M. F. Wiles, "Theodore of Mopsuestia as Representative of the Antiochene School," *CHB* 1:508.

22. J. B. Rogers and D. K. McKim, *The Authority and Interpretation of the Bible: An Historical Approach* (San Francisco: Harper and Row, 1979), p. 21.

23. Partly because Theodore of Mopsuestia was suspected of an unorthodox Christology; see J. D. Wood, *The Interpretation of the Bible* (London: Gerald Duckworth, 1958), p. 71.

24. Grant, *A Short History*, p. 109.

25. G. Bonner, "Augustine as a Biblical Scholar," *CHB* 1:541–63.

26. For biographical aids to the study of Augustine see E. A. Blum, "Augustine: The Bishop and Theologian," BibSac 138 (1981): 57–67.

the Middle Ages is the history of the most elaborate and thoroughly integrated system of religious thought and practice the world has ever known."[27] While politically the medieval world struggled in the midst of a decentralized feudal system, ecclesiastically the church came to dominate virtually every aspect of human endeavor. Since there were fewer doctrinal controversies than in previous ages, the church was free to contemplate Scripture within the confines of the monastery. Exegesis was largely an effort to assure that interpretation of Scripture squared with the tradition of the church. The dominance of Augustinian allegory and the tendency to strain Scripture through the theology of the Latin Fathers assured the desired results.

Smalley refers to the early Middle Ages as the "age of innocence."[28] Most exegetes continue the tradition established by the Latin Fathers, especially as reflected in Augustine. Gregory the Great (540–604) emphasized an allegorical interpretation by comparing exegesis to erecting a building. First we lay the historical foundation; next we steady our faith by pursuing the typical sense; and last, by the grace of moral teaching, we color the whole structure.[29] Venerable Bede (673–735), considered to be the "father of English history," contributed to medieval exegesis by making accessible the interpretations of the church fathers.[30] Exegetes, armed with allegory and patristic theology, found Scripture and church tradition to be in perfect agreement.

By the ninth century, there were trends toward a more historical exegesis. An interest in linguistics, along with a reluctance to depend heavily upon the church fathers, produced a major departure from earlier exegetical methods. Anselm (1033–1109) and Abelard (1079–1142) symbolize the movement toward the use of reason in interpreting Scripture. The latter contributed to medieval exegesis by his work on the exegetical anthology called *Glossa Ordinaria*.[31] Abelard challenged early medieval exegesis by arranging contradictory statements from the Scriptures and the church fathers and challenging his students to reconcile them.[32] Peter

27. R. W. Southern, *Western Society and the Church in the Middle Ages* (New York: Penguin, 1970), p. 15.

28. B. Smalley, "The Bible in the Middle Ages" *The Church's Use of the Bible*, ed. Dennis Nineham (London: SPCK, 1963), p. 57.

29. V. P. Furnish, "History of Interpretation," IDB, ed. G. A. Buttrick (Nashville: Abingdon, 1976), 5:452.

30. B. Smalley, *The Study of the Bible in the Middle Ages* (Oxford: Blackwell, 1952), p. 36.

31. A gloss "can be described as a text of the Bible on which tracts of patristic and earlier medieval commentaries are written in the margin or between the lines;" see Furnish, "History of Interpretation" IDB 5:453. The gloss became the norm for biblical exposition.

32. His work is entitled *Sic et Non* (1122); see R. D. Linder, "Peter Abelard," *Dictionary of the Christian Church*, ed. J. D. Douglas (Grand Rapids: Zondervan, 1978), p. 3.

Lombard (1095–1160) went one step further by organizing citations from the church fathers and contemporary exegetes into doctrinal categories. His work *Four Books of Sentences* became the standard theological textbook until the Reformation.

The transition into Scholasticism must go through Paris and the work of the exegetical school at the Abbey of St. Victor. Hugh of St. Victor (1096–1141) gave prominence to the historical sense of Scripture as a means to discover the theological significance.[33] His students, especially Andrew, elevated reason as the means to defend and understand the Christian faith.[34] Many scholars have pointed to the influence of Jewish exegetes, especially Rashi (d. 1105), on Christian exegetes of the twelfth century.[35]

With the rise of the universities in the thirteenth century, serious Bible study became centralized. The quantity of biblical commentaries and aids to study that came out between 1230 and 1270 would not be surpassed until the Reformation.[36] With the translation of Aristotle, Christian thinkers were once again challenged by a world view that made reason the ultimate source of knowledge. Thomas Aquinas (1225–1274) attempted to reconcile Aristotelian metaphysics with the Christian faith. Since the Aristotelian view of nature did not encourage the idea of symbolism, scholastic theologians elevated the literal and historical over the symbolic. While the spiritual interpretation continued to flourish, it was primarily reserved for homiletics.[37] Grant observes that although Aquinas and other scholastic theologians helped to curb the subjective flights of exegetical fancy associated with allegory, they did so at the expense of divorcing theology from exegesis.[38]

The Franciscan Nicholas of Lyra (d. 1340) provides a bridge from the Middle Ages to the Reformers. Being greatly influenced by the Jewish Rabbi Rashi, he was concerned to expound the literal sense of Scripture, over against the allegorical. His exegetical emphasis greatly influenced Luther and opened the door for a new wave of interpreters, the Reformers.

Interpretation in the Reformation

The Renaissance (1300–1600) provided the cultural background for the exegetical methods of the Reformers. Renaissance humanism began in

---

33. J. S. Preus, *From Shadow to Promise* (Cambridge: Harvard University, 1969), pp. 24–37. This survey of hermeneutic theory in the Middle Ages takes into account the most recent historical research into medieval interpretation of the Old Testament.

34. See Smalley, *Bible in the Middle Ages*, pp. 112–95.

35. See S. B. Hoenig, "History of Interpretation: Medieval Jewish" IDB 5:449–52.

36. B. Smalley, "The Bible in Medieval Schools." CHB 2:206.

37. Smalley, "Bible in the Middle Ages" *Church's Use of the Bible*, p. 68.

38. Grant, *A Short History*, p. 116.

Italy and was characterized by a renewed interest in antiquity, especially the Greek and Roman classics. M. W. Anderson notes that the concern for historical accuracy produced a method of study that interpreted classical texts "within the parameters set by the historical setting and linguistic composition of the texts themselves."[39] Humanists such as Erasmus, Cajetan, and John Colet inevitably employed the same methods on the Greek text of the New Testament. They gave the first impulse toward the historical understanding of the biblical text.[40] Humanism's historical and linguistic sensitivity contributed philosophical tools which deeply influenced the exegetical efforts of the Reformers. Grant's assessment is probably correct: "Historical exegesis is even more the child of the Renaissance than of the Reformation."[41]

While the Reformers adopted the linguistic methods and historical concerns of the humanists, their departure from the humanists was essentially theologically motivated. Humanism tended to make reason and its use of historical and linguistic tools the ultimate source for interpreting the New Testament. Martin Luther (1483–1546) subjected reason to the Holy Spirit and chose to interpret Scripture "Christologically." In the preface to his Commentary on James, Luther wrote: "What does not teach Christ is not apostolic, even though St. Peter or Paul taught it; again what preaches Christ would be apostolic even though Judas, Annas, Pilate and Herod did it."

Paul Lehmann points out that the Reformers also departed from Rome and the medieval interpreters by shifting the authority of the Bible from a *supplementary* guide to truth and life, to the *sole* norm for faith and conduct.[42] No longer did the interpretation of Scripture rest on ecclesiastical authority or fanciful allegorizations designed to support church tradition. At the risk of opening the door to a diversity of interpretations, the Reformers stressed that exegesis was the responsibility of the individual, not a select few.

While Luther rejected medieval allegorization as mere "monkey tricks," exhibiting only the ingenuity of the exegete,[43] his Christological method led to a "canon within a canon." According to Grant, his emphasis on the Pauline letters, especially Romans and Galatians, as containing the truest gospel, reveals the subjective emphasis of his own thought.[44] John Calvin (1509–64) was more decisively influenced by the Renaissance

39. M. W. Anderson, *The Battle for the Gospel: The Bible and the Reformation 1444–1589*, (Grand Rapids: Baker, 1978), p. 22.

40. E. Krentz, *The Historical-Critical Method* (Philadelphia: Fortress, 1975), p. 8.

41. Grant, *A Short History*, p. 128.

42. P. L. Lehmann, "The Reformers Use of the Bible," *TToday* 3 (1946): 332.

43. E. C. Blackman, *Biblical Interpretation* (London: Independent Press, 1957), p. 121.

44. Grant, *A Short History*, p. 131.

humanists, as evidenced by his method of exegesis. Most scholarly inquiry into Calvin's thinking has focused on his exegetical conclusions contained in his massive *Institutes of the Christian Religion*. However, Calvin as a biblical expositor is best reflected in his commentaries, which form the major portion of his writings.[45] Like Luther, Calvin rejected the allegorical method and devoted himself exclusively to clarifying the literal sense of Scripture. While he did not follow Luther into a forced Christology, he did, like most Reformers, place heavy emphasis upon the inward testimony of the Holy Spirit to confirm his exegetical conclusions.[46]

Space forbids analysis of other Reformers whose exegetical methods also reflect the polemical conditioning of the sixteenth century. The Reformers sought to chart a path between at least three determining factors: (1) spiritualistic sectarians who claimed the guidance of the Spirit apart from Scripture; (2) a humanism that increasingly drifted toward human autonomy; and (3) a rationalistic scholasticism rooted in the authority of the church.[47] The course they pursued involved the abandonment of the allegorical method for the literary-historical method ultimately controlled by either Christological concerns or the inner testimony of the Holy Spirit. Since the Bible could no longer have its meaning imposed by eccelesiastical authority, the meaning of Scripture must ultimately come from Scripture.[48] The exegetical methods of the Reformers can best be appreciated against the background of conditioning factors that gave rise to new methods of interpreting Scripture, which will be discussed below.

The Effect of Rationalism on Exegesis

Farrar offers a rather grim description of the direction of biblical exegesis in the two centuries following the Reformation: "It was a period in which liberty was exchanged for bondage; universal principles for beggarly elements; truth for dogmatism; independence for tradition; religion for system."[49] Once again polemical concerns determined exegetical pro-

---

45. J. T. McNeill, "History of the Interpretation of the Bible: Medieval and Reformation Period," *IB*, vol. 1 (New York: Abingdon, 1951), p. 124. "He omitted from formal exposition only one book of the New Testament and eight of the Old." see also T. H. L. Parker, "Calvin the Biblical Expositor" *Courtesay Studies in Reformation: John Calvin* (Appleford: Courtesay, 1966), pp. 176–86.

46. G. W. Bromiley, *Historical Theology: An Introduction* (Grand Rapids: Eerdmans, 1978), p. 224.

47. Rogers and McKim, *The Authority and Interpretation*, p. 106.

48. W. G. Kümmel, *The New Testament: The History of the Investigation of Its Problems*, trans. by S. Maclean Gilmour and H. Kee (Nashville: Abingdon, 1972), p. 21.

49. Farrar, *History of Interpretation*, p. 358.

cedures. The Counter-Reformation of the sixteenth and seventeenth centuries produced Jesuit theologians who challenged Protestant doctrinal positions. Socinian rationalism constructed a system that subordinated Scripture to reason.[50] The fanaticism of the Anabaptists also challenged traditional Protestant interpretation of Scripture. If one adds to these factors the revolutions in scientific thinking, along with the new philosophies of Descartes, Hobbes, and Spinoza, one is confronted with a myriad of conditioning factors that shaped exegesis in the centuries following the Reformation.

The second generation of Reformers sought to preserve their identity by barricading faith behind creedal affirmations deduced from disconnected proof-texts. Under polemic pressure, theologians in the post-Reformation period resorted to scholastic argumentation cast in the Aristotelian mold in order to clarify and systematize the basic doctrines of the Reformation.[51] Ironically, the position of rationalism became a viable alternative to the dogmatic system of Protestant Orthodoxy.[52] By the end of the seventeenth century, biblical authority had been severely restricted by scientific and historical advances. No longer could investigation of the Scripture be tempered with the uniqueness of biblical history. Objectivity demanded that exegetes treat the Bible the same as any other historical document.

Once human reason was freed from dogmatic concerns, the groundwork was laid for a totally objective and free historical investigation of Scripture. Krentz describes the problem: ". . . few Orthodox scholars learned historical method without taking over rationalistic antisupernaturalism."[53] Once Scripture was disrobed of authoritative value, the study of Scripture was motivated solely by historical interests. The insights of reason attained through the new philosophies became the ultimate confirmation of Scripture's credibility.

The influence of rationalism did produce some positive advances in the textual study of the New Testament. Fundamental for the historical inter-

---

50. The movement was named after two Italian teachers, uncle and nephew, L. F. M. Sozini (1525–1562) and F. P. Sozini (1539–1604). The movement subjected Scripture to (1) reason, and (2) moral significance and utility. O. Zoeckler, "Socinus, Faustis, Socinians" in *The New Schaff-Herzog Encyclopedia of Religious Knowledge*, ed. S. M. Jackson (Grand Rapids: Baker, 1969) 10: 488–93.

51. Rogers and McKim, *The Authority and Interpretation*, pp. 186–87.

52. P. Shuhlmacher, *Historical Criticism and Theological Interpretation of Scripture: Towards a Hermeneutics of Consent* (Philadelphia: Fortress, 1977), pp. 36–37. Historical-critical research in the eighteenth century was largely carried on in opposition to the dogmatic tradition and supervision of the church.

53. Krentz, *The Historical-Critical Method*, p. 22. Initially, rationalism was not a system of beliefs antagonistic to Christianity, but an attitude of mind which assumed that in all matters of religion reason is supreme; see W. Neil, "The Criticism and Theological Use of the Bible, 1700–1950: *CHB* 3:239.

pretation of the New Testament was ascertaining the exact wording and meaning of Scripture. Eighteenth-century historical investigations led scholars into an "unprejudiced examination of the textual transmission of the New Testament."[54] Names such as John Mill (1707), J. A. Bengel (1734), and J. J. Wettstein (1751–52) helped to lay the groundwork for a critical Greek Testament. Later (1774–75) J. J. Griesbach printed the first reconstructed Greek text. Bruce comments that Griesbach also "advanced beyond the historical criticism of his immediate predecessors by applying himself to the problems of literary criticism, in that area of New Testament where these problems are most obvious—the Gospels and their interrelationship."[55] Not all exegesis represented the rationalism of the eighteenth century. J. A. Bengel's word-by-word explanation of the Greek text entitled *Gnomon novi testamenti* (1742) is still in use within evangelical circles.

Although scholars such as J. J. Semler (1725–91) and J. D. Michaelis (1717–1791) sought total objectivity through a rigorous historical-grammatical approach, the rationalism of their day heavily influenced their conclusions. The quest for objectivity was commendable. But with the rush to escape ecclesiastical presuppositions, many biblical exegetes of the seventeenth and eighteenth century became shackled to the conclusions of secular rationalism.

Interpretation in the Nineteenth Century

The nineteenth century brought an intellectual and social revolution that affected not only the way man viewed the world, but also his method of investigating the varied fields of human thought and activity. Critical methods of investigating the classical world introduced a new approach to biblical criticism and interpretation.[56] Historical studies were dominated by the concept of some divine or rational idea moving through history, whether it was Hegel's dialectical process or the Darwinian theory of evolution. In every field the century was characterized by developmentalism, historical-critical methods, and scientific criticism.[57]

The first half of the century witnessed an extremely radical approach to the New Testament on the part of German scholarship. Grant observes that the shift of biblical instruction from the church to the secular univer-

54. Kümmel, *History of Investigation*, p. 47.

55. F. F. Bruce, "The History of New Testament Study," in *New Testament Interpretation*, ed. I. H. Marshall (Grand Rapids: Eerdmans, 1977), p. 38.

56. S. Neill, *The Interpretation of the New Testament 1861–1961* (London: Oxford University, 1964), pp. 7–8. Neill shows the influence of G. B. Niebuhr's two volumes on the history of Rome.

57. E. Achtemeir, "History of Interpretation: Nineteenth and Twentieth Century Christian" IDB 5:455.

sity, where Hegelian philosophical assumptions guided historical investigation, contributed to a new sense of freedom in dealing with the biblical record.[58] The exegetical methods emerging from Germany were dominated by the quest for the "essence of Christianity." If the value of the Bible is to be preserved, the "kernel" of divine truth must be detached from the historical "husks" of first-century mentality. Since the Scriptures should be examined like any other historical document, the categories of divine revelation and the miraculous were replaced with the "assured results" of Historical Criticism. Free from dogmatic concerns, exegetes pursued an "objective" analysis of the text designed to take them to the heart of the biblical message. The varied and highly subjective results clearly demonstrate the limitations of this endeavor.

The early decades of the nineteenth century were dominated by the influence of Friedrich Schleiermacher (1768–1834). Granting the conclusions of rationalism, Schleiermacher sought to preserve the value of Scripture by shifting exegetical concerns from the historical to a "psychological understanding"[59] of the text. No longer need the Bible be taken seriously in every detail. The essence of the biblical message was to be found in its record of religious experience. The task of exegesis, then, involves an analysis of religious experiences and the development of sensitivities to enter into that experience in a modern context. Schleiermacher's blending of rationalism and pietism led him to a pragmatic view of Scripture's worth. The holy books have become the Bible in virtue of their own power, but they do not forbid any other book from being or becoming a Bible in its turn.[60]

Schleiermacher's theology was largely responsible for initiating an interest in the historical Jesus.[61] Armed with rationalism and the romantic incentives of Schleiermacher, biographies of the life of Jesus tended to reflect contemporary theological convictions. D. F. Strauss (1808–74) attempted to reduce the tension between first-century supernaturalism and modern rationalism by a synthesis resulting in a "mythological interpretation." His *Life of Jesus* was an attempt to surface spiritual truths by penetrating beneath the "legendary and naive perceptions of the gospel authors." It is amazing how every so-called significant truth excavated by Strauss and other nineteenth-century biographies of Jesus perfectly reflected liberal values and perceptions.[62]

58. Grant, *A Short History*, p. 131.
59. Kümmel, *History of Investigation*, p. 116.
60. W. Neil, "The Criticism and Theological Use of the Bible, 1700–1950" CHB 3:274.
61. S. Terrien "History of the Interpretation of the Bible: III Modern Period," 1:132. Schleiermacher's *Life of Jesus* was published posthumously in 1864.
62. A. Schweitzer, *The Quest of the Historical Jesus* (New York: MacMillan, 1968), p. 80.

F. C. Baur (1762–1860), leader of the Tübingen school of biblical criticism, reinterpreted the history of the early church around an alleged conflict between a Jewish party led by Paul and a Hellenistic party led by Peter. Guided by this presupposition, Baur proceeded to dissect the Pauline Epistles accordingly. The result was the acceptance of only four letters—Romans, 1 and 2 Corinthians, and Galatians—as authentic, while the rest were categorized as second-century productions. While few scholars outside the Tübingen school accepted Baur's conclusions, his historical procedure heightened the recognition that primitive Christianity can only be understood within the historical context. The attempt to penetrate the historical context led many scholars into a commitment to Source Criticism. H. J. Holtzmann (1863), following the lead of C. H. Weisse (1823–1866), argued for Markan priority along with the use of a common source for Matthew and Luke, called Q. Although Baur's conclusions did not survive, his methodology gave impetus both to the "salvation history" school and the "history of religions" school.[63]

By the end of the nineteenth century, the Bible "was firmly anchored in its own world."[64] Biblical criticism had succeeded in thoroughly secularizing Scripture. Research in the nineteenth century was largely dominated by the literary-critical approach, with its inquiries about sources and literary links within the New Testament writings.[65] With the works of Julius Wellhausen (1844–1918) in the Old Testament, and Adolf Von Harnack (1851–1930) in the New, biblical criticism on the continent achieved a considerable measure of stability.[66]

The reader should not get the impression that all biblical scholarship and creativity in the nineteenth century resided in Germany. Neither should one conclude that Germany was without a conservative voice of protest against the assumptions of Historical Criticism. Scholars such as E. W. Hengstenberg, Carl F. Keil, Franz Delitzsch, H. A. W. Meyer, Theodore Zahn, and G. F. Oehler avoided the extremes and biases of the critical schools and employed the grammatical-historical method in their production of monumental commentaries that, according to A. B. Mickelsen, "carefully blended together grammar, lexicography, and historical background with the message and particular truths of the book."[67] The Cambridge trio of B. F. Westcott (1825–1901), J. B. Lightfoot (1828–89), and F. J. A. Hort (1828–92) made significant contributions in both the literary and textual study of the New Testament. Lightfoot sin-

---

63. Kümmel, *History of Investigation*, p. 207. Kümmel regards Otto Pfeiderer, one of F. C. Baur's pupils, as the "Father of history-of-religious theology in Germany."

64. Krentz, *The Historical-Critical Method*, p. 28.

65. W. G. Kümmel, *Introduction to the New Testament*, trans. by H. C. Kee (Nashville: Abingdon, 1973), p. 33.

66. Neil, "The Criticism and Theological Use of the Bible," p. 284.

67. A. B. Mickelsen, *Interpreting the Bible* (Grand Rapids: Eerdmans, 1976), p. 47.

glehandedly destroyed the cornerstone of the Tübingen theory by demonstrating the early date for the Ignatian letters, which show no awareness of the Petrine and Pauline factions postulated by Baur.[68] While English scholars were concerned about theological and critical questions, they were less likely to follow the philosophical presuppositions that implicitly guided continental scholars.[69]

The nineteenth century closed with most continental scholars confident of the "assured results of criticism." American and English scholars avoided many of the extremes of Historical Criticism and produced some of the best exegetical and historical commentaries on the New Testament text. But, even by the turn of the century, scholars from a diversity of backgrounds began to question the "assured results of criticism." Theological considerations and linguistic advances, combined with archeological discoveries were to force hermeneutic trends along a different path in the twentieth century.

Interpretation in the Twentieth Century

Stimulated by the accomplishments of critical thinking, the twentieth century opened with a religious and cultural optimism. Although some voices of opposition had arisen, it seemed that the assumptions of historical-critical thinking would dominate and determine the direction of biblical interpretation in the twentieth century. However, World War I dealt a severe blow to the confidence in rational thinking and the inevitable progress of mankind. The political and social catastrophes of 1918 spelled a decisive turning point for New Testament research.[70] Another factor that shaped this research in the early decades of the twentieth century was the enormous wealth of information suddenly made available for scholarly appraisal. Archeological, philological, and textual research and developments resulted in a mass of information that illuminated virtually every page of the Bible. Scholarly appraisal of the contributions demanded that biblical interpreters become extraordinarily specialized.[71] The result was a multiplicity of disciplines within New Testament research, each tending to emphasize its diversity rather than its unity. Isolation within the varied fields of research always runs the risk of oversimplification. And, certainly, any attempt to trace the trends of theological thinking in the twentieth century is immediately confronted with the varied fields of research and the difficulty of determining exactly what contributions each specialized study makes to the whole.

68. Neill, pp. 40–41.
69. Grant, *A Short History*, p. 132.
70. Kümmel, *History of Interpretation*, p. 325.
71. Terrien, "Interpretation of the Bible: Modern Period" *IB* 1:137.

Not only was the optimism of nineteenth-century liberalism shaken by political factors; vigorous opposition also challenged some of its most cherished presuppositions. The "assured results of criticism" were dealt a severe blow by William Wrede (1859–1906), who employed the historical-critical method with radically different conclusions. Wrede's *Das Messiasgeheimnis in den Evangelien* appeared in English in 1972 under the title *The Messianic Secret*. The book attacked the conventional critical treatment of the Gospels by arguing that Jesus' messianic consciousness in Mark's Gospel reflected the reading back of the Church's theological concept into the life of Jesus, rather than an unbiased historical presentation of the consciousness of Jesus. Thus, Mark could never be used as a source for a history of Jesus, since it only reflects the testimony to the messianic faith of early Christianity.[72] Albert Schweitzer (1875–1965) published *The Quest of the Historical Jesus* in 1906 under the German title *Von Reimarus zu Wrede*. His work jolted the liberal camp with an assault upon nineteenth-century biographies of Jesus, showing that they had ignored the eschatological element in Jesus' teaching.

While both Schweitzer and Wrede remained within the liberal tradition, the work of Karl Barth (1886–1968) signaled a new direction of biblical interpretation.[73] Once a student of Harnack, Barth's disenchantment with liberal theology was articulated in the first edition of his commentary on Romans (1919):

> The critical historical method of Biblical research has its validity. It points to the preparation for understanding that is never superfluous. . . . But my whole attention was directed to looking through the historical to the spirit of the Bible, which is the eternal Spirit.[74]

Barth's attempt to guide the exegete through literary and historical considerations to the deeper truths living within often does so at the expense of the biblical writer.

Rudolph Bultmann (1884–1976) also reacted strongly to the older liberal school of thought, which looked for the "real" historical Jesus, freed from theological interpretation of his person and work. He agreed with Barth that the essence of Christianity is the kerygmatic proclamation that addresses man, demanding the response of faith.[75] However, he differed

---

72. Kümmel, *History of Interpretation*, pp. 281–88.

73. J. M. Robinson and J. B. Cobb, ed., *The New Hermeneutic* (New York: Harper & Row, 1964), pp. 22–23. Robinson begins with Barth in his discussion on new hermeneutical trends.

74. K. Barth, *The Epistle to the Romans*, trans. by E. C. Hoskyns (London: Oxford University, 1933), p. 1; see the preface to the first edition.

75. J. Macquarrie, "Rudolf Bultmann," *A Handbook of Christian Theologians* (Cleveland: William Collins, 1965), p. 446.

with Barth concerning the value to be put on the historical form of the New Testament. Bultmann's exegetical efforts were largely governed by his radical skepticism concerning the factual content of the gospel narrative, on the one hand, along with his continual high regard for what he considered the central message of the New Testament. In his book *Jesus Christ and Mythology*, Bultmann clarifies his method of interpretation:

> We must ask whether the eschatological preaching and the mythological sayings as a whole contain a still deeper meaning which is concealed under the cover of mythology. If that is so, let us abandon the mythological conceptions precisely because we want to retain their deeper meaning. The method of interpretation of the New Testament which tries to recover the deeper meaning behind the mythological conceptions I call *de-mythologizing*—an unsatisfactory word, to be sure. Its aim is not to eliminate the mythological statements but to interpret them. It is a method of hermeneutics.[76]

While others before Bultmann attempted to de-mythologize, Bultmann is unique in his insistence that the interpretation of the New Testament must ultimately be an "existential" one that addresses human existence.[77]

However one may judge the efforts of Barth and Bultmann, it must be recognized that for the most part their aim was to understand the Bible, not to destroy it; to enhance its value, not to undermine its authority. In their reaction to the historical abuses of previous generations, they have been rightly criticized for undervaluing history. Doty remarks that they "concentrated upon meaning-history to such an extent that 'facticity' in the usual sense was no longer a vital concern."[78] But the issues raised by these two men are questions that scholars have only begun to take seriously in the last two or three decades.

Literary research into the Synoptics continued basically along the lines stimulated by nineteenth-century Source Criticism. Kümmel's assessment that the "source critical work on the Synoptics has reached an end in the two-source theory[79] demonstrates that little progress has been made beyond nineteenth-century thinking. Efforts to reconstruct the pre-literary tradition by an analysis of literary forms (Form Criticism) has led many scholars to conclude that the formulation and preservation of the tradition about Jesus was stimulated not by historical concerns but by

76. R. Bultmann, *Jesus Christ and Mythology* (New York: Scribner's, 1958), p. 18.

77. R. H. Fuller, *The New Testament in Current Study* (New York: Scribner's, 1962), pp. 6–7.

78. W. G. Doty, *Contemporary New Testament Interpretation* (New Jersey: Prentice Hall, 1972), p. 92.

79. Kümmel, *Introduction to the New Testament*, p. 76.

interests that are related to faith. Travis describes the task of the form critic as the classification of Gospel pericopes according to their form, in order to assign them their respective *Sitz im Leben*.[80] One of the more helpful trends in Synoptic research involves shifting the emphasis from studying the sources used by the Evangelists to examining each writer's theological purpose for writing his Gospel. The Gospel writers were not only preservers of historical detail; they also interpreted and arranged the historical content to fit their theological purpose. Scholars from a diversity of backgrounds have recognized Redaction Criticism as a useful tool for ascertaining the theological interest of the Evangelists.[81] Recent evangelical evaluation of the Gospels has pictured the narratives as a kind of "slow-action replay," with expert commentary provided by the Evangelist after the conclusion of the game.[82] Another evangelical prefers the metaphor of a "portrait" whereby one "seeks to convey an impression, create an aura, develop a perception."[83] While the Gospel narratives reflect a limited degree of literary editing, we must avoid the "documentary mentality" that turns every verbal correspondence into documentary borrowing.[84] Many of the current efforts to determine literary or oral dependency within the Synoptic tradition have led some into a kind of "unhistorical theologizing." A detailed examination of practically any pericope will show that the writers would have had to perform "literary gymnastics" with their sources to produce their Gospels by merely copying oral or written sources. Redaction Criticism helps us to see the theological purpose to which they put the historical data available to them. Because the Evangelists wrote from a theological purpose, the literary structure of their writings reflect each writer's distinctive interpretation of the historically based kerygma.

New trends in linguistic studies have attempted to make the Bible intelligible and relevant to modern man. Taking up where Bultmann leaves off, the hermeneutics of J. Robinson and a host of German scholars reflect a new understanding of the nature and function of language.[85] Attempting to understand the "new hermeneutic" is no easy task. The

80. S. H. Travis, "Form Criticism," *New Testament Interpretation*, p. 155.

81. See R. H. Stein, "What is Redaktionsgeschichte" JBL 88 (1969), 45–56; G. R. Osborne, "The Evangelical and Redaction Criticism: Critique and Methodology," JETS 22 (1979): 305–22; W. Marxen, *Mark the Evangelist*, R. A. Harrisville (Nashville: Abingdon, 1969); G. Bornkamm, G. Barth, H. J. Held, *Tradition and Interpretation in Matthew* (Philadelphia: Westminster, 1963).

82. D. A. Hager, "Interpreting the Gospels: The Landscape and the Quest," JETS 24 (1981):23–27 .

83. R. A. Guelich, "The Gospels: Portraits of Jesus and His Ministry," JETS 24 (1981): 117–25.

84. See D. Wenham, "Source Criticism," *New Testament Interpretation*, pp. 139–49.

85. Robinson and Cobb, *The New Hermeneutic*; The principle proponents of the movement are G. Ebeling and E. Fuchs.

exponents of the movement essentially call upon the interpreter to enter into dialogue with the text in order to be subjectively confronted by language and events from a different historical context. When the language from a biblical context touches one's life in a meaningful way, it becomes truth for that person. As Thiselton points out, the "new hermeneutic" is more concerned with understanding the New Testament more "deeply and creatively" than to "understand it correctly."[86] One wonders if the proponents of the "new hermeneutic" would dare to apply the same linguistic principles to their own writings.

Another contemporary linguistic revolt against historicism comes in the form of "structuralism." Bernard Lategan considers structuralism to be a "major methodological shift in exegetic procedural."[87] Like the "new hermeneutic," structuralism is an extraordinarily difficult movement to define. With the risk of ambiguity and simplistic definitions, the reader is referred to more lengthy discussions of this exegetical method.[88] Suffice it to say here that, like many efforts, structuralism lends itself to both positive and negative contributions. Some of the more positive contributions are reflected in the current use of "structural principles" in translating the Bible for diverse and primitive cultures.[89] Criticism has been leveled against the structuralist method because of its lack of historical sense.

As in previous generations, the twentieth century has witnessed its share of hermeneutical methods spurred by reactionary pens. However, since the turn of the century, there has been an increased readiness to accept the historical reliability of the New Testament documents. The reborn awareness of the primarily theological intentions of the biblical writers[90] has reflected an intense desire to interpret the text in terms meaningful to twentieth-century man. It seems fitting to conclude this survey with an assessment from Jack P. Lewis on the state and direction of New Testament study in our century:

86. A. C. Thiselton, "The New Hermeneutic," *New Testament Interpretation*, p. 323.

87. B. C. Lategan, "Direction in Contemporary Exegesis: Between historicism and structuralism," *Journal of Theology for South Africa* 25 (1978): 18.

88. See D. Patte, *Structural Exegesis: From Theory to Practice* (Philadelphia: Fortress, 1978); D. Y. Hadidian, *Structuralism and Biblical Hermeneutics: A Collection of Essays*, Pittsburgh Theological Monograph Series, No. 22 (Pittsburgh: Pickwick, 1979); V. S. Poythress, "Structuralism and Biblical Studies," JETS 21 (1978): 221–37; E. Armerding, "Structural Analysis," *Themelios* 4 (1979): 96–104.

89. E. Nida encourages translators to "the use of techniques which are proving so indispensable in so many phases of scientific inquiry involving communication." E. Nida, "Implications of Contemporary Linguistics for Biblical Scholarship," JBL 91 (1972): 89; see also J. Beekman and J. Callow, *Translating the Word of God* (Grand Rapids: Zondervan, 1974).

90. Terrien, "Interpretation of the Bible: Modern Period," 1:137.

If any one indictment could be made of New Testament study of the century, it would be its failure to deal adequately with the revelatory aspect of the New Testament in a way that would put men right with God. A proper method must make allowances for both aspects of God's word—the historical and the revelatory. That God has revealed Himself in these events and words is the claim of the Bible itself (1 Tim. 3:16; 2 Tim. 1:21). Analysis alone is not adequate. The Word must become a living acting word in each of us, bringing us into a relationship with God.[91]

91. J. P. Lewis, "The New Testament in the Twentieth Century," RQ 18 (1975): 215.

16

New Testament
Textual Criticism

Frank Pack

The purpose of Textual Criticism of the New Testament is to recover, as far as possible, what the authors originally wrote from all the available ancient copies and fragments of the New Testament books that exist. As is true with almost all ancient literature, the original autographs of the New Testament books have not survived. All copies were done by hand until the invention of printing about 1455, and each copy differs from every other copy. The task is complicated by the tremendous number of copies preserved from antiquity and the Middle Ages. The twenty-sixth edition of the Nestle-Aland *Novum Testamentum Graece* (the most recent 1981 edition) lists 88 papyri, 274 uncials, and 2,785 minuscules, to which can be added almost 2,000 lectionaries in Greek. In addition, there survive numerous copies of the ancient translations or versions, including more than 10,000 copies of the Latin Vulgate. The many quotations from Scripture by the early church fathers are also a part of the available evidence. Since nothing comparable to this occurs in the works of any ancient Greek or Latin author, the task of classical Textual Criticism is much easier.

While the overwhelming majority of differences in the copies involve word order, spelling, grammar, or stylistic details and are minor in importance, there is a significant group of differences or "variants" that do materially affect the text's meaning. B. M. Metzger comments that the United Bible Societies' *Greek New Testament* (third edition) notes 2,040 sets of variants worthy of attention by Bible translators.[1] Many others

1. B. M. Metzger, *A Textual Commentary on the Greek New Testament* (London and New York: United Bible Societies, 1971) p. v.

affect the meaning of passages in varying ways. Yet M. M. Parvis restates what has been said before: "It is true that not one of these variant readings affects the substance of Christian dogma."[2]

Manuscript Witnesses to the New Testament Text

The collection of Greek manuscripts, ancient versions, patristic quotations, and lectionaries is sometimes called the Apparatus Criticus, the total body of available materials for Textual Criticism of the New Testament.

A brief survey of the materials available for textual study follows. **Papyri** are among the most exciting discoveries of the late-nineteenth and twentieth centuries. These fragile paperlike manuscripts were mainly preserved in the dry climate of Egypt, and they have brought us much nearer to the first-century texts than we had previously been. Such notable groups as the Chester Beatty Papyri from the third century (P^{45}, P^{46}, P^{47}); the Bodmer collection, ranging in date from the late-second to the seventh centuries (P^{66}, P^{72}, P^{73}, P^{74}, P^{75}); and the John Rylands fragment on John 18 (P^{52}) from the first half of the second century—as well as our oldest New Testament manuscript—have brought fresh insights into the history of the text.

Uncial manuscripts were written on parchment in capital letters without word division (called "the book hand") and include all the manuscripts until the tenth century A.D. These have been of prime value in efforts to restore the original text. Designated by a zero followed by an Arabic number, the more famous manuscripts also are known by capital letters taken from Hebrew, Latin, and Greek.

Aleph or *Sinaiticus* (01) contains our earliest complete Greek New Testament. It is dated in the fourth century and was discovered by Tischendorf in St. Catherine's Monastery at Mount Sinai.

A or *Alexandrinus* (02) is the earliest manuscript containing the whole Greek Bible (with some gaps) and is now located along with *Sinaiticus* in the British Museum in London.

B or *Vaticanus* (03) in the Vatican, Rome, is also from the fourth century and has suffered considerable mutilation. It lacks 1 and 2 Timothy, Titus, Revelation, and Hebrews after 9:14.

D or *Bezae* (05) has Greek and Latin texts on opposite pages and is the best example of the Gospels arranged in the Western order: Matthew, John, Luke, and Mark. It is also valued for expressing the Western type of text, especially in Acts.

2. M. M. Parvis, "Text, New Testament." IDB, Vol. 4 (Nashville: Abingdon, 1962) p. 595.

D^P or *Claromontanus* (06) is also a Greek and Latin manuscript containing Paul's writings. It includes Hebrews.

W or *Washingtonianus* (032) is in our nation's capital and is a fifth-century copy of the Gospels in the Western order. There are some interesting readings here, especially in Mark.

Minuscules or cursive manuscripts are those written in small letters and date from the ninth century to the seventeenth or eighteenth centuries. Each is designated by an Arabic numeral. They are by far the largest group preserved, probably because they are the latest in date. Some have been studied and grouped into families such as family 1 (1, 118, 131, 209, 1582) and family 13 (13, 69, 124, 174, 230, 346, 543, 788, 826, 828, 983, 1689, 1709). Family 13 puts the section about the adulterous woman (John 7:53–8:11) after Luke 21:38. Other important minuscules textually are 28, especially in Mark; 33, often called "the Queen of the cursives"; 81, very important for the text of Acts; 565, a purple vellum manuscript with gold letters, written about the ninth century. Number 700 is an eleventh century manuscript containing many interesting variants, including the petition in Luke's form of the Lord's Prayer: "Thy Holy Spirit come upon us and cleanse us" instead of "Thy kingdom come."[3] Minuscule 1424, a ninth- or tenth-century copy of the entire New Testament, forms the first in family 1424; 1739 contains Acts and the Epistles, following in Paul's letters a text similar to Origen's in the third century; 2053 is regarded as one of the best sources of the text of the Book of Revelation.

Versions—the most important of which were made from the Greek New Testament before A.D. 1000—include (1) Latin (Old Latin and the Vulgate of Jerome); (2) Syriac (Old Syriac, Peshiṭta, Philoxenian and/or Harclean, and the Palestinian); (3) Coptic or Egyptian (Sahidic, Bohairic, and fragmentary versions); (4) Armenian; (5) Georgian; (6) Gothic; (7) Ethiopic; and (8) Old Slavonic. Some of these early versions (Old Syriac, Old Latin, Coptic) are very important because they reflect text forms translated in the second and third centuries. But no manuscript of the versions exists today from earlier than the fourth century.

Early church fathers quoted extensively from the New Testament in their writings, using forms of the text known to them. Thus, their quotations enable the dating and locating of certain textual readings and contribute greatly to the history of the text in the early centuries. It has been said that if all the New Testament manuscripts were destroyed, the text could be restored from the many quotations made by the church fathers. For instance, one can date the variant reading *Bethabara* for *Bethany* (John 1:28) to Origen's time (ca. 230), since he could not locate Bethany on the Jordan in his travels in Palestine and suggested the name Bethabara, a

---

3. B. M. Metzger, *The Text of the New Testament*, 2nd ed. (New York: Oxford University, 1968) p. 64.

town in existence on the Jordan.[4] Critical editions of the patristic writings help greatly in textual study.

Lectionaries also provide insight into the text of the Greek New Testament. These were service books used in the church's worship, following the practice of the Jewish synagogue where portions of Scripture were read during the service. The Greek church selected certain passages for Sundays, Saturdays, weekdays, and feast days and later placed them in books known as lectionaries. These are important because the form of the text preserved in service books tends to be conservative and even archaic. Lectionaries preserve an older form of the text than the date of the manuscript itself, but these books have not been studied extensively and await further exploration for their contributions to textual study.

The Transmission of the Text

Before Constantine

Constantine is important in church history because he granted toleration to the Christians in 311, marking the end of persecution by the state. Many of the errors in the transmission of the text occurred during the period before Constantine, when the Christians suffered severely and their scribes were not trained professionals. During this time many errors unintentionally crept into the copies, and other changes were intentionally made to "correct" what appeared to be errors or difficulties in obscure passages. In addition, differences in Gospel accounts were changed so that they would conform in wording. In some cases, changes in the text were motivated by doctrinal interests. One must not think the intentional changes perverse, since the scribe's motivation was mainly to make the accounts pure and free from various heresies that troubled the church within. Lest the wrong impression be gathered, it should be said that because of their high regard for the text, the scribes copied the material with great care, even in places where the reading did not make sense to them.

The most important person in this period was Origen, considered the first great textual scholar of the church. He found and noted variations in the church's copies and assigned reasons for the errors: carelessness of the scribes, large and smaller corrections made arbitrarily, the corrupting influences of the heretics, and so on. Origen noted with great care in his commentaries and homilies the variant readings he found in the copies, and he indicated his preferences as a scholar for a certain reading. In determining the "better reading," he utilized contextual meanings, internal probability, harmonization, and the tradition of the church, for which

4. *Commentary on John* VI:40, *Ante-Nicene Fathers*, vol. 10, p. 370.

he had the greatest respect. Because he had such a high regard for the tradition of the church, one cannot be sure that Origen actually changed the readings in the church's copies he used. He was able to find meaningful messages, even from the variations he discovered, through his use of allegory—seeking a deeper "spiritual" meaning beyond the literal problems and difficulties of the text. Origen died in 254, and his scholarly work influenced others in this early period of the church's history.

The Period of Manuscript Transmission (311–1516)

Under Constantine's favorable attitude toward Christianity, the age of the great uncial manuscripts was ushered in. The emperor ordered fifty copies prepared for the churches in his new capital, Constantinople. The earliest uncials came from this age and reflect earlier forms of the text. Primarily, two forms are in evidence in them: the Alexandrian type of text, reflecting the careful scribal traditions of Egypt (note B and Aleph); and the somewhat later manuscripts, which contained a so-called Western text-type showing much conflation of readings and longer forms of the text in many places (note D, D^p and W). But the growing influence of the church in Constantinople spread the type of text used there, and it gradually became the standard for the majority of the later copies in the Greek church.

As the spread of Islam and the conquest of Egypt brought the decline of Alexandrian influence in the Greek church, Latin became the dominant language of the West. Due to the many discrepancies in the Old Latin manuscripts, Jerome was authorized (about 384) to make a careful translation, which was known as the Vulgate. Yet it was almost two hundred years until the Vulgate superseded the earlier Old Latin versions and became the Bible of the Roman Catholic Church. Gutenberg's invention of printing by movable type about 1455 enabled the printing of many copies at one time and ushered in a new period in the history of the biblical text.

The Textus Receptus (1516–1633)

The first complete Greek Testament was printed as part of the Complutensian Polyglot in 1514 at Alcala, Spain, under the direction of Cardinal Ximenes, but it was not circulated until 1522. The first Greek Testament printed and published was edited by the famous humanist scholar Erasmus in 1516 in Basel, Switzerland. In 1515 he hastily gathered six Greek minuscule manuscripts, none of which contained the whole New Testament, and he used five of the latest in date to compile his text. Erasmus included some verses in Revelation that he translated into Greek from the Latin because his manuscripts lacked those verses. His Testament went through four more editions (1519, 1522, 1527, 1535). Robert Stephanus, a French printer, used Erasmus's fifth edition for his third edition, printed in 1550. Stephanus's fourth edition (1551) contained the first numbered chapters and verses, which remain in our Bibles today. Theodore Beza from Geneva used Stephanus's third edition as the basis for his Greek Testament, which went through ten editions. Beza also printed the Latin Vulgate as well as his own Latin text with the Greek text. Beza's 1588–89 and 1598 editions were used extensively by the King James translators.

The Elzevir brothers, Dutch printers, used Stephanus's third edition as the basis for their first Greek Testament (1624). In their 1633 edition, they wrote, "You have the text, now received by all in which we give nothing altered or corrupted."[5] From this arose the title *Textus Receptus*, or "Received Text," which became standard on the Continent, as Stephanus's third edition had become in Great Britain. Actually, the third edition of Stephanus and the Elzevir second edition differ only in 287 places.

Accumulating Textual Evidence (1633–1831)

The *Textus Receptus* so completely dominated as the printed text that the major advances in textual study for the next two centuries consisted of the marginal notes of scholars. Brian Walton's Polyglot Bible of 1657 printed the variant readings of A and 13 other newly examined manuscripts. John Mill's Testament in 1707 noted 30,000 variants from about 100 different manuscripts. He was the first scholar to see the importance of the ancient versions and the patristic quotations in textual study. Johann Bengel, the first to attempt an evaluation of the manuscripts, began to set forth rules or "canons" to guide textual scholars. J. J. Wettstein's Testament (1751–52) used over three hundred manuscripts as well as parallels from Jewish, classical, and Christian writings. He is noteworthy for being the first to cite the uncials with capital letters and the minuscules with Arabic numbers, a system still followed today. Griesbach's editions (1774–1807) laid the foundations for all subsequent textual work, modifying Bengel's system to three major recensions: Alexandrian, Western, and Byzantine. He also formulated a list of rules for textual studies, and his text showed some surprising departures from the *Textus Receptus* in a number of places.

The Modern Period (1831–)

Lachmann was the first scholar to reject the *Textus Receptus* and construct a critical text according to the oldest manuscripts available at that time. Tregelles (1857–1872) followed the same principles, presenting a model of accuracy in his citations. Tischendorf was a noted discoverer of manuscripts, especially of Sinaiticus. His eighth edition (1872) presented

5. Metzger, p. 106.

a wealth of manuscript, versional, and patristic materials on the Greek text.

However, all previous work was supplanted by the two great Cambridge scholars, Westcott and Hort, whose Testament had an accompanying "Introduction," written by Hort and setting forth their theory of Textual Criticism. They classified texts according to groups or types, following the lines laid out by Griesbach. Westcott and Hort called the Byzantine text Syrian, and a fundamental conclusion of theirs was "that all distinctively Syrian readings may be set aside at once as certainly originating after the middle of the third century, and, therefore, as far as transmission is concerned, corruptions of the apostolic text."[6] This left them to choose between three other text-types: Western, Alexandrian, and a group closely akin to the Alexandrian, which they called the Neutral because they thought it to be relatively free from contamination. In the neutral they put Vaticanus and Sinaiticus. The English Revised and the American Standard versions are basically drawn from Westcott and Hort's text.

The work of Westcott and Hort has influenced all textual work on the New Testament since. While their position aroused strong opposition from such defenders of the Received Text as Burgon, Miller, and Hoskier, there were other scholars who felt they had not gone far enough. Their work is remarkable in anticipating the discoveries and new ideas regarding the text. Although they did not have the benefit of the papyri manuscripts, which have largely come to light since 1881, their work has been solid enough to withstand most of the criticisms lodged against it. In the succeeding century there have been some modifications of their conclusions.

As already indicated, a wealth of papyri and early manuscripts have come to light since 1881. These have greatly increased our knowledge of the textual history of the second and third centuries. Critical editions of the church fathers have likewise made contributions to the accuracy of patristic quotations. Modern techniques have facilitated the gathering of photographs and copies at centers for further study. The most important center now is the *Institut für Neutestamentliche Text-Forschung* in Münster, West Germany. The United Bible Societies' *Greek New Testament* has been supplemented with *A Textual Commentary on the Greek New Testament* (edited by B. M. Metzger), which discusses over 2,000 sets of variants and shows the process by which judgments were made by the committee of scholars.

6. B. F. Westcott and F. J. A. Hort, *The New Testament in Greek*, "Introduction" (Cambridge: Macmillan, 1881), p. 117.

The Methods of Textual Criticism

The directive principles of Textual Criticism are the same for all forms of writing, whether they be Scripture or classical text. The problems the copies present are those of determining and reestablishing the original form of an ancient text, or coming as near to that form as possible on the basis of the available evidence.

Internal Criticism

Hort outlined a method that has been helpful for scholars since his day. One starts with the manuscript, examining it to understand not only the date of writing (paleography) but, if possible, to arrive at the date of the text reflected in it. This involves Internal Criticism, which studies the ways in which the manuscript varies from a standard text such as the *Textus Receptus*. It is here that one comes to see the sources of corruption in the manuscript, both unintentional and intentional. Sometimes a scribe would accidentally add to the text because of similar words or endings of clauses. At other times he would omit details through writing only once what should have been written twice or through missing words or lines with similar endings. Letters are sometimes confused, word order changed, or words substituted for other words through poor copies. On the other hand, there are variants that are intentional, arising not from an evil intent but from the desire to keep the sacred text "pure" and free from fault. For example, the copyist may correct what he believes are errors in spelling, grammar, and/or style. Or, for the sake of harmonizing the passage with other passages, especially in the Gospels, the scribe may "correct" the reading to make it reflect readings in the other parallels. Jerome complained about this: "The first reason for the many errors in our manuscripts is that one Gospel narrative of some event has been used to complete another. Then, in order to do away with divergencies, the first copy at hand has been taken as the type and the others have been corrected so as to agree with it."[7] Old Testament quotations in the New were harmonized to conform to the Hebrew Old Testament text. A scribe may also have interpolated into the text a comment originally written on a margin to make a passage clearer, for example, John 5:3b–4 in the King James Version.

Here is where the rules or canons of Textual Criticism are to be applied. These canons are inferences rather than axiomatic rules. One of the most important rules first put forth by Griesbach is that the reading that explains the origin of the other readings is to be accepted as the original one. A second rule is that the shortest reading is to be preferred, since it is the habit of scribes to add to the text rather than omit material. However,

---

7. *Epistle to Damasus*, V. 60.

since there are omissions that do occur through the scribe's error, this rule must be used carefully. A third canon is that the more obscure reading (that is, the more difficult for the scribe) is to be preferred over the clearer reading. Scribes sometimes had a tendency to clarify what they found difficult. These all deal with what Hort called "transcriptional probability." The fourth rule involves what Hort called "intrinsic probability" and is sometimes stated as preferring the reading that accords best with the writer's characteristics and tendencies as they are derived from the context and the writer's purposes. The greatest of caution must be used in applying these canons.

External Criticism

Here one relies on the answers to such questions as: How old are the witnesses supporting this reading? How old is the text itself? How widely distributed in the church are the witnesses that have this reading? There are some real pitfalls in these answers. Those who rest their case on the mere number of documents overlook the fact that the number of later manuscripts will naturally be larger. Thus, the text they exhibit will represent the largest number, while also being the least valuable. Likewise, the age of a document may not be as important as one first thinks. An "early" manuscript may exhibit a corrupted text, while a later copy may reflect a more reliable form of the text. Neither is the general appearance of the manuscript determinative, since a beautiful copy may have a corrupted text while a poorly done manuscript may have a reliable one. All of these factors have to be kept in mind when applying the methodology of External Criticism.

Classifying the Material

Through the processes indicated, each manuscript comes to be classified according to the corruptions and mistakes as well as the peculiarities it exhibits. Both accidental and intentional variations are considered. Then the process of comparing copies arranges them into groups according to the similarities of their readings. Hort was greatly influenced by the ideas of Lachmann, a classical scholar who held it was possible to draw inferences about the lost archetypes or ancestors of manuscripts through comparing the existing copies. His test was that all the copies with the same mistakes at the same places showed kinship or dependence on an archetype manuscript that contained these mistakes.

One could construct a "family tree" (or *stemma*) of manuscripts, following the principle that community of error indicated community of origin. This is the "genealogical method." By observing the close relationships between manuscripts, versional readings, and patristic quotations, family groups and text-types can be constructed. This process is much easier to follow in classical studies than in Bible scholarship because classical authors survive in much fewer copies. E. C. Colwell stated, "In any case, it is clear that in a field where no manuscripts have parents, where centuries and continents separate witnesses, the genealogical method is not of primary importance. Its importance lies in the realm of provincial history. It can chart the history of transmission in an area narrowly limited in time and space."[8]

Hort used this method to discredit the *Textus Receptus*, but he actually did not use it extensively in making his text. He recognized that the transmission of the New Testament was too complex for one to make extensive use of it. He even acknowledged that it would lead to two major ancestors and could not be carried further. Mixture or contamination from other manuscripts also complicates the picture. A number of efforts to follow the genealogical method have been attempted in the twentieth century with disappointing success.

In view of the shortcomings of the genealogical method, there has arisen an approach that may be called eclectic because it considers each variant and uses the principles and methods of Textual Criticism to make judgments. An eclectic scholar does not regard one text-type as exclusively preserving the original text, as Hort largely did. He followed his Neutral text, except in the case of certain omissions in Luke's Gospel made by Western manuscripts he followed. According to the eclectic method, the text will show the weight given to certain text-types variant by variant. Those editors who consider the Alexandrian text-type (including Hort's Neutral) to be the better text will construct such a text. If more weight is given to Western readings, the text will be influenced accordingly. For instance, the *Revised Standard Version* reflects the Alexandrian text, as do the *New English Bible* and the United Bible Societies' *Greek New Testament*. But, the *Jerusalem Bible* reflects a Western type of text that rests strongly on early versions and certain church fathers.

J. H. Ropes in Volume III of *The Beginnings of Christianity* (edited by Jackson and Lake), did a monumental study of the text of Acts, where the Western texts present a series of expanded readings. Although Ropes admitted the early existence of the Western text, he would allow only four places in Acts where the Western text preserved the original readings over the Alexandrian (20:15; 21:1; 21:25; 27:5). Ropes thus basically confirmed the position of Westcott-Hort on the text of Acts.

Two leading British scholars are advocates of what they call "thoroughgoing eclecticism." They are Professor G. D. Kilpatrick of Oxford University and his student, J. K. Elliott. E. C. Colwell defined this approach: "The editor chooses that reading which commends itself to him

---

8. E. C. Colwell, "Genealogical Method: Its Achievements and Its Limitations," in *Studies in Methodology in Textual Criticism of the New Testament*, ed. B. M. Metzger (Leiden: Brill, 1969), p. 82.

as fitting the context, whether in style, or idea, or contextual reference. Such an editor relegates the manuscripts to the role of the supplier of readings."[9] This method has been criticized because of its neglect of external considerations and its total reliance on internal probabilities. It has a strong subjective element. Dowell Flatt, in an article in *Restoration Quarterly*, listed a number of problems with this approach, while noting some of its benefits,[10] to which J. K. Elliott replied in the same journal.[11] Elliott tried to bolster his case by appealing to the many instances that Metzger's commentary on the United Bible Societies' *Greek New Testament* uses eclecticism. Metzger writes, "One may conclude, therefore, that although considerations of the literary usage of a New Testament author will be of considerable value to the textual critic, it must not be made the primary criterion in the evaluation of variant readings to the virtual neglect of external evidence."[12]

There are places where manuscript evidence divides itself in such a way that much depends on the subjective judgment of the scholar. One can see this in reading the comments about the differences of opinion on certain passages in Metzger's *A Textual Commentary . . .*, which accompanies the United Bible Societies' *Greek New Testament*. Here one may hope that further discoveries and studies will bring more clarity to those problem passages.

Kurt Aland in the Introduction to the twenty-sixth edition of the Nestle-Aland *Novum Testamentum Graece* (1981) rejects Hort's genealogical method. He writes:

> Decisions must be made one by one, instance by instance. This method has been characterized as eclecticism, but wrongly so. After carefully establishing the variety of readings offered in a passage and the possibilities of their interpretation, it must always then be determined afresh on the basis of external and internal criteria which of these readings (and frequently they are quite numerous) is the original, from which the others may be regarded as derivative. From the perspective of our present knowledge, this local genealogical method (if it must be given a name) is the only one which meets the requirement of the New Testament textual tradition.[13]

---

9. E. C. Colwell, "Hort Redivivus: A Plea and a Program," in *Studies in Methodology in Textual Criticism of the New Testament*, ed. by B. M. Metzger (Leiden: Brill, 1969), p. 154.

10. D. Flatt, "Thoroughgoing Eclecticism As a Method of Textual Criticism," RQ 18 (1975): 102–114.

11. J. K. Elliott, "In Defense of Thoroughgoing Eclecticism in New Testament Textual Criticism," RQ 21 (1978): pp. 95–115.

12. B. M. Metzger, *The Text of the New Testament*, 2nd ed. (New York: Oxford University, 1968), pp. 178–179.

13. Nestle-Aland, *Novum Testamentum Graece*, 26th ed. (Stuttgart: Deutsche Bibelstiftung), p. 43.

While Aland differs from Kilpatrick and Elliott in his approaches and contends that he has made a break with both Tischendorf and Westcott-Hort, one is still impressed with how close the United Bible Societies' Greek text follows the patterns set forth by those three pioneers of modern textual studies more than a century ago.

Recent discoveries of papyri have broadened our understanding of the early history of the text. One can also view the future with an increasing hope that greater light will be shed on the history of the New Testament text through the advances provided by the computer age. Computer capabilities provide for the storage of great amounts of information readily available for comparative study, and they offer exciting possibilities for future advances in textual studies.

17

Greek Word Studies

Leon Crouch

The study of Greek words may vary according to the purpose of the study. One may be interested in only the general meaning of a word, or the goal may be to ascertain the precise meaning of a word in a particular verse or statement. The latter purpose involves a process that demands much effort and care.

Principles and Methodology

The following is a suggested method for doing a thorough study of a word from the Greek New Testament.

Identifying the Word's Root

The first step in the process is to discover, if possible, the root from which the word is derived. Such a step may be helpful in finding a common meaning that accounts for the different senses in which the word is used, based on the assumption that the root always conveys the basic meaning or idea in each derived meaning.[1] Although there is generally a fundamental motif in a word, which tends to endure no matter what changes occur, the interpreter must avoid the pitfall of "etymological fallacy." Be aware that the original meaning may not always apply.[2]

Some of the root meanings of Greek words are catalogued in a small pamphlet by T. Rogers entitled *A Practical List of Greek Word Roots with*

1. J. D. Grassmick, *Principles and Practice of Greek Exegesis* (Dallas, TX: Dallas Theological Seminary, 1974), p. 155; B. M. Metzger, *Lexical Aids for Students of New Testament Greek* (Princeton, NJ: Privately Published, 1973), p. 42.

2. J. W. Roberts, "The Language Background of the New Testament," RQ 5 (1962): 200.

Greek and English Derivatives. It should be kept in mind that many roots are unknown at the present.

Discovering the Word's Use Outside the New Testament

The second step in a word study is to consider the use of the word in literature apart from the New Testament. This step will help in establishing most of the possible meanings for its use in the New Testament. The procedure is a matter of historical research and involves tracing the word from its first known use to the New Testament period.

First, classical usage should be considered. The classical period for Greek covers from about 900 B.C. to 330 B.C. The actual study of most words in this period would be a lifetime project, but fortunately the evidence of word usage for this period is catalogued in *A Greek-English Lexicon,* prepared by H. G. Liddell and R. Scott. This work is of tremendous value because it covers most of the literature from Homer into the New Testament period. The references may be checked by consulting the various writings published in the Loeb Classical Library, made available by the Harvard University Press.

In order to gain the most from the Liddell-Scott lexicon, the introduction must be consulted. It is necessary to be familiar with the abbreviations of the works cited. Properly used, this source gives rich dividends.

After considering the word in the classics, one should give his attention to the use of the word in the LXX. This source will cover the period from about 270 B.C. to near 200 B.C. A study of this material will involve a look at the Hebrew word or words, translated by the Greek term. This potentially tedious task is made much simpler by using the concordance prepared by E. Hatch and H. A. Redpath. These two men included in their work not only a complete concordance to the LXX but also a complete concordance to the text of the apocryphal books as well as other Greek versions of the Old Testament used by Origen in the *Hexapla.* Hatch and Redpath also list the Hebrew word translated by the Greek word being studied and every place it is so used. There are also some good and usable editions of the LXX available. The one edited by H. B. Swete, *The Old Testament in Greek,* is useful but hard to find. Perhaps the *Septuaginta* edited by A. Rahlfs is the one most readily available.

Within this process, the exegete attempts to ascertain the original life situation within which the word was used in each period. This search will often help in learning why the author chose the particular word to express his thought and will provide a point of reference for tracing the development of meaning. It will be discovered that the LXX has given a new or modified meaning to some Greek words.

The new meaning is traceable to the influence of the Hebrew word(s) that it translates. That means that the exegete must also study the Hebrew words. For this part of the study, one of the very helpful tools is

A Hebrew and English Lexicon of the Old Testament, edited by Francis Brown, Samuel R. Driver and Charles A. Briggs. This lexicon can help shed a great deal of light on the meaning of New Testament words used in the LXX. This is especially true if we accept one scholar's view that "the language of the New Testament is a special kind of Jewish biblical Greek (both in syntax and in the thought-forms it expresses)."[3]

The next stage in the study of a Greek word requires an investigation of its use in the Koine period of the language (330 B.C.–A.D. 330). The vast number of inscriptions and papyri found over the years contribute toward understanding many New Testament words. From these sources one can learn how the word was used by the common people around the time of the New Testament writings. Since it would be impossible for the exegete to study all these sources, he needs to rely on the helpful book by James Moulton and George Milligan, *The Vocabulary of the Greek Testament*. The works of Adolf Deissmann are also useful for this period.

Examining the Word Elsewhere in the New Testament

The steps mentioned above are all basically historical in nature. When that information has been gathered, it is time for studying the word in the New Testament itself. Every use of the word should be considered, especially in those places where it is used by the author under consideration. A good concordance is essential for this part of the study. One of the better ones is the *Concordance to the Greek Testament* by W. Moulton and A. Geden.

Studying the Word in Its Specific Sentence

Finally, the word must be considered in the particular sentence being studied. Some questions that must be answered are: Does the word in this place have its roots in classical Greek, in the LXX, or in the Koine? Does this New Testament writer give the word a new and Christianized meaning? These questions must be answered in light of the immediate context. Here is the place to use such lexicons as *A Greek-English Lexicon of the New Testament and Other Early Christian Literature* by Walter Bauer (revised and translated by W. F. Arndt and F. W. Gingrich, and revised and augmented by F. W. Gingrich and F. W. Danker). It is also helpful to consult word-study books, such as the *Theological Dictionary of the New Testament*, edited by G. Kittel and G. Friedrich; and the *Dictionary of New Testament Theology*, edited by Colin Brown.

When these steps have been completed, the exegete should have recorded a summary of the earliest discoverable use of the word and its

---

3. D. Hill, *Greek Words and Hebrew Meanings: Studies in the Semantics of Soteriological Terms* (Cambridge: University Press, 1967), p. 19. Cf. J. H. Moulton, W. F. Howard, and N. Turner, *A Grammar of New Testament Greek*, 4 vols. (Edinburgh: T. & T. Clark, 1908–76), vol. 3: *Syntax*, by N. Turner, pp. 4–5.

development up to and into the sentence under investigation. Here is the point where commentaries should be consulted. Those which are based on the Greek text are most likely to be of help with any additional information about the word.

A Study of *harpazō* in 1 Thessalonians 4:17

As an example of the procedure suggested above, one may look at the word *harpazō* in 1 Thessalonians 4:17. This word is chosen because of its importance, not so much in the verse but because of the teaching that has gathered around the concept thought to be contained in it. Paul uses the future-passive-indicative, first-person-plural form of the word, and it is translated "shall be caught up" in the New American Standard Bible. The Latin translation of the Greek word is *rapere* in this verse, and from that word is derived the English word *rapture*.

The concept of those who hold premillennial views of Christ's second coming is stated by Walvoord: "The Scriptures predict that the church will be raptured or 'caught up' to heaven at the coming of the Lord for them."[4] The specifics of this vary, but most hold to the idea that 1 Thessalonians 4:16–17 teaches that only the saints, or church people, will be resurrected and that the wicked dead will remain in the grave, while the wicked living will be left on earth to enter the so-called Great Tribulation. The question is whether *harpazō* gives any basis for this view.

The purpose of this study is to ascertain exactly what the word means in the specific context and to learn if the application by Walvoord and others is valid.

Pre-Christian Use of harpazō

Etymology. The word *harpazō* is derived from the root *harp-* , which means "to seize." This root is also in *harpax,* "a robber."[5] The same root is found in *harpagmos* (robbery, prize, booty) and *harpagē* (robbery, plunder, what has been stolen).[6] The etymology of *harpazō* indicates "to snatch, seize, rob, carry off, or plunder."

harpazō in Classical Greek: From the time of Homer, *harpazō* is used to mean "to snatch away, to carry off" (*Il.* 3.444; 17.62; *Od.* 10.48). This ninth century B.C. writer also used the word to mean "to seize hastily" or "to snatch up" (*Il.* 12:445). Aeschylus (about 484 B.C.) used the word to mean

---

4. J. F. Walvoord, *The Rapture Question* (Grand Rapids: Zondervan, 1970), p. 8.

5. T. Rogers, *A Practical List of Greek Word Roots With Greek and English Derivatives* (Grand Rapids: Baker, 1981, reprint), p. 11.

6. W. Bauer, *A Greek-English Lexicon of the New Testament and Other Early Christian Literature,* 2nd ed., revised by W. F. Arndt, F. W. Gingrich, and F. W. Danker (Chicago: University Press, 1979), p. 109.

"to seize and overpower" (Aesch. *Theb.* 259). A few years later (ca. 423 B.C.), Thucydides used *harpazō* to mean "plunder" (*Thuc.* 1.5). The word is found many other times in this literature but with essentially the same meanings.[7]

harpazō *in the Old Testament:* The word *harpazō* is found in the LXX canonical books thirty-four times. It is used to translate four different words: *gāzal*, *ṭārāph*, *ḥātaph*, and *lākad.*[8]

This word is used to translate *gāzal* sixteen times in the LXX. The meaning of the word in Leviticus 6:4 (5:23 in the Hebrew text) is "to seize." In Job 20:19 the word is translated "plundered" and in Job 24:2 it has the meaning of "carry off." The root of *gāzal* has in it the implication of violence that goes beyond the mere taking by force of another's property, although that idea is clear (cf. Judg. 9:25). The word *gāzal* usually refers to shameful deeds. For example, it is used of tearing a fatherless child from the breast (Job 24:9), and Micah used this word to refer to flaying people, although his use is apparently figurative (3:2).[9]

The use of *harpazō* to translate *gāzal* seems to add a little tone of violence to it, which was lacking in the earlier uses. The basic meanings of "snatch, carry off, and seize" are still in the word, however.

One finds that *harpazō* is used to translate the Hebrew word *ṭārāph* fourteen times. The basic meaning of this Hebrew word is "tear, rend, pluck." Thus *harpazō* is used in Ezekiel 22:25, where the princes of Israel are described as "roaring lions seizing prey." It is used again in verse 27, where the princes are described as "wolves ravening to shed blood" for dishonest gain. Hosea 5:14 uses *harpazō* to describe God's treatment of the wicked. It will be like a lion that tears its prey. Israel will be like a lion's whelp which selects and carries off its prey (Mic. 5:8).[10]

The use of *harpazō* to translate *ṭārāph* continues the tone of violence, perhaps even in a stronger sense than before. The root meaning of *harpazō* is not as evident when used for this Hebrew word.

The word *harpazō* translates the Hebrew word *ḥātāph* only in Judges 21:21 and Psalm 10:9. The verse in Judges instructs the Benjaminite men to "seize for yourselves every man a wife of the daughters of Selom." The

7. H. G. Liddell and R. Scott, *A Greek-English Lexicon*, 9th ed., revised and augmented by H. S. Jones and R. McKenzie (Oxford: Clarendon, 1968), p. 228.

8. E. Hatch and H. A. Redpath, *A Concordance to the Septuagint and Other Greek Versions of the Old Testament*, 2 vols. (Graz: Akademische Druck-u. Verlagsanstalt, 1954), I:160.

9. F. Brown, S. R. Driver, and C. Briggs, eds., *A Hebrew and English Lexicon of the Old Testament* (Oxford: Clarendon, 1906; reprint ed., Oxford: Clarendon, 1939), pp. 159–60. Cf. J. Schupphaus, "gazal," in *Theological Dictionary of the Old Testament*, eds., G. J. Botterweck and H. Ringgren, trans. by J. T. Willis (Grand Rapids: Eerdmans, 1975), 2:456–58.

10. Brown, Driver, and Briggs, pp. 382–83.

meaning is evidently to take by force, and any objection would be taken care of by the Benjaminites. The verse in Psalm 10 has *harpazō* twice, and both times it refers to the ungodly man who lies in wait to ravish the poor. These uses of *harpazō* add nothing to the study.

The fourth Hebrew word translated by *harpazō* is *lākad*. It is found only in Amos 3:4, where the prophet asks if a lion will utter his voice if he has taken nothing. Basically, *lākad* means "to capture, seize, take." The use of *harpazō* here is with the same meaning indicated in the root.

Finally, *harpazō* is used in the LXX noncanonical books several times with the meaning of "to captivate, ravish" (cf. Judt. 16:9).[11] The only use of the word in these books that has the meaning closely related to the idea of rapture or being caught up is in Wisdom 4:11, which says that Enoch "was caught up."[12] A different word is used everywhere else that the idea of rapture or being caught up is found in the LXX or secular Greek, from Homer onward.

The use of *harpazō* in the LXX sheds almost no light on the use of the word in 1 Thessalonians 4:17. The passage in the Book of Wisdom has a connection but helps very little.

harpazō *in the Papyri:* This word is used in the papyri several times, according to Moulton and Milligan's *The Vocabulary of the Greek Testament*. They show that it is found in a papyrus in the British Museum (dated about A.D. 14–15), where it refers to the taking away by force the things that fell to one's lot (P Lond 357[8]). A compound form of the verb is found in P Oxy 1:37, which says that someone "carried the small body off." This last statement is dated A.D. 49. Most of the occurrences of *harpazō* in the papyri are later than the New Testament and are not important for this study.

harpazō *in the New Testament*

Harpazō is found in the New Testament fourteen times.[13] The writers use the word to mean "carry off one's property," as in Matthew 12:29 and 13:19. It is also used to describe a wolf coming into a flock of sheep so that he might "snatch them" away (John 10:12). Jesus knew that the Jews were intending to "take him by force" to make him king (John 6:15). Jesus used *harpazō* in his words of assurance to his disciples in the sense that no one could "snatch" them out of his hand (John 10:28, 29). Luke tells of the concern of the Roman commander about Paul's being torn to pieces by the mob, so that he ordered his men to "take him away from them by

---

11. Liddell and Scott, p. 228.
12. E. Tiedtke, "harpazō," in *The New International Dictionary of New Testament Theology*, ed., C. Brown (Grand Rapids: Zondervan, 1975–1978), 3:601–02.
13. W. F. Moulton and A. S. Geden, *A Concordance to the Greek Testament*, 4th ed., rev. by H. K. Moulton (Edinburgh: T. & T. Clark, 1963), pp. 107–8.

force" (Acts 23:10). Jude uses the word to indicate the need to "snatch" or "pull" some from the fire (Jude 23).

The word *harpazō* is also used to describe the Spirit of the Lord "snatching" Philip away to another place (Acts 8:39). A similar use of the word is in 2 Corinthians 12:2, 4, where Paul speaks of a man who "was caught up to the third heaven" or "caught up into Paradise." The same idea is apparently found in Revelation 12:5, where the child of the woman "was caught up to God and to His throne."[14]

The use of *harpazō* in Matthew 11:12 is difficult to determine. The meaning of this passage depends on whether the verb *biazetai* is taken as a passive or a middle voice and whether it is used with or without a favorable meaning. Five possible views of the passage are given by Frank Pack, who concludes that it is to be taken as a middle voice and with a favorable meaning. He also shows that *harpazō* is elsewhere used with both a good and bad meaning, but takes the favorable meaning in this verse. The two verbs harmonize.[15] The verse seems to be saying something like "from the days of John the Baptist until now the kingdom is pressing forward vigorously and vigorous men are eagerly taking possession of it."[16]

harpazō *in 1 Thessalonians 4:17*

The use of *harpazō* in this verse may have some of the concepts found in the word elsewhere, but the nearest parallel is in 2 Corinthians 12:2, 4. The verb implies violent action, which may be for the benefit of its object (Cf. Acts 23:10),[17] but the word may also imply some harm to its object (cf. Judg. 9:25; John 10:12).

In the context of this verse, Paul is giving assurance to the Christians who were troubled over the fate of their loved ones who had died. They evidently thought that since they had died, the promises about heaven had been missed. The apostle, therefore, gives additional information about the coming of Christ.

The point is that those who had died would be raised from the dead before any of those still living on earth received any of the promised blessings. The resurrection of the dead is based on the fact of Christ's resurrection, which they had already accepted. The dead would be raised and together with those still living would be "snatched away" at the same time to meet the Lord in the air. The dead will miss nothing.

It would seem that *harpazō* in this verse has the same meaning that it does in its root form and in classical Greek. The LXX Book of Wisdom has

---

14. Bauer, Arndt, Gingrich, and Danker, p. 109.

15. F. Pack, "Biblical Exegesis: An Exegesis of Matthew 11:12, 13," *The Exegete* 1 (1981): 4–6.

16. W. Hendriksen, *Exposition of the Gospel According to Matthew* (Grand Rapids: Baker, 1973), pp. 488–89.

17. Bauer, Arndt, Gingrich, and Danker, *Lexicon*.

the same meaning in its use of *harpazō*. There is also basically the same thought in the word as in Paul's use of it in 2 Corinthians 12.

In 1 Thessalonians, *harpazō* has nothing to do with a secret snatching away of Christians or the church. There is no point in the context that indicates a second resurrection for those who were wicked, since the wicked are not mentioned. Therefore, the use of *harpazō* to imply a secret rapture or to imply a second resurrection is not in harmony with this passage nor with the rest of the New Testament.

18

Interpreting Greek Syntax

Carroll D. Osburn

The Greek Testament remains the ultimate source to which one must turn in a quest for biblical certainty. In order to be understood accurately, however, the Greek text must be read by utilizing the normative Greek syntax in common usage at the time the text was written. For centuries, the failure in this regard has resulted in considerable abuse of the Greek text. Robertson has noted: "It is the commonest grammatical vice for one to make a conjectural translation into English and then to discuss the syntactical propriety of the Greek tense on the basis of this translation."[1] Unfortunately there are any number of functionally monolingual individuals who are insistent upon pressing their notions by appealing to "the Greek," arriving at such syntactical monstrosities as "*eth* in the King James Version correctly preserves the continuous action of the Greek present tense." Exemplary of what can happen with such pretentiousness is the *Concordant Literal Translation*, in which obligatory norms of the Greek language are dismissed in cavalier fashion, resulting in nonsensical readings.[2] It is tragic indeed that the biblical text must be subjected to the abuse brought about by such superficial acquaintance with Greek syntax. In this brief essay it is impossible to treat the broad range of syntactical matters of importance to New Testament

This essay was presented originally to the Wycliffe Bible Translators, Guatemala City, October 20, 1982.

1. A. T. Robertson, *A Grammar of the Greek New Testament in the Light of Historical Research* (Nashville: Broadman, 1934), p. 821.
2. See my "How Not to Translate the Bible," *Firm Foundation* 96 (1979): 246.

exegesis,[3] but perhaps selected examples will suffice to illustrate the vital importance of idiomatic Greek syntax as an alternative to the superficiality often encountered when zealous but misinformed persons attempt to prove preconceived notions by distorted appeals to "the Greek."

The Greek Article—John 1:1

The *New World Translation* of the Jehovah's Witnesses renders John 1:1 as "and the Word was a god," a translation that discounts Jesus as the second person of the trinity and considers him merely "a god" in a pantheon of lesser divinities. The attempt to justify this reading in the *NWT* appendix (p. 774) is:

> The reason for their rendering of the Greek word "divine," and not "God," is that it is the Greek noun *theos* without the definite article, hence an anarthrous *theos*. The God with whom the Word or Logos was originally is designated here by the Greek expression *ho theos, theos* preceded by the definite article *ho,* hence an articular *theos.* Careful translators recognize that the articular construction points to an entity, a personality, whereas an anarthrous construction points to a quality about someone.

Thus a rule has been formulated: *ho theos* = God; *theos* = a god. But is this rule consistent with ancient Greek usage?

Although R. W. Funk has analyzed the Greek article in both classical and Hellenistic Greek (concluding that the use or nonuse of the Greek article is frequently only a matter of literary style),[4] as early as 1933 an attempt was made by E. C. Colwell to formulate a definite rule for the use of the Greek article: ". . . a definite predicate nominative has the article when it follows the verb; it does not have the article when it precedes the verb."[5] The importance of this grammatical norm is stated succinctly by R. H. Countess:

1) Definite predicate nouns here regularly take the article.
2) The exceptions are for the most part due to a change in word order: (a) Definite predicate nouns which follow the verb (this is the usual order) usually take the article; (b) Definite predicate nouns which precede the verb usually lack the article; (c) Proper names regularly lack the article in

---

3. See also J. H. Greenlee, "The Importance of Syntax for the Proper Understanding of the Sacred Text of the New Testament," EvQ 44 (1972): 131–146.

4. R. W. Funk, "The Syntax of the Greek Article: Its Importance for Critical Pauline Problems" (Unpublished Ph.D. dissertation, Vanderbilt University, 1953).

5. E. C. Colwell, "A Definite Rule for the Use of the Article in the Greek New Testament," JBL 52 (1933): 12–21.

the predicate; (d) Predicate nominatives in relative clauses regularly follow the verb whether or not they have the article.[6]

In John 1:49, for instance, Nathaniel refers to Jesus with two titles. "You are the Son of God" is articular; "You are King of Israel" is anarthrous but must not be misread to mean only "a king of Israel." Further, in John 19:21, "King of the Jews" occurs twice. In the first occurrence, the Jews demanded that Pilate alter the inscription over the cross, which read "The King of the Jews" (articular). In the second occurrence, they wanted instead the inscription to read "I am King of the Jews" (anarthrous and preceding the verb). Again, to read "a king of the Jews" would be to miss the point, for the objection was to the factualness of the inscription. Equally illustrative are the seven instances of Colwell's rule in the parable of the sower in Matthew 13:37–39. The first five predicate nouns are articular and follow the verb. The last two are anarthrous and precede the verb. The last two are just as definite as the five above; the only difference is that John omitted the article when the noun preceded the copula. Colwell has performed a genuine service for those interested in Greek syntax in pointing out that a predicate noun that precedes the verb and has no article is definite, whereas a predicate noun that follows the verb and has no article is less definite.

Colwell concludes his assessment by citing John 1:1 as an example in which the anarthrous predicate noun is to be translated as definite, observing that calling Jesus "God" cannot be regarded as strange here in John's prologue when, in fact, the Fourth Gospel concludes in 20:28 with the confession of Thomas, "My Lord and my God!" Countess rightly concludes his analysis of the *NWT* of John 1:1 that Jesus was "a god" with three telling criticisms: (1) this rendering ignores an established nuance of the Greek language; (2) it follows a fabricated rule that the *NWT* translators themselves ignore 94 percent of the time[7]; and (3) it alters the text to accommodate a preconceived theological position.

The Present Indicative—Matthew 19:9

For this writer the intricate problem of divorce and remarriage is a matter of continuing study. One postulate detrimental to this study is the "present tense argument," in which it is advanced that *moichatai* in Matthew 19:9 *must* mean "continues to commit adultery" because the Greek present tense *necessitates* continuity. However, like the example men-

6. R. H. Countess, "The Translation of *THEOS* in the *New World Translation*," BETS 10 (1967): 153–160. See also B. M. Metzger, "Jehovah's Witnesses and Jesus Christ," TToday 10 (1953): 65–85.

7. Countess (p. 160) notes that in John 1:1–18 the *NWT* reads "God" four times in which the noun is anarthrous.

tioned above, this argument (1) is oblivious to established Greek usage; (2) follows a fabricated rule which cannot be carried consistently through the Greek New Testament; and (3) is an attempt to find in "the Greek" justification for a theological position previously arrived at.[8]

1. The attempt to require continuity in *moichatai* in verse 9 based upon the present tense is an abuse of Greek syntax resulting from a misunderstanding of Greek mood distinctions. In moods other than the indicative, such as the imperative, subjunctive, and infinitive, the aorist tense is normally used regardless of the type of action involved. However, when the writer wishes to call special attention to the continuity of an action, he uses the present tense of those moods. In the indicative mood, though, a different situation prevails. Whereas the imperfect indicative generally denotes continuity in past time—as opposed to the aorist indicative, in which continuity may or may not be involved but is not specified[9]—in the present indicative no clear distinction can be drawn from the tense between that action which is specifically ongoing and that which is not. When those making the "present tense argument" on Matthew 19:9 appeal to the present imperative *dzeteite*, "keep on seeking," (Matt. 6:33; Col. 3:1), they evidence confusion regarding this vital Greek mood distinction.

As Turner puts it:

> In order to say *I walk* without reference to time, English can be unambiguous; not so Greek. It must use the indicative of the present. . . . Thus in Greek one seldom knows apart from context whether the pres. indic. means *I walk* or *I am walking*. In other moods than indic., of course, the problem does not arise. . . . One must always bear that in mind for exegesis.[10]

Actually, this elementary point is made in the opening chapters of beginning grammars, such as lesson 3 of Machen: "In the present tense there is in Greek no distinction between *I loose*, which simply represents the action as taking place in present time; and *I am loosing*, which calls attention to the continuance of the action."[11] Accordingly, while it is true that in moods other than the indicative the present tense denotes continuing action, in the indicative mood itself no distinction can be drawn

---

8. See further discussion in my "The Present Indicative in Matthew 19:9," RQ 24 (1981): 193–203. Cf. R. Deaver, "The Present Indicative in Matthew 19:9 (A Response)," *The Spiritual Sword* 13 (1982): 27–32, who claims to have originated the "present tense argument."

9. F. Stagg, "The Abused Aorist," JBL 92 (1972): 222–231.

10. *A Grammar of New Testament Greek* (Edinburgh: T. & T. Clark, 1963), 3, p. 60.

11. J. G. Machen, *New Testament Greek for Beginners* (Toronto: Macmillan, 1923), pp. 21–22.

from the present tense between that action which is continuing and that which is not so specified. That is to say, it is not legitimate to argue solely from the present tense apart from the indicative mood that continuity must be involved in verse 9. Thus, *moichatai* may involve continuity here, but is not required to do so by the tense.

2. The attempt to require continuity in *moichatai* in verse 9 is oblivious to the distinction between the "descriptive present," denoting the simple action of the verb in present time without regard to its continuance, and the "iterative present," which specifically denotes continuity. Now the "present tense argument" is predicated upon *moichatai* being, not descriptive ("commits adultery"), but iterative ("continues to commit adultery"). Yet those advocating the argument confusedly appeal to the "descriptive present" to specify continuity, apparently unaware (a) that while the "descriptive present" is durative, nothing is specified as to the extent of the duration; (b) that it is the "iterative present" that they need for their argument; and (c) that while every iterative is durative, not every durative is iterative. Robertson rightly notes the durative action of the "descriptive present," which he graphically depicts as (——), illustrating with Matthew 8:25, *apollumetha*, "we are perishing," a term that aptly describes the action going on at the moment but does not *specify* a repetitive or continual perishing, which would be iterative (. . . . .) rather than descriptive.[12] One has only to turn the page in Robertson's grammar to see clearly this vital distinction. Just because a verb may be durative does not necessitate its being iterative. The appeal to the vast number of "descriptive presents" in the New Testament to prove continuity in Matthew 19:9 is of no value in view of the facts that the "descriptive present" does not specify continuity, and that the "present tense argument" must read verse 9 as an iterative.

Now the "descriptive present" is common, occurring over 700 times in Matthew to describe an action going on at the time, but with *no specific reference to continuity or repetition*. On the other hand, the "iterative present" occurs only infrequently, as in Matthew 15:23, where the Canaanite woman "keeps crying out" for Jesus to heal her daughter. That the present indicative in this verse is "iterative" is clear from the imperfect indicative in the preceding verse, in which the woman is said *specifically* to have been "continuing to cry out." As Robertson notes, "The verb and the context must decide."[13] Similarly in 1 John 3:9, "does not continue to sin" is warranted from the following present infinitive, which cannot mean other than "is not able to continue in sin." There is nothing so explicit in Matthew 19 or in the verb *moichatai* to necessitate an iterative in verse 9.

---

12. Robertson, p. 879.
13. Ibid.

3. The attempt to require continuity in *moichatai* in verse 9 ignores the fact that in this context "commits adultery" is a "gnomic present," customarily employed when a general truth is under consideration. It is treated by Robertson as a usage of the present tense that does not *specify* continuity.[14] There are several uses of this "gnomic present" in Matthew, as in 7:17. It is this "gnomic present" that occurs in Matthew 19:9, when Jesus states the general truth that "whoever divorces his wife except for unchastity and marries another commits adultery." In this "gnomic present," continuity may or may not be involved, but if it is, it is not *specified*.

4. The attempt to read every present-tense verb in the Greek language as ongoing action would lead to ridiculous renderings. For instance, the verb *agoradzei*, "buys a field" (Matt. 13:14), must not be misconstrued to mean that the man "kept on buying the field," and *staurountai*, "they crucify him" (Matt. 27:38), would be nonsensical if seen as continuous action. In both instances, Matthew has employed the "historic present" with no notion of continuity involved. Failure to become thoroughly acquainted with the wide range of idiomatic uses of the Greek present tense has resulted in a fabricated rule that is not in concert with established Greek syntax.

In view of these considerations, it cannot be said that the present indicative in Matthew 19:9 cannot mean other than continuous action, for any such assertion (1) blatantly ignores vital mood distinctions as far as the present tense is concerned; (2) confusedly makes no distinction between the "descriptive" and "iterative" present; (3) disregards the "gnomic" use of *moichatai* in verse 9, in which continuity is not explicit; and (4) is a contrived argument designed to support a previously arrived at understanding. The "present tense argument" on Matthew 19:9 originated as a polemical maneuver and is a grammatical oddity best forgotten.

The Third Person Imperative—Acts 2:38

The phrase "for the remission of sins" in Acts 2:38 is commonly understood as modifying both of the preceding imperatives, "repent" and "be baptized." For instance, Lake and Cadbury observe that "*eis aphesin ton hamartion* should be connected with *metanoesate* as with *baptistheto* (cf. Luke iii. 3 *baptisma metanoias eis aphesin hamartion*) since this association of ideas is shown to be Lukan by xxiv. 47 . . . and Acts v. 31."[15] Similarly, "remission of sins" is unhesitatingly connected with both im-

---

14. Ibid., p. 866.
15. K. Lake and H. J. Cadbury, *The Beginnings of Christianity: Part I, The Acts of the Apostles*, F. J. Foakes Jackson and K. Lake, eds. (London: Macmillan, 1933), iv, 26.

peratives by F. F. Bruce,[16] B. Newman,[17] G. H. C. Macgregor,[18] and most others. Nevertheless, M. Barth has suggested that "for the forgiveness of sins" in Acts 2:38 means that baptism is received *in hope of* forgiveness,[19] a postulation that led even the Baptist writer G. R. Beasley-Murray[20] to point out that "this is surely pressing language expressive of purpose in a manner never intended." As Beasley-Murray puts it, "Peter calls for his hearers to repent and be baptized, with a view to receiving forgiveness and the Spirit,"[21] and E. Schweizer writes, "2:38 teaches nothing other than that for Luke baptism belongs to the much more important fact of conversion."[22] Even the Roman Catholic writer Schnackenburg[23] takes to task the Baptist writer Schneider[24] for separating conversion and baptism, thus virtually denying any inner connection between the two. The only reason for the attempt to separate the two imperatives in 2:38 is to evade the force and necessity of baptism for salvation due to a "faith only" predisposition.

It has been argued in certain Baptist circles that (1) since verbs must agree with their subjects in person and number, and (2) since "repent" here is second person plural and "be baptized" is third person singular, (3) it necessarily follows that repentance and baptism in Acts 2:38 cannot be combined so as to have both modified by the phrase "for the remission of sins." For instance, Ben Bogard, former dean of the Missionary Baptist Institute in Little Rock, argued in his debate with N. B. Hardeman in 1938[25] that "You can't join the second person plural to the third person singular by the conjunction 'and' with the same predicate to save your life without violating the rule of Greek, Latin, and English grammar." Similarly, L. S. Ballard argued in his debate with T. B. Warren[26] that "'repent' cannot have the same nominative or subject that 'be baptized' has, neither can 'be baptized' have the same nominative or subject that 're-

16. F. F. Bruce, *The Acts of the Apostles*, 2nd ed. (Grand Rapids: Eerdmans, 1952), p. 98.

17. B. Newman and E. Nida, *A Translator's Handbook on the Acts of the Apostles* (London: U.B.S., 1972), p. 60.

18. G.H.C. Macgregor, *The Acts of the Apostles* (Nashville: Abingdon, 1954), p. 49.

19. M. Barth, *Die Taufe ein Sakrament?* (Zürich: Zollikon, 1951), p. 140.

20. G. R. Beasley-Murray, *Baptism in the New Testament* (Grand Rapids: Eerdmans, 1973), pp. 102–108.

21. Ibid., p. 105.

22. E. Schweizer, *"pneuma,"* T.W.N.T., 6:411.

23. R. Schnackenburg, *Baptism in the Thought of St. Paul*, trans. by G. R. Beasley-Murray (Oxford: Blackwell, 1964), p. 63, fn. 122.

24. J. Schneider, *Die Passionsmystik des Paulus* (Leipzig: 1929), p. 34, fn. 2.

25. N. B. Hardeman and B. M. Bogard, *Hardeman-Bogard Debate* (Nashville: Gospel Advocate, 1938), pp. 106–107.

26. T. B. Warren and L. S. Ballard, *Warren-Ballard Debate* (Jonesboro, AR: National Christian Press, 1979), pp. 168–169.

pent' has." It may be suggested that the matter cannot be resolved by reading theological presuppositions into the Greek text. The syntactical question that must be asked is: How does the third person imperative function in Acts 2:38?

Initially it must be observed that normal Greek usage expects concord in person and number between subject and verb. Robertson, however, notes several idiomatic Greek usages in which such agreement in person and number does not exist between subject and verb.[27] For instance, in Attic a neuter plural inanimate subject takes a singular verb. This idiomatic usage continues in various New Testament texts, such as John 9:3, "in order that the works of God [nominative neuter plural] may be made manifest [third person singular]" and Luke 8:30, "many demons [nominative neuter plural] entered [third person singular]." Another established idiomatic usage in which concord between subject and verb does not exist is in the "Pindaric construction," in which, when several subjects are united, the verb is put in the singular (James 5:2f; Matt. 6:19; Mark 4:41; and 1 Cor. 15:50). Similar idiomatic usages without concord in person and number are "collective substantives," such as "multitude" and "crowd," which often take singular verbs, and the tendency for the verb to have the singular when it serves a subject having both a singular and a plural, as in John 2:2; 3:22; 18:15; and Acts 11:14. It is vital to note that these idiomatic usages are not violations of a rule but established usages in their own right. Consequently, it is syntactically incorrect to appeal to a "rule" about concord in person and number between subject and verb and to overlook established idiomatic usages that vary from the usual.

Aside from passing remarks in descriptive grammars,[28] there is a paucity of precise information concerning the third person imperative. Goetchius has noted that the third person imperative is not always imperatival,[29] and introductory primers employ such auxilliary words as "let" or "may," but Nida rightly cautions that this use of auxilliary words is not always appropriate for the third person imperative.[30] Bakker's study of the imperative[31] is limited to the aspectual differences between the present and aorist imperatives in Greek prayers, and other studies do not treat fully the third person imperative.[32] Judy Glaze, in a recent M.A. thesis at

27. Robertson, *A Grammar of the Greek New Testament*, pp. 403–407.

28. J. H. Moulton, *A Grammar of New Testament Greek* (Edinburgh: T. & T. Clark, 1908), I, 175; and Robertson, *A Grammar of the Greek New Testament*, p. 943.

29. E. V. N. Goetchius, *The Language of the New Testament* (New York: Scribner's, 1965), p. 332.

30. E. A. Nida, *Toward a Science of Translating* (Leiden: Brill, 1964), p. 201.

31. W. F. Bakker, *The Greek Imperative* (Amsterdam: A. M. Hakkert, 1966), p. 154ff.

32. A. Moreschini Quattordio, "L'uso dell'infinitivo e dell'imperativo in Omero e nella tradizione epigrafica," *Studi Classici e Orientali* 19–20 (1970–71): 347–358; C. Grassi, "Imperativo presente e aoristo nelle preghiere agli dei," *Studi Italiani di Filologia Classica* 35 (1963): 186–198; S. Amigues, "Les temps de l'imperatif dans les ordres de l'orateur au greffier," *Revue des Etudes Grecques* 90 (1977): 223–238.

Harding Graduate School of Religion, has addressed the function of the third person imperative in the LXX, isolating several idiomatic usages.[33] Ray Elliott[34] has listed New Testament usages of the third person imperative, but he provides no analysis.

However, Greek literature itself evidences an idiomatic usage that is pertinent to Acts 2:38, in which the third person singular imperative functions in concert with a second person plural imperative so as to bring emphasis to a command by allowing the speaker addressing a group to address members of that group individually. In this emphatic imperatival usage, the speaker attaches such tremendous importance to the command that he makes it clear with the third person imperative that not a single member of the group is exempt. For instance, in Exodus 16:29 the keeping of the Sabbath is expressed with the second person plural imperative: "Remain each one of you in his house," and this is made emphatic with the following third person singular imperative: ". . . no man is permitted to go out of his house on the seventh day!" In Joshua 6:10, a command is given in which the second person plural imperative, "Do not shout," is followed by a third person singular imperative, which addresses the members of the group individually with added emphasis: ". . . do not let the voice of anyone be heard!" In 2 Kings 10:19, Jehu commanded, "Call [second person plural imperative] to me all the prophets of Baal; let not one of them be missing [third person singular imperative]." In Zechariah 7:10, the command is given, "Do not oppress [second person plural imperative] the widow, the fatherless, sojourner, or poor, and let no one of you devise evil [third person singular imperative] against his brother." This usage is also found in apocryphal literature at I Maccabees 10:63, for instance, "Go with him [second person plural imperative] into the midst of the city and proclaim [second person plural imperative] that no one is to bring charges against him about any matter, and do not let anyone annoy him [third person singular imperative] for any reason." In the Apostolic Fathers, this usage occurs several times, as in Didache 15:3, "Reprove one another [second person plural imperative] not in wrath . . . and let none speak [third person singular imperative] with any who has done a wrong to his neighbor, nor let him hear [third person singular imperative] a word from you until he repents."

One particular sentence in Ignatius (*Magn.* 6:2) has striking affinity with the sentence in Acts 2:38, "Be then all in conformity with God [imperatival participle], respect one another [second person plural im-

33. J. Glaze, "The Septuagintal Use of the Third Person Imperative." (Unpublished M. A. thesis, Harding Graduate School of Religion, Memphis, TN, 1979).

34. R. Elliott, "Functions of the Third Person Imperative Verb Forms in the Greek New Testament," *Notes on Translation*, 69 (1978): 30–31, to which must be added Matt. 5:31; 8:13; 1 Cor. 7:17; 1 Tim. 4:12; and 2 Pet. 3:8.

perative], and let no man regard [third person singular imperative] his neighbor according to the flesh, but in everything love [second person plural imperative] one another in Jesus Christ." In view of the abundance of such examples, there is no syntactical basis for the assertion that the second person plural imperative and the third person singular imperative cannot refer in Greek to the same subject. To argue as Ballard and Bogard do is to ignore customary Greek usage in order to find justification for a preconceived notion.

In conclusion, the importance of Greek syntax for New Testament exegesis must be emphatically underscored. As many a preacher and debater has allowed his syntax to run away with him, it is the vital but unenviable duty of the Greek scholar to remind the preacher and debater to keep his feet on the ground. Especially is this true when men ill-equipped in Greek language and literature would use the Greek text to prove theological points. Greek syntax must escape from theological manipulation and from English syntactical categories. To treat Greek syntax with the circumspect precision required in New Testament study, one must become thoroughly familiar with the nuances and idioms of the language, as well as with its customary usages, a time-consuming task for which there is no substitute. As Alexander Pope put it well over two hundred years ago: "A little learning is a dangerous thing; Drink deep, or taste not the Pierian spring."

19

Using Historical Background in New Testament Interpretation

Le Moine Lewis

The New Testament is a book that appeared in the course of history and is an integral part of the historical stream. It had antecedents that prepared the way for it—roots in antiquity and many references to the past—and it has had a history of its own. This book did not appear in a vacuum. Each book in the New Testament was produced in a particular historical context and first spoke to that situation and to its problems. If the student of the New Testament wishes to receive anything approaching the fullness of its riches, he must master as much as possible of the history that is relevant.

What can be known of the world and of the events that prepared the way for and gave birth to the New Testament is limited—it is partial and there are many gaps. Although one can ask many questions that cannot be answered with the certainty one might wish, what can be learned can help put New Testament teachings and the problems that evoked them into their original settings and throw light on the authors' original intentions. Knowledge of history helps the student identify accidents of time and place and allows him to look beyond these accidents to eternal truths that speak to other times and places.

In the New Testament, people and churches are located in cities and countries. They are in life situations with temptations, problems, opportunities, challenges. History helps view them with sympathy and understanding. Mastery of the text calls for a knowledge of the history of Jerusalem and Palestine, of the Roman Empire of which Palestine was a part in the first century, and of the territory around Palestine—the neighbors with whom the people had their closest dealings. Jewish history and Roman history set the stage on which the New Testament is the center. Most introductions to the New Testament give concise summaries of this history. These can lead to larger histories of Rome and Palestine, which in turn will guide the student to the works of Josephus, the Jewish historian of the first century; to Suetonius, with his lives of the emperors; and to Tacitus with his history of Rome. The study goal of this general historical background is to make the student at home in the world of the New Testament.

Basically, this world was Jewish. Even the great apostle to the Gentiles went first, in almost every city, to the Jews. All through the New Testament, one encounters people with Jewish backgrounds. To them the Scriptures were the Old Testament, which told of their history and had come to them through ancestors who lived through the times of the Persians, the Macedonians and Greeks of Alexander, the Seleucids of Antioch, and the Ptolemies of Egypt. After these came the Romans, who ruled Palestine in the days of Jesus, his apostles, and the early Christians.

The period between the Testaments prepared the scene for the New Testament. Jewish history of those years, preserved in their apocryphal and pseudepigraphal books, prepares the student's mind to empathize with the Jewish people of the time. Historians of the Hellenistic Age add their bit, since they help the student understand Palestine as a land through which many conquering armies had marched, an area whose people had paid tribute to many conquering lords.

The writers of the New Testament may not have been conscious of much of the background history that had shaped their world, and their readers may have been even less aware of it. However, the more the modern reader looks back and knows of history, the better tuned his mind will be to catch the message of the New Testament for that time and for this.

The Old Testament History

Once the student opens the New Testament he begins meeting Old Testament characters and events. There are the people mentioned in the genealogies of Jesus, many of whom have interesting histories in the Old Testament. There is the mention of "Emmanuel" in the annunciation to Joseph. Over and over, the student meets such people as Abraham, Isaac, Jacob, David, Elijah, and Isaiah. Only when the student is familiar with the history of these persons will he get the full message of the passages that refer to them.

The sermon in Acts 2 refers to Joel and passages from David's psalms. The second sermon in Acts 3 contains references to Jesus as fulfilling promises and prophecies of Abraham and Moses, of Samuel, and of the prophets who came after him. The defense of Stephen in Acts 7 and Paul's sermon in Acts 13 have many ties to Old Testament history. Understanding the point of Stephen's defense depends on knowing the history of Joseph and the jealousy of his brothers, the trials suffered by Moses as he led the Israelites out of Egypt and through the wilderness, the rebellions of the people and their persecutions of their prophets, and the story of the building of the temple. Paul's speech at Antioch presupposes in his listeners a knowledge of the exodus from Egypt, the wilderness wanderings, the conquest of Canaan, the reigns of Saul and David. There are quotations from Psalms, Isaiah, and Habakkuk.

The Book of Romans presupposes an understanding of Jewish history—the failure of the Jews as the covenant people and the whole story of Abraham and his faith. The Letter to the Galatians builds on a knowledge of Old Testament history that includes the covenant with Abraham, the story of Hagar and Ishmael and of Sarah and Isaac.

The Letter to the Hebrews takes for granted a knowledge of the role of angels in the Old Testament; the office and functions of the high priest of Israel; the story of Moses, the exodus, and wilderness wandering; Joshua and the conquest of Canaan; Abraham and Melchizedek; the priests, tabernacle, and temple; and the sacrifices of the old covenant.

To understand and fully appreciate the message of the Letter of James one must know the history of Abraham, Rahab, the trials of Elijah and other prophets, and the sufferings of Job. The First Letter of Peter likewise assumes a general knowledge of the prophets, especially of Isaiah; an understanding of the role of the priests and God's priestly nation and their covenant with God at Mount Sinai with the Law of Holiness; a familiarity with Abraham and Sarah and with Noah and the flood. The Second Letter of Peter presupposes some knowledge of the prophets and their rivals, the false prophets; Noah and the flood; Abraham, Lot, and Sodom and Gomorrah. The Second Letter of Paul to Timothy takes for granted an understanding of the laws of purification from the Book of Leviticus and later traditions that circulated among the Jews, embellishing the ancient story of Moses and the Egyptian magicians. To get the message of the Letter of Jude one must know the story of the exodus; the account of Lot and Sodom and Gomorrah; the stories of Cain, Balaam, and of Korah and his rebellion; the apocryphal *The Assumption of Moses*, and the pseudepigraphal *Book of Enoch*.

The Book of Revelation builds on an understanding of the priesthood of the Old Testament; the imagery of the prophets; Isaiah and Ezekiel; the role of Babylon in the destruction of Jerusalem; and the role of Michael in the Book of Daniel.

Without a knowledge of Old Testament history, anything like a satisfactory understanding of the New Testament is impossible. The New builds on the Old—and together they are one great revelation from God.

Palestinian Politics in the Time of Jesus and Religion in the Time of Jesus and the Apostles

References to Herod and the Archelaus in Matthew 2 should drive the serious student to the Jewish historian, Josephus, and to modern studies of the political situation in Palestine at the birth of Jesus. The Herods and the priests of Luke 1 and 3 reinforce the significance of Josephus' work. The beheading of John the Baptist by Herod, and the trials of Jesus before Annas and Caiaphas and before Pilate and Herod, make Josephus even more important. Another source, the Qumran Scrolls and the community they reveal, makes modern scholars appreciate the fact that John the Baptist preached in the wilderness rather than in the cities.

All through the Gospels, students meet Pharisees, Sadduccees, and Herodians. To understand the clash of Jesus with the Jewish leaders, his criticism of his contemporaries, and the rising opposition against him, one must delve into the history of the religious parties in Palestine in the time of Jesus—into the rabbinical schools of Hillel and Shammai, the traditions of the Elders, the oral traditions of the rabbis. These form the background to Jesus' clash with the Jews on the clean and unclean, the Sabbath, the questions of divorce and remarriage.

In the Gospels, Jesus is pictured as going to the synagogue "as his custom was." This synagogue of first-century Judaism sheds light on the early church. When one comes to Acts, it takes only a small measure of curiosity to drive the student to seek more history. In Acts 5, there is Gamaliel and his references to Theudas and Judas the Galilean; in Acts 6, the Hellenists murmur against the Hebrews; in Acts 7, there are the synagogues of the Freedmen, of the Cyrenians, of the Alexandrians, and of those from Cilicia and Asia disputing against Stephen. Later, as the student meets Herod the King, Felix, Festus, and Agrippa, he looks for light from Jewish history.

Rome and the Church in the Roman Empire

The desire to see and understand Jesus in his own world will drive the student to search Roman history when he reads in Luke's Gospel that when Jesus was born, Augustus was ruler; that when Jesus began his public ministry, Tiberius was Caesar. When reading that the Jewish leaders said to Pilate, "If you release this man, you are not Caesar's friend; everyone who makes himself a king sets himself against Caesar," the student asks, "Who was Caesar at the time of the crucifixion?" The account of Paul's meeting with Aquila and Priscilla at Corinth, after Claudius had expelled the Jews from Rome, compels the student to dig into Roman history for all the light he can find. When Paul says, "I appeal to Caesar," and when Festus announces that he is sending him to Caesar, the student may well wonder about the identity of the "Caesar" who would have to deal with Paul's case. The serious exegete will be anxious to learn as much as possible of the man who heard Paul's defense.

Each reference in Acts to a place where Paul planted a church calls for digging into the history of that city for any light that can be found on the kind of people Paul preached to and the kind of problems these people would have to face when they embraced Christianity. Every letter written to the church in one of these cities calls for all the knowledge of this city that can be discovered.[1]

The very mention of Epicurean and Stoic philosophers in Acts 17 should lead the student into the history of these schools.[2] The Gnostic vocabulary in Colossians and the Pastorals, the mention of "philosophy and empty deceit, according to human tradition," and "all the riches of assured understanding and the knowledge of God's mystery, of Christ, in whom are hid all the treasures of wisdom and knowledge," makes it necessary for the student to look into the Gnostic library and gather the historical background that will shed light on the church problems that called for exhortations to seek "spiritual wisdom and understanding."[3]

Before one can with confidence declare the implications for today of Paul's answers to the problems in Corinth, he must look as deeply as possible at these problems in their original first-century setting. The search will lead not only to ancient geographers, travelers, and literary works but also to modern archeological discoveries.[4] For each Epistle in the New Testament, the student must learn what he can of the city where the church was located and to whom the letter was addressed, and must try to determine as closely as possible the time of the writing so as to be able to put the problems faced in the letter in their original setting.

Representative Problems of Interpretation

Marriage, Divorce, and Remarriage

Some problems call for the light of history more insistently than others. One of these is Jesus' teaching on marriage, divorce, and remarriage.

---

1. See E. M. Blaiklock, *Cities of the New Testament* (Westwood, NJ: Fleming H. Revell, 1965); W. M. Ramsay, *The Cities of St. Paul* (London: Hodder and Stoughton, 1907; reprinted Grand Rapids: Baker, 1960). There are articles on each of the cities in IDB (New York: Abingdon, 1962), updated in the Supplementary Volume of 1976.

2. F. W. Beare's articles on each of these schools in IDB, 2:122–123 and 4:443–445 include good bibliographies.

3. *The Nag Hammadi Library*, ed. J. M. Robinson (New York: Harper & Row, 1977); R. M. Grant, *Gnosticism and Early Christianity* (New York: Columbia University, 1959); R. McL. Wilson, *Gnosis and the New Testament* (Philadelphia: Fortress, 1968).

4. For example, Strabo (Loeb Classical Library). Available material will be found in the references listed in note 1.

In the Gospel of Matthew, the very position of the Sermon on the Mount highlights the sermon as a declaration of the kingdom principles that the teacher wanted to stand out clearly at the very beginning. Here the demands of the old covenant are contrasted with the demands of the kingdom. It had been said, "You shall not commit adultery." Jesus warns against the lustful eye. This is followed by the quotation from the old law, "Whoever divorces his wife, let him give her a certificate of divorce." In contrast with this, Jesus says, "But I say unto you that every one who divorces his wife, except on the ground of unchastity, makes her an adulteress; and whoever marries a divorced woman commits adultery."

In reporting the final journey to Jerusalem after the end of the great Galilean ministry, Matthew, Mark, and Luke record that the Pharisees interrupted Jesus' journey, testing him on his attitude toward divorce. Jesus attributed divorce under the law of Moses as a concession to "hardness of heart" and pointed them back to God's original intention of one man and one woman for life. Matthew records, "And I say to you: whoever divorces his wife, except for unchastity, and marries another, commits adultery." But in some ancient texts we find, after the word *unchastity*, "makes her commit adultery." Other ancient authorities insert "and he who marries a divorced woman commits adultery." In Mark it was after Jesus and his disciples entered the house that he said to the disciples, "Whoever divorces his wife and marries another, commits adultery against her; and if she divorces her husband and marries another, she commits adultery." In Luke the record is much briefer, but it appears in that long section that follows his setting his face to go to Jerusalem after his ministry in Galilee. Jesus' words are given without any context: "Every one who divorces his wife and marries another commits adultery, and he who marries a woman divorced from her husband commits adultery."

A study of Jesus' teaching on marriage, as recorded in these three gospels, forces one to look into history. Such a study leads to discovering the contrast between the teaching of Hillel and Shammai shortly before the time of Jesus. The great Shammai allowed divorce only on the grounds of unchastity. Hillel, his pupil, allowed divorce on the most trivial grounds, such as the wife's burning her husband's bread.[5] In Matthew and Luke, Jesus' teaching is directed to the men, but in Mark, Jesus lays down the same teaching for men and women. This raises the question of whether only men could bring divorce proceedings under Jewish law. Was Mark written in Rome and for Romans, and under Roman law could women also institute divorce proceedings? How is one to explain the exception clause in both of the records in Matthew? Do Mark and Luke

5. See the discussion in J. P. Lewis, *The Gospel According to Matthew*, Living Word Commentary (Austin, TX: Sweet, 1976), 2:64–68.

represent the original words of Jesus and Matthew the later expansion by the church? Or does the whole record illustrate Jesus' method of teaching? Thus, he would first throw out the stark, naked paradox—the harsh, strong declaration of Mark and Luke. Later, after letting the disciples stew with the harshness of his declaration, did Jesus himself enlarge on the original declaration, relieving the paradox? Was the "unchastity" he refers to "unfaithfulness to the marriage vow to be faithful until death," or did it refer to the discovery that the marriage partner did not come to the marriage as a virgin and hence the marriage could be nullified?[6] In the floating pericope about the woman taken in adultery, which sometimes occurs at the beginning of John 8 and sometimes at the end of John or after Luke 21:38, the proposal of the Pharisees was that the law of Moses said that she should be stoned. Was stoning a live option in the time of Jesus? Would this have been the sentence on unfaithfulness in marriage instead of divorce?

In 1 Corinthians 7, when Paul concludes his discussion of all the marriage problems the Corinthian Christians faced in their pagan environment, and says that the widow "is free to be married to whom she wishes, only in the Lord" (v. 39), did he have in mind the kind of problem over which Kallistos and Hippolytus were later to clash at the beginning of the third century? The Christian widow was free to marry, but must she really marry or could she practice concubinage—as did some noble women who could not find noblemen and took personal slaves without paying the price of losing rank and estate by marrying under their class? Kallistos felt Roman law was unjust, and he deemed that what was concubinage in the eyes of the law was allowable to the Christian, since the concubinage was "marriage" in the eyes of the church. Hippolytus took the position that if a woman wanted a slave for a husband, she must be willing to pay the price of losing her rank and her estate. She could not say to the government that the man was her slave and to the church that he was her husband.[7] Was Paul saying that a widow must marry a Christian, or was he saying that the marriage must be real marriage and not concubinage? Even in the days of Kallistos and Hippolytus there was not enough historical evidence available to resolve this question.

The Problem of the Samaritans

Jesus' home in Nazareth and his great work in Galilee were separated from the center of Judaism, the temple at Jerusalem, by an area of Palestine called Samaria. The Gospels record at least two journeys Jesus attempted through that country: the well-known trip when he visited

---

6. F. C. Grant, *The Growth of the Gospels* (New York: Abingdon, 1933), p. 187.

7. H. Lietzmann, *The Founding of the Church Universal*, The Beginnings of the Christian Church, vol. 2 (New York: Scribner's, 1938) p. 327.

with the Samaritan woman at the well and preached to her townspeople, and the lesser-known occasion when the Samaritans, knowing Jesus was traveling toward Jerusalem, refused to allow him to preach.

These neighbors of the Jews provided Jesus' definition of "neighbor" in the story of the good Samaritan. In the account of the healing of the ten lepers, it was the Samaritan leper who came to express gratitude—a sharp contrast to the lack of response from the Jewish nine.

Clearly, Jesus recognized the Jewish prejudice against Samaritans and did not share it. His apostles learned this lesson, and the early church accepted it. When Philip preached to Samaritans and baptized them, the Jerusalem church sent Peter and John to Samaria, where they laid their hands on those Philip had baptized, and they received the Holy Spirit.

Just who were these Samaritans? The New Testament student will want to know.[8]

Antioch as Base of the Gentile Mission

Antioch has a very special place in the Acts of the Apostles and in early church history. There is a beautiful and clear scheme of preparation for the Gentile mission. After the story of the Jerusalem church, there are accounts of Samaria as the halfway house to the Gentiles; the conversion of the treasurer of Ethiopia, as an indication of things to come; the conversion of the missionary to the Gentiles; and Cornelius as the test case of preaching to Gentiles. Then comes Antioch as the base for the Gentile missions. This should make any reader curious about the history of Antioch. Did anything in its past make it a fit place for a church composed of both Jews and Gentiles? Why should Antioch be the church to send help to Jerusalem? Why would Paul keep returning to Antioch? What of the tradition that Luke was a physician from Antioch? Once again, answers are available.[9]

The Jerusalem Conference

By the time of Jesus, the law of Moses had been embellished with an oral tradition—indeed, an oral law. Without some knowledge of the burden that this law put on the working peasant, the student can understand neither Jesus' denunciation of this tradition nor Peter's stand at the Jerusalem Conference. Peter called the law a yoke hard to bear, and later Judaism has resented Peter's metaphor.

To appreciate the final decision of the conference the student must know not only the history of God's covenant with Noah after the flood but

---

8. J. A. Montgomery, *The Samaritans* (Philadelphia: John C. Winston, 1907); T. H. Gaster, IDB, 4:190–197.

9. G. Downey, *A History of Antioch in Syria* (Princeton: Princeton University, 1961), pp. 163–201, 272–287, 582, 583; W. A. Meeks and R. L. Wilken, *Jews and Christians in Antioch*, pp. 13–18.

also what the rabbis had made of the Noachite Code in the centuries that followed. The concessions the Jerusalem Conference asked Gentile Christians to make were terms of the Noachite Code as viewed by Judaism. The Jews had conceded that Gentiles who kept the Noachite Code were acceptable to God.[10]

The Resurrection of the Dead

The scorn that Paul met in Athens when he referred to the resurrection, and the problems at Corinth over the resurrection, call for a look at the history of Greek thought on the nature of man, the relation of soul and body, and the Greek ideal of immortality as opposed to a resurrection of the body.[11]

Meat Sacrificed to Idols

Probably nothing in Paul's Epistles seems more foreign to modern thinking than the problem of eating meat offered to idols. Here one needs the light that history can shed on the problem. Behind the history of the meat market—operated to dispose of the excess of meat given to pagan priests as their portion of the sacrifices—and the dinners where meat bought at such markets was served to guests, lie important lessons concerning one's influence as a Christian and an uncompromised stand for Christ in a complex society.[12]

Paul's Roman Citizenship

At Philippi on his second journey, Paul's appeal to his Roman citizenship led to his being freed from prison with an apology from the officials. In Jerusalem after the third journey, when he brought Gentile money to Jerusalem, his appeal to his Roman citizenship saved him from scourging by Roman soldiers. What were the privileges of a Roman citizen? How could one prove Roman citizenship in crises far from home and far from Rome?[13]

As a Roman citizen in Caesarea, Paul appealed to Caesar. While waiting for his trial in Rome, Paul lived in his own rented house. Paul preached

---

10. G. F. Moore, *Judaism* (Cambridge: Harvard University, 1932), 1:247f.

11. A. D. Nock, *Conversion* (Oxford: Clarendon Press, 1933), pp. 247–249. See also the commentary of K. Lake and H. J. Cadbury on Acts 17:32–33 in *The Beginnings of Christianity*, vol. 4, ed. by F. J. Foakes Jackson and K. Lake (London: Macmillan, 1933), p. 219; on 1 Corinthians 15, H. Conzelmann, *I Corinthians*, Hermeneia (Philadelphia: Fortress, 1975), pp. 248–293; cf. J. D. Tabor, "Resurrection and Immortality: Paul and Poimandres" in *Christian Teaching:* Studies in Honor of LeMoine G. Lewis, ed. Everett Ferguson (Abilene: Abilene Christian University, 1981), pp. 71–91.

12. K. Lake, *The Earlier Epistles of St. Paul* (London: Rivingtons, 1930), pp. 198–202.

13. A. N. Sherwin-White, *Roman Society and Roman Law in the New Testament* (Oxford: Clarendon, 1963), pp. 48–98, 108–119, 144–193.

and wrote letters. Onesimus, the runaway slave, was converted. Onesiphorus searched for the prisoner and visited him. Epaphroditus of Philippi brought him a gift. Some of Caesar's household were converted by this prisoner waiting for trial. The praetorian guard heard the gospel. What can history tell us of the functioning of Caesar's court?

History and the Book of Revelation

Nowhere is a knowledge of historical background more desirable than in studying the Book of Revelation. An interpreter can have little confidence in his understanding of this book until he has made a thorough effort to settle the time of its writing and has searched out extensively the relations of the Christians to the Roman empire of this time. Is the book at home in the reign of Domitian? What can be learned about Domitian and his persecution of Christians? The serious student must look into the facts behind such an expression as "the synagogue of Satan." Is the throne of Satan at Pergamum a reference to emperor worship and the temple erected there to Domitian? References to two beasts and the worship of the image of the beast call for searching the history of the time for light. What were the pressures put on Christians of Asia Minor to secure the libellus that certified their having sacrificed to the gods of Rome?[14]

Under the Judgment of History

Through the providence of God, Christian principles that belong to every age have been richly illustrated by the accidents of history. Paul wrote, "For whatever was written in former days was written for our instruction, that by steadfastness and by the encouragement of the scriptures we might have hope" (Rom 15:4, RSV). In his trial before Festus and Agrippa he declared ". . . this was not done in a corner" (Acts 26:26 RSV). Paul had great confidence that anyone who knew the historical background of his gospel would accept the truth of that gospel.

It has become clear in the twentieth century that any interpretation of Scripture must be judged by history.

14. R. H. Mounce, *The Book of Revelation*, NICOT (Grand Rapids: Eerdmans, 1977), pp. 31–36, 90–99.

20

Using Historical Foreground in New Testament Interpretation

Everett Ferguson

If the relevant Roman, Greek, and Jewish literature, history, and customs may be labeled the "background" to the New Testament, then early Christian literature, history, and practices may appropriately be termed the "foreground" of the New Testament. The use of historical background materials in the interpretation of the Bible is generally accepted and is at the foundation of the historical-grammatical approach to the Bible. Not so generally recognized is the value of early church history as an aid to the interpretation of the New Testament. What Christianity became in its early history was largely shaped by the New Testament documents, although not by these exclusively, of course. This development also deserves to be considered in attaining a proper historical perspective on the meaning of the text itself.

Two aspects of the Christian material are to be considered: (1) the actual interpretation of New Testament passages, sometimes expressed consciously and explicitly but at other times expressed only allusively or implicitly (especially in the earliest writings outside the text); (2) the faith and practice of early Christianity, which reflect the understanding of the apostolic message and often preserve early customs, presuppositions, and structures of thought. Both aspects are in view in the following discussion but are not sharply distinguished in some of the comments.

Value of Church-History Materials in Interpreting the Bible

Let it be noted that the point being made is that although early Christian materials are valuable for the interpretation of the New Testament, they are not themselves the authority. The author has no desire to substitute church tradition for Scripture as the standard for Christian faith and life, nor even to supplement Scripture as a norm with ecclesiastical tradition. The plea here, rather, is that church history may give information helpful for understanding what the Scriptures meant, or in other words, may aid one to understand and interpret correctly the biblical standard.

A knowledge of church history is essential for grasping the total historical context of the New Testament. Consideration of the background gives only half of that historical context. It tells what went before. Church history tells what came after the New Testament. Both are necessary to complete the picture that provides the proper setting for the texts.[1] It is essential to see the New Testament in its historical context. This principle has long been recognized in the study of the Bible, but the principle is imperfectly applied if the church historical foreground is neglected. The New Testament is part of a continuity from its background to its foreground. The student can more clearly define the meaning of the text and sharpen its message by seeing it against both what preceded and what followed. The New Testament is part of a historical continuum, and this total context is necessary if one is to avoid taking the Bible in a vacuum or leaving it floating in airy unreality.

The historical background and foreground set the boundaries of possible meanings for the New Testament texts. They may not tell precisely what a given text meant, but they will tell certain things that it cannot have meant and will set the range of most likely meanings. Some interpretations are historically impossible; others are historically possible. Background and foreground together determine these parameters. To give an absurd illustration, a text in the first century could not be giving a strategy for nuclear warfare, for such was unknown. Similarly, although not equally impossible, a mid-twentieth-century manual of warfare would not include a lengthy section on the use of a troop of archers. These are far-fetched ideas but may serve to demonstrate that exegesis has to do with what is historically possible. History, customs, and literature surrounding the New Testament make known what was historically possible. Even more so, they make known what was historically likely or probable in a given situation.

Even those developments in the early church that one may judge on a biblical or doctrinal basis to be erroneous may still contribute positively to a correct understanding of the text. Historical continuity requires that

---

1. J. P. Lewis, *A Study of the Interpretation of Noah and the Flood in Jewish and Christian Literature* (Leiden: Brill, 1966) provide an example by its comprehensive collection of background and foreground materials surrounding the New Testament references to the flood.

even error must have been derivable in some way from the apostolic setting, either as a direct line of development (but into an area outside the bounds of New Testament authorization) or as a reaction to an apostolic teaching. Thus the later developments in church history have to be accounted for from the historical circumstances that gave them rise, and these circumstances include the beginnings of the Christian movement. A scholar's understanding of early Christianity must be such as will explain the later ecclesiastical developments, even if he considers these wrong or simply unfortunate. In this regard, many have taken an unhistorical view of Christian origins or Christian teachings. (A specific illustration will be given below.) Again, it is a matter of what is possible or likely in a given historical setting: even "error" must have been of a kind derivable from what is determined to have been the "truth."

Early Christian authors, such as the Apostolic Fathers, the second-century Apologists, the early Theologians and Anti-Heretical Writers, were nearer in time and place to the New Testament church than either modern scholars or even the "background" sources cited. They were therefore in a good position to preserve and transmit authentic information. They understood the customs, spoke the same language, and lived in the same tradition of faith and nearly the same historical context in which the New Testament was written. They were in a good position to preserve the original sense of a passage or intention of a teaching. They most certainly were not always right. A stream may become contaminated quite near its source, but it is much less likely to become so until farther away from its origins.

Moving from such general considerations to some things more specific, consider the meaning of words, which is determined by usage. The usage of biblical words by the early Christians and the meanings they gave to those words are important data to be considered along with other evidence in deciding the meaning to be given to a word in a given passage.[2] For instance, *cheirotoneō* became the ecclesiastical word "ordain." That meaning must be considered in deciding the meaning of a passage such as Acts 14:23. Even if not settling the meaning in a given text,[3] the direction in which the usage of a word was moving makes it possible to plot the

---

2. Unfortunately G. Kittel, *Theological Dictionary of the New Testament*, 9 vols., trans. G. Bromiley (Grand Rapids: Eerdmans, 1964–74), generally gives very brief notice to the post-New Testament usage of words. W. Bauer, *A Greek English Lexicon of the New Testament and Other Early Christian Literature*, trans. W. F. Arndt and F. W. Gingrich, second edition revised by F. W. Gingrich and F. W. Danker (Chicago: University of Chicago, 1979), gives full attention to the Apostolic Fathers but does not include later authors, for which one must consult G.W.H. Lampe, *A Patristic Greek Lexicon* (Oxford: Clarendon, 1961).

3. See my discussion in "Ordination in the Ancient Church (IV)," RQ 5 (1961): 137–139.

course of development of its meaning and so helps to locate a text in that development. Sometimes the immediate background and foreground make the meaning of a word in the New Testament virtually certain.[4]

Another specific value of church-history materials to an understanding of the New Testament is in the interpretation of the Old Testament. The types of Old Testament interpretation practiced by early Christian writers would not be allowed now, and there should be no desire to return to such uncritical "unhistorical" approaches. However, the kind of interpretation employed in literature close in time to the New Testament makes more intelligible the use made of the Old Testament by New Testament writers.[5] The latter were simply approaching their Bible according to the ways in which sacred literature was employed in their time. A modern scholar should not expect them to study text the way he does, nor should their methods dictate today's exegesis, however theologically normative their interpretations are for Christians of all ages. In fact, New Testament interpretations of the Old Testament may seem quite sober and restrained in contrast to what some early Christian authors later did. However, even allowing for extremes, the evidence of church history allows one to see that meanings possibly strange to us were not arbitrary but were arrived at in accord with recognized practices.

Dangers to Be Avoided

Along with the plea on behalf of the values to be found in considering the historical foreground to the New Testament, certain cautions are in order. There are pitfalls that have not been avoided in the past and into which the student rushing into this area may fall.

Replacing Scriptural Authority by Tradition

This danger has already been mentioned: taking the early church, not Scripture, as authority. Some churches that accept tradition as well as Scripture as normative do this on principle. They are often as arbitrary in what they accept out of early Christian tradition as others are about what they select out of Scripture to follow. To listen attentively to the early Christian development as a testimony to the meaning of the Bible is not the same as making that development normative for present Christian practice. Nonetheless, one may unintentionally allow that development to usurp a position of authority belonging only to God's Word.

4. E. Ferguson, *A Cappella Music in the Public Worship of the Church*, revised edition (Abilene: Biblical Research Press, 1972), pp. 1–27 on *psallō*.

5. See my "Christian Use of the Old Testament," in *The World and Literature of the Old Testament*, ed. J. T. Willis, The Living Word Commentary on the Old Testament, Vol. 1 (Austin, TX: Sweet, 1979), pp. 346–357.

Reliance on Reverse Chronology

Another danger is perhaps closely related to the preceding: reading later positions back into the New Testament. Even someone who does not accept the authority of the early church may do this. It is often an instructive technique to take a fully developed doctrine or institution and trace it back from its fullest formulation to its roots in the New Testament.[6] This reverse historical process often reveals connections unexpected or unnoticed in the usual order of study. The person approaching the question in this way has to be especially conscious of the danger of allowing the development that did occur to control his thinking about what was true at the beginning or about what the development should have been or, under the circumstances, might have been. There were many changes in Christian practice, some occurring quite early. There were fundamental changes in the structure of thinking as the church moved from its matrix in Judaism to become predominantly Greek and Roman in membership. This shift profoundly altered the understanding of certain biblical teachings. Although this essay has argued that one should pay attention to the later Christian development, there is other evidence and other principles of exegesis (as discussed elsewhere in this volume) to serve as controls over a one-sided dependence on the Christian historical development. After all, the church's early history is to aid, not determine, the interpretation of the New Testament.

Overgeneralization

The next danger to be mentioned is of a different order. The student may take an isolated or individual view out of the historical testimony and consider it to be the general position. Of course, a single writer or source may preserve the correct understanding overagainst the majority position. The amateur is particularly likely to seize on an isolated quotation and attribute to it a significance it does not deserve. Such an "amateur" may be a perfectly competent scholar in some other area but not knowledgeable in church history or patristics. Here the quantity of material is important. It is more likely for an individual writer or church in a certain region to go astray than for such a thing to happen to the church over a broader territory. Given enough time, of course, this consideration diminishes in force. It is important to determine if there is a uniform testimony of many witnesses so as to establish a definite tradition of teaching. The earlier and more extensive such a consensus can be established, the stronger and more persuasive it becomes as traceable to earliest Christian times or resting on something other than individual

---

6. This method is followed in my series on "Ordination in the Ancient Church," 4 parts, RQ 4 (1960): 117–138, 5 (1961): 17–32, 67–82, 130–146.

innovation. Still, the opposite caution is also in order: a majority does not necessarily establish truth.

Missing the Writer's Purpose

The earliest Christian writers outside the New Testament text were living in a creative time. The apostolic writings were authoritative, but they were not yet collected and identified as an exclusive "canon."[7] Early second-century authors did not treat the New Testament writings as later authors did, because there was not yet an entity known as the "New Testament." Therefore, the reader has to be careful about identifying use of a given passage found in our present New Testament as a conscious interpretation of what that passage meant in its original context. Polycarp, bishop of Smyrna in the early second century, is a good example of an author who was throroughly imbued with the language of the New Testament (especially Paul, but also John and Peter) but did not use it in a way helpful to the modern exegete. He uses the language of the text allusively and to provide a vocabulary to express his own ideas, not in order to explain the ideas of the New Testament author. The new meanings and contexts that he gives to certain passages were not misunderstandings on Polycarp's part, still less any effort to deceive. However, if one takes him as a guide to the meaning of the passages he cites, one misunderstands both Polycarp and the authors he uses. Hence, a student must be careful to determine what kind of use is being made by any early Christian author in order to assess the significance to be given to that usage in adducing it as a testimony to the meaning of a New Testament text.

To summarize, church history—that is, the historical foreground to the New Testament—is not the judge that decides the meaning of the text. Rather, it is a witness in the exegete's court of inquiry. The testimony of this witness is evidence that deserves consideration and needs to be heard.

Some Examples

1. We read in 1 Corinthians 14:16 that the person who does not know the "tongue" in which another says thanks cannot say "Amen" to that prayer because he does not understand what has been said. Both the background information about the practice in the Jewish synagogue and the foreground information about early Christian assemblies provide a precise explanation for Paul's reference. Jews and Christians alike re-

---

7. For some reflections on this development see my "Lectures on the New Testament Canon," *The Seminary Review* 24 (1978): 113–143.

sponded to prayer in a corporate, unison "Amen,"[8] meaning "May it be so." It served as a ratification of the prayer, a way by which the whole congregation gave its endorsement to a prayer spoken by the leader and so made that prayer its own. A person who did not understand what was spoken, however, could not meaningfully join in this congregational acclamation. (It should be remembered that Paul's instructions in 1 Corinthians 14 have as their context the assembly of the church.)

The background and foreground information give an explanation of what exactly was meant by the passage. The statement does not refer to a private agreement with what was said, but rather to participation in a corporate act that was a regular part of the assembly of early Christians. The historical context confirms that Paul referred to a real "speaking" when he said, "How shall he *say* the 'Amen'?"

2. Another example of the way historical foreground gives clarity and specificity to the understanding of a New Testament text is provided by 1 Timothy 2:8. The reader might take the phrase "lifting up holy hands" to be a symbolic expression for purity of motives and life. That would be included, but the historical context explains that something more specific provides the point of reference. Arms outstretched and hands held up represented the symbol of prayer in the ancient world. Both literary texts and early Christian art confirm that the normal Christian posture in congregational prayer was standing with hands extended.[9] Paul was referring to this posture in prayer in these instructions (once more the Christian assembly is the context for the practice). The thrust, of course, is that these hands are to be "holy" and not engaged in wicked deeds; but the reference is still to what was actually done with the hands in the approach to God in prayer.

3. The confirmation of the correct understanding of a passage whose interpretation has been disputed in modern times may be illustrated in regard to John 3:5. The modern evangelical Protestant interpretation that "born of the water" refers to natural birth revives the ancient Gnostic effort to remove the necessity of water baptism from the plan of salvation. The uniform testimony of church history for many centuries, however, is that John 3:5 was referring to baptism.[10] In fact, one could claim that this passage was the favorite baptismal text of the early church. Only some Gnostics—and that on the doctrinal basis that material elements were bad and so could not be part of the design of the spiritual Father—denied the baptismal reference in this text. The interpretation of John 3:5 in the

---

8. For some of the church history evidence see my *Early Christians Speak*, reprint edition (Abilene: Biblical Research Press, 1981), pp. 94, 101f., 144.

9. Ibid., p. 141, esp. nn. 16–17 for some of the evidence.

10. Ibid., p. 38; E. Ferguson, "Baptismal Motifs in the Ancient Church," RQ 7 (1963): 211.

early church indeed provides a good illustration of the principle stated earlier that in historical development even error must be derivable in some way from truth. The emphasis on the statement that "Except one be born of water . . . he cannot enter the kingdom of heaven" led to a teaching that put the saving efficacy of baptism in the water, instead of in the accompanying response of faith. It also led to the practice of infant baptism as necessary for salvation.[11]

These developments were departures from the New Testament gospel and its emphases, yet they were possible from an isolated and exaggerated interpretation of John 3:5—but those who would dehydrate this text have no convincing way to explain these developments. If baptism had not been related positively to the forgiveness of sins and salvation in the apostolic teaching, it becomes all but impossible to account for the development of sacramental doctrine in the post-apostolic church. It is similarly all but impossible to give a historical explanation of how there was such a total misunderstanding of John 3:5 and other teaching on baptism and salvation throughout orthodox Christian literature in the second century. The historical foreground is a powerful argument for uniting water and the Spirit in one's understanding of baptism.

Resources and Tools

The interpreter who wants to use the Christian foreground material in understanding the New Testament is advised to obtain a working knowledge of early church history. For his course on ancient church history, the author uses as the textbook J. G. Davies, *The Early Christian Church* (paperback reprint [Grand Rapids: Baker, 1980]). For an evaluation of books that would give a good survey of the field, see "A Review Article: Histories of the Early Church" in *Restoration Quarterly* 14 (1971):205–214. There are also good surveys of early Christian literature that will give a student a working knowledge of what is available in this field: E. J. Goodspeed and R. M. Grant, *A History of Early Christian Literature* (Chicago: University of Chicago, 1966); and F. L. Cross, *The Early Christian Fathers* (London: Duckworth, 1960). More comprehensive treatments are found in the patrologies. Particularly recommended are those of J. Quasten, *Patrology*, 3 vols. (Utrecht: Spectrum, 1950–60), and B. Altaner, *Patrology* (London: Nelson, 1960).

The interpreter who wishes to make use of early Christian literature in his exposition of the biblical text now has available an excellent time-saving aid. The *Biblia Patristica*, three volumes at the time of writing with

11. See my "Inscriptions and the Origin of Infant Baptism, JTS New Series 30 (1979): 37–46.

more to come,[12] is a computer-aided publication (prepared by the *Centre d'analyse et de documentation patristiques*, published by the *Editions centre national de la recherche scientifique*). For each verse of the Bible, the *Biblia Patristica* lists the author and reference for every known citation in early Christian literature. A caution must be offered to users of these lists of references, since no effort was made to evaluate the quality of the references. If an editor of the patristic text thought he saw an allusion to the biblical text and listed it in his edition, the reference is repeated in the *Biblia Patristica*. An allusion may or may not have relevance for understanding the biblical text, and what someone saw as an allusion to text may not have been intended by the original author in the first place.

There are also indexes to biblical quotations in the *Ante-Nicene Fathers* (see below) and in most individual editions of works from early Christian literature. These may be consulted to locate references to the text being studied, although the indexes are not complete and not every patristic work is included in any set. The ordinary student will therefore have to accept that his exploration will not be comprehensive.

For detailed technical work, the student will want to consult patristic works in their original language. The latest or best editions of an author's works may be found by consulting one of the standard patrologies mentioned above or the *Clavis Patrum Graecorum*.[13] Where only the general sense of a passage is sufficient (and for most persons this is adequate), a good English translation suffices. Often the best English translation is to be found in an individual work devoted to a single treatise or to a single author, and these may be found in the standard reference works. Most often, however, the student will want to go to one of the sets of collected works. Perhaps most widely used is the *Ante-Nicene Fathers* and *Post-Nicene Fathers*.[14] It remains the most nearly complete and most accessible series, but the language and style is Victorian, more recently discovered documents are not included, and homiletic and commentary writings are for the most part not included (for instance, most of the homilies of Origen await an English translator). The highest quality of translation is most consistently maintained in *Ancient Christian Writ-*

12. J. Allenbach *et al.*, ed., *Biblia Patristica: Index des Citations et allusions bibliques dans la litterature patristiques*, 1. *Des origines à Clément d'Alexandrie et Tertullien* (Paris, 1975), 2. *Le troisième siècle (Origène excepté)* (Paris, 1977), 3. *Origene* (Paris, 1980).

13. Edited for Corpus Christianorum by M. Geerard, 4 vols. (Turnhout: Brepols, 1974–). One may also consult F. L. Cross and E. A. Livingstone, *The Oxford Dictionary of the Christian Church*, 2nd ed. (London: Oxford University, 1974).

14. A. Roberts and J. Donaldson, ed. *The Ante-Nicene Fathers*, Reprint of the American Edition, 10 vols. (Grand Rapids: Eerdmans, 1951); Schaff and H. Wace, *A Select Library of Nicene and Post Nicene Fathers*, First Series, 14 vols.; Second Series, 14 vols., Reprint (Grand Rapids: Eerdmans, 1956–1966).

ers.[15] The volumes in this series provide copious notes, but with a few exceptions it has aimed "to fill the gaps" by translating works not otherwise available or in need of more adequate treatment. The most comprehensive of the newer sets is *Fathers of the Church*,[16] although some of the early volumes are of indifferent quality, and the series has been more frankly Roman Catholic in orientation.

There is now in progress at the University of Laval at Sainte Foy, Quebec, Canada, a project to put on computer tape bibliographical information on all patristic literature. The project is named *Banque d'information bibliographique en patristique* (Bibliographic Information Bank in Patristics). One item to be included is a listing of major treatments of biblical texts in patristic works studied in the articles included in the bank. When assembled, this will be a valuable resource tool.

An important new source for early Christian history is the Nag Hammadi Library. This is a collection of codices written in Coptic in the fourth century, but the works themselves are translations of earlier Greek writings. Most of the works are Gnostic; some were only used by Gnostics. They are being much exploited now in the interpretation of the New Testament and for understanding early Christian history. Gnosticism was previously known almost exclusively from the writings of its more orthodox opponents. Gnosticism presented a rival interpretation of the Christian message, and this material adds a new dimension to understanding the early Christian period. Provisional translations of all the writings found at Nag Hammadi are available in the work edited by James Robinson (*The Nag Hammadi Library* [New York: Harper, 1977]). The major edition with English translations and notes is also edited by Robinson (*The Coptic Gnostic Library*, 15 volumes [Leiden: Brill, 1975–]).

15. Forty volumes at time of writing (New York: Newman Press, 1946–).
16. Sixty-nine volumes at time of writing (Washington: Catholic University of America, 1947–).

21

The Contributions of Archeology to New Testament Interpretation

John F. Wilson

Archeology may be defined as "the techniques and results of excavations and the means of dating and interpreting ancient material remains."[1] Note especially the word *interpreting*. Field archeologists excavate and discover buildings, pottery, tools, inscriptions, documents, and so on. But artifacts cannot speak; they become a valuable source of information only when they are correctly interpreted. Archeology, then, involves two indispensable activities: excavation and interpretation.

The Present State of New Testament Archeology

Biblical archeology deals primarily with interpretation, and G. E. Wright calls it a special "armchair variety of general archeology."[2] "The biblical archaeologist," he continues, "may or may not be an excavator himself, but he studies the discoveries of the excavations in order to glean from them every fact that throws a direct, indirect, or even diffused light upon the Bible."[3] Biblical archeology is not a special kind of field archeology; the artifacts studied are excavated in exactly the same way as any others. Rather, biblical archeology is a special kind of Bible study.

1. J. P. Kane, "Palestinian Archaeology and the New Testament," *Religion* 2 (1972): 69.
2. G. E. Wright, *Biblical Archaeology*, 2d ed. (Philadelphia: Westminster, 1962), p. 17.
3. Ibid.

According to H. D. Lance, it is "that subspeciality of biblical studies which seeks to bring to bear on the interpretation of the Bible all the information gained through archaeological research and discovery."[4]

New Testament archeology interprets discoveries that throw light on the New Testament text. It is commonly believed that archeology is much less valuable in New Testament studies than in studies of the Old. One scholar even notes that "'New Testament archaeology' scarcely exists as a field of inquiry, much less an academic discipline."[5] There are at least two reasons for this sad state of affairs—sad because it is depriving students and scholars of a great deal of useful information. First, since specifically "Christian" artifacts from the New Testament period are mostly nonexistent, many scholars have concluded that there is nothing to study. Even G. Ernest Wright, the great biblical archeologist, maintained that for New Testament studies, "archaeology cannot be expected to be as helpful as it has been with the Old Testament."[6] This, he says, is because the time period involved is much shorter (only a century or so), and because the early Christians were a tiny group "scattered throughout a vast realm" and therefore left nothing behind.[7] Because of this kind of thinking, New Testament archeology seldom attains more than a few pages in the final chapter of most books on biblical archeology—a sort of stepchild of the discipline.

Even more damaging is the attitude of the majority of New Testament scholars, especially those whose methods follow the line of Higher Criticism, running from F. C. Baur's "Tübingen School" through Dibelius's and Bultmann's "form-critical school" into the more recent approach of Redaction Criticism. Many of these scholars regard the Gospels as "late" and mostly historically unreliable documents that along with Acts were created to promote theological positions almost entirely unrelated to actual geographical locations or historical events. Obviously, sifting through dirt for coins, potsherds, and smashed buildings can contribute little to those who hold rigidly to such an understanding of the New Testament. For these reasons, the tremendous explosion of archeological information that has surfaced in recent years has been mainly ignored— despite the fact that some of it not only illuminates the text and the history of the primitive church, but even requires a reevaluation of some of the most cherished critical theories.

William F. Albright once noted that "all important radical schools of New Testament criticism of the nineteenth and twentieth centuries are

4. H. D. Lance, "American Biblical Archaeology in Perspective," BA 45 (1982): 100.
5. W. Dever, "What Archaeology Can Contribute to an Understanding of the Bible," BArRev 7 (1981): 41.
6. Wright, p.238.
7. Ibid., p.250.

prearchaeological."[8] Since their initial formulation, vast numbers of papyrus documents have surfaced in Israel and adjacent countries, especially Egypt. The Dead Sea Scrolls have burst onto the scene. Yet the critical theories, Albright charges, are not primarily based on such historical evidence but rather simply float *"in der Luft"* (in the air). They should be revised to fit the new evidence, but such a revision has not occurred, he concludes, because "New Testament scholars have not been accustomed to trouble themselves about history, archaeology, or other fields outside of their immediate specialty."[9]

As a result of the situation described by Albright, scholarly work on New Testament texts is often highly speculative, consisting mainly of textual reconstructions and theories about the intentions of the authors of the texts, and contributing very little to the understanding of the text. William Dever strikes home with his conclusion that "archaeology—in the broad sense of the deliberate or chance recovery of ancient remains, including epigraphic evidence—is obviously the *only* possible source of new factual data capable of elucidating the Bible, without which scholars are reduced to endless manipulation of the received texts, or application of ingenious but frequently inconclusive hypotheses."[10] If critical scholarship is to free itself from the maze of subjectivity in which it now wanders, it may have to face courageously the challenges of recent archeological discoveries and readjust its theories and methods accordingly. As Dever predicts, "it may be that the future of biblical studies will rest largely with the increasing sophistication of archaeology . . . in combination with improved historical and text critical studies."[11]

As the prevailing literary-critical presuppositions are more widely questioned and more and more New Testament scholars become disillusioned with the diminishing results of literary analysis, archeology may enjoy a resurgence of interest. Developments in the field of archeology itself suggest a brighter future for biblical, especially New Testament, archaeology. For example, since the birth of the modern state of Israel, archeology has become a kind of national passion in that nation. Major digs and important finds are numerous. A veritable explosion of new discoveries has occurred, with much of it only now becoming known outside Israel. Many of the most dramatic finds are dated precisely in the period of most interest to New Testament students—the "Second Temple Period," to use a favorite Israeli phrase. At the same time, archeological methodology has been vastly improved in recent years. Gone are the

8. W. F. Albright, "Retrospect and Prospect in New Testament Archaeology," *The Teacher's Yoke: Studies in Memory of Henry Trantham,* ed. E. J. Vardaman and J. L. Garrett, Jr., (Waco: 1964), p. 29.

9. Ibid., p.33.

10. Dever, p. 41.

11. Ibid.

romantic days when rich amateurs set out for the exotic lands of the East to search for treasure or for the graves of ancient heroes. Archeology is much more mundane now—but infinitely more useful. Archeologists today can work with historians to reconstruct the past in amazing detail, by studying no more than broken walls and floors, shattered pottery, layers of sand and gravel, shriveled seeds, broken bones, and barely discernible inscriptions. It is not necessary to find treasures, or museum pieces, or monumental buildings. In fact, such dramatic discoveries are often less useful than the lowly materials mentioned above.[12]

Both archeology and New Testament studies seem ready for an extremely fruitful new phase in their interrelationship.

The Goals and Limitations of New Testament Archeology

New Testament archeology deals with any artifact in any location and of any historical period, if that artifact throws light on the New Testament. But most of the contributions archeology can make in this field fall between certain limits of time and space. Geographically, the most important areas are Israel, Jordan, Syria, Lebanon, Arabia, Egypt, Asia Minor (modern Turkey), Greece, and Italy. Some of these countries contain the actual sites of New Testament events, while others provide useful background for the first century or have some other special significance. For example, Egypt, with its dry climate, provides most of the papyrus discoveries.

The most significant time period lies between 63 B.C., when Rome began to rule Palestine and much more of the East, and A.D. 138, when the second and last Jewish revolt was put down. During this time the world of the New Testament developed, Jesus carried out his ministry, the Christian church began and expanded throughout the Roman Empire, and the New Testament documents were written. Within these perimeters of time and space, archeology can make at least five kinds of contributions to New Testament studies:

Apologetics

In many conservative-evangelical circles archeology is conceived of primarily as an apologetic tool, as a way to prove the truthfulness of the Bible. The story of William Ramsey, the late-nineteenth-century scholar whose research in Asia Minor confirmed many historical details in the Book of Acts, is told and retold as the example *par excellence* of the way in

---

12. See W. Dever, "Archaeological Method in Israel: Continuing Revolution," BA 43 (1980): 41–8; J. F. Strange, "New Developments in Greco-Roman Archaeology in Palestine," BA 45 (1982): 85–8.

which archeology can validate the biblical record.[13] Care must be taken not to overemphasize such a claim. Sometimes dramatic "proofs" are later found to be based on misinterpretation of the artifacts.[14] Furthermore, to prove that an ancient writer was correct on some historical point does not prove that writer to be inspired. Excavations have time and again verified the accuracy of passages in the works of the first-century Jewish historian Flavius Josephus, sometimes in astonishing detail.[15] This fact in no way verifies Josephus's religious statements, let alone proves him to be inspired! D. J. Wiseman, a highly respected evangelical archeologist and ancient historian, cautions that extra-biblical sources such as archeology "indicate the contemporary thought and methodologies but cannot themselves directly relate to the historical doctrines of revelation and inspiration."[16]

This is not to say that archeology has no apologetic function, however. In fact, the overwhelming impression one gets from an investigation of the archeological record is of the historical and cultural reality of the persons, places, and events described in the New Testament. Fairy tales have their own imaginary times, places, and characters—"Once upon a time, in a faraway land, there lived a king. . . ." Not so are the narratives of the New Testament, which are anchored to the geography and history of *terra firma*.

Sometimes, for example, we can even know what a biblical character looked like. King Herod Agrippa I, who persecuted the early church and killed the apostle James (Acts 12:2), left an excellent likeness of himself on a coin minted in Caesarea in 43 A.D., shortly before his grisly death (described in Acts 12:19–23 and Josephus's *Ant.* 19. 8. 2). The coin's inscription illustrates the egotism and political opportunism for which Acts 12 condemns him: "The Great King Agrippa, Lover of Caesar."[17] Another coin provides us with an actual portrait of Salome, the girl who danced before Herod Antipas and was rewarded with the head of John the Baptist.[18]

The geographical and historical context of a New Testament story is often vividly confirmed by archeology. Excavations on the northern peak

13. E.g., E. M. Blaiklock, *The Archaeology of the New Testament* (Grand Rapids: Zondervan, 1974), pp. 99–106.

14. The fallen walls discovered in Jericho, widely cited as confirming Joshua 6, are now known to predate Joshua by centuries. Other examples abound.

15. Josephus correctly describes the paint job done by the decorators of Herod's private apartments at Masada; excavations uncovered the very walls, painted as he described them. See Y. Yadin, *Masada* (London: Sphere, 1966), pp. 41–52.

16. D. J. Wiseman, "Archaeology and Scripture," WTJ 33 (1970/1): 133–52.

17. See J. Meyshan, "The Coinage of Agrippa the First," IEJ 4 (1954): 186–200.

18. Mark 6:17–29. See D. Hendin, *Guide to Ancient Jewish Coins* (New York: Attic, 1976), p. 42.

of Mount Gerizim, the sacred mountain of the Samaritans, revealed a large altar of uncut stones, apparently the altar of sacrifice. Further investigation indicated this altar to have been in ruins in Jesus' day, destroyed by the Jewish King Hyrcanus in 128 B.C. This shows us why the Samaritan woman with whom Jesus talked at Jacob's well (John 4:4–24) used the aorist tense in her statement, "Our fathers worshiped on this mountain" (v. 20, RSV), indicating that worship once had taken place there, but no longer did. Furthermore, using surveying techniques, the archeologists showed that the site of the ruined altar was in full view from the well, accounting for the word *this* in the woman's question and Jesus' reply ("a time is coming when you will worship the Father neither on this mountain nor in Jerusalem"). Although such evidence does not prove that the conversation in John 4 took place, it does prove that the story is set in an actual geographical location at a very specific time and that both time and place are verifiable as real.[19] Such minute and verifiable details suggest that the New Testament writers were not creating whole stories out of thin air.

Devotional Data

Archeology is of value in judging the historical validity of so-called Christian holy places, sites where notable New Testament events are said to have occurred. Greco-Roman religion considered certain spots to be "holy," that is, to be places where the "other world" of gods and spirits touches this world. It was believed that prayers offered on such spots were more likely to be answered and that touching them meant coming in physical contact with the divine. The Christianity of the post-Constantinian era, which adopted so many Greco-Roman pagan practices, also adopted this one. Sometimes the pagan divinity was simply Christianized and the holy place and its veneration continued. Of particular interest were sites where Jesus had been or where miracles had occurred.

From the fourth century on, hundreds of pilgrims began coming to the Holy Land to visit the places where Jesus was born and raised, taught and performed miracles, and was crucified, buried, and resurrected. Their motive in coming was not historical curiosity; they hoped by such pilgrimages to actually experience the transcendent—to touch the "other world."[20]

Sometimes the holy places were in fact preserved in the memory of the pre-Constantinian churches and were most probably the actual sites of Jesus' activity. Many others have little or no claim to authenticity. The

19. See R. Bull, "An Archaeological Context for Understanding John 4:20," BA 38 (1975): 55–7; and "The Excavation of Tell er-Ras on Mt. Gerizim," BA 31 (1968): 58–72.

20. See J. Wilkinson, *Jerusalem Pilgrimages Before the Crusades* (Jerusalem: Ariel, 1977), pp. 33–43.

sites have usually been covered with a series of churches where the pilgrims could pray. Often the construction of these churches, which sometimes date to Constantine (early fourth century) or even earlier, quite literally destroyed the actual historical site. An example is the Church of the Holy Sepulcher in Jerusalem, where an ancient tomb which may in fact have been Jesus' burial place, and an ancient rock outcropping, which may in fact have been his place of execution, have been almost entirely obliterated due to efforts to "venerate" them.

Most of the work done at such sites is not "New Testament archeology" as has been defined above. It is rather the study of early Christian architecture. Still, there are cases where the excavations do shed light on the possible authenticity of a site and provide interesting and helpful historical information. Examples include the excavations at the Church of the Annunciation in Nazareth and the so-called House of Saint Peter in Capernaum. Still, even if a site proved to be the very spot where a New Testament event transpired, for most modern students and scholars the value of such verification will depend on whether light is thrown on the meaning of the text.

Illustrative Material

By far the most fruitful use of archeology in New Testament studies may be called illustrative. Any text becomes more understandable when it can be placed in context—not simply a literary context but also a cultural, historical, geographical, and religious context. The New Testament has a definite context in time and space: roughly the first century A.D. in the eastern Greco-Roman world. Some literature has survived from this environment—the writings of Josephus, Strabo, Tacitus, the papyri, and so on. Alongside these written records must be added the growing list of archeological discoveries that furnish parallel material to clarify and illustrate the New Testament text.

Numerous examples could be given. The rage of the crowds and the ensuing riot when Paul was thought to have brought a Gentile into the temple in Jerusalem (Acts 21:27–36) is better understood in the light of two stone inscriptions. Found in 1871 and 1938, these inscriptions seem to be the very ones described by Josephus (Ant. 15. 11. 5) Their message is clear: "No foreigner is to enter within the balustrade and enclosure around the temple area. Whoever is caught will have himself to blame for his death which will follow."

Here the literary and archeological evidences come together to provide a clear "context" for the biblical text. What might otherwise have appeared to the reader to be a tempest in a teapot can now be understood to represent a serious outrage in the eyes of the crowd and thus a real threat to Paul's life.

In 1968 archeologist Vasilios Tzaferis reported the discovery of a first-century tomb at Giv'at Mivtar in north Jerusalem. Among the skeletons was one of a young man (24 to 28 years old) who had met death by crucifixion. The evidence was unmistakable: a large nail, about sixteen centimeters long, still held the man's calcanean (ankle) bones together. The arm bones just above the wrist were scratched where the nails had passed through them. Although thousands of people were crucified in the first century, no remains had ever been found, probably because the corpses of those so despised as to undergo such a punishment were simply tossed on the dump heap. In some way this man's body had been rescued and placed in the tomb of a wealthy family, just as was the body of Jesus (Mark 15:42–47; John 19:38–42). Also, both leg bones were broken in two between the knee and ankle, just as was the case with the criminals crucified with Jesus (John 19:31–33). Not only does this dramatic find provide medical experts an opportunity to study the physiology of crucifixion, it also gives New Testament scholars a context for the accounts of the crucifixion of Jesus.[21]

Many other finds with implications for New Testament study come from the vast Jerusalem necropolis, the ancient graveyard of the Second Temple period. For example, names familiar in the New Testament are common in tomb inscriptions (Martha, Salome, Simon, Saul, Sapphira, and so on). There is even an inscription that seems to read "Alexander of Cyrene, Simon's son" (cf. Mark 15:21).[22]

These few examples represent a veritable avalanche of discoveries, appearing in field reports at a mind-boggling rate. Through them the context of the New Testament is becoming clearer and the implications for text studies more and more unavoidable.

Exegetical Implications

Exegesis is the process by which one determines what a text meant to its original author and readers. Archeology can be very helpful in doing exegesis, although its use in New Testament studies is still limited. Major New Testament commentaries seldom make adequate use of archeological discoveries.

An example of the use of archeology in New Testament exegesis may be drawn from the Jerusalem necropolis excavations. Fortunately, Second Temple Jewish tombs are easy to identify since they exhibit distinctive

---

21. See V. Tzaferis, "Jewish Tombs at and Near Giv'at ha-Mivtar, Jerusalem," IEJ 20 (1970), 18–32; N. Haas, "Anthropological Observations on the Skeletal Remains from Giv'at ha-Mivtar," IEJ 20 (1970): 38–59; V. Moller-Christensen, "Skeletal Remains from Giv'at ha-Mivtar," IEJ 26 (1976): 35–8.

22. N. Avigad, "A Depository of Inscribed Ossuaries in the Kidron Valley," IEJ 12 (1962): 1–12.

burial customs. The typical tomb was carved from rock,[23] often on a steep valley side. The entrance displayed a memorial structure carved from rock. Several such memorials of various designs have survived from Jesus' day and may still be seen in the Kidron Valley. A small doorway, which could be sealed with a rolling stone, led into a square burial chamber. Around the edges of this chamber were stone benches, and cut into the walls were *kokhim* or *loculi*, slots for individual burials.

Sometimes sarcophagi (large stone coffins) are found in the tombs, especially those of very wealthy or important persons. But usually the tombs contain stone boxes called ossuaries, just long enough to accommodate the longest bone in the human skeleton, the femur. The skeleton having been disassembled, the bones of the deceased are carefully stacked inside the ossuary. Sometimes several skeletons are placed together in an ossuary, and often the names of the deceased are scratched on the outside.

Ossuary tombs are found in abundance in Jerusalem and Jericho. They confirm the practice of secondary burial by at least some Jews of the time. In such burials the body was first laid on one of the stone benches in the tomb and left for a year or longer, until all the flesh decayed. The bones were then placed in an ossuary, with suitable ceremony, as a final resting place. Apparently this custom was exclusively Jewish and was limited to the Jerusalem-Jericho area. The burials can be dated from the time of Herod I (37–4 B.C.) to the early third century A.D. and in Jericho even more narrowly—between A.D. 10 and A.D. 70.

Why did such a custom arise? The evidence seems to point to a Pharisaic origin, and the reason is theological. The Pharisees believed quite literally in resurrection (cf. Acts 23:8) and were thus concerned to preserve the bones of the dead. But special care was taken not to preserve the flesh. Even when the final resting place was a sarcophagus, holes were cut in the sides of the coffin so that the flesh, reduced to liquid by putrefaction, would drain away. Why this care to preserve the bones but destroy the flesh? Because sin resides in the flesh, and lest one's sins be carried into the day of judgment, the "sinful flesh" must quite literally be stripped off! (cf. 2 Cor. 5:1–5).[24]

The custom and the theology behind it must have impressed a young theology student, Saul of Tarsus, whose education in Jerusalem occurred precisely when this custom was most prominent. This fact is significant in exegeting the many Pauline texts that use the word *flesh*. Statements that should be studied with this archeological data in mind include:

23. Cf. Matt 27:60; Mark 15:46; Luke 23:53.
24. See L. Y. Rahmani, "Ancient Jerusalem's Funerary Customs and Tombs," BA 45 (1982): 109–19; R. Hachlili, "Ancient Burial Customs Preserved in Jericho Hills," BArRev 5 (1979): 28–35; R. Hachlili, "A Second Temple Period Necropolis in Jericho," BA 43 (1980): 235–40.

Romans 7:18: "I know that good does not dwell in me, that is, in my flesh."

Romans 7:25: "In my flesh I serve the law of sin. . . ."

Romans 8:3: "God, sending his son in the likeness of sinning flesh, and for the sinning. . . ."

1 Corinthians 15:50: "Flesh and blood cannot inherit the kingdom of God, nor does the perishable inherit the imperishable."

Galatians 3:3 "Are you trying to reach perfection by means of the flesh?"

Galatians 5:19: "These obviously are works of the flesh. . . ."

Galatians 6:8: "The one who sows in his flesh will harvest decay, but the one who sows in the spirit will harvest eternal life."

Perhaps one might even include the difficult statement regarding the scandalous relationship in the church at Corinth: "Hand this man over to Satan for the destruction of the flesh, so that the spirit may be saved in the day of the Lord" (1 Cor. 5:5).

Lexigraphy

Archeology is also of great value in determining more precisely the meaning of words used by the New Testament writers. The Egyptian papyri, which revealed the common, day-to-day Greek language of the first century, show that the New Testament is written in *Koine* (that is, "common") Greek, rather than classical or the special "Holy Ghost" Greek. This discovery has been of inestimable value in improving our translations of the New Testament.

Inscriptions can serve the same purpose. For example, Jesus condemns those who avoid the commandment to honor father and mother by pronouncing a proposed gift to them as "Corban, that is, a gift dedicated to God" (Mark 7:10–13). Archeologists have found the word *corban* at least twice in the very period Jesus made his accusation. First, near the south wall of the temple enclosure in Jerusalem, a stone vessel was found incised with pictures of doves or pigeons and marked with the word *KPBN:* "corban."[25] One is immediately reminded of Luke 2:22–24, where Jesus' parents bring him to the temple and sacrifice "a pair of doves or two young pigeons." The inscription apparently pronounces such birds "corban," or set aside for holy use. Second, an ossuary found in the Kidron Valley, a short distance from the temple mount to the south, has the following inscription (as translated by J. A. Fitzmeyer):

25. B. Mazar, "Excavations Near Temple Mount Reveal Splendors of Herodian Jerusalem," BArRev 6 (1980): 59.

All that a man may find-to-his-profit in this ossuary (is) an offering [corban] to God from him who is within it.[26]

In other words, "you cannot use anything you find here, because it is Corban!" These inscriptions clearly indicate the meaning of *Corban* in Mark 7:11.[27]

A final example will suffice. Excavators at Beth Shean-Scythopolis, one of the Decapolis cities mentioned in the Gospels, found two inscriptions using the Greek word *amphodon*. These were apparently what we would call "street signs" identifying "the *amphodon* of Demetrius" and "the grain *amphodon*." An *amphodon* is thus seen to be a building containing a group of shops or a "bazaar," such as is still common in the Middle East.[28] Mark, alone among the Synoptics, notes that Jesus' disciples, whom he sent to secure a colt for his triumphal entry into Jerusalem, found the colt *pros thuran exō epi tou amphodou* (Mark 11:4). That is, he was tied "outside the doorway leading to an arcade of shops," surely a more vivid and accurate picture than "by a door without in a place where two ways met" (KJV).

Conclusion

Archeology seems likely to assume a more prominent place in the study of the New Testament. The various forms of literary-critical studies are like veins of silver, some of which have been mined out during the last century, resulting in less and less recovery of value. Meanwhile, archeologists have quite literally discovered rich new deposits of information that offer new and exciting possibilities for students and scholars to understand better the foundational documents of the Christian faith. For those who are willing to devote themselves to the task, the future seems bright.

A Basic Bibliography

Note: only a few works are listed, but they form a good beginning point and will themselves lead to a wealth of further bibliographical references.

26. J. A. Fitzmeyer, "The Aramaic Qorban Inscription from Jebel Hallet et-Tur; and Mark 7:11/Matthew 15:5," *Essays on the Semitic Background of the New Testament* (Missoula, Montana: Scholars Press, 1974), p. 96.

27. It is interesting that in the parallel passage, Matt 15:5, in the supposedly more "Jewish" gospel, this Aramaic term has been dropped in favor of the *Greek* word for "offering."

28. G. M. Fitzgerald, "Two Inscriptions from Beisan," PEQ (1926): 150–4. Note appended by F. C. Burkitt, p. 154.

Books

1. Finegan, Jack. *The Archaeology of the New Testament. The Life of Jesus and the Beginning of the Early Church*. Princeton: Princeton University, 1969.
2. ———. *The Archaeology of the New Testament. The Mediterranean World of the Early Christian Apostles*. Boulder, CO: Westview Press, 1981.
3. Meyers, Eric M., and Strange, James F. *Archaeology, the Rabbis and Early Christianity*. Nashville: Abingdon, 1981.
4. Wilkinson, John. *Jerusalem as Jesus Knew It. Archaeology as Evidence*. London: Thames and Hudson, 1978.
5. Yamauchi, Edwin. *The Archaeology of New Testament Cities in Western Asia Minor*. Grand Rapids: Baker, 1980.

Periodicals

1. *The Biblical Archaeologist*
2. *The Biblical Archaeology Review*
3. *The Israel Exploration Journal*
4. *The Palestine Exploration Quarterly*

22
Use of the Old Testament in the New

Neale Pryor

"The Old Testament is the New Testament concealed. The New Testament is the Old Testament revealed." This adage has long been the clear expression of believers regarding the relationship of the two testaments. Paul bound the two together in this statement, "For whatever was written in earlier times was written for our instruction, that through perseverance and the encouragement of the Scriptures we might have hope" (Rom. 15:4, NAS).

The relationship between the two testaments is not as simple as might seem at first, especially in the way New Testament writers make use of passages from the Old. The problems fall into two general categories. First, some Old Testament passages that are applied to New Testament situations do not seem in their original context to refer to the events of the Christian era. Second, the New Testament sometimes does not seem to quote the Old's text faithfully, sometimes even changing the reading to fit the purpose of the writer.

Is there evidence of dishonesty in the New Testament writers? Do they take unallowable liberties with the text? How could the Jews be convinced that the Old Testament predicted New Testament events by inaccurate quotes or strained exegesis? Or, did the New Testament writers employ exegesis from the Old Testament that was accepted in their day? A frank and open look at this problem should be helpful to any serious student of the Bible.

The Application of Old Testament Prophecies in the New

It would be nice if the Old Testament always predicted an event that was clearly fulfilled in the New and there was never any more question about it. This is the general view of the naive student of the Bible. Upon closer examination, however, there is often evidence that a New Testament writer was applying a passage that seems not to have anything to do with that situation and perhaps was never in the mind of the Old Testament writer.

Perhaps other categories could be given, but there are at least four ways in which New Testament writers applied passages from the Old. First, there are those prophecies that have direct fulfillment. The Old Testament predicts the event, and the New shows its fulfillment. Those are the easy ones. Second, there are double prophecies. These passages have a fulfillment in the time of the prophet and also have a second, more remote, fulfillment in Christ. Third, there is the typological fulfillment, where something in the Old typifies an event in the New. Fourth, there are instances where the wording in the Old just fits, and it seems that the writer in the New has appropriated it and applied it to fit his situation.

J. W. McGarvey saw three different types of fulfillment in Matthew 2:

> Verses 6, 15, and 18 give us three kinds of prophecy. The first is direct and relates wholly to an event which was yet future; the second is a case where an act described is symbolic of another later and larger act; the last is a case where words describing one act may be taken as fitly and vividly describing another later act, though the acts themselves may bear small resemblance.[1]

Examples for all four categories are given below, using quotations from the New American Standard Version of the Bible throughout.

Examples of Direct Fulfillment

1. *Matthew 2:6:* The wise men followed the star to Jerusalem and there inquired where the King of the Jews was to be born. The chief priests and scribes said that he was to be born in Bethlehem, ". . . for so it has been written by the prophet:

> And you, Bethlehem, land of Judah,
> Are by no means least among the leaders of Judah;
> For out of you shall come forth a Ruler,
> Who will shepherd My people Israel.

The quotation, except for the last line of the verse, basically reflects the words of Micah 5:2. It would seems that Micah is directly prophesying that the Messiah is to be born in Bethlehem, the birthplace of King David.

---

1. J. W. McGarvey, *The Fourfold Gospel* (Cincinnati: Standard Publishing, n.d.), pp. 51–52.

How appropriate that the king to take over David's throne should also be born in that place!

There is no indication from the text of Micah that the prophet had any incident of his day in mind. (This conclusion is debated.) He was looking forward to the coming of the Messiah and predicting his birth at Bethlehem. Jesus was born in Bethlehem as a direct fulfillment of this prophecy. The prophet foretold it, and it was fulfilled as he foretold it. This is the simplest of the examples of direct prophetic fulfillment.

2. *Matthew 4:15–16:* A second example of this type of fulfillment is regarding the glorification of the land of Zebulun and Naphtali. Matthew told of Christ leaving Nazareth and moving to Capernaum. He then cited Isaiah 9:1–2:

> The land of Zebulun and the land of Naphtali,
> By the way of the sea, beyond the Jordan, Galilee of the Gentiles—
> The people who were sitting in darkness saw a great light,
> And to those who were sitting in the land and shadow of death,
> Upon them a light dawned.

Although there may be those who maintain that Isaiah 9 is not messianic but predicts the glorious return of Israel from Babylonian captivity, the context of verses 1–7 seems to demand a messianic fulfillment all the way. In verses 4 and 5 God will break the power of the enemy. In verse 6 the child is to be born, and in verse 7 he will sit upon the throne of David and reign forever in justice and righteousness.

The land of Zebulun and Naphtali had suffered greatly in the days of Isaiah through the Assyrian invasions: "In the days of Pekah king of Israel, Tiglath-pileser king of Assyria came and captured . . . Gilead and Galilee, all the land of Naphtali; and he carried them captive to Assyria" (2 Kings 15:29). Isaiah was saying that this land had suffered much, but in days to come it would be most glorious. This was the land of Galilee in New Testament times. This was the very land most frequently trodden by the Son of God. Jesus' move to Capernaum and his setting up this town as his base of operation made the land of Zebulun and Naphtali a most enviable place.

Here is another example of direct prophetic fulfillment. The prophet predicted the event; it was fulfilled in the New Testament. It was easy for the writer to point back to the words of the prophet and say, "This is that which was fulfilled."

Examples of a Double (or "Fuller Meaning") Prophecy

1. *Matthew 1:23:* Matthew tells of Joseph's dream, in which he was informed by the angel that Mary was with child conceived by the Holy Spirit (v. 20). He then sees in Isaiah 7:14 a prediction of this event:

> Now all this took place that what was spoken by the Lord through the prophet might be fulfilled, saying, "Behold, the virgin shall be with child, and shall bear a Son, and they shall call His name Immanuel," which translated means, "God with us."

If one looks to Isaiah 7 and reads this passage in its context, he will see that the prophet was not primarily speaking of the birth of Christ. Isaiah had gone to Ahaz, king of Judah, with a message of hope. Judah was being threatened at that time (about 734 B.C.) with an invasion from the combined armies of Syria and Ephraim. Isaiah told Ahaz not to fear these "two stubs of smoldering firebrands" (v. 4). The invasion would not materialize and soon both Syria and Ephraim would be destroyed.

Isaiah then offered to give Ahaz a sign that this would occur, even if the king did not want a sign. "Therefore the Lord Himself will give you a sign: Behold, a virgin will be with child and bear a son, and she will call His name Immanuel" (v. 14). The sign was further explained in verse 16: "For before the boy will know enough to refuse evil and choose good, the land whose two kings you dread will be forsaken." In other words, before a woman can conceive and bear a child and that child gets old enough to know right from wrong, Syria and Ephraim will both be destroyed. The time span would cover about thirteen years. Within two or three years of this prophecy, Syria was destroyed (732 B.C.). Within another ten years, Ephraim was taken into captivity (722 B.C.).

There is really no way that one can make this prophecy apply exclusively to the birth of Christ without totally disregarding the context of Isaiah 7. Here seems to be an example of a prophecy that has two applications. It applies to the situation in the prophet's time. The sign of the birth of the child gives the time within which the kingdoms of Syria and Ephraim will be gone. But there is also a more remote fulfillment in the birth of Christ.

It is significant that the word that Isaiah used for virgin, 'almah, is one that may connote either a virgin or a young woman. In the days of Isaiah it was a young woman who would give birth to a child, and there is no way to tell which young woman this may be. Perhaps it is not any specific young woman, but just a manner of speaking: before any woman can conceive and bear a child and that child know right from wrong. Isaiah used a similar expression to denote a time span in 8:4, ". . . for before the boy knows how to cry out 'My father' or 'My mother,' the wealth of Damascus and the spoil of Samaria will be carried away before the king of Assyria."

Nothing in the context of Isaiah 7 would demand a virgin birth. Yet, in the birth of Jesus, the woman was a virgin. While 'almah may just mean a young woman of marriageable age, it may also mean virgin. The LXX translated *'almah* by the Greek *parthenos* (virgin) in Isaiah 7:14, even though the usual translation was *neanis* (young woman). Matthew used the LXX translation, *parthenos*, in his citation of the passage.

3. *Matthew 2:17–18:* There is a possibility that this passage could be a double prophecy. First the slaughter of the infants by Herod is described. Then Matthew adds:

> Then that which was spoken through Jeremiah the prophet was fulfilled, saying,
> "A voice was heard in Ramah,
> Weeping and great mourning,
> Rachel weeping for her children;
> And she refused to be comforted,
> Because they were no more."

If one examines the context in Jeremiah 31:15, he would find no evidence that the author had in mind Herod's slaughter of the children. The passage in Jeremiah is a message of hope. Here, as in Matthew, Rachel symbolized the mothers of Israel. The mothers were weeping for their children who had gone into captivity. In verses 16–17 they are told to weep no more, for their children were coming home:

> Thus says the LORD,
> "Restrain your voice from weeping,
> And your eyes from tears;
> For your work shall be rewarded," declares the LORD,
> "And they shall return from the land of the enemy.
> And there is hope for your future," declares the LORD,
> "And your children shall return to their own territory."

It is possible that Matthew was merely appropriating the words of Jeremiah and applying them to the situation in Jesus' day. But it is likewise possible that this passage is a double prophecy. It had an application in the days of the prophet: the exile would be over soon, and the children of the mothers of Israel would return home. It also had a more remote fulfillment in the time of Christ, when the mothers of Israel would weep for their children whom Herod had killed. At any rate, it is obvious that Jeremiah did not primarily have the slaughter of the infants in mind when he penned these words.

Examples of Typological Fulfillment

1. *Matthew 2:15:* In telling of the flight into Egypt, Matthew saw a prophecy of this event in Hosea 11:1. Matthew 2:14–15 reads:

> And he arose and took the Child and His mother by night, and departed for Egypt; and was there until the death of Herod, that what was spoken by the Lord through the prophet might be fulfilled, saying, "Out of Egypt did I call My Son."

Again, by looking at Hosea 11:1, the reader would never get the idea that the prophet had in mind the flight into Egypt. God was recalling those tender moments of Israel's infancy, when the nation was just leaving Egypt. The parallel of a father's remembering those tender moments when his child was but a babe is evident. In Hosea 11:3, God recalls the times he taught Ephraim to walk, taking him by the arms and helping him along. Another possible reading would give the sense that God took Ephraim up in his arms. Either reading shows the sweet and tender relationship that once was. Then Hosea says that the ungrateful child grew up and rebelled against God.

There is really no way this could prophesy of the flight into Egypt by Jesus and his parents except typologically. God's "son" in the Old Testament was Israel. God's Son in the New Testament is the Christ. In this parallel, the events of God's "son" in the Old Testament foreshadowed—and in a sense were prophetic of—what the Son did in the New.

2. *First Corinthians 10:4:* Paul says that the children of Israel all ate the same spiritual food and drank "from a spiritual rock which followed them; and the rock was Christ." This is a possible parallel to the first example. The Rock that gave Israel water in the wilderness was a type of Christ, the source of living water (cf. John 4:10; 7:38).

3. *Other examples:* The writer of Hebrews sees many parallels and lessons to be drawn from the tabernacle. He sees typified in the tabernacle the redemption provided by Christ. The Most Holy Place represents heaven (9:24), the veil represents the flesh of Christ (10:20), the washing of the priests represents baptism (10:22). These and many other lessons can be learned from typological fulfillment. The whole Old Testament system of sacrifice was prophetic in that it typified Christ's offering of himself.

Similarly, to Peter, the salvation of Noah and his family through water was a type of salvation through the water of baptism (1 Pet. 3:21). Peter's emphasis was not that Noah was saved by the ark from the water, but that he was saved through the water. The water was the division between the old world of sin and the new world cleansed of sin. Likewise, baptism is that division in the conversion of a sinner.

Examples of Appropriated Texts

1. *Matthew 13:34–35:* After telling of the seaside parables—the sower, the tares, the mustard seed, and the leaven—Matthew includes the summary statement in 13:34–35:

All these things Jesus spoke to the multitudes in parables, and He did not
speak to them without a parable, so that what was spoken through the
prophet might be fulfilled, saying,
"I will open My mouth in parables;
I will utter things hidden since the foundation of the world."

Again, one would never think from reading the Old Testament passage
here quoted (Ps. 78:2) that it had any reference to Jesus' speaking in
parables. Psalm 78 begins with the author's invitation to the people to
listen to what he has to say. He then proceeds to rehearse the history of
Israel, emphasizing her continued rebelliousness and God's continued
goodness and blessings. In inviting the people to listen to what he has to
say, the psalmist says (vv. 2–3):

> I will open my mouth in a parable;
> I will utter dark sayings of old,
> Which we have heard and known,
> And our fathers have told us.

Here seems to be an example where Matthew appropriated the text
and applied it to Jesus simply because the wording fit so perfectly. It could
be argued that this is a double prophecy, but it does not seem likely.
Perhaps there is some typological connection in that the teacher in the
psalm was a "type" of the greatest Teacher of all.

2. *Matthew 2:18:* As was suggested earlier, it is possible that Matthew's
use of Jeremiah 31:15 in Matthew 2:18 is an appropriation of the text. The
wording fit the situation, so Matthew saw no reason not to include it
among his prophecies of Christ.

The Manner in Which Old Testament Prophecies Are Quoted in the New

There seems to be no consistency in the way Old Testament passages
are quoted in the New. Frequently it is evident that the LXX is the basis of
the quotations, even though it is not possible to know exactly how the
LXX text of the first century read. Second, there are other occasions
where the quotations seem to be independent translations from the
Hebrew. Third, there are those quotations which seem to follow neither
the LXX nor the Hebrew text but may be deliberate alterations of the text
to suit the needs of the author.[2]

---

2. See E. E. Ellis, *Paul's Use of the Old Testament* (Edinburgh: Oliver and Boyd,
1957), pp. 155–85.

Examples of Quotations from the LXX

Particularly interesting are those passages in which the New Testament writer follows the LXX when it fits in with what he is saying, but the Hebrew text gives a totally different sense. Is he following the true original reading, or is he choosing a translation that suits his purpose when the original does not?

One such example is the quotation by James of Amos 9:11–12 in Acts 15:16–18. The problem is seen in Acts 15:17, where James quotes to show that God included the Gentiles in the Church: "'In order that the rest of mankind may seek the LORD,/And all the Gentiles who are called by My name."

In Amos 9:12 the passage reads: "'That they may possess the remnant of Edom/And all the nations who are called by My name'. . . .'"

It is easy to see how the variant reading came about. The Hebrew words for *Edom* and *mankind* are identical except for the vowel pointings, which were added after the time of Christ. In Hebrew the words for "seek" and "possess" are very similar and could be easily confused by a scribe. But the sense of the passage is completely changed. Amos is saying that Israel will possess the land of Edom in the latter days. The LXX, which James quotes, says that all mankind will seek the Lord.

One must first ask which text is the original one. Perhaps James is quoting the original, and the Hebrew text is defective here. Perhaps James, an inspired apostle, is giving a reading that he knows is at variance with the Hebrew but he believes does not lessen the truth of what he says. He was teaching that Gentiles are to be included; he was not at that time becoming a textual critic!

Examples of Quotations from the Hebrew Independent of the LXX

Matthew gives twelve quotations introduced by the formula, "that that which was spoken by the prophet might be fulfilled." These have been identified as "formula quotations" or *Reflexionszitate*. They are 1:22–23; 2:5–6; 2:15; 2:17–18; 2:23; 3:3; 4:14–16; 8:17; 12:17–21; 13:35; 21:4–5; 27:9–10. Another feature characteristic of all of these is that they seem to be direct translations from the Hebrew, independent of the LXX. This has raised an interesting question as to whether they may be part of a Book of Testimonies that the early church used in teaching Jews. Could this Book of Testimonies be the Logia that Matthew composed in Aramaic, spoken of by Papias?

Ellis discussed this possibility as seen in the way Paul quoted the Old Testament: "The NT contains quotations which vary from the LXX and MT but which agree with parallel NT and patristic citations."[3] Could even

3. Ibid., p. 99.

the church fathers be acquainted with this Testimonia and be quoting it in their citations from the Old Testament?

Perhaps the New Testament writer was making his own translation from the Hebrew text in these instances. Or perhaps he had a Greek translation of key texts in the Old Testament from which he was quoting, maybe even a Book of Testimonies.

Examples of Quotations that Deviate from the Hebrew and the LXX

There are occasions where the New Testament writers are quoting from no known text. It even looks as if they may be deliberately changing a reading in order to make it fit the point they are trying to make. Two of the most flagrant examples of these will be discussed.

1. *Ephesians 4:8:* It seems that Paul was quoting Psalms 68:18 here, but he deliberately changed the text to suit his needs. In the Psalms passage the king is honored for having won a great victory with the help of God. He is pictured as sitting triumphant while the conquered bring their tribute to him: "Thou hast ascended on high. Thou hast led captive Thy captives;/Thou hast received gifts among men. . . ."

Paul applied this to Christ, but spoke of Christ's *giving* gifts to men instead of receiving them: "When He ascended on high,/He led captive a host of captives,/And He gave gifts to men."

Paul changed the second person (Thou) to the third (He). This may be understandable, but why did he change "received" to "gave"?

One attempt to harmonize the passages is that the king in the Psalms verse received gifts from men in order to bestow them on his subjects. In like fashion Christ received gifts from heaven to bestow them upon his children. An additional insight comes from the Aramaic Targum. According to F. Foulkes:

> The Targum on the Psalms, that may involve an interpretation going back into pre-Christian times, has 'Thou ascendest up to the firmament, O prophet Moses, thou tookest captives captive, thou didst teach the words of the law, thou gavest them as gifts to the children of men.'[4]

It seems that the rabbinic interpretation of this passage made it apply to Moses ascending Mount Sinai and bringing the gifts of the law down to Israel. It is interesting that the Syriac Peshitta version also gives this reading of Psalms 68:18.

Paul was not drawing from a totally unknown rendering of the passage in Psalms. He was reflecting the current rabbinic interpretation of the

---

4. F. Foulkes, *The Epistle of Paul to the Ephesians* in *The Tyndale New Testament Commentaries*, ed. R. V. G. Tasker (Grand Rapids: Eerdmans, 1978), p. 115.

passage and used that particular rendering to explain how Christ bestowed the various gifts and offices of the church.

2. *Hebrews 10:5:* The writer of Hebrews was showing that the blood of bulls and goats could not avail to take away sin; therefore, the offering of the body of Christ was necessary. In his argument he quoted from Psalms in Hebrews 10:5: "Therefore when he comes into the world, He says, 'Sacrifice and offering Thou hast not desired,/But a body Thou hast prepared for Me.'"

The relevant passage in Psalms 40:6 reads: "Sacrifice and meal offering Thou hast not desired;/My ears Thou hast opened. . . ." Literally the Hebrew says "ears thou hast digged for me." Perhaps it refers to opening the ears so one can hear and obey. The idea in the psalm seems to be that more than sacrifices, God wants men to hear him and obey him.

But what led the writer of Hebrews to make the change from "ears Thou hast digged" to "a body Thou hast prepared"? Bruce saw this not as a translation from the psalm:

> . . . it is rather an interpretative paraphrase of the Hebrew text. The Greek translator evidently regarded the Hebrew wording as an instance of *pars pro toto;* the "digging" or hollowing out of the ears is a part of the total work of fashioning a human body.[5]

The writer could be quoting the accurate text, which has long since been lost, but that is unlikely. He seems to be taking liberty as an inspired writer to give an interpretation on the text that the original writer never intended.

Summation

Before one can sit in judgment on New Testament writers in their use of the Old Testament, he needs more information. They may be citing the original text, although the available evidence does not seem to point in that direction. They may be using exegesis that by our standards may not be acceptable yet was totally acceptable in their day. How else could so many have been convinced by the way in which the writers proved that Christ fulfilled the Old Testament Scriptures?

There may be more in the word *fulfill (plēroō)* than meets the eye. It seems that the early Christians felt that the whole testimony of the Old Testament was toward the Christian dispensation. Every shadow, action, and statement of the men of old could find some fulfillment in the New Testament.

5. F. F. Bruce, *"The Epistle to the Hebrews"* in *The New International Commentary* (Grand Rapids: Eerdmans, 1964), p. 232.

One must also bear in mind that the writers of the New Testament could make changes that uninspired men would dare not attempt. If they saw fulfillment in a passage, whether or not it was originally intended, the truth was still there. If they saw fit to change the wording in order to make their point, they took that liberty. The truth they spoke was still to be accepted, whether or not the prophet they cited knew it.

23

The Function of Critical Methods in New Testament Interpretation

Duane Warden

The word *critical* has suffered in popular usage. As used here, it has reference to a willingness to look at all the knowable facts, to make intelligent inferences, and to draw conclusions with some claim to objectivity. With regard to biblical studies, a critical outlook is essential. Religious experience is universal, but from time to time and place to place the experiences, doctrines, and ethics of men with regard to their religions have been and are greatly varied. The question from a critical standpoint is: What claim, if any, to ultimate validity does the Christian faith have? That question cannot be dealt with without soon considering the historical revelation of God in Christ and in the history of Israel. That in turn brings one immediately to the Bible, because it is in this book that the historical process is related and the message revealed.

With reference to biblical studies, "critical" is a rather technical term that suggests that the Scriptures are to be approached with the same historical-critical methods used to evaluate the claims and reliability of any other piece of literature. If it is truth that one seeks, it appears foolish to deny the legitimacy of such an approach. One may object to the philosophical presuppositions of critics of the New Testament or may reason differently from the same evidence and draw different conclusions, but if his results are to have any claim to legitimacy, he must agree that there is nothing to be feared from subjecting the New Testament literature to the closest possible examination.

It is difficult to argue with Gerhard Ebeling's statement in regard to the need for a thorough and conscientious treatment of the Bible: "This conscientiousness demands the carrying out of every kind of study that can serve the coming to understanding of what the biblical text seeks to bring to understanding."[1] Whatever can be learned in regard to the formation and transmission of the Bible can only aid in understanding its message.

To a considerable degree, interpreting the Bible is a function of one's presuppositions and conclusions with regard to critical questions. If one begins with the presupposition that all religious expressions, including those of the Christian tradition, must be understood as simply human phenomena (as commerce and trade, for example, are human phenomena) whose investigation consists in the delving into man's psychic experiences, one's conclusions with respect to critical questions asked about the Bible have been largely predetermined. Obviously, one's conclusions are apt to be quite different with respect to the same questions if he presupposes that God, a personal being, has stepped into human history to reveal himself and to give guidance to man. Presuppositions are inevitable in approaching the biblical text, or any other document for that matter. The question is whether it is possible for one to take his presuppositions to the biblical text and have them challenged and instructed by the data. While it is probably neither possible nor desirable to have one's presuppositions completely isolated from his conclusions, it may at least be hoped that presuppositions are not the only or even the chief contributor to the conclusions. If such a possibility is not granted, the whole enterprise of critical investigation is in question. On the other hand, if one is unalterably committed to defending a given view of biblical material regardless of the data, his conclusions are predetermined and his results are suspect.

Once one has dealt with philosophical considerations and the possibility that presuppositions may be informed by the data, there is still the matter of interpreting that data. In John's Gospel, for example, Jesus is presented as acting and speaking in a clearly defined way. The answers to certain critical questions make a considerable difference in the way one interprets what is said of Jesus. If the words and acts presented are largely the creation of the early church, developed by oral traditions to meet specific needs of the community (cf. L. Martyn, *History and Theology in the Fourth Gospel*, 2nd ed., Abingdon, 1979), the Gospel will be interpreted considerably differently than if it is an accurate and reliable record of historical events. Moving from presuppositions to interpretation is not an easy step devoid of pitfalls. The interpreter must always challenge himself with respect to what he brings to the text, his eisegesis—as well as what he gets from the text, his exegesis.

---

1. G. Ebeling, *Word and Faith*, trans. J. W. Leicht (Philadelphia: Fortress, 1963), p. 427.

The specific critical concerns of the student of the New Testament are generally related to broad categories. The following are not all-inclusive, but they do touch on principal areas of concern.

Language Studies

It is axiomatic that before translations are made, the Bible must be read and interpreted in its original languages. Even the most "literal" translation is to a considerable degree an interpretation. Because modern man is removed by several centuries from the languages of the Bible, sometimes specific words and idioms are difficult to understand. For example, the words *hilasmos* (1 John 2:2; 4:10) and *hilasterion* (Rom. 3:25) are of obvious theological significance, but much is to be desired in regard to our knowledge of the range of meanings for the words among the peoples to whom the New Testament books were originally addressed. To use another example, in John 10:24 Jesus is asked a question by the Jews. The question literally translated reads: "How long do you lift up our souls?" The phrase apparently is an idiom that is translated in the Revised Standard Version: "How long will you keep us in suspense?" There is disagreement in regard to this interpretation, however, and others have thought that the Jews were asking, "How long will you trouble us with this matter?"[2] For the interpretation of this passage and many like it, there is need for constant critical study of biblical languages. As more literature from the early centuries of Christianity is made available, increasing insight is possible. All the questions with regard to the languages in which the Bible is written are by no means solved. Critical inquiry is a continuing necessity.

Historical Considerations

The range of topics in need of critical evaluation under this heading is very broad. There is first a consideration of the actual historical context from which arose New Testament books and the events they describe. A remarkable example of how recent criticism has considerably altered a long-held view is with respect to Palestinian Judaism during the time of Christ. It was long believed that Judaism was fairly homogeneous in the first century before the destruction of Jerusalem. The Dead Sea Scrolls have played a major role in changing that view. It is now recognized that the Judaism encountered by John the Baptist and by Jesus was quite diverse. Critical studies, based on new evidence in this case, have changed

2. A. Pallis, *Notes on St. John and the Apocalypse* (Humphrey Milford: Oxford University, n.d.), pp. 23–24.

the way one understands the peoples of Jesus' day. One may now better understand the context in which Jesus taught and the early church grew.

Historical questions go beyond this, however, to basic questions about the New Testament documents themselves. Do the Gospels, for example, present an accurate record of Jesus' words and deeds? It is not enough to answer, "Of course; they must because they are given by God's inspiration." For many years after the Protestant Reformation, questions with regard to the authenticity and reliability of biblical books were seldom asked. Those who challenged the traditionally accepted authorships, or the historical reliability of biblical documents—such as Hobbes (1588–1679) and Spinoza (1632–77)—were generally raged against by churchmen. Few felt the need to seriously examine their reasoning and conclusions. That day has long past. It is no longer those on the fringes who challenge the inspiration of biblical books, but those in the mainstream. Their learning, careful examination of the data, and close reasoning require those of a contrary view to meet them where they are. The alternative is to abandon the field by resorting to superstition and tradition. It is demonstratively possible to obtain a following in this way, but it cannot satisfy the person who insists on truth as an ingredient of his faith.

Let it be said, however, that those who come to the biblical text with a more conservative view of the Bible as a divinely inspired book are not the only ones open to the charge of allowing their presuppositions to determine their conclusions. The person who comes to the text with the presuppositions of inspiration and finds data there reinforcing his views is no more to be charged with intellectual dishonesty than the one who goes to the text with a presupposition that a mechanical, cause-effect relationship is the only basis for understanding historical phenomena and then finds his views confirmed.

Many students will concede the possibility of God's having stepped into human history. Or they will affirm that he in fact has, but they will nevertheless maintain that—because God has mediated his word through human agency—the Bible is to be understood as subject to the same foibles, errors, and limitations of any other ancient document. They reason that a close examination of the biblical documents themselves demands that conclusion. If such a view is not defensible theoretically, and if the examination of the evidence does not warrant that conclusion, the battleground is within the confines of the text. Critical questions must be asked and reasonable answers proposed.

Literary Considerations

Literary Criticism of biblical documents cannot be altogether separated from Historical Criticism, yet there is a decided difference in emphasis. Any document may be historically reliable, and yet the author may have made use of diverse sources for what he writes. Conservative and liberal students of the Bible alike acknowledge that the author of a given biblical book would have used all his human resources, his own memory of events, and documents at his disposal in compiling the book. The understanding of every Bible student will be enhanced to the extent that written and oral sources are identified within various documents and their characteristics delineated.

The analysis of various literary methods employed by biblical authors assists the reader in following the thought and grasping the writer's point. It can only aid understanding if, for example, the last discourse of Jesus to his disciples is seen against the background of a genre of literature where a great man (Jacob, for example, in Gen. 49) had made a final address to a close-knit following before his death. Many students of the New Testament have seen in various documents remnants of early Christian hymns (Phil. 2:5–8; Col. 1:15–20; John's prologue); others have seen the frequent employment of chiastic patterns. Literary Criticism of the New Testament is, among other things, a continual effort to discover such devices and evaluate their significance. Any Literary Criticism of the Bible also implies the need for a healthy criticism of the critic. Every hymn and every chiastic structure "discovered" in the text is not necessarily that, and a blind acceptance of all such assertions will hinder and not aid biblical understanding.

Literary critics have at times extensively rearranged the material of biblical books, as for example, Bultmann on the Gospel of John.[3] A fuller understanding of the Bible requires a serious look at such assertions and an evaluation on the basis of the text.

Although Hermann Gunkel was principally an Old Testament scholar, his work in the early part of this century has stimulated a great deal of interest in oral tradition, which may lie behind documents of both Old and New Testaments. That the Christian message existed in oral form for several years after the death of Christ can hardly be denied. One aspect of Literary Criticism is the attempt to isolate various types of oral tradition in the New Testament. The interests of the literary critic range over a consideration of the synoptic problem, the relationship of the Fourth Gospel to the Synoptics, the authorship and nature of Acts as a literary document, a consideration of the vocabulary, style, and content of the Pastorals as opposed to other Epistles of Paul and the implications of this for authorship, and a whole range of similar questions.

The considerations and conclusions of the literary critics have presented, and will continue to present, serious challenges to the conservative student of the Bible. That literary critics such as R. Bultmann

---

3. R. Bultmann, *The Gospel of John: A Commentary*, ed. R. W. N. Hoare and J. K. Riches, trans. G. R. Beasley-Murray (Philadelphia: Westminster, 1971).

and D. E. Nineham (to name only two) have had great influence on biblical studies can hardly be denied. By no means are all the insights of liberal literary critics totally incompatible with a conservative view of inspiration, although many of them are. Not only must the validity of the various findings of literary critics be carefully evaluated, but the implications of the conclusions for the whole field of biblical studies must be thought through.

Theological Considerations

To a considerable extent, all that has been discussed to this point has dealt with theological implications of the criticism of the New Testament. Every person who deals with the text on any level must do so with some notion of what the book essentially is. Critical studies focus on this point. K. Grobel is undoubtedly correct when he writes, "Biblical criticism within its proper framework—the totality of the theological reflection— is all prolegomena to biblical theology."[4]

Much of current Literary Criticism, particularly form-critical and redaction-critical thought, hardly gives consideration to the worth of the New Testament as a historical record. Worse than denying its historical worth, which at least might be challenged, based on theological considerations history is treated as if it were of little consequence. That is not the view of the New Testament itself. The First Epistle of John begins, "That which was from the beginning, which we have heard, which we have seen with our eyes, which we have looked upon and touched with our hands, concerning the word of life" (1 John 1:1, RSV). Whatever else may be said of the New Testament, its writers presented the historical figure of Jesus as central to the faith.

Is it possible to have a Christian message that does not consider history? If the New Testament has no reliable historical record of Jesus, it may be questioned whether the document has any message of ultimate worth. If literary and historical critical efforts leave us with a book that is only an interesting chapter in man's religious history, is it really worth the attention given it? We are not asking whether religion, or even Christianity, is worth the effort, but whether the New Testament is worth the effort. It may be answered, of course, that the book has had great influence on the religious life of the Western world, that it represents a noble tradition of ethics and an artistic portrayal of man's search for and longing for communication with God. But these are not the great questions. Should it have influenced history? Is its ethics or its search for God really any more noble than the holy traditions of any other religion? By whose standard is it more noble, and what gives validity to that standard?

4. IDB, 1962 ed., s.v. "Biblical Criticism," by K. Grobel, p. 413.

Is there an inherent contradiction in the theological stance of the liberal? To them, the New Testament is somehow normative, but its existence is purely a human phenomenon. It may be answered that the results of scholarship and honest inquiry lead in a given direction, and honesty requires that necessary conclusions be accepted. A certain amount of credence can be given to that answer, but once it has been discovered that the New Testament is a wholly human document, is one justified in considering it normative? Has a similar amount of work gone into the examination of any other ancient document, the Gilgamesh Epic, for example, or the philosophy of Plato? Yet, if the liberal critic is correct, these documents possess as much significance as the biblical documents, perhaps more significance even from a religious standpoint.

In an interesting essay, R. Preston postulates two basic presuppositions of Christian theology. The first of these, he says, is that the ground of the universe is at least personal, and the second is that Jesus Christ was not basically mistaken.[5] While both of these presuppositions are assuredly necessary for Christian faith, it seems that there must be at least one more: that the Bible is a reliable record of God's deeds and words in human history. Without a record that is somehow from God and hence somehow normative, subjectivism reigns.

R. Bultmann, by any estimate one of the most influential biblical scholars of modern times, presents the view that the Bible can speak to modern man in his existential situation only when the myths have been removed and it is seen as a call on man for a spiritual encounter with God. The final redactor of John, according to Bultmann, was a sophisticated man who never placed much stock in the miracle stories of Jesus and did not intend for them to be taken literally. Bultmann begins his *Theology of the New Testament* with the bold and often-quoted words: "The message of Jesus is a presupposition for the theology of the New Testament rather than a part of that theology itself."[6] With this, of course, he dismisses any need to know of the historical Jesus or his words. The *kerygma* of the primitive church, its traditions of Jesus shaped and altered by its *Sitz im Leben*, is all that we can learn from the New Testament. Beyond the mere fact of Jesus' existence, nothing is known. With this view, the New Testament has been altered from the document that it presents itself as being.

It is not to be denied that anyone who believes that the Bible is an inspired and an inerrant record from God to man has his presuppositions tested, and at times severely tested, by a close examination of the text. Even a relatively conservative critic such as R. Brown writes, ". . . true

5. R. Preston, "The Presuppositions of Christian Theology" in *Vindications*, ed. A. Hanson (London: SCM, 1966), p. 18.

6. R. Bultmann, *Theology of the New Testament*, trans. K. Grobel, 2 vols. (New York: Scribner's, 1951), p. 3.

critical studies demand a humble submission to evidence and a willingness to accept truth no matter where it may be found. In the long run this humility and docility to truth serve the ecumenical movement better than do the hidden presuppositions of an over-literalistic approach to the Bible."[7] Brown assumes that the presuppositions of which he speaks are hidden from the conservative scholar and that such a view of the Bible is indefensible. That such a view is intellectually defensible is the burden of the conservative Bible scholar.

The following assessment by W. Doty is generally accepted as true: "The basic presuppositions for the modern historical-critical approach to the New Testament writings were set in the last part of the eighteenth century under the influence of deism and rationalism."[8] The presuppositions of the literary critic, formed "under the influence of deism and rationalism" deserve as careful consideration as any other. They are not the historical presuppositions of the church, and they are not the presuppositions of the New Testament itself. One wonders at what point one's presuppositions so alter his mental framework that the designation "Christian" no longer applies.

Conclusion

Shortly after the turn of the century A. Schlatter voiced some forceful objections to attempts to approach the New Testament from a detached, historical perspective. Schlatter suggested that if it were possible to step outside one's own frame of reference and view the historical record of the text with complete objectivity, the detached, impersonal approach would in itself be the most powerful attack possible. He argues that the New Testament is a book calling for involvement, faith, and commitment and that there cannot be and ought not to be an artificial separation between dogmatics and biblical theology.[9]

Schlatter's observations are very much in order today. One cannot deny the apologetic task of Christians to defend their presuppositions and conclusions with respect to what the New Testament as a document essentially is. That apologetic task will either convince or fail to convince as it examines the text.

It cannot be expected of the Christian, however, that he look at the Bible with detachment. He is of necessity personally involved with its message, which is to say that he is involved in its historical statement.

7. R. Brown, "The Unity and Diversity in New Testament Ecclesiology," NovT 6 (1963): 298.

8. W. G. Doty, "The Discipline and Literature of New Testament Form Criticism," ATR 51 (1969): 286.

9. A. Schlatter, "The Theology of the New Testament and Dogmatics," in *The Nature of New Testament Theology*, trans. and ed. R. Morgan (London: SCM), pp. 122–23.

Literary critics of recent decades increasingly have sought to relegate history to the sidelines of theological considerations. The New Testament, however, proclaims itself to be a document of history. Its historical witness will either be defended in the critical arena, or the nature of Christian faith will have been considerably altered.

24

The Wall Broken: An Interpretation of Ephesians 2:11–22

James E. Howard

In his observation, "Something there is that doesn't love a wall," Robert Frost exhibited a keen grasp of human nature.[1] There seems to be something in the baser side of man's makeup that almost inherently sets him to the task of building walls between himself and his fellowman. The walls in today's world come in all shapes and sizes. Barriers have been erected between races, nations, economic classes, educational levels, age groups, and religions. The result is a world in which man finds himself alienated and estranged. From the moment of Adam and Eve's first tinge of guilt at disobedience of God's command and their desire to hide from God's presence, man has continued to find himself cut off—horizontally from his fellow creatures and vertically from God who created him.

The one greatest fact in human history is God's love for man and his desire to heal broken relationships vertically and horizontally. Nowhere is this divine purpose more clearly stated than in the biblical revelation of Paul's Epistle to the Ephesians.[2] Chadwick states the theme of the book as

1. Robert Frost, "Mending Wall," in *One Hundred and One Famous Poems*, ed. Roy J. Cook (Chicago: Reilly & Lee, 1958), p. 158.
2. In the present study there is neither occasion nor need to examine the Pauline authorship of Ephesians. Aside from the strong and early attestation for authorship by the great apostle, one might simply list as of the same persuasion the names of such great critical scholars as H. Chadwick, T. K. Abbott, C. H. Dodd, R. Grant, and M. Barth. In fact it is Dodd who describes the epistle's thought as "the crown of Paulinism." For a thorough discussion of the issue cf. D. Guthrie, *New Testament Introduction: The Pauline Epistles* (London: Tyndale, 1968), pp. 99–128; A. Van Roon, "The Authenticity of Ephesians," *Supplements to Novum Testamentum*, vol. 39 (Leiden: Brill, 1974).

"the Church, one, holy, catholic, and apostolic, divinely planned and founded for the redemption of humanity in Christ in virtue of his reconciling work."[3] The key word here is "catholic," because God's desire was for a universal fellowship of the redeemed. Wherever man is alienated from the Father or from another of the Father's created children, God's purpose is thwarted and his desires unfulfilled.

The method of this all-encompassing divine plan is described in Ephesians 2:11–22, the focus of the present study. Ephesians is usually understood to consist of two main parts roughly equal in length: 1:3–3:21 and 4:1–6:22.[4] While the first three chapters are described as dogmatic or kerygmatic, the contents of the last three are labeled ethical, didactic, or parenetic.[5] The section here under discussion serves as the apex of the apostle's statement of God's universal plan for reclaiming his lost creation.

Literary Background

As a background for looking at Ephesians 2:11–22 in detail, it is necessary first to place the passage in its literary context by examining its literary genre or type as well as smaller literary or originally oral units of expression found within the passage.[6] The larger unit is the epistle. The pattern used in the New Testament epistle is, for the most part, the usual one of the Hellenistic epistles of the time. Its elements are as follows: At the beginning is a formula of salutation, with the names of sender and recipient; then a thanksgiving to God; and for a conclusion a message of greeting and good wishes in one's own hand to take the place of a signature.[7] It has been argued that the apostle Paul adapted Greco-Roman letter models for Christian purposes.[8] It has likewise been suggested that Paul wrote by a basic understanding of structure but modified that understanding on occasion.[9] Since the time of Deissmann it has been under-

3. H. Chadwick, "Ephesians," in *Peake's Commentary on the Bible*, ed. M. Black and H. H. Rowley (London: Nelson, 1964), p. 980.

4. M. Barth, *Ephesians 1–3*, Anchor Bible, vol. 34 (Garden City, N.Y.: Doubleday, 1974), p. 53.

5. Ibid.

6. The discipline known as "form criticism" or "form history" attempts to give fuller meaning to a given unit of biblical material by focusing attention on the realization that any people or culture is understood by the spoken and written patterns it uses to express itself. For example, how would some future generation understand our present civilization if it were to unearth such diverse forms of expression as a rock music record, romance novel, newspaper advertisement, business letter, recorded telephone message, or printed sermon?

7. P. Feine and J. Behm, *Introduction to the New Testament*, 14th rev., ed. W. G. Kümmel (New York: Abingdon, 1966), p. 176.

8. W. G. Doty, *Letters in Primitive Christianity* (Philadelphia: Fortress, 1973), p. 21.

9. Ibid.

stood that Paul's letters are not "private personal letters" in the usual sense of that term but rather were written to communities of Christians for use in their common life.[10] Ephesians certainly seems to meet these criteria.

Ephesians 2:11–22 has also come under investigation as regards form. The larger unit of chapters 1–3 has been defined as a *berakah*, or blessing for use in public worship, possibly in connection with the Lord's Supper.[11] It is widely agreed that 2:14–18 represents an early Christian hymn used in corporate worship, either authored by Paul or more likely taken by him and modified for his specific purposes.[12] Prominent hymnic elements include the heavy use of participles, parallelism of members, and cosmic language.[13] The passage has been further identified as part of a nature hymnology concerning the peace of Christ.[14] Verses 14–16 have been isolated and identified as a reworked liturgical fragment in which had originally been celebrated the unity of heaven and earth accomplished in the reconciling work of Christ.[15] On the basis of style the theory that these verses are a baptismal hymn is untenable.[16] It seems clear, though, that verses 14–18, whether composed by the apostle, or simply employed by him, form a beautiful and powerful testimony to the centrality of Christ and his redemptive sacrifice for the reconciling purpose of God.

Context of Ephesians 1–3

Before examining the structure and meaning of 2:11–22, it is important to examine the immediate context of the first three chapters of the Ephesian epistle, which explain God's eternal purpose and plan. Perhaps the key statement for understanding the entire epistle is to be found in 1:9–10: "For he has made known to us in all wisdom and insight the mystery of his will, according to his purpose which he set forth in Christ as a plan for the fulness of time, to unite all things in him, things in heaven and things on earth." (All Scripture quotations in this chapter are from the Revised Standard Version.) The apostle Paul indicates something of the breadth of God's purpose in these words. He has introduced the letter by indicating that the saved have been chosen (v. 4) and destined in love (v. 5). This election has been accomplished through redemption by

10. Ibid., p. 25.

11. C. L. Mitton, *Ephesians*, New Century Bible (Greenwood, SC: Attic Press, 1976), p. 23. Mitton cites J. C. Kirby, *Ephesians: Baptism and Pentecost* (1968).

12. J. T. Sanders, "Hymnic Elements in Ephesians 1–3," ZNW 56 (1965): 215–218. Sanders cites H. Schlier's belief that the hymn was actually authored by Paul.

13. Ibid.

14. G. Giavini, "La Structure Litteraire D'Eph. II.11–22," NTS 16 (1970): 209–211.

15. E. Käsemann, *Exegetische Versüche und Besinnungen* (Göttingen: Vandenhoeck & Ruprecht, 1964), p. 280.

16. Ibid., p. 282.

Christ's blood (vv. 7–8). In verse 9 Paul introduces a key word for understanding the epistle, the term *mystery*. As the mystery of God *(mystērion tou theou)*, the crucifixion and glorification, the salvation event, is removed from the grasp of worldly wisdom and characterized as a history prepared and fulfilled in the sphere of God.[17] As the divine mystery is fulfilled in Christ, the creation and consummation are comprised in him and taken out of the sphere of their own control.[18] The comprehending of the whole created order in Christ, a cosmic eschatological event of immense proportions, is God's great now-revealed mystery.[19]

The apostle Paul moves from the account of cosmic salvation to the individual recipient of redemption and assures the saved that he is "sealed" with the promised Spirit (v. 13). The apostle concludes the first chapter of Ephesians by praying for those who share in salvation as well as read the words of the epistle. He prays for their reception of "a spirit of wisdom and revelation" (v. 17) as well as their enlightenment (vv. 18–19). He concludes with an affirmation of the supremacy of Christ "over all things for the church, which is his body, the fulness of him who fills all in all" (vv. 22–23).

In 2:1–10 Paul goes on to paint in vivid colors the status and nature of the "children of wrath" (v. 3) on the one hand and those made alive with Christ (v. 5) on the other. The spiritual condition of man before participation in this redemption is contrasted with that of man after he has become the recipient.[20] This section concludes with a beautiful definition of the relationship of grace and faith in salvation (v. 8) and a comforting reminder that the whole scheme of redemption is God's and that man is his greatest workmanship (v. 10).

The passage under discussion (2:11–22) is sandwiched between this treatise on salvation and chapter three, which concludes the theological section of the letter. Chapter three sets out to be a prayer in the fashion of 1:15–23 but pauses long on a note of awed wonder at the part assigned to Paul himself in this scheme involving all the universe and both eternities.[21] In 3:1–7 the apostle actually continues the discussion of Gentile salvation begun in 2:11–22. Verses 7–13 restate the now-revealed great mystery that it is through the church that God has chosen to make known his manifold wisdom to the principalities and powers in the heavenly places.

---

17. G. Bornkamm, "Mysterion," in *Theological Dictionary of the New Testament*, vol. 4, ed. G. Kittel (Grand Rapids: Eerdmans, 1967), p. 820.

18. Ibid.

19. Ibid.

20. R. Summers, *Ephesians. Pattern for Christian Living* (Nashville: Broadman, 1960), p. 31.

21. C. H. Dodd, "Ephesians," in *The Abingdon Bible Commentary*, ed. F. C. Eiselen et al. (Nashville: Abingdon, 1957), p. 1222.

Ephesians 2:11–22

One comes now to discuss 2:11–22, "the key and high point of the whole epistle."[22] The logical structure of this section is generally clear and falls under the following headings: a description of the division of humanity (vv. 11–12); praise of Christ's work of reconciliation (vv. 13–18); and the elaboration of the tangible result of peace, namely the growing church (vv. 19–22).[23]

This passage cannot adequately be understood without some grasp of the audience addressed by the apostle. Although it is widely held that Ephesians is a circular letter addressed to the churches in the province of Asia,[24] it still seems apparent that the epistle was meant "for Ephesus and her daughter churches."[25] It likewise appears that although there were both Jews and Gentiles in the Ephesian church, the Gentiles were by far in the majority.[26] This is significant because this section in particular is obviously addressed to Gentiles.

The Division of Humanity (2:11–12)

Paul calls on those who were called "the uncircumcision" to remember their past condition—"separated from Christ, alienated from the commonwealth of Israel, and strangers to the covenants of promise, having no hope and without God in the world." The term "remember" *(mnēmoneuete)* is of special significance. Paul, here reflecting his Jewish background, is not thinking of memory as a mere mental activity. The modern notion of "remembering," psychologically viewed as an act of an individual human mind, is quiet alien to the Hebraic conception.[27] To remember some event or person or past state means to actualize that reality so that it continues to live. One of the great fears of the Old Testament man was the possibility that his name might not be remembered, or live on after his death.[28] A favorite theme of Deuteronomy is, as in 5:15—"You shall remember that you were a servant in the land of Egypt, and the LORD your God brought you out thence with a mighty hand and an outstretched arm. . . ." The great cultic festivals such as Passover were

22. Barth, p. 275.

23. Ibid.

24. Based on the absence of the phrase *en Ephesoi* in the two major uncial manuscripts of the New Testament—Sinaiticus and Vaticanus.

25. H. C. Thiessen, *Introduction to the New Testament* (Grand Rapids: Eerdmans, 1960), p. 244.

26. Ibid., p. 242. See also M. Barth, "Conversion and Conversation." Int 17 (1963): 20. Barth believes that Ephesians is addressed only to Gentile Christians.

27. A. G. Hebert, "Memory," in *A Theological Word Book of the Bible*, ed. A. Richardson (New York: Macmillan, 1963), pp. 142–143.

28. Cf. 2 Sam. 18:18 for mention of the memorial that Absalom had erected to keep his name in remembrance.

intended to make the salvation event of the exodus an ever-new reality in the hearts of the people.

The act of remembrance likewise involves recognition, confession, and self-reflection.[29] Paul wishes that the Gentile Christians remember so keenly their pre-Christian lot in life that they are emotionally transported back to that time of alienation, helplessness, and despair. Circumcision was the badge of belonging. To Abraham, his household, and all subsequent generations, to be circumcised was to receive a sign of the covenant between God and man as well as a sign that indicated total commitment to God.[30] "Uncircumcision" was a term of contempt and disdain.

Because they were not of the covenant community, the Gentiles were excluded from all that made life spiritually meaningful. First of all, they were without the Messiah.[31] Second, they were alienated from Israel's commonwealth. The term *citizenship* may be preferred to *commonwealth*, which might have geographical overtones, whereas Paul wants to make it clear that the Gentiles would have been "far off" (v. 13), even if they had been living in Israel, since they did not possess the rights of citizens.[32] Third, they were strangers to the covenants of promise. Although several covenants are mentioned in the Old Testament, all are denoted as unilateral contracts based on the goodness of God. Underlying the various covenants, however, is one basic covenant relationship in which God promises that Israel will be his own possession among all peoples, a kingdom of priests, and a holy nation.[33] It is from this special relationship that the Gentiles are excluded.

Fourth, the Gentiles are described as having no hope. This sad epitaph accurately describes the pagan world of the apostle's day. Because of the commonly held cyclical view of history, the Gentile found his world moving toward no purposeful end. Although the mystery religions so prevalent in that time promised immortality, the inscriptions on tombs and the uniform pessimism of the age provide unimpeachable evidence that people of all classes faced the future without hope either for themselves or the world.[34] Fifth, the Gentiles are "without God in the world." They are

29. O. Michel, "Mnēmoneuō," in *Theological Dictionary of the Bible*, vol. 4, ed. G. Kittel (Grand Rapids: Eerdmans, 1967), pp. 682–683.

30. Cf. J. T. Willis, *Genesis*, The Living Word Commentary on the Old Testament (Austin, TX: Sweet, 1979), pp. 247–248.

31. Thus Barth, p. 256. Barth suggests that as long as the Gentiles lacked historic communion, e.g. with Israel's anointed priests, kings, and prophets, they were deprived of communion with the Messiah to come.

32. Ibid., pp. 256–257.

33. Exod. 19:5–6. For a comprehensive examination of the uniqueness of God's covenant with Israel cf. D. J. McCarthy, *Treaty and Covenant* (Rome: Pontifical Biblical Institute, 1963), pp. 168–177.

34. F. W. Beare, "The Epistle to the Ephesians," in *The Interpreter's Bible*, vol. 10, ed. G. A. Buttrick (New York: Abingdon, 1953), p. 652.

literally *atheoi* or atheists. It has been suggested that this term represents the conclusion of a series of descriptions of the pagan world from uncircumcision, which is an external mark, to being without God, which is a matter of innermost spiritual poverty.[35] It was not that the Gentiles worshiped no gods (1 Cor. 8:5) but that they had not served the living God nor shared in his covenant promises. A darker picture of hopelessness could scarcely have been painted nor a greater contrast drawn between the Jews, God's chosen people, and the Gentiles, living in a world of hopeless despair.

Christ's Work of Reconciliation (2:13–18)

The apostle begins his second division with a great time contrast—"at one time"—"but now." Whereas the Gentiles had been ostracized and alienated, now in Christ Jesus "you who once were far off have been brought near in the blood of Christ" (v. 13). In Jesus Christ the great barrier has been broken down. Through his blood the estranged have been befriended. The distant have been brought near. It is interesting that the writer Paul borrows and reapplies a passage from the Old Testament (Isa. 57:19): "Peace, peace, to the far and to the near, says the LORD; and I will heal him." Here is to be seen Paul's rabbinic method. The original subject of the Isaiah passage, the destiny of exiled, displaced Jews, now gives way to an application of the text to the formerly alienated Gentiles.[36] To those formerly far off and now near, peace is proclaimed (v. 17). While the Isaiah passage had earlier been applied to Jewish proselytes, Paul makes two major changes. First, it is the blood of Christ, not the blood of circumcision, that now brings the Gentiles near. Second, all Gentiles are now brought near, not just the "God-fearers."[37] Verse 13 actually serves as a summary statement of the fact that God has acted decisively in the cross to bring about universal redemption.

The structure of 2:13–18 is vitally important for a right understanding of the passage. Paul appears to draw one great conclusion, namely that Jesus Christ is "our peace" (v. 14), and then lists a number of truths that grow out of that one all-encompassing truth. In what sense, then, does the apostle want us to understand the Lord to be "our peace"?

First he has "made us both one." The pronoun *amphotera* translated "both" is significant. Whereas the term's primary frame of reference is Jews and Gentiles, it can also have a more universal connotation and be translated "all."[38] Christ is peace for men of all nations.

---

35. Barth, p. 260.

36. Cf. J. Muilenberg, "The Book of Isaiah. Chapters 40–66," in *The Interpreter's Bible*, vol. 5, ed. G. A. Buttrick (New York: Abingdon, 1956), p. 675.

37. Barth, pp. 276–277.

38. W. F. Arndt and F. W. Gingrich, *A Greek-English Lexicon of the New Testament and Other Early Christian Literature* (Cambridge: University Press, 1957), p. 47.

But the Lord Jesus Christ is also "our peace" because he has "broken down the dividing wall of hostility." Probably more theories have been proposed to explain this phrase than any other in the epistle. Probably the least likely interpretations are those that equate the wall with the curtain of the temple, which was torn from top to bottom at the death of Christ (Matt. 27:51).[39] Another rather ingenious interpretation sees in the wall a reference to the age-old practice of Jews to live in a section of a city separated by some natural or man-made barrier from other inhabitants.[40] Others take the term *wall* to refer to the wall around a city, possibly the wall around Jerusalem destroyed in the Roman conquest in A.D. 70.[41] It is more likely that the apostle, again reflecting his Hebraic background, is referring to the literal wall in the Jerusalem temple, which separated the Court of Gentiles from the Court of Women. Signs were posted on this wall to warn all non-Jews of the penalty of death to be imposed on any who trespassed that boundary.[42]

Perhaps Paul begins with the thought of such a literal wall. But in the total context of his discussion he seems to have transferred that idea to the concept of the Torah or Law as a wall around Israel and further transformed his concept to refer to a cosmological wall that separates the heavenly and earthly spheres.[43] The apostle wants to make quite clear the fact that on the cross Christ has destroyed the barrier between Jew and Gentile, thus symbolizing the end of all barriers between men. This act of reconciliation thus makes him the author of peace, one who destroys

39. Cf. W. Rader, *The Church and Racial Hostility*, Beiträge Zur Geschichte der Biblischen Exegese, 20 (Tübingen: J. C. B. Mohr, 1978), pp. 105–106. Rader points to J. Cocceius (1603–1669) as an early advocate of this view.

40. Ibid., p. 121. A view held by the eighteenth-century scholar C. Schoettgen.

41. D. C. Smith, "Jewish and Greek Traditions in Ephesians 2:11–22" (unpublished Ph.D. dissertation, Yale University, 1970), p. 100.

42. A. Deissmann, *Light from the Ancient East* (New York: Harper & Brothers, n.d.), pp. 79–81. Deissmann refers to one such inscription discovered in 1871 by Clermont-Ganneau, worded as follows: "Let no foreigner enter within the screen and enclosure surrounding the sanctuary. Whoever is taken so doing will be the cause that death overtaketh him." Just how strictly this prohibition was observed is seen in Acts 21:27–37, where the apostle Paul is mistakenly thought to have taken a Gentile into the temple.

43. Smith. This cosmological wall should not be confused with the wall between heaven and earth proposed by those who interpret Ephesians in thought forms of the Gnostic Redeemer myth. According to this view Ephesians reflects a system of salvation in which a cosmic redeemer comes down from heaven, breaks down the wall separating the earthly and heavenly spheres, gathers his members imprisoned in this world, and returns to heaven. For the classic statement of this theory cf. H. Schlier, *Christus und die Kirche im Epheserbrief*, Beiträge zur Historischen Theologie, 6 (Tübingen: Verlag J. C. B. Mohr, 1930). For an excellent refutation of the theory, cf. A. Richardson, *An Introduction to the Theology of the New Testament* (New York: Harper & Brothers, 1958), pp. 141–144.

hostility and opens up to all access to the Father (v. 18). Such an interpretation is consistent with the overall theme of the epistle, which is the
universal Lordship of Christ (1:10–22).

Christ is our peace because he has broken down the dividing wall of
hostility "by abolishing in his flesh the law of commandments and ordi-
nances . . ." (v. 15). While there has been a great deal of debate concerning
whether this phrase refers to the abrogation of the whole law or only the
ceremonial aspects of it,[44] it is clear that the elaborate system of legal
observances publicly marked off Jew from Gentile.[45] The bond that has
been cancelled by being nailed to the cross is a signal acknowledgement
of indebtedness in respect of the broken law.[46] Because the law was given
only to Israel, it served as a limit separating those included in God's
covenant from those yet outside the covenants and their promises.[47] On
the cross Christ put himself under the law, thereby demonstrating for all
to see that the law is incapable of healing rifts and instead widens the gaps
dividing men.[48] The death of Christ rather than the promulgation of new
decrees stood behind the abolition of the divisive statutes.[49]

Christ is our peace because he has created "one new man in place of the
two, so making peace" (v. 15). Paul again draws on his Jewish heritage in
presenting the concept of this "one new man." The strong distinction
between individuality and corporality so characteristic of the Western
enlightenment mentality was almost unknown in Old Testament
thought, particularly in the early period. Man was defined much more as
part of a group than as an individual. In fact, in Hebrew thought "the
whole group, including its past, present, and future members, might
function as a single individual through any one of those members conceived as representative of it."[50] Paul utilizes this fluidity of thought to
express the oneness of Jesus Christ with his now-reconciled new humanity. This "new man" is none other than Jesus Christ himself, and only as
his followers are drawn into intimate rapport with him do they become a
part of him and share in the resultant unity.[51] Christ incorporates within

44. Smith, pp. 60, 81, 82, 85, 116.
45. F. F. Bruce, *The Epistle to the Ephesians* (New York: Revell, 1961), p. 54. Bruce
cites Col. 2:14, which speaks of the cancellation of the bond that stood against us, with
its legal demands.
46. Ibid.
47. Barth, p. 290.
48. M. H. Scharlemann, "The Secret of God's Plan: Studies in Ephesians," *Concordia
Theological Monthly* 41 (1970): 414.
49. Barth, p. 265.
50. H. W. Robinson, *Corporate Personality in Ancient Israel*, Facet Books, Biblical
Series, No. 11 (Philadelphia: Fortress, 1964), p. 1. A prime illustration of this concept is
the case of Achan (Joshua 7), whose individual sin resulted in corporate punishment.
51. J. W. Bowman, "The Epistle to the Ephesians," Int 8 (1954): 198.

himself, and is the creator of, a new race in which age-old distinctions have lost their relevance and force.[52]

Christ is our peace because he has reconciled disparate humanity "to God in one body through the cross, thereby bringing the hostility to an end" (v. 16). By breaking down the divisive wall—which resulted in hostility not only between Jew and Gentile but also between God and man because God's purposes were being thwarted—Christ has established peace. As in verse 14, the pronoun *amphoteroi* is used, referring primarily to both Jew and Gentile but more broadly to all who have found themselves estranged from God.

The term "reconcile" *(katallaxē)* is rich with meaning. The term is to be understood against the background of the great rift between God and man, as graphically symbolized by the visible wall between Jew and Gentile. There exists within history and the heart of man a condition of total spiritual disorder.[53] It involves a state of conflict in man's relationship to God and even of internecine strife in the supernatural sphere itself.[54] The walls between Jews and Gentiles, or between any other human groups, are only symptomatic of a deeper sickness.

Jesus Christ came into this rift to be God's agent of reconciliation (2 Cor. 5:18). The word *reconcile* denotes a transformation or renewal of the state between God and man and therewith of man's own state.[55] In man's becoming a new creature there is a change, not merely in man's disposition or his legal relationship, but in the total state of his life.[56]

Because all the minor and secondary divisions among men are ultimately due to the fact that all men are separated from God,[57] the peace that Christ has created is a comprehensive one. This peace is a spiritual, political, and social event of unlimited dimensions. It reaches into the divided soul of ancient and modern man. It is inexhaustible.[58] It refers to man's total well-being when he is right with God. Verse 18 refers to the result of this peace as "access in one Spirit to the Father."[59]

---

52. R. P. Martin, "Ephesians" in *The Broadman Bible Commentary*, vol. 11, ed. C. J. Allen (Nashville: Broadman, 1971), p. 147.

53. J. A. Mackay, *God's Order. The Ephesian Letter and This Present Time* (New York: Macmillan, 1953), p. 25.

54. Ibid.

55. F. Büchsel, "Katallassō," in *Theological Dictionary of the New Testament*, vol. 1, ed. G. Kittel (Grand Rapids: Eerdmans, 1964), p. 255.

56. Ibid.

57. D. M. Lloyd-Jones, *God's Way of Reconciliation. Studies in Ephesians Chapter 2* (Grand Rapids: Baker, 1972), p. 223. Cf. R. P. Martin, *Reconciliation: A Study of Paul's Theology* (Atlanta: John Knox, 1981).

58. M. Barth, *The Broken Wall* (Philadelphia: Judson, 1959), pp. 266–267, as cited in D. J. Harris, *Shalom. The Biblical Concept of Peace* (Grand Rapids: Baker, 1970), pp. 61–62.

59. B. Gärtner, *The Temple and the Community in Qumran and the New Testament*

The Tangible Result of Peace (2:19–22)

The third division of the section under discussion describes the result of the peace effected through the reconciling work of Christ on the cross. Because the dividing wall of hostility has been broken down, those incorporated into the "one new man" are no longer "strangers and sojourners" but are now "fellow citizens with the saints and members of the household of God, built upon the foundation of the apostles and prophets, Christ Jesus himself being the cornerstone" (vv. 19–20). Recent debate has centered around the meaning of "cornerstone" *(akrogōniaiou)*. To some interpreters the cornerstone means the stone that crowns the building.[60] Citing Psalm 118:22, those of this view see Jesus Christ as the rejected stone exalted to be the crown of the whole structure.[61] Others interpret the figure to mean that Christ is the bedrock foundation out of which the building grows.[62] This view seems to fit best the centrality of Christ, which is so dominant a theme in Ephesians.

More significant, though, is Paul's combining of the growth motif from agriculture with the building motif from the sphere of architecture. The "holy temple" (v. 21) into which Gentile Christians have now been built and in which they have become "fellow citizens" is none other than the universal church of which Christ is the source of unity and harmony. The action of having been joined together implies a continual process of spiritual growth and unification within that church.[63]

Thus concludes the apostle Paul's majestic description of the reconciling work of Jesus Christ. Through the cross Christ has become our peace and has ended hostility between man and man (as symbolized by Jew and Gentile) and as a result of that reconciliation also between God and man. In hymnic language of praise is proclaimed the fact that the rift of the fractured universe has been healed and mankind may be at one with its Creator as well as with its brother. The wall is now broken.

(Cambridge: University Press, 1965), pp. 61–62. Gärtner distinguishes between this "access" and that contained in the temple symbolism of 4QFlor. in the Qumran materials, where strict entrance conditions are laid down for anyone seeking access to the new spiritual temple.

60. F. F. Bruce, "New Wine in Old Wine Skins: The Corner Stone," ExpTim 74 (1973): 231–232.

61. Ibid., p. 235.

62. R. J. McKelvey, "Christ the Cornerstone," NTS 8 (1962): 358–359.

63. M. R. Weed, *The Letters of Paul to the Ephesians, the Colossians, and Philemon*, The Living Word Commentary, vol. 11, ed. E. Ferguson (Austin, TX: Sweet, 1971), p. 145.

25

Vital Principles and Practices in Hermeneutics

J. D. Thomas

Because the Bible claims to be the Word of God to man, it behooves man to understand the Scriptures with precision. Authority should be comprehended exactly, since the meaning of life here on earth could be at stake. When approaching the New Testament, both the language and the culture gaps between the first-century eastern Mediterranean peoples and twentieth-century citizens of the world must be bridged. This must be done without any appreciable loss of equivalent meanings of the message of this significant book.

In practice the terms *hermeneutics, exegesis,* and *interpretation* are used interchangeably, or at least in overlapping ways, yet some scholars make sharp distinctions between them. In the latter case the word *exegesis* is taken to mean "the process of leading out the meaning" of the original language to the original recipients in their contextual and cultural situation. *Hermeneutics* then is thought of as the principles or theory underlying such a process, and *interpretation* is the application of the meaning to life situations today. To go a step further, *homiletics* is the technical term for the sermonizing of the meanings for desired ends.

Historically, the Bible has been interpreted in several different basic ways. Origen of the early third century was a prominent user of the allegorical method, in which he claimed that there were at least three meanings to a text, answering to "body, soul, and spirit." Some of his deeper meanings were rather far-fetched. The School of Antioch sought to be a corrective to Origen, opting for historical and typological emphases. Allegory was dominant for a long period, however, and finally, for many interpreters, a fourfold sense evolved, including allegory, anagogy, tropology, and literal (grammatico-historical). A real contest ultimately developed between the allegorical and the literal, with a live question remaining about how many valid meanings a passage can have. This question leads into the initial point of view of the interpreter. Although the emphasis in this study will be on the New Testament, the principles apply to Old Testament interpretation as well.

Presuppositions

Every interpreter comes to his task with an already-formulated point of view or set of presuppositions. He begins his work having already accepted certain things as true. Of itself this is not bad. Whether his presuppositions are, in fact, truth is the question. If he can investigate new facts with an open mind and is willing to change his conclusions if the findings so demand, there is no problem. There are about as many different sets of presuppositions as there are interpreters, and many of these are in diametrical opposition to each other. Obviously someone is wrong, and this is why there is so much confusion about biblical interpretation. The Bible is a powerful book, and people who get acquainted with it are drawn to know its message well, even though they come to it with different ideas and even reach different conclusions because of their differing presuppositions. The nature of the Bible and the import of its message make the stakes high for accurate interpretation, so emotions often become strained.

There are many differing basic philosophical stances open to persons who would interpret Scripture, so it is not surprising that people do not see the Bible alike. No doubt differing presuppositions are more responsible than any other single factor for the existence of so many different religions that claim to be Christian. Certainly all are not interpreting the Bible with precise accuracy, and it should be understood that some are wrong, even though their motives might be good. It is so easy to be controlled by presuppositions that all interpreters should constantly search their own souls to ensure that they are able to rise above prejudged conclusions.

Major topics that are important to interpretation and about which there are serious disagreements include:

1. Is the Bible a divinely given document or merely humanly produced, and does it set forth the meaning of life and a purpose for human existence? This embraces the question of the Bible's authority and whether or not it is to be thought of as a book of doctrine and practice for mankind to accept and follow.

2. Is God's revelation to man objective or subjective? Is it to be intellectually understood in reasonable, propositional statements? Numerous philosophies of today hold that reason has no place in determining truth

and that the human intellect does not contribute significantly to the obtaining of valid religious knowledge.

3. Is the same truth of God's revelation applicable to all men alike or does each individual have a different truth, with conflicts between such truths possible? In our day of "situation ethics," "existential experiences" and other relativities, it should be obvious that moral problems and other spiritual concerns make this a serious question for one who seeks to be truly God's person.

4. Is the Bible—Old Testament and New Testament—a unity, and does it all have a controlling author, the Holy Spirit? Some scholars insist that the Bible had no such inspiration and that its several parts have no special bond of unity.

There are, of course, numerous other presuppositions that people bring to the Bible and that color interpretation, but the above list covers some of the most important that interfere with good interpretation in our day. Obviously these are a major problem and must be dealt with.

Epistemology

Of all the differing views with which people come to the Bible, epistemology, or theory of valid knowledge, is probably one of the most troublesome today. What are the sources or avenues through which valid knowledge comes? How does one know anything for sure? This problem has troubled man for twenty-five centuries, without any clear-cut solution.

Liberal Theology

Liberal theologians hold that knowledge is gained through reason and experience, the latter meaning what one discerns through the five senses—"Seeing is believing." This group appreciates science and the scientific method, and the clear-cut liberal tends to want a scientific, experiential verification for whatever is to be accepted as truth, although he has a high regard for reason in the "knowing process." Again, the term *experience* can take on flexibility, sometimes ending with no more than presuppositions. There is more to reality than human experience can verify scientifically. Such things as love, beauty, happiness, goodness, and personal relationships have reality, though they are not within science's domain of reference. Thus the denial of all unverifiable realities is simply to beg the question. Everyone should face up to the text of Scripture and heed its message.

Existential Theology

Existential theology, or neo-orthodoxy, has had many different colorations and emphases and champions, but perhaps Rudolf Bultmann has been the recognized spokesman for "pure" existentialism in recent years. With others he denies reason a place in epistemology, and they all accept some type of personal confrontation experience, wherein true knowledge comes. Bultmann also denies history any valid place in "knowing," to the point that even major historical events in the Bible (as the resurrection) did not really happen—yet the telling of them has a wholesome religious value anyway. Private experience and personal choice are important to the existentialist, but there is no room or need for cognitive, propositional revelation. The Bible's words as such have no meaningful authority—any revelation comes "between the lines" or in whatever self-understanding develops. Subjectivity is the core of the knowing process, according to Sören Kierkegaard, the founder of the movement, and there is no such thing as public truth. One man's truth can differ from another's. Serious exegesis of biblical texts is thus a futile exercise, since the final answer will be the subjective, private answer the existentialist interpreter gives to it, or, in Bultmann's terminology, what is left after the passage is "demythologized."

Another existential approach bears the name of *Heilsgeschichte* (Holy History), in which God is working out an overall redemptive plan, but his revelation comes not in words, but in historical events. The history is objective and real, but the interpretation of the events is existential, mystical, and nebulous.

The New Hermeneutic

The "new hermeneutic" is a term coined to describe an idea of two of Bultmann's former pupils who, with several others, deserted his pure existentialism about 1955, because they felt his denial of historicity would not even allow him to have a real Lord. Fuchs and Ebeling claimed for this new epistemology that knowledge comes through a "language event." This particular existential thrust hopes to demonstrate the inwardness of knowledge, the interaction between the interpreter and the language-event.

Recent Epistemological Influences

More recent views making a claim upon the epistemological scene include:

1. *Social-science considerations,* whereby the historical context dominates the process. Words and propositional statements are necessary, but they are not the end products. These constitute the information that flows through the texts from a social system or matrix. The "domain of reference" is the important thing.

2. *Liberation-theology motifs,* whereby certain oppressed groups (Blacks, the poor, women, the politically oppressed) have "one issue"

concerns about what oppresses their particular group. They tend to let this concern dominate the meaning of religion and/or God's revelation.

3. *Structuralism*, is a somewhat new idea for use in determining knowledge. It claims that interpretation must be done in terms of the structures of human thought and deals primarily with the sentence and syntactical units, with a strong concern for structure. Structuralism rejects the usual epistemological approaches of both literature and history, in favor of the ordering of the body of linguistic data into its structure! It assumes that it is completely objective and that all subjectivity has been removed. Presuppositions (the normal type), attitudes, and values are neutralized, and the relations of parts and wholes are redefined. This system takes biblical hermeneutics completely out of the realm of the ordinary man's communication. It is new to epistemology and ignores the approach that man has used through ages past. Paul Ricoeur, who has become popular in this field in recent years, has said, "I myself am in favor of a hermeneutic which grafts existential interpretation upon a structural analysis. . . ."[1]

4. *Analytic philosophy*, though not especially concerned with biblical texts but rather any and all textual meanings, has done some valuable work in the analysis of texts and interrelation of their parts, their contextual backgrounds, and other relevant factors. There are numerous different emphases within this approach. A chief criticism could be made of A. J. Ayer's conclusion that "a statement is meaningful if, and only if, it is either analytic or empirically meaningful."[2]

This means that these "logical empiricists" will not accept anything as meaningful unless it can be demonstrated as true by empirical observation or experiment. All theological and ethical statements are thus automatically declared to be meaningless. These people are so much concerned with analysis and its findings that they ignore the basic content and message being communicated. John Wild has made an interesting observation in this regard: "Analytic philosophy, which surrenders objective insight to focus on the logical and linguistic tools of knowledge, is like a man who becomes so interested in the crack and spots of dust on his glasses that he loses all interest in what he may actually see through them."[3]

It is true, however, that apart from this distortion in basic philosophy, much can be learned from the analysts about semantics, linguistic relationships, and such matters as contextual influences upon both author

---

1. *Semeia*, vol. 4, Society of Biblical Literature, 1975, p. 31.
2. A. J. Ayer, *Language, Truth and Logic*, 2nd rev. ed. (New York: Dover, 1946), p. 9.
3. J. Wild, *The Challenge of Existentialism* (Bloomington: Indiana University, 1955), p. 10.

and interpreter. Truth in these matters, from whatever source, deserves to be fully considered.[4]

5. *The evangelical school of thought* probably has the largest number of adherents among Bible students in America today. Their basic theology is largely derived from that of John Calvin, one of the great reformers, who championed an "illumination of the Holy Spirit" doctrine. Succinctly, this teaching holds that the natural man, the unregenerated person, is incapable of understanding and dealing with spiritual truths and realities until he is personally and directly "illumined" by an operation of the Holy Spirit—after which he is saved, has peace of soul, and can now understand and interpret God's Word satisfactorily, at least in its major meanings.

The evangelicals consider themselves to be careful and respectful Biblicists, but they probably do not realize that by depending upon such a dominating influence of the Spirit, they are denying the powerful influence of the Word itself, which claims to be the "power of God unto salvation" (Rom. 1:16). The same book says in 10:17 that "faith comes by hearing and hearing by the message of Christ." In this light, Scripture gives a strong impetus to a rationally understood epistemology derived from propositional word statements. The "revelation" from the direct operation, however, is private, rather than public, and is said to be "better felt than told." Since it is noncommunicable, it thus differs from the message of the gospel, which is to be preached, believed, and obeyed—all of which require understanding of a public communication.

6. *Traditionalism*—all through the years we have had the idea of an "authoritative church tradition," which has been considered by some to supersede Scripture in authority. Luther opposed such thinking, and we have continually heard voices pleading for "going back to the Bible." To claim such tradition as authority is not an attempt to interpret the Word.

The Inductive Method

The epistemological approach that the present writer espouses is what D. R. Dungan, in his book *Hermeneutics,* calls the inductive method. It expects the common man of normal intellect to be able to approach the Bible with serious and careful study and be able to learn what God wants him to know, both accurately and fully enough for him to become unquestionably a man of faith! Thomas Campbell, in his *Declaration and Address,* set forth this same basic epistemology, making an appeal to what he called "the common mind," or "universal reason."

The inductive method simply involves inducing from the specific to the general, in the way that one ordinarily thinks in common communication. One very carefully studies the language, words, syntax, et cetera, to

4. Cf. E. D. Hirsch, *Validity In Interpretation* (New Haven: Yale University, 1967).

determine what is actually said, but one also takes into account any and all historical factors, contextual considerations, and the like, thereby getting the message, for all practical needs and purposes.

Methodology

Linguistic communication is the most common method of sharing ideas used by human beings, perhaps because it is the most precise and the least ambiguous, even though it is always open to some ambiguity. By this we mean that words, expressed in sentences with subjects and predicates and carrying propositional statements of cognitive and rational ideas, are the best means for one mind to communicate with another. This is, no doubt, why language was invented. Men think in logical terms that have propositional content, and they impart cognitive information to each other. These propositions are intellectually grasped and are reflected upon by reason, to the point that they are understood and a judgment is formed, which can then be stated propositionally. Nonverbal communication (e.g., body language) can exist, but it is more susceptible to ambiguity than is word revelation. Again, historical events can also convey revelation, but there is a very high likelihood of misinterpretation. The crucifixion of Jesus meant something different to the Roman soldiers who crucified him than it did to his disciples, although it was the same event to both. Word explanation makes the meaning of the event precise as to God's purpose.

Defining the Task of Exegesis

The goal of biblical interpretation is to bring the exact meaning of the text for its original recipients to the understanding of today's readers—to translate what it meant into what it means.

The task of exegesis in leading out the meaning of the text requires, first, that the historical circumstances be reconstructed, both general and immediate. This includes determining the exact shades of meaning of both words and concepts. It calls for learning the general world view of both the author and the original readers. One should have a general knowledge of their historical background and be able to "feel" their presuppositions and the problems and concerns they faced at the time of the writing of the document in question. The exegete should know the history of the New Testament period but should also realize that the text itself is part of that history and contributed much to it.

Sound exegesis will discern the nonempirical human factors in the history—e.g., what Jesus truly thought of himself. His messianic consciousness obviously cannot be learned from such empirical facts as archeological findings, yet one needs to know this if possible.

Ideally, to get the feel of the Greek language, one should study it until he can be a "Greek among Greeks." He should also try to learn to think as both the Jews and the Romans of the time, for these cultural influences are also strong in the New Testament revelation. This calls for study of primary sources rather than a dependence upon secondary ones.

Exegesis is the basic discipline for all Bible study. It is where one begins, and its conclusions must always inform and invite new study. Theological conclusions must never be drawn until the exegesis is complete. What exegesis says must control the theology that one accepts. The reverse would be mere eisegesis (reading one's own ideas into the text) and would be a denial of sincere scholarship. The scholarly exegete must ever be careful to avoid being dominated by his own presuppositions and traditions. It is easy to see this danger in others but not in oneself! Here begin both heresy and denominationalism. Truly objective and fair scholarship calls for listing all the possible alternatives to each decision, then fairly trying each in the context, without bias or undue dependence on one's own traditional background. If carefully done, this will foster one's objectivity and fairness to the text and will in general produce a higher-quality result.

Tools for Text Study

In the beginning with the text itself, the first step is to obtain good tools. The best aid for getting acquainted with what is available is F. W. Dankea's *Multipurpose Tools for Bible Study* (St. Louis: Concordia, 1960). Major tools include lexicons, concordances of the Bible (in the various languages) and of the patristic writings, word studies, commentaries, special articles, and studies of particular problems. The more one studies the original languages and their grammatical nuances, the better exegete he will be. He should be content, however, to deal with what is actually there and not try to be novel or ingenious about some new method or philosophy of interpretation. The final result should be an organic unifying of the whole text into a grand synthesis with the entire Bible, rather than a reduction of the text to atomic particles and the resultant claim that they disagree with each other.

The textual apparatus found in a good Greek Testament (Nestle-Aland, 26th ed.; or the UBS text available from the American Bible Society) should be considered in order to determine the exact wording of the original document as far as possible. For nonusers of Greek, the footnotes in good English versions can help. Where there may be major disagreements, they should be worked out carefully.

Logical Principles

In many respects the Bible is to be studied as any other literature. Ordinary language forms and grammatical rules of accidence and syntax must be respected. The Scriptures were written in human language, not that of angels, and therefore the ordinary rules of grammar and linguistic principles must be observed the same as for other books. Further, there is no peculiar biblical logic! The same laws of thought and rules for correct thinking apply for the Bible as for secular writings. Once it was thought that the New Testament was written in a peculiar "Holy Ghost" Greek, but A. Deissmann has proved conclusively that the Greek used is *Koine*, the Greek spoken by the common man of the street in that day.

Yet, the Bible must be regarded as a different book. Its nature and the time and circumstances of its production cannot be ignored. Its total context and world view must ever be kept in mind. For instance, "God" in John 3:16 ("God so loved the world") must be interpreted to mean "our loving heavenly Father"—never a mere philosophical concept, such as Tillich's "Ground of Being," or Plato's "Idea of the Good," or Roman Stoicism's "World Soul." We must impart to the Bible the meaning the author had in mind at the time of writing. Likewise the New Testament expression, "It is written," used of references from the Old Testament, means that the idea quoted is in fact the authoritative declaration of God and is to be so regarded. This is how the New Testament author considered it. A statement in one place can give force and meaning to the same statement in another place, such as "build according to the pattern."

Language

One should realize that in going from Greek or Hebrew into English (or from any other language into another), a good translation cannot be strictly on the basis of word-for-word substitutions. It does not work that way. Since every language has its own idioms and other linguistic elements that are peculiar to it, word-for-word translations would not always carry over the true meaning. A good illustration of this is the Greek term *mē genoito*. Literally this means "may this not come to be," but the expression carries a force that these English words do not reflect. Our translations read "God forbid," "certainly not," and so on. An equivalent expression for today might be "No Way!" if one wanted to translate what the Greek reader of the first century got from this phrase.

The historical development of word meanings must also be considered. *Pneuma* once meant "wind," but by New Testament times it commonly meant "spirit." Out of the 281 occurrences in the King James New Testament it was translated "wind" only once (John 3:8), this no doubt under Calvinistic influence. "Wind" does not fit the John 3:8 context, whereas "spirit" is what is under discussion. Therefore, what a word meant at a given time in history is important to know for good translation. Word meanings should be checked in concordances to determine their meaning elsewhere in Scripture, particularly in material by the same author. Then check them in other authors—in the LXX, in early Christian writers that are not included in the canon, in Jewish writers, and also in pagan literature. All these can help to determine the intended meaning of a word or expression.

The immediate and the general context tie in to the historical atmosphere and perspective. Knowing these will help determine language meaning. For example, some say that the Greek preposition *eis* in Acts 2:38 means "because of"; that is, they already had the remission of sins. Yet, one finds the same expression in Matthew 26:28 and will note that there it is stated that Christ died "for the purpose of" *(eis)* remission of sins. So one knows from other passages that he did not die "because of" or "because they already had" the remission of sins; one knows that the "because of" interpretation in Acts 2:38 is wrong.

Background and Foreground

Familiarity with the historical situation for the two or three hundred years previous to the writing of the New Testament helps in understanding Jewish and pagan attitudes and events, including governments, education, religions, economics, cultures. A knowledge of these factors will enrich our understanding and interpretation of the biblical text, as it applies to both then and now.

Again, studying the two or three centuries following the birth of Christianity shows how those early Christians, who were close to the facts of the New Testament message, understood them. This may well shed light on what our own understanding should be. In studying this material, it is wise to guard against the overinfluence of any prejudices found among today's scholars. Extreme views should be avoided.

Precision of Thought

The need for logical reasoning sometimes leads the student deeper than mere technical or mechanical rules can take him. Here such matters as commands, inferences and approved precedents of the biblical characters must be considered. Commands are logically obvious, yet not all of them apply generally. Some have exceptions, and care should be given to this possibility. An inference is a conclusion derived from reasoning, based on evidence, and logically determined. Some inferences are "necessary." If so, they must be accepted as an integral part of the message conveyed. Valid assumptions made in Scripture, such as "the existence of God," are necessary inferences. Approved precedents upon the part of the biblical characters convey a binding obligation upon today's reader in cases where the context indicates that the exemplary character understood that he was required to act or think in a certain manner. Actually, both inferences and binding examples have the force of "command authority" for today's reader, for logically a command lies behind them.

Practically every writing about hermeneutics has a list of rules pointing out the order of procedure and things to watch for, and most of them have something worthwhile to suggest. A book that this writer prefers as very practical is D. R. Dungan's *Hermeneutics*.[5] The best brief article for practical usage is probably Malherbe's "The Task and Method of Exegesis."[6]

5. D. R. Dungan, *Hermeneutics* (Delight, AR: Gospel Light, n.d.).
6. A. Malherbe, "The Task and Method of Exegesis," RQ 5 (1961): 169.

26

Bibliography for Biblical Exegesis

Edward P. Myers, Compiler

Bibliographies

A Bibliography of Bible Study for Theological Students. Princeton, NJ: Princeton Theological Seminary, 1960.

Aune, David E. *Jesus and the Synoptic Gospels: A Bibliographic Study Guide.* TSF-IBR Bibliographic Study Guides. Madison, WI: Theological Students Fellowship, 1980.

Barker, Kenneth L.; Bruce K. Waltke; and Roy B. Zuck. *Bibliography for Old Testament Exegesis and Exposition.* 4th ed., revised and enlarged. Dallas: Dallas Theological Seminary, 1979.

Bollier, John A. *The Literature of Theology: A Guide for Students and Pastors.* Philadelphia: Westminster, 1979.

Branson, Mark Lau. *The Reader's Guide to the Best Evangelical Books.* New York: Harper & Row, 1982.

Childs, Brevard S. *Old Testament Books for Pastors and Teachers.* Philadelphia: Westminster, 1977.

Danker, Frederick W. *Multipurpose Tools for Bible Study,* 3rd ed. St. Louis: Concordia, 1970.

Essential Books for A Pastor's Library. 4th ed. Richmond, VA: Union Theological Seminary, 1968.

Fitzmyer, J. A. *An Introductory Bibliography for the Study of Scripture.* Rev. ed. Rome: Biblical Institute, 1981.

France, R. T. *A Bibliographical Guide to New Testament Research.* 3rd ed. Sheffield: JSOT, 1979.

Goldingay, John. *Old Testament Commentary Survey.* With additions & editing by Mark Branson and Robert Hubbard. 2nd ed. Madison, WI: Theological Students Fellowship, 1981.

Hurd, J. C., Jr. *A Bibliography of New Testament Bibliographies*. New York: Seabury, 1966.

Johnson, S. Lewis, Jr. *Bibliography for New Testament Exegesis and Exposition*. Dallas: Dallas Theological Seminary, n.d.

Kaiser, Otto, and Kümmel, Werner G. *Exegetical Method*. New rev. ed. New York: Seabury, 1981.

Keeple, Robert J. *Reference Works for Theological Research*. 2nd ed. Lanham, MD: University Press of America, 1981.

Marrow, Stanley B. *Basic Tools of Biblical Exegesis*. Rome: Biblical Institute, 1978.

Minister's Library: A Select Bibliography. The Faculty of New Orleans Baptist Theological Seminary. New Orleans, LA. 1978.

Scholer, David M. *Basic Bibliographic Guide for New Testament Exegesis*. 2nd ed. Grand Rapids: Eerdmans, 1973.

Stuart, Douglas. *Old Testament Exegesis: A Primer for Students and Pastors*. Philadelphia: Westminster, 1980.

Thiselton, Anthony C. *New Testament Commentary Survey*. Revised by Don Carson. Leicester, England: Theological Students Fellowship, 1977.

Wagner, G., ed. *An Exegetical Bibliography of the New Testament*. Macon/Edinburgh: Mercer University/ T. & T. Clark, 1982–.

Wiersbe, Warren W. *A Basic Library for Bible Students*. Grand Rapids: Baker, 1981.

General Exegesis

Berkhof, Louis. *Principles of Biblical Interpretation*. Grand Rapids: Baker, 1950.

Bright, John. "Modern Study of Old Testament Literature." In *The Bible and the Ancient Near East* (pp. 13–31). Edited by G. E. Wright. Reprint ed. Winona Lake, IN: Eisenbrauns, 1979.

Bullinger, E. W. *Figures of Speech Used in the Bible*. Grand Rapids: Baker, 1968 (reprint).

Caird, G. B. *The Language and Imagery of the Bible*. Philadelphia: Westminster, 1980.

Clements, R. *One Hundred Years of Old Testament Interpretation*. Philadelphia: Westminster, 1976.

Dungan, D. R. *Hermeneutics*. Delight, AR: Gospel Light, n.d.

Ensign, Grayson. *You Can Understand the Bible*. Joplin, MO: College Press, 1978.

Fairbairn, Patrick. *Typology of Scripture*. 2 vols. Grand Rapids: Zondervan (reprint), n.d.

Farrar, Frederic W. *History of Interpretation*. Grand Rapids: Baker, 1961 (reprint of 1885 edition).

Grant, Robert M. *A Short History of the Interpretation of the Bible*. Rev. ed. New York: Macmillan, 1972.

Hahn, H. F. *The Old Testament in Modern Research*. Philadelphia: Fortress, 1966.

Hayes, John R., and Holladay, Carl R. *Biblical Exegesis: A Beginner's Handbook*. Atlanta: John Knox, 1982.

Henry, C. F. H. *God, Revelation, and Authority*. Vol. 4, *God Who Speaks and Shows*. Waco: Word, 1979.

Kaufman, S. A. "The Temple Scroll and Higher Criticism." HUCA 53 (1982): 29–43.

Kendrick, Carroll. *Rules of Bible Study.* Kansas City, MO: Old Paths Book Club, 1946.

Longenecker, Richard. *Biblical Exegesis in the Apostolic Period.* Grand Rapids: Eerdmans, 1975.

Mickelsen, A. Berkeley. *Interpreting the Bible.* Grand Rapids: Eerdmans, 1963.

Ramm, Bernard. *Hermeneutics.* Grand Rapids: Baker, 1971.

_____. *Protestant Biblical Interpretation.* 3rd rev. ed. Grand Rapids: Baker, 1970.

Schultz, Samuel J., and Inch, Morris A., eds. *Interpreting the Word of God.* Chicago: Moody, 1976.

Society for Old Testament Study. Series of scholarly Books reviewing the State of Old Testament Studies.

    The People and the Book. A. S. Peake, ed. Oxford: Clarendon, 1925.

    Record and Revelation. H. W. Robinson, ed., 1938.

    The Old Testament and Modern Study. H. H. Rowley, 1951.

    Tradition and Interpretation. G. W. Anderson, ed., 1979.

Soulen, R. N. *Handbook on Biblical Criticism.* 2nd ed., revised and augmented. Atlanta: John Knox, 1981.

Terry, Milton S. *Biblical Hermeneutics.* Grand Rapids: Zondervan, 1974 (reprint).

Tsevat, M. "Common Sense and Hypothesis in Old Testament Study." VT Supplement 28 (Congress Volume Edinburgh, 1974), pp. 217–30. Leiden: Brill, 1975.

Yamauchi, E. *Composition and Corroboration in Classical and Biblical Studies.* Philadelphia: Presbyterian and Reformed, 1966.

Old Testament

Introductions

Archer, Gleason L., Jr. *A Survey of Old Testament Introduction.* Chicago: Moody, 1964.

Childs, Brevard S. *Introduction to the Old Testament as Scripture.* London/Philadelphia: SCM/Fortress, 1979.

Eissfeldt, Otto. *The Old Testament: An Introduction Including the Apocrypha and Pseudepigrapha and Also Other Works of a Similar Type From Qumran.* Oxford/New York: Basil Blackwell/Harper & Row, 1965.

Fohrer, George. *Introduction to the Old Testament.* Nashville/London: Abingdon/SPCK, 1968.

Harrison, R. K. *Introduction to the Old Testament: With a Comprehensive Review of Old Testament Studies and a Special Supplement on the Apocrypha.* Leicester/Grand Rapids: Inter-Varsity/Eerdmans, 1969.

LaSor, William Sanford; Hubbard, David A.; and Bush, Frederic W. *Old Testament Survey: The Message, Form, and Background of the Old Testament.* Grand Rapids: Eerdmans, 1982.

Soggin, J. A. *Introduction to the Old Testament: From Its Origins to the Closing of the Alexandrian Canon.* Rev. ed. London/Philadelphia: SCM/Westminster, 1980.

Young, Edward J. *An Introduction to the Old Testament*. Grand Rapids: Eerdmans, 1965 edition.

Texts

Brooke, A. E., et al., eds. *The Old Testament In Greek*. 3 vols. London: Cambridge University, 1906–1940. Incomplete.
Elliger, K., and Rudolf, W., eds. *Biblia Hebraica Stuttgartensia*. Stuttgart: Deutsche Bibelstiftung, 1967–1977.
Kittel, R., ed. *Biblia Hebraica*. 9th ed. Stuttgart: Württembergische Bibelanstalt, 1954.
Rahlfs, A., ed. *Septuaginta*. 8th ed. 2 vols. Stuttgart: Württembergische Bibelanstalt, 1965.
Septuaginta: Vetus Testamentum graece autoriatate Societatis Gottingensis editum. Gottingen: Vandenhoeck & Reprecht, 1931.

Concordances

Hatch, E., and Redpath, H. A. *A Concordance to the Septuagint and the Other Greek Versions of the Old Testament Including the Apocryphal Books*, 3 vols. London: Oxford University, 1897–1906. Reprinted in 2 vols., Graz: Akademischer Druck, 1954. Cf also *An Expanded Index of the Hatch-Redpath Concordance to the Septuagint*. Jerusalem: Dugeth, 1974.
Lisowsky, Gerhard. *Konkordanz zum hebraischen Alten Testament*. 2nd ed. Stuttgart: Württembergische Bibelanstalt, 1958.
Mandelkern, Solomon. *Veteris Testamenti concordantiae hebraicae atque chaldaicae*. 9th ed. Jerusalem/Tel Aviv: Schocken, 1971.
Wigram, G. V. *The Englishman's Hebrew and Chaldee Concordance of the Old Testament Numerically Coded to Strong's Exhaustive Concordance*. Grand Rapids: Baker, 1980.

Lexicons/Lexical Aids

Brown, F.; Driver, S. R.; and Briggs, C. A. *A Hebrew and English Lexicon of the Old Testament*. Corrected edition. London/New York: Oxford University, 1952. Reissued as *The New Brown, Driver, and Briggs . . . Numerically Coded to Strong's Exhaustive Concordance*. Grand Rapids: Baker, 1981.
Davidson, B. *The Analytical Hebrew and Chaldee Lexicon*. London: Samuel Bagster & Sons, 1848. Reprint Grand Rapids: Zondervan, 1970.
Einsaphr, Bruce. *Index to Brown, Driver, and Briggs Hebrew Lexicon*. Chicago: Moody, 1976.
Gesenius' Hebrew and Chaldee Lexicon to the Old Testament Scriptures Numerically Coded to Strong's Exhaustive Concordance. Grand Rapids: Baker, 1979.
Harkavy, Alexander. *Hebrew and Chaldee Dictionary to the Old Testament*. New York: Hebrew Publishing, 1914.
Holladay, W. L. *A Concise Hebrew and Aramaic Lexicon of the Old Testament, Based upon the Lexical Work of Koehler and W. Baumgartner*. Leiden/Grand Rapids: Brill/Eerdmans, 1971.

Jastrow, M. *A Dictionary of the Targumim, the Talmud Babli and Yerushalmi, and the Midrashic Literature.* London/New York: Luzac/Putman, 1886–1900 (often reprinted by various publishers).

Koehler, L. and Baumgartner, W. *Lexicon in Veteris Testamenti libros,* 2nd ed. Leiden: Brill, 1958.

Landes, George M. *Student's Vocabulary of Biblical Hebrew: Listed According to Frequency and Cognate.* New York: Scribner's, 1961.

Mitchell, Larry A. *A Student's Vocabulary for Biblical Hebrew and Aramaic.* Grand Rapids: Zondervan (Academic Books), 1984.

Robinson, M. A. *Indexes to All Editions of Brown-Driver-Briggs Hebrew Lexicon and Thayer's Greek Lexicon.* Grand Rapids: Baker, 1981.

Tregelles, Samuel Prideaux, tr. and reviser. *Gesenius' Hebrew and Chaldee Lexicon to the Old Testament Scriptures.* Grand Rapids: Eerdmans, reprinted 1949.

Watts, John D. *Lists of Words Occurring Frequently in the Hebrew Bible.* Grand Rapids: Eerdmans, 1960.

Hebrew and Aramaic Grammars

Bauer, H., and Leander, P. *Historische Grammatik in den Semitischen Sprachen.* 2nd ed. Halle: Universtiteit Verlag, 1922.

Bergstrasser, B. *Hebräische Grammatik.* Vols. 1–2. Leipzig, 1918. Reprint, Hildesheim: G. Olms, 1962.

Brockelmann, C. *Grundriss der Vergleichenden Grammatik der Semitischen Sprachen.* Vols. 1–2. Berlin, 1908. Reprint, Hildesheim: G. Olms, 1959.

Carson, E. Leslie. *Elementary Hebrew.* Grand Rapids: Baker, 1945 (paperback, 1978).

Gesenius, W., and Kautzsch, E. *Gesenius' Hebrew Grammar.* 2nd ed. London/New York: Oxford University, 1910; 15th printing (1980) has a revised index of passages.

Harris, R. Laird. *Introductory Hebrew Grammar.* Grand Rapids: Eerdmans, 1950.

Lambdin, T. O. *Introduction to Biblical Hebrew.* New York/London: Scribner's/ Darton, Longman and Todd, 1971/1973.

LaSor, William Sanford. *Handbook of Biblical Hebrew.* 2 vols. Grand Rapids: Eerdmans, 1978, 1979.

Livingston, G. Herbert. *A New Approach To Hebrew Grammar.* Wilmore, KY: Asbury Theological Seminary, 1966.

Marks, John H., and Rogers, Virgil M. *A Beginner's Handbook to Biblical Hebrew.* Nashville: Abingdon, 1958.

Mansoor, Menahem. *Biblical Hebrew: Step by Step.* Grand Rapids: Baker, 1978.

Meyer, Rudolf. *Hebräische Grammatik.* 3 vols. Berlin: Walter de Gruyter, 1966.

Rosenthal, F. A. *A Grammar of Biblical Aramaic.* Wiesbaden: Harrassowitz, 1961.

Weingreen, J. *Practical Grammar for Classical Hebrew.* 2nd ed. New York/London: Oxford University, 1959.

Williams, R. J. *Hebrew Syntax: An Outline.* 2nd ed. Toronto/Buffalo/London: University of Toronto, 1976.

Yates, Kyle M. *The Essentials of Biblical Hebrew.* Nashville: Broadman, n.d. Reprinted from Harper and Brothers, 1938.

New Testament

Introductions

Baker, Glen W.; Lane, William F.; and Michaels, J. Ramsay. *The New Testament Speaks*. New York: Harper & Row, 1969.

Guthrie, Donald A. *New Testament Introduction*. 3rd ed. Downers Grove: Intervarsity, 1970.

Harrison, E. F. *Introduction to the New Testament*. Grand Rapids: Eerdmans, 1964.

Koester, Helmut. *Introduction to the New Testament*. 2 vols. Philadelphia: Fortress, 1982.

Kümmel, W. G. *Introduction to the New Testament*. Rev. ed. Nashville/London: Abingdon/SCM, 1975.

Marxsen, W. *Introduction to the New Testament: An Approach to Its Problems*. Philadelphia/Oxford: Fortress/Basil Blackwell, 1968.

Robert, A., and Feuillet, A. *Introduction to the New Testament*. New York: Desclee, 1965.

Thiessen, H. C. *Introduction to the New Testament*. Grand Rapids: Eerdmans, 1943.

Zahn, Theodor. *Introduction to the New Testament*. 3 vols. Edinburgh: T. & T. Clark, 1909. Reissued by Klock and Klock, 1953.

Wikenhauser, A. *New Testament Introduction*. Dublin/New York: Herder & Herder, 1958.

Texts

Aland, K., et al., eds. *The Greek New Testament*, 3rd ed. New York/London: United Bible Societies, 1975.

Aland, K. ed. *Synopsis quattuor evangeliorum: Locis parallelis evangeliorum apocryphorum et patrum adhibitis*. 9th ed. Stuttgart: Deutsche Bibelstiftung, 1976.

Aland, K. ed. *Synopsis of the Four Gospels: Greek-English Edition of the Synopsis Quattuor Evangeliorum with the Text of the Revised Standard Version*, 3rd ed. New York/London: United Bible Societies, 1979.

Greeven, H., ed. *Synopse der drei ersten Evangelien: mit Beigabe der johanneischen Parallelstellen = Synopsis of the First Three Gospels with the Addition of the Johannine Parallels*. Tübingen: J. C. B. Mohr [Paul Siebeck], 1981.

Huck, A., ed. *Synopsis of the First Three Gospels*, 9th ed., rev. by H. Lietzmann. Tübingen: J. C. B. Mohr [Paul Siebeck], 1950; English edition by F. L. Cross; Oxford: Basil Blackwell, 1957.

Kilpatrick, G. D., ed. *He kaine diatheke*, 2nd ed. London: British and Foreign Bible Society, 1958.

Nestle, E., and Aland, K., eds. *Novum Testamentum Graece*, 26th ed. Stuttgart: Deutsche Bibelstiftung, 1979.

Throckmorton, B. H., Jr., *Gospel Parallels: A Synopsis of the First Three Gospels*, 4th ed. New York/London: Nelson, 1979.

Concordances

Aland, Kurt. *Vollstandige Koncordanz sum griechischen Neuen Testament: Unter Zugrundelegung aller kirstischen Textausgaben und des Textus Receptus.* 2 vols. Berlin/New York: Walter de Gruyter, 1975–

Hatch, Edwin, and Redpath, Henry A. *A Concordance to the Septuagint.* 2 vols. Graz: Akademische Druck-u. Verlagsanstalt, 1954.

Moulton, W. F., and Geden, A. S. *A Concordance to the Greek New Testament According to the Texts of Westcott and Hort, Tischendorf, and the English Revisers.* 5th ed., rev. by H. K. Moulton, with a supplement. Edinburgh: T. & T. Clark, 1978.

Schmoller, A. *Handkonkordanz-zum griechischen Neuen Testament.* 9th ed. Stuttgart: Württembergische Bibelanstalt, 1951.

Wigram, G. V. *The Englishman's Greek Concordance Numerically Coded to Strong's Concordance.* Grand Rapids: Baker, 1979.

English Concordances

Concordance to the Apocrypha/Deuterocanonical Books of the Revised Standard Version. Grand Rapids: Eerdmans, 1982.

Ellison, J. W. *Nelson's Complete Concordance of the Revised Standard Version Bible.* 2nd ed. New York/London: Nelson, 1979.

Goodrick, E. W., and Kohlenberger, J. R. *The NIV Complete Concordance.* Grand Rapids: Zondervan, 1981.

Hartdegen, S. J. *Nelson's Complete Concordance of the New American Bible.* Collegeville/Nashville: Liturgical/Nelson, 1977.

Morrison, C. *An Analytical Concordance to the Revised Standard Version of the New Testament.* Philadelphia/London: Westminster/SCM, 1979.

Strong, J. *The Exhaustive Concordance of the Bible.* New York/Cincinnati: Hunt Eaton/Cranston Curtis, 1894; frequently reprinted by various publishers.

Wigram, G. V., and Winter, R. D. *The Word Study Concordance.* Wheaton/Pasadena: Tyndale House/William Carey Library, 1978; keyed to Strong, Moulton-Geden, Arndt-Gingrich, and Kittel-Friedrich.

Young, R. *Analytical Concordance to the Bible.* 8th ed. London/New York: Lutterworth/Funk Wagnalls, 1939; reissued by other publishers.

Lexicons/Lexical Aids

Alsop, J. R. *An Index to the Bauer-Arndt-Gingrich Lexicon.* 2nd ed. Grand Rapids: Zondervan, 1981.

Bauer, W. *A Greek-English Lexicon of the New Testament and Other Early Christian Literature.* 2nd ed., rev. by William F. Arndt, F. Wilbur Gingrich, and Frederick W. Danker. Chicago: University of Chicago, 1979.

Bullinger, E. W. *A Critical Lexicon and Concordance to the English and Greek New Testament.* London: Longmans & Co., 1877; last edition reissued London/Grand Rapids: Samuel Bagster and Son/Zondervan, 1975.

Cremer, Hermann. *Biblical-Theological Lexicon of New Testament Greek*. 4th ed. with supplement. Edinburgh: T. & T. Clark, 1895/1977.

Friberg, B., and Friberg, T. *Analytical Greek New Testament*. Grand Rapids: Baker, 1981.

Kubo, S. *A Reader's Greek Lexicon of the New Testament*. Berrien Spring/Edinburgh: Andrews University/T. & T. Clark, 1971/1979.

Lampe, Geoffry William Hugh. *A Patristic Greek Lexicon*. Oxford: Clarendon, 1968.

Liddell, H. G. and Scott, R. *A Greek-English Lexicon: A New Edition Revised and Augmented Throughout with Supplement*. 9th ed. London: Oxford University, 1925–1940; Supplement, 1968.

Moulton, H. K. *The Analytical Greek Lexicon Revised*. London/Grand Rapids: Samuel Bagster and Son/Zondervan, 1977/1978.

Moulton, J. H., and Milligan, G. *The Vocabulary of the Greek Testament, Illustrated from the Papyri and Other Non-literary Sources*. 2nd ed. London/Grand Rapids: Hodder and Stoughton/Eerdmans, 1957/1963.

Rienecker, F. *A Linguistic Key to the Greek Testament*. 2 vols. Grand Rapids: Zondervan, 1976–1980. Now available in a single volume.

Sophocles, E. A. *Greek Lexicon of the Roman and Byzantine Periods* (from B.C. 146 to A.D. 1100). 2 vols. New York: Unger, 1957. First published in 1887 but still a useful index to Koine usage although it needs to be updated. References are included on classical works, New Testament, and LXX.

Thackeray, Henry St. John. *Lexicon to Joseph*. Paris: Paul Geuthner, 1930–53.

Thayer, J. H. *A Greek-English Lexicon of the New Testament: A Dictionary Numerically Coded to Strong's Exhaustive Concordance*. Grand Rapids: Baker, 1977.

Zerwick, M., and Grosvenor, M. *A Grammatical Analysis of the Greek New Testament*. 2 vols. Rome: Biblical Institute, 1974–1979.

Grammars

Blass, F.; Debrunner, A.; and Funk, R. W. *A Greek Grammar of the New Testament and Other Early Christian Literature*. Chicago/London: University of Chicago, 1961.

Chamberlin, William Douglas. *An Exegetical Grammar of the Greek New Testament*. Grand Rapids: Baker, 1979 (paperback edition issued with permission from Macmillan, 1941).

Colwell, Ernest Cadman. *A Beginner's Reader-Grammar for New Testament Greek*. New York: Harper & Row, 1965.

Dana, H. E., and Mantey, Julius R. *A Manual Grammar of the Greek New Testament*. Toronto: Macmillan, 1927.

Davis, William Hersey. *Beginner's Grammar of the Greek New Testament*. Mt. View, CA: Omega Christian Book Publishers, n.d. (reprint of 1923 edition).

Drumwright, Huber L., Jr. *An Introduction to New Testament Greek*. Nashville: Broadman, 1980.

Funk. R. W. *A Beginning-Intermediate Grammar of Hellenistic Greek*. 3 vols. 2nd ed. Missoula: Scholars Press, 1977.

Goetchius, Eugene Van Ness. *The Language of the New Testament*. New York: Scribner's, 1965.

Kistemaker, Simon. *Introduction to Greek: A Practical Grammar of New Testament Greek.* Jackson, MS: Reformed Theological Seminary, 1976.

LaSor, William Sanford. *Handbook of New Testament Greek.* 2 vols. Grand Rapids: Eerdmans, 1973.

Machen, J. Gresham. *New Testament Greek for Beginners.* Toronto: Macmillan, 1923.

Moule, C. F. D. *An Idiom-Book of New Testament Greek.* 2nd ed. London/New York: Cambridge University, 1959.

Moulton, J. H.; Howard, F. W.; and Turner, N. *A Grammar of New Testament Greek.* 4 vols. Edinburgh: T. & T. Clark, 1929–1976.

Robertson, A. T. *A Grammar of the Greek New Testament in Light of Historical Research.* 4th ed. Nashville/London: Broadman/Hodder and Stoughton, 1923.

Smyth, H. W. *Greek Grammar.* Rev. ed. Cambridge: Harvard University, 1963.

Thackeray, H. St. J. *A Grammar of the Old Testament in Greek According to the Septuagint.* Vol. 1. London: Cambridge University, 1909.

Werner, John R. *Greek: A Programmed Primer.* 3 vols. Phillipsburg, NJ: 1980.

Word Books

von Allen, J. J., ed. *Vocabulary of the Bible: A Companion to the Bible.* London/New York: Lutterworth/Oxford University, 1958.

Bauer, J. B., ed. *Sacramentum verbi: An Encyclopedia of Biblical Theology.* 3 vols. London/New York: Sheed and Ward/Herder and Herder, 1970.

Bengel, John Albert. *New Testament Word Studies.* 2 vols. Originally published under the title: *Gnomen of the New Testament* (1864). Grand Rapids: Kregel, 1971 (reprint).

Botterweck, J., and Ringgren, H., eds. *Theological Dictionary of the Old Testament.* Grand Rapids/London: Eerdmans/SCM, 1977–.

Brown, Colin, ed. *The New International Dictionary of New Testament Theology.* 3 vols. Grand Rapids/Exeter: Zondervan/Paternoster, 1975–1978.

Harris, R. Laird; Archer, Gleason L.; and Waltke, Bruce K. *Theological Wordbook of the Old Testament.* 2 vols. Chicago: Moody, 1980.

Kittel, G. and Friedrich, G., eds. *Theological Dictionary of the New Testament.* 10 vols. Grand Rapids/London: Eerdmans/SCM, 1964–1976.

Leon-Dufour, Xavier. *Dictionary of Biblical Theology.* Rev. ed. London/New York: Geoffrey Chapman/Seabury, 1973.

Richardson, Alan, ed. *A Theological Word Book of the Bible.* London/New York: SCM/Macmillan, 1950/1951.

Robertson, A. T. *Word Pictures in the New Testament.* 6 vols. New York/London: Harper & Brothers, 1930–1933.

Silva, Moises. *Biblical Words and Their Meaning: An Introduction to Lexical Semantics.* Grand Rapids: Zondervan, 1983.

Turner, Nigel. *Christian Words.* Nashville: Nelson, 1981.

Vincent, Marvin R. *Word Studies in the New Testament.* 4 vols. New York/London: Scribner's 1887–1900; reprinted, Grand Rapids: Eerdmans, 1946.

Vine W. E. *Expository Dictionary of New Testament Words.* 4 vols. London: Oliphants, 1939–41; reissued in one volume, London/Grand Rapids: Oliphants/Zondervan, 1952/1981.

_____. *An Expository Dictionary of Old Testament Words*. Edited by F. F. Bruce. Old Tappan, NJ: Revell, 1978.

White, William, Jr. *Theological and Grammatical Phrasebook of the Bible*. Chicago: Moody, 1984.

Archeology

Aharoni, Y. *The Archaeology of the Land of Israel*. Philadelphia: Westminster, 1982.

Albright, W. F. *History, Archaeology and Christian Humanism*. New York: McGraw-Hill, 1964.

_____. *The Archaeology of Palestine*. New ed., rev. by W. G. Dever. Gloucester: Peter Smith, 1976.

Avi-Yonah, M., ed. *Encyclopedia of Archaeological Excavations in the Holy Land*. 4 vols. Englewood Cliffs: Prentice-Hall, 1976–1979.

Baez-Camargo, Gonzalo. *Archaeological Commentary on the Bible*. New York: Doubleday, 1984.

Blaiklock, E. M., and Harrison, R. K., eds. *The New International Dictionary of Biblical Archaeology*. Grand Rapids: Zondervan, 1983.

Cornfeld, Gaalyah. *Archaeology of the Bible: Book by Book*. New York: Harper & Row, 1976.

Dever, William G. *Archaeology and Biblical Studies: Retrospects and Prospects*. The Winslow Lectures at Seabury-Western Theological Seminary. Evanston: 1973.

Frank, Harry T. *Discovering the Biblical World*. Maplewood, NJ: Hammond, 1975.

Finegan, Jack. *Archaeological History of the Middle East*. Boulder/Folkestone: Westview/Dawson & Sons, Ltd., 1979.

_____. *The Archaeology of the New Testament: The Life of Jesus and the Beginning of the Early Church*. Princeton: Princeton University, 1969.

_____. *The Archaeology of the New Testament: The Mediterranean World of the Early Christian Apostles*. Princeton: Princeton University, 1981.

Gray, John. *Archaeology and the Old Testament World*. New York: Harper & Row, 1965.

Kenyon, K. M. *Archaeology in the Holy Land*. 4th ed. London/New York: Ernest Been/W. W. Norton, 1974.

_____. *The Bible and Recent Archaeology*. London/Atlanta: British Museum/John Knox, 1978.

Kitchen, K. A. *Ancient Orient and Old Testament*. Chicago: Inter-Varsity, 1966.

Lance, H. D. *The Old Testament and the Archaeologist*. Philadelphia: Fortress, 1981.

Lapp, Paul W. *Biblical Archaeology and History*. New York: World Publishing, 1969.

Lewis, Jack P. *Archaeology and the Bible*. The Way of Life Series. Abilene, TX: Biblical Research Press, 1975.

_____. *Historical Backgrounds of Bible History*. Grand Rapids: Baker, 1971.

_____. *Archaeological Insights into the Interpretation of the Minor Prophets*. Second Annual Inman Bible Forum Lectures: Ohio Valley College. Parkersburg, WV., 1984.

Pfeiffer, Charles F., ed. *The Biblical World: A Dictionary of Biblical Archaeology.* Grand Rapids: Baker, 1966.

Schoville, Keith N. *Biblical Archaeology in Focus.* Grand Rapids: Baker, 1978.

Williams, Walter G. *Archaeology in Biblical Research.* New York: Abingdon, 1965.

Wright, G. E. *Biblical Archaeology.* Rev. ed. Philadelphia: Westminster, 1962.

Atlases and Geographies

Aharoni, Y. *The Land of the Bible: A Historical Geography.* Rev. ed. by A. F. Rainey. Philadelphia: Westminster, 1980.

Aharoni, Y., and Avi-Yonah, M. *The Macmillan Bible Atlas.* Rev. ed. New York: Macmillan, 1977.

Avi-Yonah, Michael. *The Holy Land from the Persian to the Arab Conquests (536 BC to AD 640): A Historical Geography.* Rev. ed. Grand Rapids: Baker, 1977.

Baly, D. *Geographical Companion to the Bible.* New York: Harper & Row, 1963.

_____. *The Geography of the Bible.* 2nd ed. New York: Harper and Row, 1979.

Grollenberg, L. H. *Atlas of the Bible.* London/New York: Nelson, 1956.

May, Herbert G. *Oxford Bible Atlas.* 3rd ed. New York: Oxford University, 1984.

Smith, George A. *Historical Geography of the Holy Land.* 4th ed. London: Hodder and Stoughton, 1896; reprinted by various publishers.

27

Bibliography of the Scholarly Writings of Jack P. Lewis

Annie May Lewis, Compiler

"Ability," "Communion of Saints," and "Transcendentalism." In *Baker's Diction-ary of Theology* (pp. 16, 131–132, 528). Edited by E. F. Harrison. Grand Rapids: Baker, 1960.

"Ah, Assyria, the Rod of My Anger." *Twentieth Century Christian* 45 (April 1984):16–19.

"And Why Not You?" *World Vision* 12 (March–April 1946):16, 17.

"Apocrypha," "Luke," and "Matthew." In *Wycliffe Bible Encyclopedia* (pp. 111–12, 1056–57, 1090–91). Edited by C. F. Pfeiffer, H. F. Vos, and J. Rea. Chicago: Moody, 1975.

Archaeological Backgrounds to Bible People. Grand Rapids: Baker, © 1977, 1981.

"Archaeological Fictions." *Christian Light* 2 (November–December 1980):53, 62; and (March–April 1981):86–87, 93.

Archaeology and the Bible. Abilene, TX: Biblical Research Press, 1975.

"Archaeology and the Bible." In *Harding College Bible Lectures* (pp. 140–48). Aus-tin, TX: Firm Foundation, 1976.

"As One Having Authority." *Campus Journal* 16 (1973):14–16.

"Australia and New Zealand," jointly with B. Terry. In *The Harvest Field* (pp. 47–48). Edited by H. Schugg and D. H. Morris. Abilene, TX: Abilene Christian College, 1942.

"Authority." *Harding Graduate School of Religion Bulletin* 18 (June 1978).

"The Authority of the Scriptures." In *Harding College Bible Lectures* (pp. 184–203). Austin, TX: Firm Foundation, 1977.

"Banquet," "Bread," "Cup," "Drink," "Drunkenness," "Famine," "Fast, Fasting," "Food," "Leaven," "Meals," "Table," "Vinegar," "Wine," "Winepress." In *Nelson's Illustrated Bible Dictionary*, pp. 130–31, 190–91, 268–69, 313, 377, 378, 389–91, 640–41, 689–90, 1026, 1087, 1101–2, 1103. Edited by Herbert Lockyer, Sr. Nashville: Nelson, 1986.

"Baptismal Practices of the Second and Third Century Church." RQ 26 (1983):1–17.

"Berlin and the Bible." *Voice of Freedom* 22 (March 1974):41–42.

"Better Than Denominationalism." *Gospel Broadcast* 5 (January 18, 1945):42, 43, 47.

"The Bible and Archaeology." *The Spiritual Sword* 1 (January 1970):26–27.

"The Bible and Archaeology." In *White's Ferry Road Bible Lectures* (pp. 117–29). West Monroe, LA: School of Biblical Studies, 1979.

"Bible Archaeology and Geography." In *The World and Literature of the Old Testament* (pp. 71–116). Edited by J. T. Willis. Austin, TX: Sweet, 1979.

"Bible Characters Really Lived." *Gospel Advocate* 127 (July 18, 1985):426.

"Bible Lesson for January 12, 1964: Isaiah's Call." *Gospel Advocate* 106 (January 2, 1964):3, 7.

"Bible Study in the Churches of Christ." *Seminary Review* 31 (December 1985):177–96.

"Bible Translation and Doctrinal Error." *Firm Foundation* 94 (June 7, 1977):356, 363.

"The Biblical Field." *Harding Graduate School of Religion Bulletin* 14 (July 1975).

"The Books of Kings." *Minister's Monthly* 12 (September 1966):22–25.

"Bring the Books and the Parchments." *Firm Foundation* 86 (February 11, 1969):89.

"But What Is One Among So Many?" *Gospel Advocate* 126 (May 3, 1984):277.

"The Christian School as the Educator Sees It." In North Central *Christian College Lectures: Christian Education* (pp. 76–90). Austin, TX: Firm Foundation, 1960.

"The Church—'A Called Out' Body." *Gospel Broadcast* 5 (August 2, 1945):438, 447.

"The Church a Mighty Army." *Gospel Broadcast* 5 (May 10, 1945):296–297.

"The Church as a Building." *Gospel Broadcast* 5 (April 5, 1945):214, 219.

"The Church—Body of Christ." *Gospel Broadcast* 5 (April 12, 1945):234, 238.

"The Church—Family of God." *Gospel Broadcast* 5 (April 19, 1945):252.

"Church—Vineyard of the Lord." *Gospel Broadcast* 5 (June 14, 1945):362–363.

"A Cloud of Witnesses: Hebrews 12:1." *Gospel Advocate* 125 (April 21, 1983):233, 237.

"Commencements I Remember." *Harding Graduate School of Religion Bulletin* 22 (July 1982).

"Confused Holy Spirit?" *Firm Foundation* 95 (August 15, 1978):520; and *Voice of Freedom* 27 (March 1979):36.

"Cooperative Evangelism." *Harding Graduate School of Religion Bulletin* 29 (January 1987):1.

"Courage" and "Despair." In *Baker's Dictionary of Christian Ethics* (pp. 146, 176–177). Edited by C. F. Henry. Grand Rapids: Baker, 1973.

"Demythologizing the New Testament." In *Harding College Bible Lectures* (pp. 163–75). Nashville: Christian Family Books, 1965.

"Difficult Texts from the Psalms and Proverbs." In *Difficult Texts of the Old Testament Explained: The Fifth Annual Fort Worth Lectures* (pp. 311–23). Hurst, TX: Winkler Publications, 1982.

"Doctrinal Problems and the King James Version." RQ 14 (1971):142–54.

"Eastern Turkey and the Bible." *Firm Foundation* 85 (November 12, 1968):726.

"Edna," "Ekron, Ekronite," "Elhanan," "Eliab," "Fast, Fasting," "Feasts," "First Fruits," "Food," and "Leaven." In *Zondervan Pictorial Encyclopedia of the Bible* (pp. 201, 259–62, 279, 289, 501–504, 521–526, 541, 581–87, 910–13). Edited by M. Tenney. Grand Rapids: Zondervan, 1975.

"The Effect of Affluence on the Church." *Contact* 15 (Fall 1968): 10–13.

The English Bible from KJV to NIV: A History and Evaluation. Grand Rapids: Baker, 1981.

"The Ethical Teaching of the Prophets." In *Ethics for Daily Living,* pp. 161–75. Edited by Winford Claiborne. Freed-Hardeman College Lectures, 1986. Henderson, TN: Freed-Hardeman College, 1986.

"An Exegesis of Romans 13:1–7." In *Harding College Bible Lectures,* pp. 100–112. Austin, TX: Firm Foundation, 1966.

"External Only?" *Firm Foundation* 97 (June 17, 1980):388.

"Ezekiel." In *Fort Worth Christian College Lectures* (pp. 333–46). Fort Worth, TX: Fort Worth Christian College, 1961.

"Faith Only." *Gospel Advocate* 128 (March 6, 1986):145, 148.

"First Century Jews and the Messiah." *Twentieth Century Christian* 41 (February 1979):3–5.

"Following Paul with Hertz." RQ 15 (1972):129–51.

"From the Beginning It Was Not So." In *Your Marriage Can Be Great* (pp. 410–19). Edited by T. B. Warren. Jonesboro, AR: National Christian Press, 1978.

"Fruit of the Vine." *Firm Foundation* 93 (February 17, 1976):101.

"Gambling." *Gospel Broadcast* 5 (March 8, 1945):150–151.

"Genesis 3:15: The Woman's Seed." *Firm Foundation* 92 (April 22, 1975):248.

The Gospel According to Matthew. 2 vols. Austin, TX: Sweet, 1976.

"The Graduate School as I Remember It." *Harding Graduate School of Religion Bulletin* 19 (February 1979):1–3.

"Great News From Jerusalem." *The World Evangelist* 12 (May 1984):4.

"Greek Word Studies on the Function and Authority of Preachers." *Firm Foundation* 97 (September 1980):567, 572, 583, 599, 615, 631, 635.

"Greek Words for Elders." *Firm Foundation* 96 (June 26–July 31, 1979):407, 423, 439, 455, 471, 475, 487, 491.

"The Hardest Commandment." *Twentieth Century Christian* 34 (April 1974):7–9.

"A Historical Background of the Prophets." In *Living Lessons from the Prophets,* pp. 71–86. Edited by John Waddey. Knoxville, TN: East Tennessee School of Preaching and Missions, 1985.

Historical Backgrounds of Bible History. Grand Rapids: Baker, 1971.

"How Many Times Was Cain Killed?" *Harding Graduate School of Religion Bulletin* 22 (October 1982).

"I Must See Africa." *Voice of Freedom* 23 (March 1975):37–38.

"I Was in the Isle Called Patmos." *Firm Foundation* 88 (December 14, 1971):789, 795.

"If I Had One Sermon to Preach: Our Greatest Need." *Minster's Monthly* 3 (May 1958):13–16.

"In Journeyings Often." *Firm Foundation* 93 (October 5, 1976):629, 634, 635.

"In Search of Gilgal." RQ 11 (1968):137–43.

"Inspiration and Authority of the Bible." In *Harding College Bible Lectures* (pp. 90–122). Austin, TX: Firm Foundation, 1972.

"Inspiration and Authority of the Bible." *Alternative* 5 (Spring 1979):3–8.

"The Intermediate State of the Dead." In *Harding College Bible Lectures* (pp. 169–90). Austin, TX: Firm Foundation, 1974; and *Magnolia Bible College Lectures* (pp. 87–96). Kosciusko, MS: Magnolia Bible College, 1984.

"An Introduction to the Testaments of the Twelve Patriarchs." Ph.D. dissertation, Harvard University, 1953.

"Italics in English Bible Translation." In *The Living and Active Word of God: Studies in Honor of Samuel J. Schultz* (pp. 250–70). Edited by M. Inch and R. Youngblood. Winona Lake, IN: Eisenbrauns, 1983.

"I've Heard That You Do Not Believe That Isaiah 7:14 Predicts the Virgin Birth and Yet Matthew 1 Says That It Does: How Do You Explain This?" *Harding Graduate School of Religion Bulletin* 24 (March 1983).

"I Wish She Would Stay Here with Me." *Harding Graduate School of Religion Bulletin* 27 (March 1986):1, 3; and *Gospel Advocate* 128 (May 15, 1986):300, 308.

"Jesus Gave His Blood." In *Bible Foundations*, 2:2:273 (pp. 9–16). Nashville, TN: Gospel Advocate, 1973.

"The Jewish Background of the Church." RQ 2 (1958):154–63.

"The Jewish Background of the New Testament." RQ 5 (1961):209–15.

"Kizzie, Stay Put!" *Firm Foundation* 98 (January 6, 1981):3.

Editor of *The Last Things; Essays Presented by His Students to Dr. W. B. West, Jr., Upon the Occasion of His Sixty-fifth Birthday.* Austin, TX: Sweet, 1972.

"Lay Up Treasures in Heaven." *Firm Foundation* 100 (March 1, 1983):135; (March 8, 1983):151, 156.

Leadership Questions Confronting the Church. Nashville: Gospel Advocate Co., Christian Communications. 1985.

"Let Me Write Their Songs." *Firm Foundation* 99 (July 13, 1982):436, 443.

"Liberality in the Early Church." *Gospel Advocate* 109 (March 30, 1967):195, 200–201.

"Living Soul." *Firm Foundation* 93 (March 16, 1976):166.

"Loaves and Fishes." *Firm Foundation* 85 (July 30, 1968):484, 491.

"A Look at the New International Version." *The Apostolic Reflector* 1 (April 1974):56–57.

"Lords Over God's Heritage?" *Firm Foundation* 94 (June 14, 1977): 372, 379.

"The Louvre and the Bible." *Voice of Freedom* 22 (January 1974):12–13.

"Love—Its Meaning." In *Your Marriage Can Be Great* (pp. 110–14). Edited by T. B. Warren. Jonesboro, AR: National Christian Press, 1978.

"The Majority of the Men." In *What Lack We Yet?* (pp. 37–42). Edited by J. D. Thomas. Abilene, TX: Biblical Research Press, 1974.

"Mark 10:14, *Koluein*, and *Baptizein*." RQ 21 (1978):129–34.

"Mark Them Which Cause Divisions." *Firm Foundation* 100 (February 22, 1983):118.

"Meeting Modernism." In *Abilene Christian College Annual Bible Lectures* (pp. 238–52). Abilene, TX: Abilene Christian College, 1969.

"The Ministry of Study." *Harding Graduate School of Religion Bulletin* 8 (April 1970); *The Campus Journal* 13 (Spring 1971):6–8; and *Christian Bible Teacher* 15 (November 1971):368–369, 371.

The Minor Prophets. Grand Rapids: Baker, 1966.

"Modern Speech Translations." *Firm Foundation* 88 (April 13, 1971):231, 236, 247, 252–253; and (April 20, 1971):247, 252–53.

"The Mosaic Authorship of the Pentateuch." In *Harding College Bible Lectures* (pp. 73–108). Austin, TX: Firm Foundation, 1971.

"The New American Standard Bible." In *Harding Graduate School Bible Lectures* (pp. 90–105). Nashville, TN: Gospel Advocate, 1971.

"The New English Bible." *Firm Foundation* 87 (May 19, 26, 1970):312, 313, 315, 326, 332.

"The New English Bible." *Twentieth Century Christian* 34 (March 1972):36–39.

"The New International Version." RQ 24 (1981): 1–11.

"The New Testament in the Twentieth Century." RQ 18 (1975):193–215.

"The New World Translation of the Holy Scriptures." *The Spiritual Sword* 6 (October 1974):32–36.

"Noah and the Flood in Jewish, Christian, and Muslim Tradition." BA 47 (December 1984):224–239.

"The Northeast." In *Harding College Lectures* (pp. 228–32). Austin, TX: Firm Foundation, 1952.

"Notes to Hosea and Joel." In *The NIV Study Bible*, pp. 1321–44. Edited by Kenneth Barker. Grand Rapids: Zondervan, 1985.

"The Office and Function of a Prophet." In *Living Lessons from the Prophets*, pp. 40–55. Edited by John Waddey. Knoxville, TN: East Tennessee School of Preaching and Missions, 1985.

'ōhel, 'ārôn, bā'ar, bᵉ'ēr, bᵉ'ēr laḥay rō'î, bᵉ'ēr sheba', bō'r, bôr, bûr, gāmal, gᵉmûl, gᵉmûlâ, tagmûl, gāmāl, zāqēn, zāqān, zāqēn, zōqen, ziqnâ, zᵉqûnîm, ḥāqâ, ḥāqaq, ḥōq, ḥûqqâ, ḥātam, ḥōtām, ṭal, yāda', dē'āh, da'at, yidde'ōnî, môda', môda'at, maddā', yā'ad, 'ēdâ, mô'ēd, massā', qāhāl, qōhelet, qāṣēr, qōṣer, qāṣar, qāṣir. In *Theological Wordbook of the Old Testament*. Edited by R. L. Harris. Chicago: Moody, 1980.

"The Old Testament and Homosexual Acts." In *Counseling Homosexuals* (pp. 1–32). Edited by B. W. Flatt, J. P. Lewis, and D. E. Flatt. Jonesboro, AR: National Christian Press, 1982.

"Old Testament Ethics." *Twentieth Century Christian* 44 (September 1982):6–9.

"Old Testament Studies in the Past Fifty Years." RQ 9 (1966):201–15.

"Only Begotten Son." *Firm Foundation* 93 (June 22, 1976):388, 395.

"Overcoming Modernism." In *Abilene Christian College Bible Lectures* (pp. 82–113). Austin, TX: Firm Foundation, 1954.

"Personality of the Month: W. B. West, Jr." *Gospel Advocate* 120 (March 2, 1978):133, 136.

"The Preacher Needs to Know the Old Testament." *Harding Graduate School of Religion Bulletin* 12 (September 1973).

"Preaching." *Firm Foundation* 98 (June 2, 1981):339.

"Pretexting?" *Firm Foundation* 98 (May 19, 1981):310.

"Priest and Prophet, False and True Prophet." In *Harding College Lectures* (pp. 156–68). Austin, TX: Firm Foundation, 1953.

"The Priesthood: 1 Peter 2:5–9." *The Exegete* 1 (May 1982):1–5.

"The Priority of Bible Study." *Gospel Advocate* 128 (October 2, 1986):593, 604.

"Putting Away and Divorce." *Gospel Advocate* 128 (November 6, 1986):665, 668.

"Read from the King James or the American Standard." *Harding Graduate School Bulletin* 23 (December 1982):1–2; *The Seed* 1 (Spring 1983):7; and *Mission Journal* 17 (July 1983):3–5.

"Real Estate in Palestine." *Firm Foundation* 85 (May 14, 21, 28, 1968):308, 327, 343, 346.

"Red or Green?" *Image* 1 (June 15, 1985):28.

"Reflections on Preaching." *Harding Graduate School of Religion Bulletin* 19 (November 1979):1ff; *The Harvester* 61 (February 1981):7–9; and *Firm Foundation* 98 (June 2, 1981):339.

Review of *Bible, Archaeology and Faith*, by H. T. Frank. *Christian Bible Teacher* 17 (July 1973):286, 303.

Review of *The Bible in Modern Scholarship*, edited by J. P. Hyatt. RQ 9 (1966):118–20.

Review of *The Consequences of the Covenant*, by G. W. Buchanan, JBL 91 (March 1972):108.

Review of *Genealogy and History in the Biblical World*, by R. R. Wilson. RQ 23 (1980):249–51.

Review of *Hosea: A New Translation with Introduction and Commentary*, by F. I. Andersen and D. N. Freedman. BA 45 (Summer 1982):190–91.

"A Review of Loraine Boettner's Postmillennialism." *The Spiritual Sword* 9 (January 1978):8–11.

Review of *The Living Bible Paraphrased*, by K. Taylor. *Christian Bible Teacher* 16 (August 1972):328, 346–47.

Review of *Luke and the Gnostics*, by C. H. Talbert. RQ 9 (1966):53–55.

Review of *The Noah's Ark Nonsense*, by H. M. Teeple. BA 42 (Summer 1979):190–91.

Review of *The Prophets*. Vol. 1: *The Assyrian Period*, by K. Koch. *Hebrew Studies* 24 (1983):205–6.

Review of *The Prophets Speak*, by S. J. Schultz. JETS 13 (1970):132.

Review of *Protestant Biblical Interpretation*, 3d ed., by B. Ramm. *Christian Bible Teacher* 15 (October 2, 1971):349.

Review of *The Quest for Noah's Ark*, by J. W. Montgomery. *Mission* 6 (April 1973):314–15; and *Christian Bible Teacher* 17 (May 1973):200.

Review of *Where is Noah's Ark?*, by L. R. Bailey. BA 42 (Summer 1979):190–91.

"Reviewing 'The Friends' Church.'" *Gospel Broadcast* 5 (July 19, 1945):406–407, 415.

"The Revised Standard Version of the Bible after Twenty-Five Years." *Firm Foundation* 89 (January 25, 1972):7; (February 1, 1972):7; (February 8, 1972):7.

Reviser of sections V–Z. *Smith's Bible Dictionary*. Edited by R. Lemmons. Garden City, N.Y.: Doubleday Doran & Co., 1966.

"The Schools of the Prophets." RQ 9 (1966):1–10.

"A Self-Perpetuating Board?" *Firm Foundation* 99 (June 8, 1982): 356, 363.

A Self Study Report of the Harding College Graduate School of Religion. Memphis: Harding College, 1964.

"Shall I Preach a While First?" *Christian Bible Teacher* 17 (July 1973):266, 273; and *Harding Graduate School of Religion Bulletin* 21 (July 1980):1ff.

"Shall I Speak Falsely for God?" *The Mission Studies Quarterly* 1 (July 1967):25–34; *Mission Strategy Bulletin* 5 (November-December 1977):1–4; and *Abilene Christian University Annual Bible Lectures*, pp. 117–35. Abilene, TX: Abilene Christian University, 1981.

"The Signs of the Times." *Twentieth Century Christian* 42 (December 1979):18–21; and *Campus Journal* 24 (Spring 1981):4–6.

"Signs of These Times." *Harding Graduate School of Religion Bulletin* 21 (January 1981):1ff.; *Firm Foundation* 98 (April 28, 1981):259; and *Gospel Light* 51 (September 1981):135.

"Silence of Scripture." *World Evangelist* 15 (January 1987):10–12.

"Some Verses Involving Textual Critical Problems." In *Lubbock Christian College Bible Lectures* (pp. 193–209). Lubbock, TX: Lubbock Christian College, 1972.

"The Soul." *Bible Beacon* 9 (May 1971):34, 39.

"'Spiritual Words' or 'Spiritual Men'? (1 Cor. 2:13)." *Firm Foundation* 100 (April 19, 1983):262, 267.

"Stewards of Our Minds." In *Harding University Bible Lectures* (pp. 140–54). Austin, TX: Firm Foundation, 1980.

"A Study of the Effectiveness of Poetry in Sermon Technique." M.A. thesis, Sam Houston State Teachers College, 1944.

A Study of the Interpretation of Noah and the Flood in Jewish and Christian Literature. Leiden, The Netherlands: Brill, 1968.

"Study to Show Thyself Approved to God." *Christian Bible Teacher* 3 (November 1959):4–5; (December 1959):4, 13, 17; (January 1960):5; (February 1960):4–5.

"The Suffering Servant." *Twentieth Century Christian* 27 (July 1965):15–16.

"A Sunday Morning in Russia." *Voice of Freedom* 20 (February 1972):24–25.

"The Synagogue." RQ 4 (1960):199–204.

"The Teacher in the Christian College." *Minister's Monthly* 15 (October 1969):56–58.

"Tell Us the Dream." *Firm Foundation* 85 (October 8, 1968):643, 645.

"The Text of the New Testament." The Restoration Quarterly 27 (1984); 65–74.

"That Which Every Joint Supplies." *Firm Foundation* 91 (May 21, 1974):232; and *Christian Bible Teacher* 20 (October 1976):410.

"Those Who Rule." *Image* 1 (August 15, 1985):10.

"To Study, To Do, and To Teach." *Christian Bible Teacher* 17 (October 1973):404–7, 409.

"Too Little and Too Late." *Gospel Broadcast* 5 (April 26, 1945):266; and *World Vision* 11 (May-June, 1945):9.

"Topography and Archaeology of the Gospel of John." In *Lubbock Christian College Bible Lectures* (pp. 224–35). Lubbock, TX: Lubbock Christian College, 1976.

"Tradition." *Firm Foundation* 90 (January 2, 1973):3, 12–13.

"Translation Problems." In *Pepperdine College Lectures* (pp. 44–47). Los Angeles: Pepperdine College, 1968.

"Translation Questions." *Firm Foundation* 98 (October 6, 13, 1981):631, 647.

"The Transmission of the Text of the Bible." In *Harding College Bible Lectures* (pp. 46–51). Austin, TX: Firm Foundation, 1962.

"Virgin Daughter." *Firm Foundation* 93 (January 6, 1976):6.

"A Visit to Ephesus." *Voice of Freedom* 21 (March 1973):38–40.

"A Visit to Pergamum." *Voice of Freedom* 21 (June 1973):88–89.

"A Visit to Philippi." *Voice of Freedom* 21 (January 1973):4–5.

"W. B. West, Jr." *Harding Graduate School of Religion Bulletin* 22 (February 1982).

"What Do We Mean by Jabne?" *Journal of Bible and Religion* 32 (April 1964):125–32; and *The Canon and Masorah of the Hebrew Bible* (pp. 254–61). Edited by S. Z. Leiman. New York: KTAV, 1974.

"What Is Christian Love?" *The Spiritual Sword* 3 (July 1972):50–52.

"What Shall I Major In?" *Firm Foundation* 90 (June 26, 1973):406.

"What the Bible Teaches about God." In *Harding Graduate School of Religion Bible Lectures* (pp. 93–108). Nashville: Gospel Advocate, 1972.

"What the Old Testament Claims for Itself." *The Spiritual Sword* 5 (October 1973):24–27.

"What the Restoration Movement Has Accomplished." *Firm Foundation* 99 (March 2, 9, 16, 23, 30, 1982):135, 151, 167, 183, 199.

"When a Man . . .: An Exegesis of Deut. 24:1–4." In *Abilene Christian University Annual Bible Lectures* (pp. 144–61). Abilene, TX: Abilene Christian University, 1979.

"When God Says 'You are Unworthy.'" *Twentieth Century Christian* 39 (August 1977):25–27.

"Where Are the Dead Now?" *Twentieth Century Christian* 20 (April, 1958):15.

"Why I Am Not a Denominationalist." *Gospel Broadcast* 4 (November 30, 1944):744–45.

"Why New Bibles?" *Firm Foundation* 87 (October 13, 1970):647, 651; (October 20, 1970):663; (October 27, 1970):679, 685.

"Why Stop Here? The New King James in Perspective." *Christianity Today* 26 (October 8, 1982):108, 110.

"Why Study the Old Testament?" *Teenage Christian* 1 (April 1960): 20–21, 31.

"Women, Keep Silent in the Church." *Christian Bible Teacher* 17 (April 1973):138–139, 145.

"The Word of Prophecy Made Sure." In *Pillars of Faith* (pp. 151–74). Edited by H. O. Wilson and M. M. Womack. Grand Rapids: Baker, 1973.

"The Work of the Preacher." In *Jesus Calls Us*, pp. 202–17. Harding University Lectures, 1985. Delight, Ark.: Gospel Light Publishing Co., 1985.

"You." *Firm Foundation* 84 (May 2, 1967):275; *Twentieth Century Christian* 31 (December 1968):29–31.

"You Shall Love the Lord Your God with All Your Mind." *Twentieth Century Christian* 34 (July 1972):17–18, 27; and *Christian Bible Teacher* 16 (January 1973):6–7, 36–37.

"The Zero Milepost." *Firm Foundation* 93 (December 7, 1976):771, 779.

0-8010-5472-9 $12.95

Theology

Are you concerned to interpret and apply Scripture
accurately? Could you profit from what a team of
experts, each writing in his area of specialty, can teach
you on this subject? If so, *Biblical Interpretation* belongs
in your library.

In this volume twenty-four college professors and two
preachers combine their knowledge and
communication skills to help those who preach, teach,
and study the Bible. They review for you the history of
biblical interpretation, the method for doing word
studies, the contributions of archaeology and history to
interpretation, and many other useful aspects of the
subject. They also provide two exemplars of biblical
interpretation, one of Jeremiah 4:23-26 and one of
Ephesians 2:11-22.

Biblical Interpretation was written in honor of
Jack Pearl Lewis, a leading evangelical scholar and
professor of Bible at Harding Graduate School of
Religion since 1953.

F. Furman Kearley is editor of the *Gospel Advocate*.
Edward P. Myers is Academic Dean at Alabama
Christian School of Religion, Montgomery, and
Timothy D. Hadley is Associate Professor of Bible
and Biblical Languages at Lubbock Christian College.

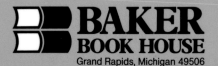

**BAKER
BOOK HOUSE**
Grand Rapids, Michigan 49506